THE OBSERVER GUIDE TO EUROPEAN COOKERY

Also by Jane Grigson

CHARCUTERIE AND FRENCH PORK COOKERY
GOOD THINGS
FISH COOKERY
ENGLISH FOOD
THE MUSHROOM FEAST
JANE GRIGSON'S VEGETABLE BOOK
FOOD WITH THE FAMOUS
THE FRENCH COOKERY SCHOOL (with Anne Willan)
JANE GRIGSON'S FRUIT BOOK

THE OBSERVER GUIDE TO EUROPEAN COOKERY

JANE GRIGSON

MICHAEL JOSEPH
LONDON

First published in Great Britain by
MICHAEL JOSEPH LIMITED
44 Bedford Square, London W.C.1.
1983

ISBN 0 7181 2233 X

Phototypeset by MS Filmsetting Limited, Frome, Somerset
Printed and bound in Belgium
by Brepols, Turnhout

CONTENTS

ACKNOWLEDGEMENTS

Many people helped with information and recipes for this book and most of them are acknowledged in the text. I should also like to thank the *Observer* team: editor Polly Pattullo, art director Graeme Murdoch, copy editor Jose Northey, research Liz Strauli, picture editor Colin Jacobson, photo stylist Mary Hamlyn, home economists Ann Page-Wood and Claire Ferguson. The book editor was Caroline Schuck.

My three main helpers were Patricia Bellman who shared the cooking, Elisabeth Bond who advised me about Austrian food, and Maria Holden who gave much help with Portugal.

Other information came from Fiona Andrews, Katalin Bencze, Luca and Anna Benedetto, Robert and Betty Bolgar, Antoinette Daridan, Joan Duckworth, Christopher and Helle Grigson, Jean Grønbårg, Mark Lake, Steve Liddle, John Lipitch, Olivia Mills, Ariane Nisberg, John Noble, Bríd Mahon, Laure Olive, Lisanne and Giles Radice, Laszló Ránky, David Robey, Eva Rodés, Deirdre Ryan, Victor Sassie, Geneviève Stehli, Jean-Sébastien Stehli, John Sullivan, Michèle Tapponier, Baillie Tolkien, William Tullberg, Jacqueline Vettier, Pauline Viola, Anne Willan, Lena Wickman, Carol Wright.

INTRODUCTION

In the spring of 1981, Peter Crookston, then editor of the *Observer* magazine, wrote me a brief letter. Would I like to go on a cook's tour of Europe and write about it for him?

We were in France at the time, in the quiet village where we live for several months every year. Would I like ... yes, I would. The planning started in the *Observer* offices where we began to argue about the countries to be included. Omissions were sad. Holland because of the importance of Indonesian food there. Poland because 1981 was a year when Poles were not eating much, and queuing for what there was in endless hopeless lines: how could I write about their delicacies? Bulgaria, Czechoslovakia, Yugoslavia were cut out by time and routes. As the weeks went by I thought Russia would have to go, too, as officialdom was delaying the journey with efficacious inefficiency: luckily the friend in Moscow whom I had first turned to for advice came to our rescue and produced the remarkable section, the most informative part of the book, which tells us exactly what Soviet citizens eat and give their friends. Nowhere else can you find this, since most books on Russian food draw mainly on past splendours, rather than on what is cooked today.

My own great surprises were Hungary and Portugal. Especially Portugal, since Hungary I was prepared for by reading one of the best cookery books I know, a book that traces the history of the country so well, describes its geography so completely, that one has a general idea of what one will find. Portugal has its enthusiasts, but no book to compare with George Lang's on Hungary. Dish after dish was new to me; the baroque pâtisserie was as unexpected as the baroque architecture of Bom Jesus; the cabbage women of Barcelos market and the sucking pig restaurateur of Mealhada, the riverside restaurants of Oporto, the festoons of inflated gut hanging by the open butchers' shops in Viseu market, had a directness about food that is rare in northern Europe. For sheer delight, I remember the clean tasting and lavish open tables of Bergen, Roskilde and Stockholm, the tenderness of reindeer steaks, the spicy herring and cheese eaten by candlelight in a restaurant that had been a favourite drinking place of Sweden's great poet, Bellman. For the excitement of food, the lavishness of Europe's supplies, the grey concrete market of Rungis at dawn, in December, is my best memory of all. Lorries from all over Europe bringing in and taking away the finest possible ingredients were parked by the vast hangars, each containing a separate market. Later that day and the next day, that early visit explained what was on the menus of Paris restaurants, and what was missing. No sole—far too dear—but excellent John Dory and sea bass and oysters. Suivant les marchés, that current phrase of the good restaurateur, that guarantee of honest cookery, acquires its meaning at a place like Rungis.

The market is no small concept. In the Middle Ages our northern ships were taking salt cod down to the Mediterranean and Portugal, bringing back wheat, spices and dried fruit—dried fruit in such quantities that the people who produced it wondered what on earth we did with it in the north. I think everyone would agree that Portuguese and Mediterranean cooks do far better things with salt cod than Scandinavians, and that the British know far more about using currants and raisins than the Greeks.

Food and ideas about cooking it have been passing from one part of the world to another ever since the neolithic revolution began in the Middle East. They were part of the spread of civilization though, since people will change their tastes in painting and architecture much faster than their tastes in food, knowledge of what was eaten is far sparser than knowledge of the houses that were lived in or the clothes that were worn. Cookery books were few before the 17th century—and how close is the general diet at any period to the cookery books published? Change owed more to the movement of people, of armies, merchants, chefs, wealthy landed travellers, than to books. Before canals, the railway, good roads, most places ate what could be produced within a 30-mile radius. Ports did better of course, if they were on a big trade route. For most people food was essentially regional food and not always enough of it either. Even in good areas, peasants ate a meagre diet, since most of what they produced went for sale at local markets. Only wealthy men could buy special seeds to grow exotic vegetables, or employ gardeners who understood how to grow fine fruit unfamiliar to the place they lived in, or afford chefs trained elsewhere to provide variety and elegance at mealtimes.

These reflections uncover a pattern in European eating that dictates the order of this book. Greece comes first, with classical and Hellenic chefs already theorizing about food in terms that do not seem odd today. In terms that make perfect sense. Italy took on the skills of Greece, since well-off Romans employed chefs from Athens just as well-off Northerners have looked to Paris for their chefs. Through Spain, Arab dishes and Arab gardening, as well as new vegetables and foods from America, were handed on to the rest of Europe. Portugal comes in here, in its great phase of travel and discovery. France next, in the perfect, unique position between Mediterranean and Atlantic seas, exactly poised to take advantage of the Renaissance and the New World.

Through France, where cookery took off in the 17th century, northern Europe received the shaping ideas about food that influence our standards and practice today. French influence has been welcomed, resented and resisted, but always in the end absorbed. Because of this over-riding influence it has been difficult to follow a scheme of exact order for the most northerly countries; in the end they are placed from west to east starting with Britain, which has looked to France as the source of culinary ideas from the time of the Norman conquest. The prickly relationship between the two countries, the mixture of admiration and resentment, is well exemplified in attitudes of 18th century English cookery writers. They forswear French recipes and 'extravagance', sneer at decadent refinements —and then fill their books with French recipes. And sometimes the recipes they think of as English came first from France two or three generations back and fitted so neatly into our lives at the time that they were rapidly naturalised. When the nationalist movements made people turn to their own countries in 19th century Germany, say, or Hungary, they looked more and more consciously at their native food—but the peasant dishes they took up were often much refined by French chefs and by chefs trained in the French tradition, to make them suitable for 'polite' tables. This is especially interesting in Hungary, where paprika was not mentioned in a cookery book until the 1820s and did not become a polite food until a process was discovered that tamed and varied the heat of different peppers to a reliable scale. Károly Gundel, from Hungary's most distinguished family of chefs, points out that it was through the influence of French chefs that Hungarian food, especially in restaurants, made great advances and 'became lighter without losing its originality . . . it adapted itself to the more refined taste of other lands'. He observed that there are four different dishes made with paprika, gulyás, pörkölt, tokány, paprikás—'these names were not adopted from popular usage but were rather the result of a gentleman's agreement among restaurateurs' in the interests of uniformity, 'these names do not always exactly coincide with the corresponding dishes in the different regions of the country'.

Internationalism in the business of food seems today to be developing into something monstrous. The deep-freeze cuisine, the theory of Hiltonism, lie over Europe—over the world—like a grey duvet, protecting people, especially travellers, from culture shock and surprises. In a word, depriving them of experiences that make life exciting or a little disturbing or that challenge received ideas. The undoubted advantages of large scale manufacture and organization—outstanding hygiene, efficient distribution, prices that enable far more people than ever in the past to satisfy their hunger—have not so far been allied with outstanding quality of flavour. This has depressed me for a long time. In a world where possibilities are infinite, commerce seeks continually to restrict choice beyond a certain level. The 300 varieties of pear that are listed by one French 17th-century gardener—though he had to admit that only 30 of them were really worth eating—are reduced in Europe's economic community to about half a dozen. The Golden Delicious apple, not the most distinguished of apples by a long way, accounts now for 75% of the world's apple production. Only the assiduous gardener, living in the right sort of place, can keep old varieties alive. Officially he does not have the right to sell them or to sell grafted trees or cuttings.

As the tour progressed, as the photographers came back with their own discoveries, as friends and agencies contributed information, as the researcher brought in new material and the copy editor asked tricky questions, an enormous diversity emerged. A diversity so lavish and intriguing that we could hardly do justice to it. We had never aimed for completeness but had had no idea how far away from it we were going to be. Natives of the thirteen countries concerned will miss favourite specialities I am sure, but I hope they will mainly approve my choice of the good things of Europe, the things that have especially appealed to me not just in recent journeys for the *Observer* but over thirty years of modest travelling.

Jane Grigson

AMERICAN MEASUREMENTS

All spoon and volume measurements are level.

When following a recipe, stick to one kind of measurement; do not mix them as proportions will then be wrong.

Yeast I generally use dried fermipan yeast that is added directly to the flour—in Britain it is sold under the brand name of Harvest Gold. Each packet contains a scant 2½ teaspoons, and is equivalent to 30 g (1 oz/1 cake compressed yeast) fresh yeast or 15 g (½ oz) dried yeast. If you are using either of the two latter forms of yeast they need to be reconstituted in a little of the liquid from the recipe, which should be at blood heat. Whisk or mash the yeast with the liquid and leave it in a warm place until it bubbles and froths into a spongy looking head of foam, allow 10–15 minutes.

Cream American heavy cream is equivalent to English whipping cream, with a butterfat content of 36% minimum.

There is no equivalent to English double cream. In recipes where double (48%) and single cream (18%) are mixed, use all heavy cream.

English soured cream has a butterfat content of 18%. This means that it is lighter than French crème fraîche, though it has something of the same sharp flavour. To make a passable approximation of crème fraîche, turn to p.132 in the French section.

English clotted cream, butterfat content 55% at least, is richest of all, very thick and crusty.

Sugar caster = American superfine granulated sugar
icing = American powdered sugar

Cling film called plastic wrap in America

Bakewell paper called silicone non-stick paper for baking in America

GREECE

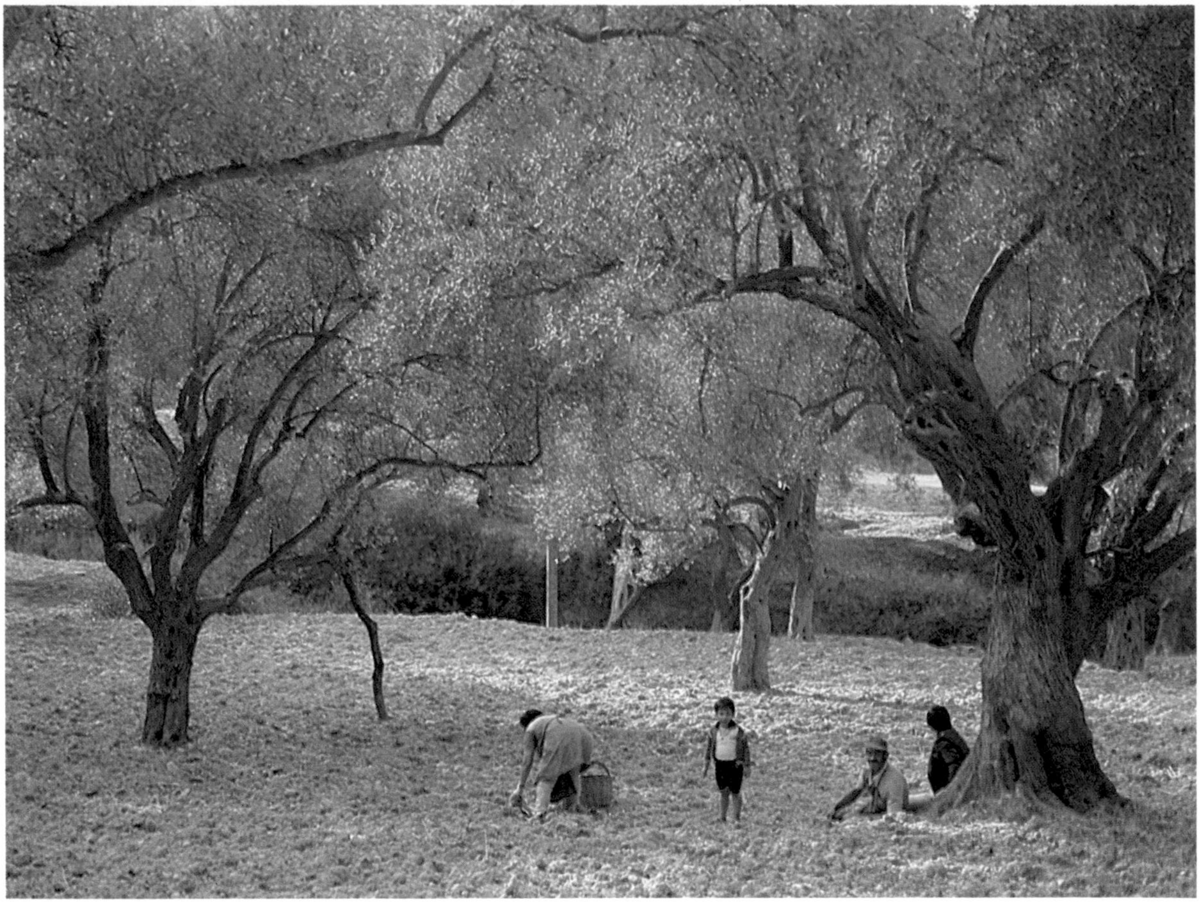

In late autumn, olives are shaken and beaten from the trees and gathered by the family

Sitting outside a small taverna on Rhodes, hard by the water's edge, sipping retsina and nibbling olives, pistachio nuts, little cubes of cheese and bits of octopus, I realised that two thousand years ago and more, Greeks were drinking the same resinated wine and eating the same food. Only the very rich would have enjoyed extra dishes of consummate skill.

Greek chefs then had the same reputation as French chefs have today—'Cook and poet are alike: the art of each lies in his brain,' said one Greek writer. And he reported a chef's remarks to a young commis: 'I'm a gourmet—that's the key to our skill. If you aren't to spoil the ingredients entrusted to you, you must love them passionately ... Cook and taste often. Not enough salt? Add some. Something lacking? Keep tasting and adding until the flavour is right. Tighten it, as you would a harp, until it's in tune. Then when everything is in harmony, bring on your chorus of dishes, singing in unison.'

Such statements have been made again and again since then, each chef in turn heralding a revolution (nouvelle cuisine?) whereas he is really restating the principles of fine cookery that, for Europe, were first enunciated in Greece. Our Greek chef saw good food, food in its season, as an integral part of the harmony and pleasure of life.

Meat and game were plentiful. Our chef dealt with lamb, veal, pork, ham, sausages, and hare. Flour came, perhaps, from one of the new watermills. For dessert, he was able to produce almonds, walnuts, pine kernels, pistachio nuts with their green and purple tones, and dried raisins. If his cheesecakes were not quite up to Athenian standards, he would serve them with Hymettus honey, a much prized delicacy from the nearby Mount Hymettus.

He might have agreed with the chefs of Kos that cooked lettuce stalks were the best of vegetables, in spite of their reputation for cooling sexy desires. His salads contained bitter rocket and green coriander, with sorrel added for sharpness. And, of course, he had olives and olive oil. He was sharp, too, in the market, poking down into the punnets of figs to see what was beneath the fine ones on top, and bargaining with fish-sellers.

Then, as now, fish was the favourite food of chefs and other discriminating eaters. They knew the best parts of the tunny fish, that octopus needs bashing to tenderness on the rocks, how squid should be stuffed, and the special deliciousness of red mullet. They loved shellfish like oysters, mussels, crabs, lobsters, and prawns, as well as the apricot-orange creaminess of sea urchins, enclosed in purple-brown spikes. The best foods of Greece have not changed.

I wonder what our chef would have thought of new foods that came later with Arab merchants and Turkish invaders, or after the discovery of America? If he considered the tomato to be over-used today, he would surely enjoy spinach in flaky pies ... the elegance of okra. Or the transforming lemon and the clarity its flavour brings to food. He might also envy modern pastry-cooks the neutral sweetness of sugar (the assertive sweetness of honey, the only sweetener he had, limits variety in dishes), but what would he make of the thick black coffee needed to balance the tooth-piercing syrups? And the accompanying glass of water?

Except in top restaurants or hotels, the way of ordering a meal in Greece demands nerve. You will be handed the universal printed menu, listing every Greek dish you can think of—there are no great regional differences. Here and there, inky smudges on the plastic indicate the day's dishes. Or yesterday's. You must at this point, earlier for preference, make for the kitchen to see what bubbles on the stove. On account of Greek willingness to feed you at any time of the day, meat dishes can be overcooked. Best to stick to the little meze dishes—the appetisers, such as stuffed vine leaves and vegetables, little pastries and so on. Then grilled fish, which came out of the sea that morning, with a Greek salad. Then figs, oranges or grapes and the superb coffee: if you value your teeth, order metrios (lightly sugared coffee), or sketos (without sugar).

Buying picnic food is another great pleasure. You find the baker's shop simply by looking out for people carrying pans of meat and potatoes under white cloths, or a tray of buns on their head. They are going to and from the baker's ovens, where these foods are baked for them as they have always been. Butchers' shops are stark and you may prefer to look for sausage and cooked meats at the grocery, along with honey and cheese, fruit, wine and olives.

On leaving a village one day in November to look for a sheltered picnicking place, I stopped at a spot where people were knocking down olives from their tree. I joined in, and later was rewarded by dipping bread into the green-gold stream of oil that came from the presses. Everything in the pressing shed had a soft sheen of oil—sacks, mats, walls, floor, the dog—even the farmers, who had brought in their crop and were watching it pass through the unchanging process, the centuries-old system hurried along by machinery.

FISHERMAN'S SOUP
Kakavia

This is the old soup of romantic association, and still a reality for some fishermen—a soup cooked over the fire on shore or in a boat, in the three-legged pot known as a kakavi. The fish used will depend on what have been caught. Greeks claim that kakavia is the origin of bouillabaisse, taken by Ionian Greeks in ancient times when they set off to colonise the place now known as Marseilles.

Enough of the same types of Greek fish can be bought in England to make a reasonable showing—red and grey mullet, snapper, bream, whiting, and John Dory. The problem comes when you try to get hold of small live lobsters and live Mediterranean prawns. You may have to be content with buying frozen ones or substituting mussels and cooked prawns, whose shells at least can be added to the basic stock.

When you choose the fish, allow extra weight to compensate for any mussels used as their shells are so heavy. Ask the fishmonger to give you bones and heads left over from filleting. When you get home, divide up the fish according to the time they take to cook, putting them on separate plates as you prepare them. Add their trimmings to the trimmings you already have.

Serves 6–8
fish trimmings, well washed
250 g/8 oz/2 cups sliced onion
125 ml/4 fl oz/$\frac{1}{2}$ cup olive oil
2 bay leaves
2 good sprigs of parsley
$\frac{1}{2}$ teaspoon rigani or dried thyme
250–500 g/8 oz–1 lb tomatoes, peeled (optional)
level teaspoon peppercorns; salt
2 litres/4 pts/10 cups water
2 kg/4 lb mixed fish and shellfish, cleaned
lemon juice

Put the fish trimmings, onion, oil, herbs, tomatoes, peppercorns and a good pinch of salt into a large pan. Add the water, bring to the boil and cook steadily, uncovered, for 45 minutes. Sieve into a clean pan so that you now have a thick soup base.

Bring to simmering point and add the fish in batches—the thickest, firmest pieces first, together with the lobster if using, and ending up with mussels and cooked prawns, which only require a minute or two. Correct the seasoning with salt and lemon juice. Serve with bread or croûtons.

Variation psarosoupa, meaning fish soup, is a domesticated version of kakavia. The choice of fish can be simpler, but buy some cheaper fish to give strength to the broth—say a slice of conger—as

Kakavia, the Greek bouillabaisse, is made from whatever fish is on sale at the market that morning.

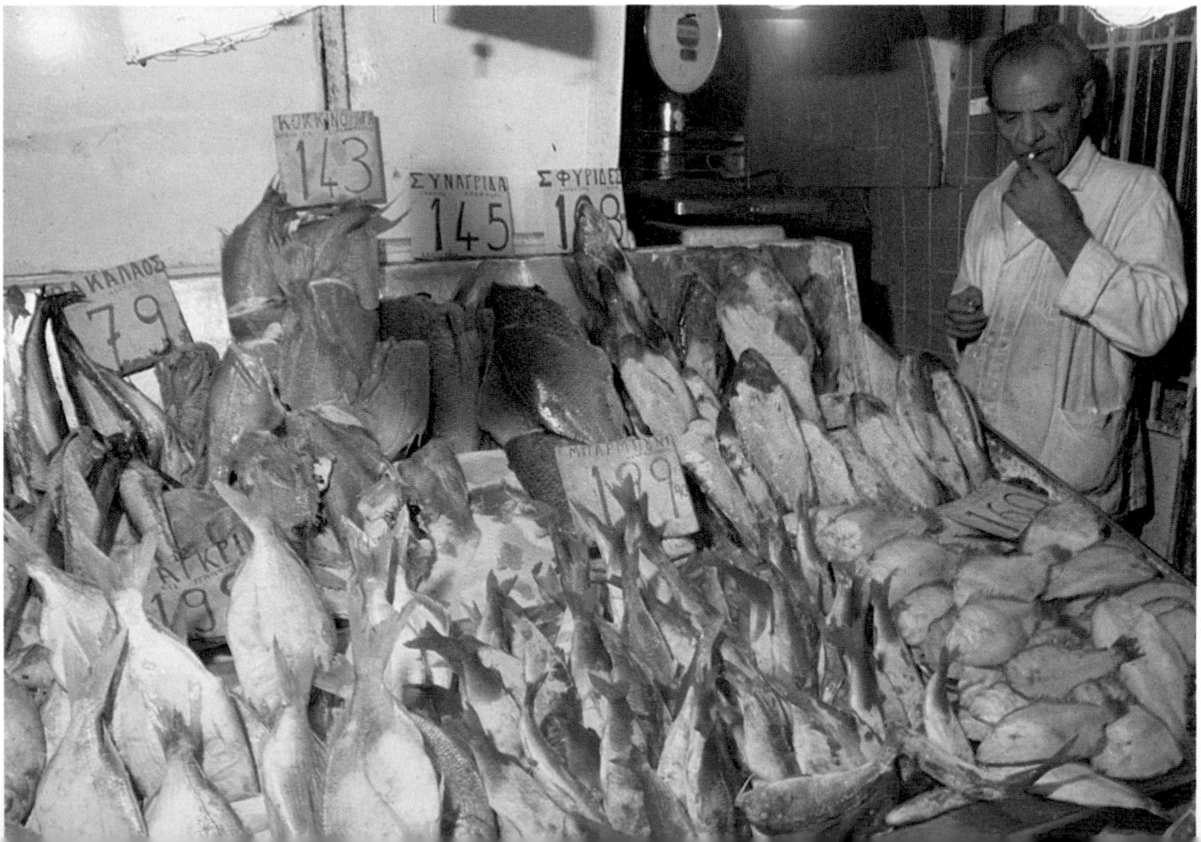

well as the fishmonger's trimmings. The difference between psarosoupa and kakavia is that with psarosoupa the best fish is extracted from the broth and kept warm to provide a main course. The snag is obvious—the fish gets overcooked. It may be unauthentic, but you will have a much better meal if you allow the fish to cool completely; it can still be served with an oil and lemon dressing, or a lemon mayonnaise, and potatoes.

Start off by making the stock base for kakavia, with extras such as white wine, garlic, carrot, leek, spring onion, according to what you have. Include the trimmings and some cheaper fish. When you prepare the main fish, sprinkle it with lemon juice.

After 35 minutes cooking, put in the main fish and some small scrubbed potatoes. Lower the heat to a simmer. When the fish turns opaque while remaining slightly pink at the bone, remove it to a plate, sprinkle with salt and leave to cool. Take out the potatoes, peel and put them round the fish.

Strain the stock into a clean pan, pressing slightly on the debris to get as much moisture out as possible. Season to taste, cook rice in it and finish with egg and lemon (see avgolemono box on page 26).

BEAN SOUP
Fassolada

The simple, basic vegetable soup of Greece, easy to make, easy to vary according to what you have in the house.

Most recipes simply boil the vegetables together in a pot, but I have come across one or two in which all the vegetables, except the beans, are lightly fried in olive oil before the main cooking begins. I think this complication is unnecessary in a soup of such rustic simplicity.

Serves 6
500 g/1 lb/2 cups dried white beans
2 large tomatoes, peeled and diced, or 2 tablespoons/3 tbs tomato paste
large leek, sliced, or large onion, chopped
1–2 carrots, diced
2 potatoes, diced
3 stalks of celery with their leaves, chopped
2 cloves of garlic, peeled and split
4 tablespoons/⅓ cup olive oil
salt and black pepper
chopped parsley
black olives

Pour boiling water over the beans to cover and leave for 1 hour. Drain, rinse and put into a large saucepan with plenty of water. Put on the lid and simmer for 30 minutes, then add all the vegetables, the garlic, and the oil, plus extra water to keep everything covered. Continue to simmer until the beans are tender and beginning to split (about 1½ hours in all). Add salt and pepper, and more water to give the consistency you like.

Put in a handful each of chopped parsley and black olives and leave the soup to murmur for another 5 minutes. Taste and correct the seasoning again. Serve with plenty of bread, and dry white rather than red wine.

APPETISERS
Mezedes

Greeks delight in serving a spread of tasty little dishes with a drink before meals. These appetisers can be hot or cold, simple or elaborate, and the ones I've chosen reflect the variety you may be offered all over the Eastern Mediterranean as well as in Greece. Each recipe is enough for about four people, unless I state otherwise, should you wish to serve them singly instead of dipping into lots of them.

CUCUMBER AND YOGURT SALAD
Tzatziki

This also makes a refreshing sauce with grilled meat or fish, or with fried fish—in which case grate the cucumber instead of dicing it, and after salting it, squeeze out the liquid. Or on a hot day, add iced water, and a splash of vinegar to the cucumber when you salt it.

The cream in the recipe is my own addition to make up for the thin quality of much of our commercial yoghurt. If you make you own yoghurt including cream, you need add no more here.

1 cucumber, peeled and diced small
salt and pepper
1–2 cloves of garlic, peeled
heaped tablespoon chopped mint or dillweed, or 2 level teaspoons dried mint or dillweed
tablespoon lemon juice or white wine vinegar
500 ml/¾ pt/scant 2 cups plain yoghurt
4 good tablespoons/⅓ cup double cream
olive oil

Put the cucumber into a colander. Sprinkle with 1 level tablespoon salt, cover with a plate and leave to drain for at least 1 hour. Dry on kitchen paper.

Meanwhile crush the garlic with a little salt until it is creamy. Mix in a bowl with the herbs and lemon juice or wine vinegar. Beat in the yoghurt

Mezedes include stuffed peppers; dolmades; brain, aubergine, cucumber and yoghurt salads; taramasalata

and double cream. Add a spoonful or two of olive oil, if you like, to add flavour and extra smoothness. Finally add the cucumber, taste and adjust the seasonings.

BEAN SALAD
Fassolia salata

Greeks go mainly for dried white beans, but you can make a beautiful salad by mixing different coloured beans (dried and/or fresh) together, or arranging them in banks or wedges separately on a dish.

250 g/8 oz/good cup large dried white beans
bouquet garni
150 ml/$\frac{1}{4}$ pt/$\frac{2}{3}$ cup dressing (made as for Brain salad see page 17)
heaped tablespoon chopped sweet onion or spring onion

Soak the beans in cold water for at least 6 hours, then tip the water away and cook the beans in a large pan of water with the bouquet garni. Drain and toss while hot with the dressing, with the onion added.

HUMUS ME TAHINI

For this popular dish a liquidizer or processor is essential, I would say. Unless you use canned chick peas which are soft enough to sieve easily—but then the flavour is not so good.

Soak 150 g (5 oz) chick peas for 24 hours, then simmer them in water until soft. Drain and save the liquor. Put 4 tablespoons of the liquor into your machine, with the juice of a lemon and 2 halved cloves of garlic. Whizz at top speed, adding the chick peas alternately with about 100 g (3–4 oz) tahini (sesame paste). If the mixture clogs, add more liquor or lemon juice, and some olive oil. Keep tasting, and do not overdo the tahini. Season and scrape into a bowl. Cover with a thin layer of olive oil and a sprinkle of cayenne and parsley.

FRIED CHEESE
Kefalotyri saganaki

A delicious appetizer but an awkward one that has to be made at the last minute. Serve with beer, white wine or ouzo.

Cut slices of kefalotyri cheese; you will need about 175 g (6 oz) or enough to make a single layer in a small frying pan. Turn the slices in flour and shake off surplus. Fry them on each side until a nice crusty brown. Put on to a plate, squeeze lemon juice over them and a little pepper. No salt, as the cheese is salty.

BRAIN SALAD
Miala salata

A salad one can never have enough of. I came across it first in Claudia Roden's *Middle Eastern Food*, then discovered it was popular in Greece. A good excuse to include it here.

500 g/1 lb lamb's or calf's brains
salt and pepper
level teaspoon peppercorns
2 tablespoons/3 tbs lemon juice
FOR THE DRESSING
125 ml/4 fl oz/½ cup olive oil
juice of 1 large lemon
½ teaspoon each rigani and dried mint
tablespoon chopped spring onion or chives
heaped tablespoon chopped parsley

Soak the brains for a good hour in salted water after rinsing themrain and put them into a large pan in a single layer and cover with cold water. Add the peppercorns, lemon juice and a good pinch of salt, then bring to simmering point and cook for 15 minutes. Lamb's brains will be cooked through and opaque; larger brains need longer.

Drain and cut the brains into cubes while still warm. Pour over a dressing made by beating together the olive oil, lemon juice, rigani and mint, spring onion or chives and parsley. Season to taste with salt and pepper. There may seem to be a lot of herbs, but apart from the delicious flavour they add, they also help to veil the reality of brains from the squeamish.

AUGERGINE SALAD
Melitzanosalata

I find this a tricky salad to make, not because it is difficult—it is very easy—but because it's impossible to know whether the aubergines are bitter or not. Many recipes suggest grilling or baking them to burn the skin brittle, so that it can be peeled away easily. But, to my mind, this emphasises any bitterness there may be.

Never having solved this problem to my satisfaction, one day I was delighted to be given the mildest and yet most recognisable aubergine salad in a quayside taverna at Elounda in Crete. It came with grilled swordfish, lemon quarters and chips. I ate it with enthusiasm—just right with the dryish swordfish—and asked for more.

This delighted the owner, who told me how he made it. Boil 2 large aubergines—I halve them first—until they are tender, then scrape the pulp from the skins. Mash it, or chop it to a mush, drain off any liquid and gradually add about 150 ml (¼ pt/⅔ cup) mayonnaise to taste. Very simple, and easy to control.

If you decide to grill the aubergines, squeeze the pulp after peeling off the skins whole. This way you get rid of some of the bitterness. Then you can mash or chop the pulp with olive oil, vinegar, grated onion, salt and pepper. Serve sprinkled with chopped parsley, and olives.

STUFFED VINE LEAVES
Dolmades

Dolmades comes from a Turkish verb, meaning to stuff. Other leaves can be used—cabbage or large spinach leaves—but they cannot rival the lemony flavour of vine leaves and their lean firm texture.

Fresh vine leaves should be a young green and about the size of the palm of your hand: dunk them, in bundles tied with thread, into boiling water and boil for 2 minutes, then remove, drain and cool them. Pickled vine leaves from the barrel or in polythene packets need soaking to reduce the brine strength—allow at least 30 minutes and taste a bit to see if they are all right. Canned leaves are the least easy to handle, because they are so delicate. Remove the wodge carefully from its can and put into a large bowl of cold water. After 15–20 minutes separate the leaves. Use broken leaves to patch the holes and line the cooking pan.

Dry the leaves and spread them out on a large surface, underside up, stalks towards you. Cut the stalks away and put a teaspoon of rice filling (see page 18) at stalk end of each leaf. Flip the sides over and roll up loosely—to allow for the rice swelling.

Line a heavy pan with broken leaves, then put in the little rolls, smooth side up, fitting them close together in two or three layers. Intersperse with 3 large cloves of garlic, cut into slivers. Add the juice of a large lemon, 1 teaspoon sugar and 250 ml (8 fl oz/1 cup) water for a meat filling, or 125 ml (4 fl oz/½ cup) each water and olive oil for a plain rice filling.

Put a plate on top, or a clean pan lid, to keep the rolls in place. Cover the pan tightly and simmer for 1 hour. Check the liquid level after 30 minutes, adding more boiling water if necessary and lowering the heat if the rolls are drying out too fast. After 1 hour, taste one of the rolls to see if it is cooked. If made with canned leaves, they will probably be ready and it will be wise to take them off the heat; other kinds will benefit from 1½–2 hours cooking.

To eat hot either drain them and serve with plain yoghurt. Or drain off the cooking liquid and use to make avgolemono sauce I (page 26), keeping the dolmades hot meanwhile. Pour the sauce over just before serving them.

To eat cold cool the dolmades in the cooking pan. Most of the liquid will have disappeared, so add a little lemon juice to what remains and a little oil and strain it over the cold dolmades as a dressing. If you want to serve them before a meal with a glass of ouzo or other aniseed-flavoured spirit, or retsina, drain them first or they will be messy to eat.

To freeze dolmades drain and open-freeze them on a tray. Once they are hard, range them closely together in boxes with greaseproof paper or clear film between the layers so that you can remove a few at a time.

If you have a freezer—or intend giving a large party—it is well worth making 50 dolmades.

FISH ROE PÂTÉ
Taramasalata

One of Europe's oldest surviving luxuries is salted mullet roe, which the Greeks first imported from Ancient Egypt and then began to make themselves (as they still do). It was always a rare, expensive item, and to make it go further, Greek cooks extended it with cheap local ingredients—olive oil and bread. This mullet roe is the true tarama—a word which like the Italian bottarga and the French poutargue comes from Coptic, from a word meaning 'the mummy', which is a good description of the embalmed roe covered in pearly-grey wax.

Nowadays, economy means abandoning the proper bottarga, which is kept for eating in tiny slivers with an aperitif, and using other preserved fish roes, usually cod's. Alas in Greece—the best restaurants apart—economy has reduced taramasalata to a nasty heap of bright pink mashed potato, vaguely flavoured with something fishy. Avoid it. You are more likely to eat good taramasalata at your own table, than in a taverna looking across the Aegean sea.

With a processor or blender, it is easy to make. Quantities are variable, but here are the ones I use. With a processor or blender, it is easy to make taramasalata. Although olive oil belongs to ancient tradition, Greeks these days prefer to use a tasteless oil, or a mixture of the two. In any case mixtures of this kind (see humus on page 16) should be made to taste, which makes them an agreeable task for the cook.

Serves 8
250 g/8 oz smoked cod's roe
125 g/4 oz/2 cup crustless white bread, soaked in a little water
up to 250 ml/8 fl oz/1 cup mixed plain and olive oil, or plain oil
juice of 1 large lemon
large clove of garlic, crushed
heaped tablespoon finely chopped sweet onion
black olives, for serving

Remove the skin from the roe. Break it up into large lumps and soak these in plenty of water for an hour or more to reduce the saltiness. Be guided by your taste, as the saltiness varies.

Drain the roe and put it into the processor or blender. Squeeze the bread dry and add it to the roe. Switch on and pour in the oil gradually, as if you were making mayonnaise. When you have a pale pink purée, taste and add lemon juice, then more oil if you like. Put in the garlic, mix briefly, then stir in the onion (without further electrical mixing) and scoop the mixture into a bowl. Arrange black olives round the taramasalata, and serve with toast or bread.

RICE FILLINGS FOR VEGETABLES

There are two main classic fillings, one consisting of flavoured rice, the other of flavoured rice and meat. Having said that, I must admit that variations are legion. Whether or not the filling is pre-cooked, or the length of the pre-cooking, all depends on the amount of time that the final dish will be cooked.

KEBABS

Souvlakia comes from the Greek word, souvla, which describes any kind of skewer or spit. And the cry, 'Souvlakia, souvlakia,' is a familiar sound everywhere in Greece as street vendors urge you to buy their kebabs—tiny pieces of delicious-tasting meat speared on small thin wooden sticks.

Kebabs were as popular among the ancient Greeks as they are today. Homer tells us how Achilles organised a barbecue when he had envoys from Troy to dinner. First he gave a drink, then 'Patroclus set the chopping block by the fire, and laid on it the loin of a sheep and a goat, and the chine of a fat pig. Automedon held the meat while Achilles chopped it; then he sliced the pieces and put them on spits while Patroclus made the fire burn high. When the flames subsided, he spread out the coals, and laid the spits across them propped on spit-rests. He sprinkled them with salt. When the meat was cooked, he put it on to dishes and handed round baskets of bread while Achilles served everyone his portion.' We can get an idea of Achilles' spit-rests from a pair excavated at Thera—two walls of pottery, each with a handle on one side so that they can be moved easily, and the tops of the walls nicked in a scallop effect to hold the little spits. I wonder nobody has copied this idea today—one that dates back about three and a half thousand years and is so practical.

Homer's advice is excellent. Obviously he had watched the process many times, or taken part himself. Only one thing is missing—the marinade. This is particularly good with small cubes of meat. Whisk together more or less equal quantities of olive oil and lemon, with rigani as flavouring. Turn the spits of meat in the liquid every so often and leave at least 1 hour before cooking. Always use a prime cut of meat; a marinade improves the flavour but it is no miracle cure for toughness of cuts which should be stewed.

Unless you are skilled at grilling kebabs, confine their make-up to meat cubes, with an occasional bay leaf for flavouring. Additions like onions, mushrooms, tomatoes and peppers are best kept, I think, for accompanying dishes if you want to dress the kebabs up a bit.

The point is to get the grill and its rack, which should be oiled, very hot before you start cooking. Put the kebabs on the hot rack, and turn them as they brown outside. If you can get the heat high enough to achieve a crusty outside and a tender pink inside, that is success for lamb or beef. Pork can be seared outside briefly, but should then be cooked more slowly, i.e. farther from the heat so that it cooks through—10–15 minutes depending on size.

For dolmades made with fresh leaves, for instance, the cooking time can be up to 2 hours; this gives the rice plenty of time to swell and become tender.

For baked stuffed vegetables half-cook the filling before stuffing.

FILLING I

250 g/8 oz/2 cups chopped onion
1–2 large cloves of garlic, finely chopped
125 ml/4 fl oz/½ cup olive oil
250 g/8 oz/good cup long grain rice (brown, Basmati or Patna)
heaped teaspoon tomato paste, optional
150 ml/¼ pt/⅔ cup water
level tablespoon each chopped mint and dillweed, or 2 level teaspoons each dried mint and dried dillweed
¼ teaspoon powdered cinnamon
salt and pepper
sugar, to taste

OPTIONAL EXTRAS

60 g/2 oz/½ cup pine kernels or chopped walnuts
60 g/2 oz/⅓ cup currants or raisins

Soften the onion and garlic in the oil over a low heat until golden and transparent. Stir in the rice and tomato paste, if used, and the water. Simmer until the liquid is absorbed and the mixture juicy, then add the remaining ingredients. Stir well, take off the heat and leave for 5 minutes, then taste for seasoning.

FILLING II

250 g/8 oz beef, veal or lamb, finely chopped or minced, uncooked or cooked rare
125 g/good 4 oz/good ½ cup long grain rice
medium onion, chopped, or 6 spring onions, chopped
2 level tablespoons/3 tbs tomato paste
2 level teaspoons salt
teaspoon freshly ground pepper
heaped tablespoon chopped parsley
teaspoon each chopped fresh mint and dillweed
salt and pepper, to taste
¼ teaspoon powdered cinnamon

OPTIONAL EXTRAS

60 g/2 oz/½ cup pine kernels or chopped walnuts
60 g/2 oz/⅓ cup currants or raisins
2 tablespoons/3 tbs sherry, port or fortified wine

If the cooking time of the final dish is to be long, mix the meat with the rest of the ingredients. If the cooking time is short, first gently cook the onion in a little olive oil until soft and transparent, then raise the heat and put in the meat. When it is slightly browned, add the rice and 125 ml (4 fl oz/½ cup) water. Cook, uncovered, about 10 minutes until the liquid is absorbed, then remove the pan from the heat and add the remaining ingredients.

BAKED STUFFED VEGETABLES

These are often included as a meze, but a large dish of mixed stuffed vegetables makes a beautiful first course, or accompaniment to a main course.

Aubergines Slice long ones down from the stalk end, but for round ones, slice off a lid from the stalk end and cut round inside to loosen the flesh. Sprinkle the cut sides with salt and leave upside down in a colander to drain for at least 1 hour. Rinse and wipe them free of moisture, then fry lightly in oil or butter or simmer them in boiling salted water until they are just tender. Scoop out the pulp with a pointed spoon (add to the stuffing mixture), leaving a shell to take the stuffing.

Artichokes (globe) Cook in boiling salted water, with lemon juice or vinegar. Run under cold water, pull out the centre leaves and scrape out the hairy choke to form a cup.

Courgettes Prepare and cook lightly as for aubergines, above.

Peppers Slice off the tops for lids, discard seeds and white membranes.

Tomatoes Slice off the tops for lids, hollow out the insides, season with salt and put upside down to drain.

Fill the vegetables loosely with a rice stuffing (see page 19), half-cooked; replace the lids or scatter with breadcrumbs, grated cheese and melted butter. Put in a shallow ovenproof dish and bake at 180°C (350°F), gas 4 for 30–45 minutes, depending on their size.

AUGERGINE SLIPPERS
Melitzanes papoutsakia

Moussaka baked in aubergine halves can be served hot or cold. Slice aubergines in half from stalk end. Sprinkle with salt and leave to drain for at least 1 hour.

Rinse and wipe them dry, then fry in oil or butter or simmer in boiling salted water until tender. Scoop out the pulp and reserve. Fill each 'shell' two-thirds full with the meat sauce (see Moussaka recipe, page 30) mixed with the reserved pulp. Place close together in buttered baking dish.

Set oven at 180°C (350°F), gas 4. Make a cheese sauce. Pour a little into each 'slipper'. Bake for 30–45 minutes until set.

GREEK SUMMER SALAD
Salata

This is the dish that makes me most homesick for Greece. Not because it was the best thing I ate there, but because it appeared in every small taverna on every beach, at every market or monument or site that I visited.

Serves 6
a lettuce, separated into its leaves
6 fine large tomatoes, peeled and quartered or sliced
½ cucumber, scored with a fork or zester, sliced
salt and pepper
12 spring onions, or 1 sweet onion
12 sprigs of fresh mint, chopped
heaped teaspoon rigani
4 tablespoons/⅓ cup olive oil
2 tablespoons/3 tbs lemon juice
about 175 g/6 oz feta cheese, crumbled, or sliced or cubed
18 black olives

Roll up the lettuce leaves and slice the rolls across thinly with a stainless-steel knife. Scatter all over a serving dish. Arrange the tomatoes and cucumber on top of the lettuce, leaving a good lettuce rim, in receding layers, seasoning as you go. Scatter with onion and herbs. Beat the oil with lemon juice and pour over the whole salad. Put the cheese and olives on top (sometimes rings of sweet pepper are added, too).

Serve straightaway—if this salad stands around for long the shreds of lettuce will wilt and the cucumber will weep.

SPINACH PIE
Spanakopitta

Some of the Greek spinach pies have béchamel or rice additions to give body to the vegetable, cheese and egg filling. I find this too heavy, particularly if the pie is eaten cold, and recommend the following version. Frozen leaf spinach can be used instead of fresh.

Serves 8
12 sheets/½ packet filo pastry
250 ml/8 fl oz/1 cup olive oil
FOR THE FILLING
1.5 kg/3 lb fresh spinach or two 500 g/1 lb packets frozen leaf spinach, thawed
75 g/2½ oz/7 tbs butter
6 large spring onions, chopped, or 60 g/2 oz/½ cup chopped onion
200 g/7 oz/1¾ cups grated feta cheese or grated Cheddar and Parmesan cheeses, mixed
4 large eggs
2 teaspoons dried dillweed
rounded tablespoon chopped parsley
salt and pepper
shallow baking pan at least 20 × 30 × 3 cm (3 × 12 × 1½ in)

Make the filling first. Wash and trim the stalks from the spinach and cut the leaves into thin strips. Sprinkle with 1 tablespoon salt. Leave for 1 hour in a bowl, then rub and squeeze out the juice.

Meanwhile, heat the butter and cook in it the chopped onion until soft but not browned. Add it with the cheese, eggs and herbs to the spinach. Mix well, taste and correct the seasoning.

Set oven at moderate, 180°C (350°F), gas 4. Oil or butter the baking pan well.

Brush a sheet of pastry with oil and put it into the pan, which it will overlap. Brush 5 more sheets and put them on top. Put in the filling, sprinkling it with 2 tablespoons (3 tbs) of the olive oil. Bring the overlapping pastry up over the filling. Cut the last 6 sheets to the size of the tin, brush them with oil and lay them on top. Score the top into squares and sprinkle with water to prevent it curling. Bake in the heated oven for about 45 minutes or until the top is golden brown. Serve hot or cold.

THREE-CORNERED SPINACH PIES
Trigona spanakopittes

Cut filo pastry into strips longways, each sheet into three or four. Brush with oil or melted butter and put one strip on another, so that for each pie you have a double strip. Put a teaspoon of filling more or less, depending on the width of the strip, at one end. Take one corner and fold it over the filling end, down to meet the long edge. Now take the corner of this filled triangular end, fold it over to meet the long edge of the strip, so that you have a straight narrow end again. Repeat this folding process until all the strip is used up to leave a plump triangular package. Repeat with more double strips of filo to use up the filling. Makes 15–18 pies.

The pies can be deep-fried, preferably in olive oil, or they can be put on to buttered trays for baking. Brush them with melted butter and bake until golden brown as in the recipe for Spinach pie.

Many other fillings can be used instead of spinach. Try the chicken one on page 24, or a thick fish stock-based velouté sauce with chopped seafood and a couple of eggs beaten into it, with chopped onion or grated cheese and nutmeg added to bring out the flavour.

THREE-CORNERED CHEESE PIES
Trigona tiropittes

Crumble or grate 500 g (1 lb) feta cheese, and add 125 g (4 oz) kefalotiri cheese (or mizithra cheese for a mild creaminess). Mix with 3 beaten eggs. If you wish to make a large pie like the spinach pie on page 20, add 150 ml (¼ pt/⅔ cup) thick nutmeg-flavoured béchamel sauce. Then fill, fold and deep-fry or bake as for three-cornered spinach pies. Makes 15–18.

OKRA WITH TOMATO
Bamies me domates

For 4–6 people, choose a shallow pan that will take 500 g (1 lb) okra in a single layer. In it cook a large chopped onion gently in a little olive oil. When it is soft, push to one side and brown the okra lightly. Stir in 1–2 tablespoons water, then place on top the same weight of tomatoes as okra, peeled and sliced. Add the juice of a lemon, chopped parsley and a little pepper and sugar.

Simmer without a lid for 15–20 minutes or until the okra is tender (fast cooking will split the pods), and the sauce is reduced. With watery tomatoes, you may have to remove the okra to its serving dish before boiling the sauce down hard. Add salt to taste, and serve the okra with its sauce, hot, warm or cold, sprinkled with chopped parsley.

Chicken, lamb or veal stew with okra Use the same quantities of okra and tomatoes as above, together with enough meat (chicken joints or cubed lamb or veal) for 4–6 people. Cook an onion as above, then brown the chicken joints or cubed meat in the same pan and cook with the tomatoes and lemon juice, together with 150 ml (¼ pt/⅔ cup) wine. When the meat is nearly cooked, put in the okra, allowing some of the pods to burst. If the pan is too full, remove the cooked meat and keep hot while cooking the okra in the sauce.

OKRA

Okra (bamies to the Greeks) or ladies' fingers are not a native vegetable. As they come from Africa, I assume they were brought to Greece by Arab traders. Beautiful shape apart, the unusual quality of okra is its gluey juice. In stews this is allowed to escape from some of the pods to smooth and thicken the consistency of the sauce. When served on its own as a vegetable or first course, considerable care is taken to keep the juice inside the pods, and the tomato sauce they are cooked in is thickened by reduction.

Okra is not as easy to buy in England as it should be, considering that it's imported all the year round. You have mostly to go to immigrant shops for it. Avoid rough, dry-looking pods that are spotted with dark brown; go for small, fresh green ones. Cut off the stalk and pare away the tough outer part of the top cone, leaving it intact so that the seeds and juice cannot escape. Put in a dish and sprinkle with vinegar—125 ml (4 fl oz/½ cup) for every 500 g (1 lb)—and salt, if you want to make extra sure of preventing the okra from splitting. Rinse and dry, then use according to your recipe.

FISH FRITTERS WITH GARLIC SAUCE
Psari me skordalia

Skordalia is a garlic sauce of a mayonnaise consistency. It is very popular with fish in batter but also goes well with fried slices of aubergine and courgette as well as boiled beetroot and potatoes. A Greek reader sent me the recipe here, which I find the best of all the different versions. Use a processor or blender if you can, but in any case, crush the garlic before putting it into the machine.

Salt cod, soaked, drained and cut into convenient, not too large pieces, is a favourite of the Greeks but any white fish fillets can be used as well.

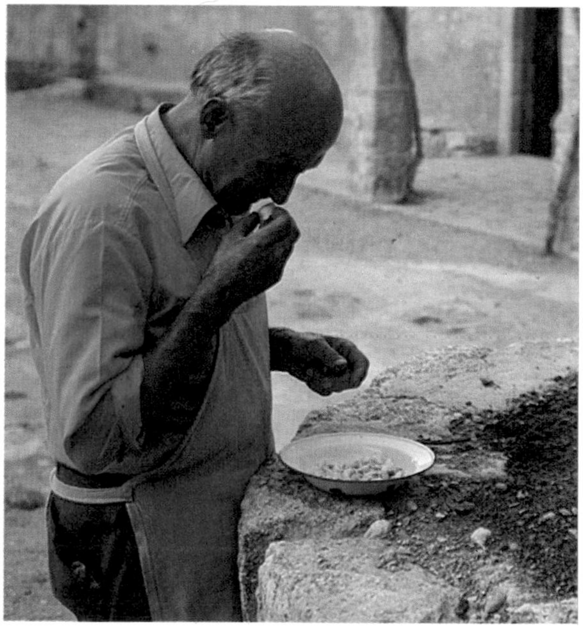

Serves 2–3
4–6 fish fillets
oil, for frying
FOR THE BATTER
125 g/4 oz/1 cup flour
level teaspoon baking powder
1 egg
tablespoon olive oil
dessertspoon ouzo or other aniseed-flavoured spirit
¼ teaspoon each powdered bay leaf and rigani
FOR GARLIC SAUCE
3 or more large cloves of garlic
salt
5 cm/2 in slice of stale white bread, from a small loaf, crusts removed
100 g/3½ oz/scant cup ground almonds
125 ml/4 fl oz/½ cup olive oil
white wine vinegar

Beat the batter ingredients together in the order given, using just enough water to bring it to a batter consistency. Do not make it too thick and clogging; if you are not sure, cook a trial fritter.

Make the sauce: crush the garlic thoroughly with a little salt until it is a thick cream. Soak the bread briefly in a little water, then squeeze dry to give a thick paste. Add to the garlic, pounding well, then blend in the almonds. When you have a smooth thick mixture, add the oil, drop by drop at first, as for mayonnaise. Season to taste with wine vinegar and salt.

Dry the fish fillets well, dip them in the batter and deep-fry, preferably in olive oil for the best flavour. Serve at once with garlic sauce.

Planting garlic cloves in a monastery garden

STUFFED SQUID
Kalamarakia yemista

My favourite Greek dish, which can be made every bit as well elsewhere in Europe. The best-sized squid to use has a bag measuring 12–15 cm (5–6 in) long. The trick of success is to keep the liquid barely simmering; if it boils hard, the squid can burst. This does not matter from a flavour point of view, but it spoils the effect of plump little cushions in a rich sauce.

Serves 6
1 kg/2 lb squid
250 g/8 oz/2 cups chopped onion
olive oil
125 g/4 oz/½ cup brown or long grain rice
75 g/2½ oz/good ½ cup pine kernels
100 g/3½ oz/good ½ cup currants or raisins
small bunch of parsley
salt and pepper
150 ml/¼ pt/½ cup dry white or red wine
375 ml/12 fl oz tomato juice, or 397 g/14 oz can tomatoes, chopped, or 500 g/1 lb tomatoes, peeled and chopped
wooden cocktail sticks or needle and thread

Prepare the squid (see box below). Set the bag(s) aside. Chop the triangular fins and tentacles.

Cook the onion slowly until soft in a little oil. Stir in the tentacles and fins, rice, pine kernels and currants or raisins. Chop the parsley leaves and add them too; season. Stuff the squid half full, leaving room for the stuffing to swell, and close up with cocktail sticks or sew up.

Brown the squid lightly in olive oil in a sauté pan, over a high heat. Pour off any surplus oil, then put the pan back over a low heat, adding the wine and tomato juice or canned tomatoes with their juice, or

CEPHALOPODS

The prized parts of squid, cuttlefish and octopus—kalamari, soupia, chtapodi—are the same, the bag, the tentacles and, in the case of the first two, the ink sac. They are prepared and cooked in similar ways, with appropriate adjustments of cooking time according to age and toughness rather than kind. When frying tiny cuttlefish or squid rings, remember than the briefer the cooking the better: too long and they will be tough.

Squid First remove the fine purple veil (skin) from the bag, if this has not already been done, by peeling it off and away from the head. Draw back the edge of the bag, then grasp the head, with its tentacles, and pull it free of the bag. (The innards, including the ink sac, should come away cleanly.) Cut the triangular fins from the bag, then rinse it out, removing the transparent plastic-like 'pen' (shaped like a quill pen, hence its name) and any innards that have not come away with the head. Cut the tentacles free just above the eyes. Inside the fleshy rim, joining the base of the tentacles, lies a hard, beak-like mouth. Squeeze it out with your fingers and throw it away.

Examine the soft innards. You will see a thin, silver streak with dark undertones: this is the ink sac, and sacs from 2–3 squid will give you enough blackest of black liquid to colour a sauce. Free it with a small knife and put into a bowl. Slit it and add a few tablespoons of water to dissolve the ink (this mixture will be poured through a sieve into the sauce at the end of cooking time) and press gently on the sac to push through as much ink as you can. The remaining head and innards of the squid can be used to give extra flavour to fish stock, if you like. Well rinse squid pieces before using (recipe above for Stuffed Squid).

Cuttlefish The pen, instead of being transparent and unattached, is thick and chalky and tightly stuck to the sac (you will recognize this 'pen' if you have ever kept cage birds). For this reason, you will find it easier to cut the bag into strips to make a stew, rather than stuff it. Tiny cuttlefish, barely 3 cm (a good inch) long, are eaten whole, deep-fried, and are, I would say, more popular in Provence than Greece.

Octopus By the time it appears in shops and markets here, the octopus has received its ninety-and-nine bashings. It will also have been cleaned, and the bag may well have been cut away too, since the tentacles are the delicacy. If you see two kinds of octopus, one with two rows of suckers down the tentacles, the other with only one, go for the former as they are more tender. The single sucker ones are from our own waters and tend to be very tough. Always buy generously, since octopus can lose a great deal of liquid as it cooks. It is prudent to put it into a covered glass dish in a low oven for an hour or two: keep an eye on it and you will see a pinkish liquid gradually rising up the dish. This should be drained off before the tentacles are briefly fried. For stewed octopus, make use of some of the liquid for the sauce, cut up the octopus and cook it briefly in the sauce, since it has already had a preliminary slow cooking.

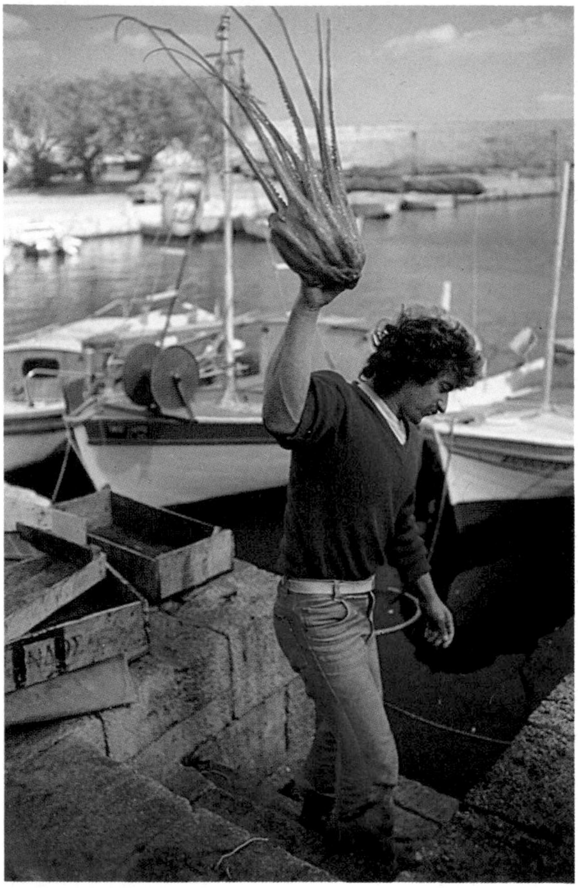

The fisherman beats his octopus to tenderness

the fresh tomatoes. Half-cover and cook for about an hour until the squid are tender and plump and the sauce is reduced and fairly thick. Turn the squid from time to time. Season at the end of cooking, 5–10 minutes before serving. Serve hot or cold.

PORK WITH QUINCES
Hirino me kydonia

This dish can be made with a stewing cut of veal, beef or lamb, or with a chicken, if you do not care for the idea of stewed pork. And if quinces do not appear in your local greengrocer's, substitute pears, apples or prunes, reducing the weight slightly. If you are unfamiliar with the flavour of quince, or find it strong, start by using half the weight of quince given below. This in fact means a small quantity, since much of the weight is lost with the peel and core (do not throw them away, but use to flavour apple jelly). This style of meat with fruit is popular in North Africa, not far from Crete where the recipe comes from.

I visited Crete once in late November, expecting little by way of flowers and fruit. First surprise was the bunches of tiny wild narcissi in the markets, then the sight of them bobbing in the windy, stony fields. Second surprise in Chania market was a box of the largest quinces I have ever seen. They are known as Kydonian apples here and in other Mediterranean countries as well, Kydonia being the ancient name of Chania.

As I left the market, I glanced up at a woman by a first-floor window. From a nail in the wall beside her hung a long curling strip, the thinly-cut zest of an orange, drying in the clear sunshine. I suspect it had been cut with an apple peeler, and was destined for a stew such as this one.

Serves 6
1 kg/2 lb boned meat (pork, veal, beef or lamb), or a similar weight of chicken, jointed
60 g/2 oz/$\frac{1}{4}$ cup butter
250 g/8 oz/2 cups chopped onion
250 ml/8 fl oz/1 cup red wine
strip of dried orange peel
short stick of cinnamon
300 ml/$\frac{1}{2}$ pt/1$\frac{1}{4}$ cups water
500 g/1 lb quinces, peeled, cored and sliced
tablespoon clear light honey
salt and pepper
coriander leaves or parsley, chopped

Cut up the meat into cubes. Heat the butter in a deep sauté pan and stew the onion until soft and golden. Push to one side, or put on a plate. Raise the heat and brown the meat in the remaining fat. Pour off the surplus fat, put in the wine, peel and cinnamon, plus the onion if you removed it. Add the water. Bring to simmering point, cover, cook 1 hour for stewing meat, $\frac{1}{4}$ hr for chicken.

Put the quinces on top of the meat and drip the honey all over. Cover again and cook, keeping the simmering low, until the meat and fruit are tender —allow another hour, but check after 45 minutes. Taste, season with salt and pepper and leave another 10 minutes. Scatter with chopped coriander or parsley, and serve with bread.

In Heraklion market, on Crete

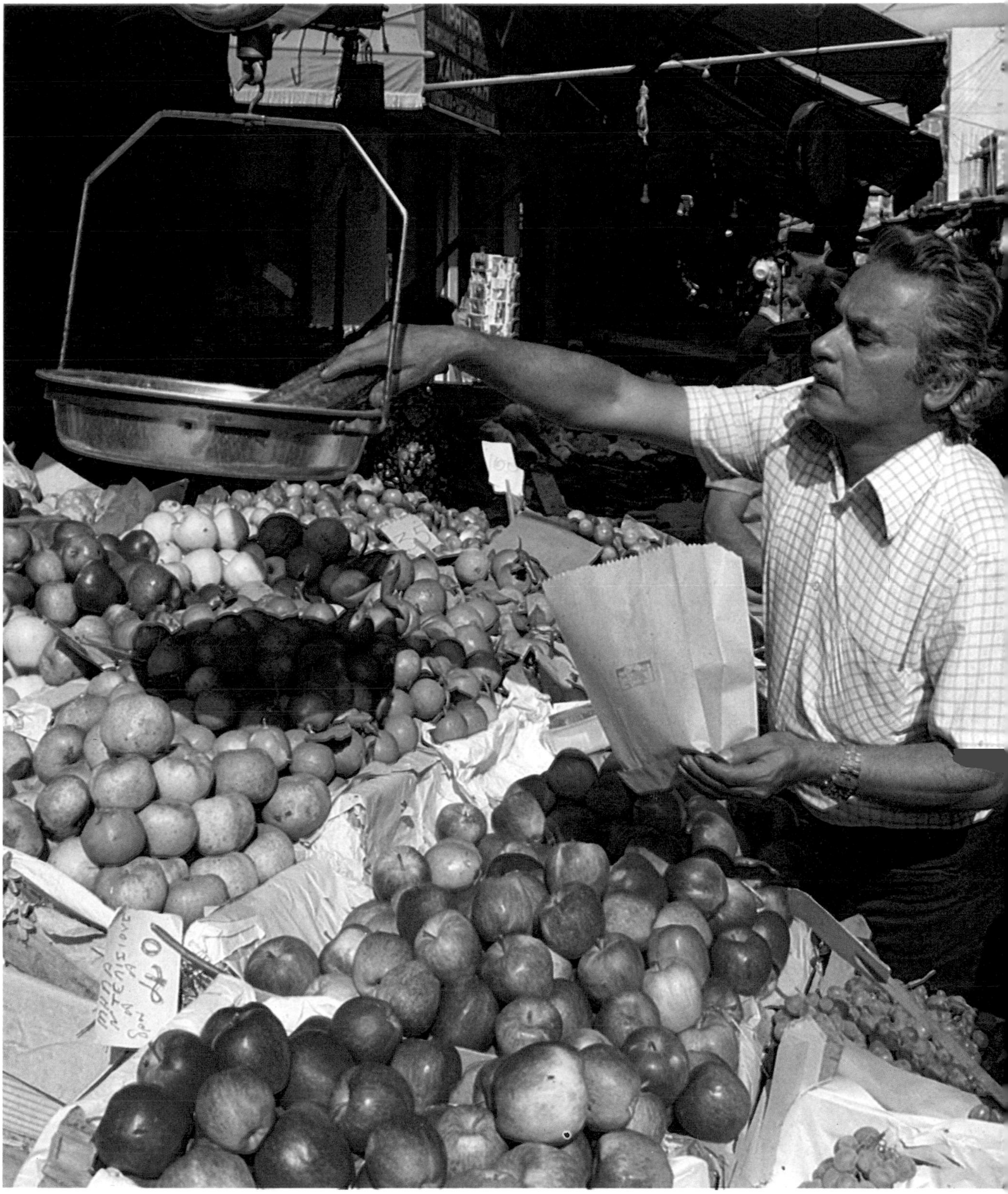

CHICKEN PIE
Kotopitta

This is made just like the spinach pie. Our chickens tend to be fatter and have less flavour than Greek ones, so to compensate for this, use chicken stock rather than water in which to cook the chicken.

Fit a large roasting chicken, breast up, into a saucepan with as little room to spare as possible. Put a butter paper over the breast, and pour in enough stock almost to cover the legs. Bring to simmering point, cover with a lid and leave until just cooked and a little on the pink side. Remove and set aside. Add 500 g (1 lb/4 cups) sliced onions and 150 ml (¼ pt/½ cup) milk to the pan of stock and boil hard, uncovered, until you're left with a pulpy onion sauce equivalent to a generous 300 ml (½ pt/good 1¼ cups).

Meanwhile, remove the skin from the slightly cooled chicken, then cut the meat from the bones into neat pieces and put them into a large basin. Add the reduced onion sauce, 60 g (2 oz/¼ cup) butter, 100 g (3½ oz/scant cup) grated kefalotiri or Parmesan cheese, with plenty of salt, pepper and grated nutmeg, then mix in 2 large beaten eggs. The filling will be fairly juicy but more or less coherent. A little liquid may flow out but no matter if you are making a large pie. If you want to make three-cornered pies (recipe on page 11) instead of one pie, pour off any watery juices.

When you make up the pie, use melted butter rather than oil to brush the sheets of filo pastry.

LEMON CHICKEN
Kotopoulo lemonato

One of the best and simplest chicken recipes, clear and vigorous yet delicate.

Serves 6
large roasting chicken
125 g/4 oz/½ cup butter
grated zest and juice of 2 lemons
level tablespoon rigani
125 ml/4 fl oz/½ cup giblet stock or water
2 level teaspoons salt
plenty of freshly ground black pepper
3 eggs
extra lemon juice

Set oven at moderate, 180°C (350°F), gas 4.

Stuff the bird with half the butter mashed with lemon zest and some of the rigani. Brown it in the rest of the butter and put into a deep casserole. Pour over the juice of the 2 lemons, plus the stock or water, salt, pepper and the rest of the rigani. Cover and bake in the heated oven, basting every 15–20 minutes until the chicken is cooked (about 1 hour). Transfer the chicken to a heated dish and keep warm.

Beat the eggs vigorously and strain in the chicken juices, to make an avgolemono sauce (see box on page 26), using extra lemon juice to heighten the flavour. Serve the chicken with boiled rice.

AVGOLEMENO

As its name implies, the popular sauce of Greece is made from eggs and lemon. It tastes rich and clear, more lemonish than our northern hollandaise egg sauce, and lighter since the bulk consists of stock rather than butter. It is served with vegetables, poultry, meat or fish, either separately or poured over.

The basic mixture is 4 egg yolks or 3 eggs beaten with the juice of a large lemon (to extract the maximum juice, pour boiling water over the lemon and leave a few minutes before squeezing it). First beat the yolks or eggs in a large bowl or in the top of a double boiler, using an electric beater if you have one, then beat in the lemon juice. Now you are ready to complete it:

Sauce I Pour 250 ml (8 fl oz/1 cup) hot liquid slowly into the egg and lemon mixture, beating all the time. The liquid should be appropriate to the dish or from it (see the lemon chicken recipe above). Place the bowl or pan over simmering water and stir or beat until the sauce is thick, light and smooth. As with any egg mixture, do not overheat or the egg will curdle. When the consistency seems right, dip the base of the bowl or pan into very cold water to prevent overheating.

Sauce II A much richer version of the one above. Make a velouté sauce (recipe on page 114) with 30 g (1 oz/2 tbs) of butter and 30 g (1 oz/¼ cup) flour, moistened with 500 ml (¾ pt/scant 2 cups) appropriate liquid. Cook well, allowing the sauce to reduce a little. Use yolks only for the egg and lemon mixture. Pour a ladle of the hot sauce on to the egg mixture, beating all the time; pour back into the pan, off heat. Reheat, without boiling, and stir until thickened. Add chopped parsley.

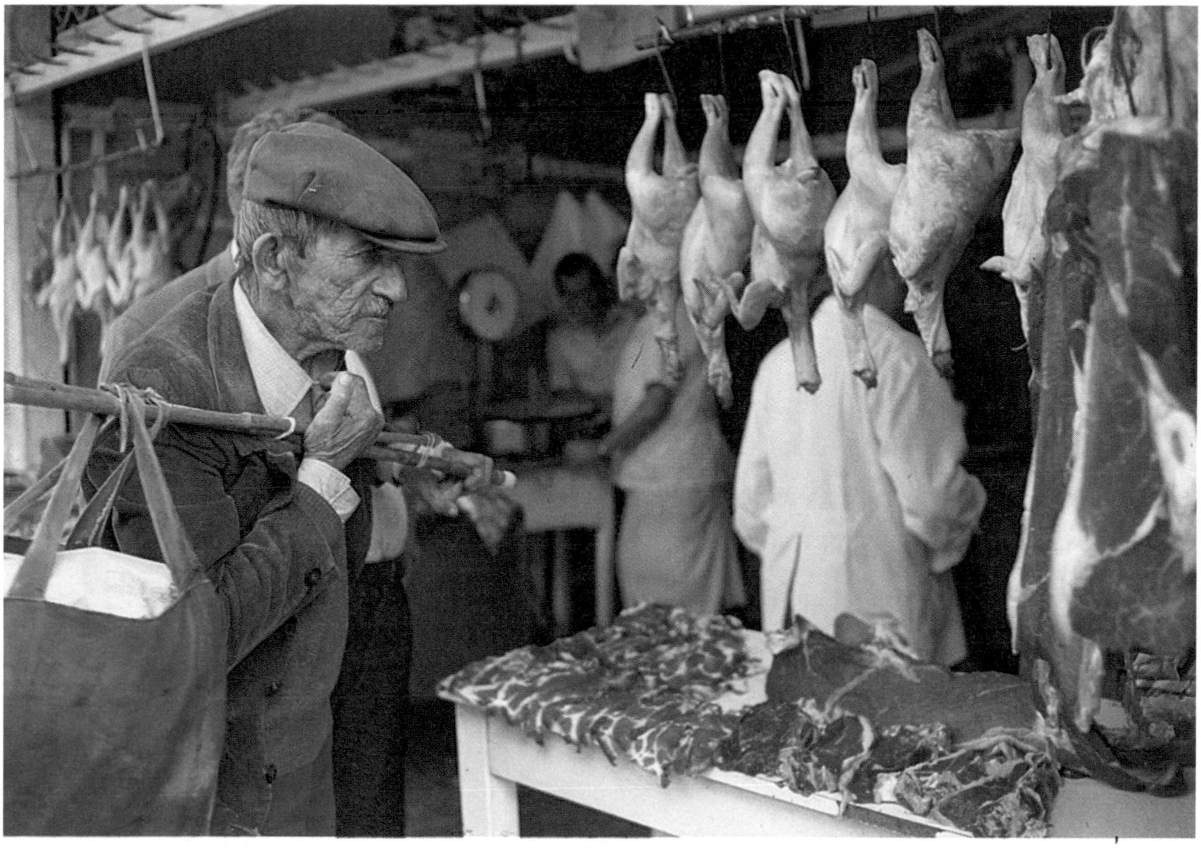

Many butchers' shops are open-fronted which makes it easier—if dustier—to choose meat

VEAL OR BEEF STEW
Stifado

If you visit Greece in one of the cooler times of the year and walk through to a taverna kitchen in the customary way, one of the pans bubbling away on the stove is likely to be a stifado. It will not, I am afraid, always be very well cooked unless you happen to have arrived early on. The romantic thought of stews simmering to perfection for hours on some homely stove often proves disappointing in reality; the liquid has boiled hard, the meat is tough, the sauce is swimming with fat, the taste is coarse, the texture stringy.

A home-made stifado is the thing, where you have had a chance to keep an eye on it. The point is that the liquid should have reduced to a sauce by the time the meat is tender. Not an English technique at all. What you need to do is to keep the lid tightly on the pot for a good hour, then remove it or tilt it to half-cover the pot, so that the liquid gently but steadily reduces to a rich burnished sauce.

Serves 6–8
1 kg/2 lb stewing veal or chuck steak, cubed
olive oil
3 large cloves of garlic, peeled and halved
250 ml/9 fl oz/good cup red wine
500 ml/¾ pt/scant 2 cups tomato juice
2 tablespoons/3 tbs wine vinegar
bouquet garni, with sprig of rosemary
500–750 g/1–1½ lb pickling onions
2 rounded tablespoons/3 tbs currants or seeded raisins
salt and pepper

Brown the meat over a high heat in the oil, in a deep sauté pan. Pour off any surplus fat, put in the garlic and red wine. Bubble for a few minutes, scraping any brown residue into the liquid. Lower the heat, add the tomato juice, vinegar and bouquet garni. Reduce to a mild simmer, cover and leave to

RIGANI

In Greece meat dishes are often flavoured with rigani—the dried leaves and flowers of a Mediterranean marjoram, *Origanum dictamnus*, stronger and sharper than our own wild marjoram and sweet marjoram. People go out and pick their own at the beginning of May, tying the stalks with the flower buds into bunches for drying.

I have never seen rigani in spice racks in grocers here, though a Greek or Cypriot shop, if you have one near you, should be able to supply this herb. Otherwise bring it home with you from Greek market stalls or look for it in shops in Sweden, Denmark and Germany where it is known as 'Spanish hops'—'Spanish' because it comes from the south, and 'hops' because it was used in brewing.

If you cannot obtain rigani, use oregano instead—known to Americans, I believe, as the 'pizza herb'—which belongs to Italian cooking. It doesn't have the same flavour, but comes nearer to it than ordinary marjoram.

Green herbs that you might not expect to find are dillweed (used in meat stuffings, or with broad beans), coriander leaves which give a flat bitterness and which are sold here as 'Chinese parsley' in oriental stores, and mint which is used fresh or dried.

Cumin and orange-tasting coriander seeds give a special taste to meat cookery. So, too, does cinnamon—try adding a small pinch or stick of cinnamon to a lamb or veal stew. Cinnamon sticks are much used to flavour syrup for the various syrup-soaked cakes: rose-water and orange-flower water give a Greek character to straightforward shortbread biscuits, and soothe the sweetness of baklavas (buy triple-strength rose-water from a grocer, not rose-water mixed with glycerine from a chemist).

Buy sesame seeds for bread and biscuit-making from Middle Eastern stores: they're usually the cheapest.

Bundles of dried herbs, including rigani (top left)

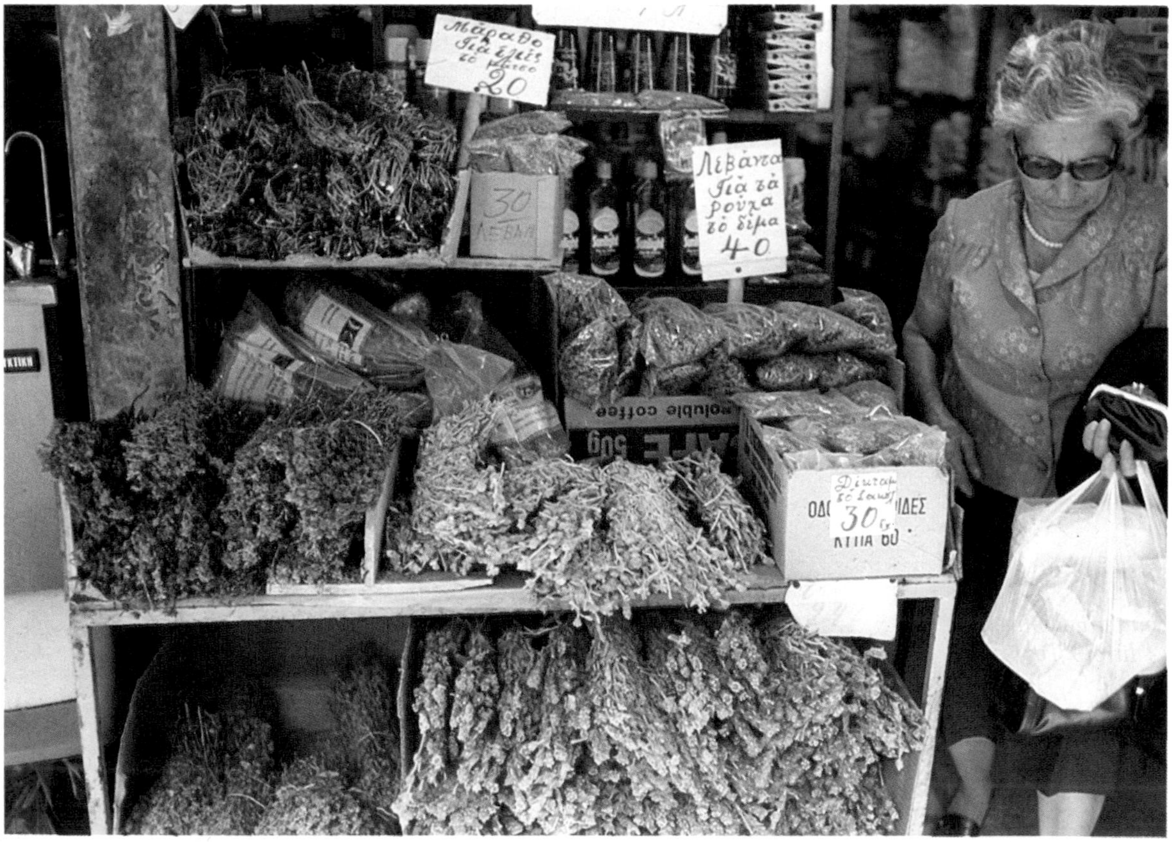

cook for 1 hour (transfer to a cool oven, 140°C (275°F), gas 1) if this is more convenient.

Meanwhile, pour boiling water over the onions, and leave for 2 minutes or until the silvery skins can easily be removed. Nick a cross in the firm root base of each onion, to prevent the centre part popping out as it cooks.

After the meat has simmered 1 hour, put in the onions and the currants or raisins. Stir round and check on the meat and the liquid level. Complete the cooking with the pan uncovered or half-covered, so that the meat is finally bathed in a rich sauce (about 45 minutes). Season with salt and pepper and leave to murmur gently for a further 10 minutes. Keeping back the salt to the end of the cooking time is essential when you are reducing the liquid of the dish. Salt, too, can have a toughening effect on meat, so hold your hand until the meat is already tender.

HARE STEW
Laghos stifado

'Let us sing of hares,' wrote Oppian, the 2nd century AD poet and zoologist, 'rich harvest of the hunt'. Long ears, narrowing head, unsleeping, lustful and prolific, but above all good to eat. The Greeks cook them as I suspect they always have—with red or white wine and onion or garlic. Tomato is a more recent addition, but it cooks down to a dark unity with the other ingredients.

The recipe is basically the same as for beef or veal stifado, as far as the cooking is concerned. The difference comes with the vinegar wash and marinade.

Serves 6–8
1 hare, jointed
100 ml/3½ fl oz/½ cup wine vinegar
MARINADE
large onion, coarsely chopped
large carrot, diced
3 cloves
large bouquet garni
½ litre/¾ pt/scant 2 cups white or red wine
STEW
butter and olive oil
¼ litre/9 fl oz/scant 1¼ cups tomato juice
head of garlic, or ½–¾ kg/1–1½ lb/scant 1¼ cups pickling onion
salt, pepper, sugar

Soak hare in water to cover plus the vinegar, for 30 minutes or so. Drain the pieces and pat them dry with kitchen paper or a cloth. Put them into a pot with the marinade ingredients. Cover and keep in a cool place, larder or refrigerator, for 2 days, turning the pieces occasionally.

To cook the hare, drain the pieces and dry them. Pour the marinade through a sieve into a basin, throwing nothing away.

Make up the stew as for veal or beef stifado (see page 27), browning the marinade vegetables after the hare, and including the bouquet garni and the marinade liquid.

If you decide to use garlic, add it at the start of simmering. Separate the cloves and remove their papery skins, but leave them whole. Onions are prepared and added in the same way as for a beef stifado. Rabbit can be substituted in this recipe if you cannot get hare.

HARE IN WALNUT SAUCE

A dish for October when the new walnuts come in, fresh and yellow, with fine bitter skins. It comes from Robin Howe's *Greek Cooking*.

Serves 6–8
1 hare jointed, or 6–8 hare pieces
wine vinegar
2 stalks celery, chopped
4 slices lemon
sprig or two of marjoram
60 g/2 oz/½ cup butter
4 tablespoons/⅓ cup olive oil
juice of half a lemon
liqueur glass brandy
½ litre/¾ pt/scant 2 cups meat stock or water
large bay leaf
½ teaspoon cinnamon
15 walnuts, shelled, or 30 walnut halves
salt, pepper
level tablespoon flour

Soak hare for 2 days in half water/half wine vinegar to cover. Add celery, lemon slices and herb. Drain, dry and brown the meat in butter and oil. Add lemon juice and brandy and bubble down vigorously. Lower the heat and add stock or water, bay leaf and cinnamon. Simmer until hare is tender, turning the pieces occasionally.

Meanwhile, pour boiling water over the walnuts and remove the fine skin. Grind and mix with salt, pepper and flour. Use to thicken the sauce, when the hare is tender. It should cook down almost to a purée. Serve on pieces of fried bread.

The recipe can also be made with rabbit: of course, it will taste quite different and cook more rapidly.

MOUSSAKA

The nice thing about moussaka from the cook's point of view is that you have a certain liberty of choice. The meat can be fresh from the butcher or left over from a joint (the rare meat close to the bone is the best part to use). It can be made with beef or lamb, or veal, together with brains, which must always be pre-cooked whether or not the veal is. Although aubergines are the best vegetable to use, potatoes and/or courgettes are also popular.

Bear in mind that moussaka can be ruined by wateriness or fattiness. The first comes from too timid a cooking of the meat sauce, the second from using butcher's mince or frying the vegetables too richly; browning them lightly on one side only reduces the oiliness without ruining the mellow flavour of the dish.

The usual Greek topping for moussaka is a cheese sauce enriched with eggs or egg yolks. You can cut down labour and heaviness by using a plain custard mixture of yoghurt, milk, eggs and cheese instead.

Serves 6–8
1.5 kg/3 lb aubergines, peeled or unpeeled and sliced
salt
olive oil
FOR THE MEAT SAUCE
250 g/8 oz/2 cups chopped onion
3 good tablespoons/⅓ cup butter
500 g/1 lb lean lamb, beef or veal, minced or chopped, or 400 g/good 12 oz cooked lamb, beef or veal, minced, or 400 g/good 12 oz cooked veal, plus 125 g/4 oz cooked brains
500 g/1 lb tomatoes, peeled and chopped, or 397 g/14 oz can tomatoes
½ teaspoon rigani or dried oregano
2 cloves of garlic, crushed
black pepper, cayenne
150 ml/¼ pt/⅔ cup red wine
brown sugar
wine vinegar
salt
60–90 g/2–3 oz feta or kefalotiri cheese, grated, or mixed grated Cheddar and Parmesan cheeses
4 tablespoons/6 tbs breadcrumbs
FOR THE CHEESE SAUCE
600 ml/1 pt/2½ cups thick béchamel sauce, or half milk and half yoghurt
3–6 large eggs (see method below)
60–90 g/2–3 oz/½–¾ cup feta or kefalotiri cheese, grated
extra grated cheese, for the topping

Spread out the sliced aubergines in a colander and sprinkle the layers with a little salt. Put a plate on top, and leave them for at least 1 hour to exude their bitter liquid. Rinse slices, then dry them in a cloth. Fry them in oil on one side only till golden and set aside.

Meanwhile, make the meat sauce. Cook the onion gently in the butter in a large pan. When it is soft and golden, raise the heat and put in the meat, spreading it out in a layer. Allow it to brown underneath, then turn it over to brown the other side. Pour off any surplus fat. Tip in the tomatoes with their juice, add the herb, garlic, black pepper and cayenne to taste. Simmer, uncovered, for 15 minutes to make a moist rich stew. If it seems watery, raise the heat and boil off the liquid; if it seems dry, add a little water or stock.

When the meat is cooked, add the wine and boil fiercely for a few moments. Correct the seasoning with sugar, vinegar and salt. If the basic ingredients were full of flavour, you will need hardly any sugar and vinegar—such seasonings are a northern compensation. Check again for oiliness, blotting it away with kitchen paper, or pouring it off. Stir in the cheese and breadcrumbs and set aside.

For the cheese sauce, warm the béchamel or bring the milk to the boil. Beat 3 eggs into the sauce, off the heat. Or pour the boiling milk on to 6 eggs, beating in a basin with the yoghurt. Stir in the cheese. Set the oven at moderate, 180°C (350°F), gas 4.

Line base and sides of a wide, fairly shallow baking dish with a layer of aubergine slices, cooked side down, then put in a layer of meat sauce. Repeat until the two mixtures are finished (it does not much matter whether you finish with aubergine or meat). Pour the cheese sauce or custard over the top. Bake in the heated oven for about 1 hour, but check it after 40 minutes; the moussaka is ready when the top is nicely browned and set.

HONEY AND NUT PASTRIES
Baklavas

Everyone knows about baklavas but few people make them. A pity, as they are very simple—more a matter of organisation than culinary skill. You need a packet of filo pastry, and a baking tray large enough to take the pastry sheets, or two trays to take them cut in half. The quantity below may seem exaggerated, but the pastries freeze well. If you have no freezer, then halve the quantities.

Greek recipes give conflicting instructions about the syrup: some say pour it cold over the hot cake,

continued on p. 32

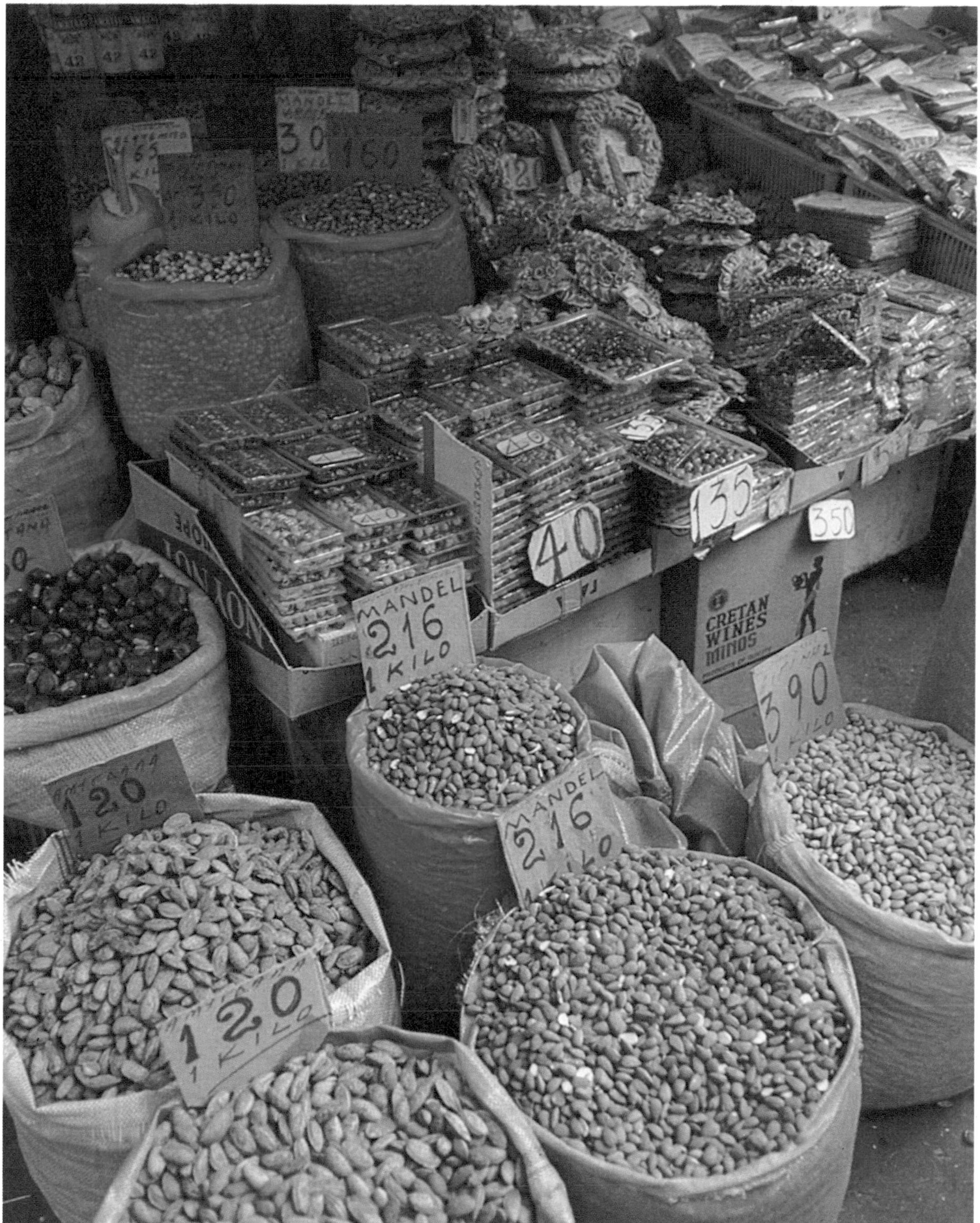

Nuts are a major ingredient in Greek cookery, especially for cakes and pastries

others hot over hot cake, while others say pour it hot over cold cake. I've tried them all, and found no difference; just avoid cold syrup over cold cake.

Enough for 20–30 people
500 g/1 lb packet filo pastry
500 g/1 lb/2 cups butter, clarified
600 g/1¼ lb/5 cups chopped walnuts
175 g/6 oz/¾ cup sugar
rounded tablespoon powdered cinnamon
½ nutmeg, grated
FOR THE SYRUP
500 g/1 lb/2 cups sugar
2 tablespoons/3 tbs lemon juice
finely cut zest of 1 orange and 1 lemon
10–12 cm/4–5 in long sticks of cinnamon
1–2 large shallow baking trays

The top and bottom layers of baklavas consist of four or five layers of pastry, each sheet of pastry and the baking tray being liberally brushed with the clarified butter. The remaining pastry, and any broken scraps, should be divided into two lots, to go in the centre with three layers of filling. Each sheet should also be brushed generously with clarified butter. Set oven at 180°C (350°F), gas 4.

To make the filling, mix together the walnuts, sugar and spices. The walnuts should be chopped fairly finely, or you might prefer to process some and chop the rest less finely by hand. Then spread over the pastry, topping with the rest of the pastry to make three layers in all.

Cut through the top pastry, lengthways, in parallel lines about 3 cm (generous inch) apart. Then cut diagonally so that you have diamond shapes. Sprinkle the top of the pastry with water and bake in the heated oven for 45 minutes or until nicely browned and golden.

Meanwhile, simmer the syrup ingredients together for 5 minutes. When the cake comes out of the oven, pour on the strained syrup evenly and leave until the next day. Cut into pieces, following the topmost cuts already made.

Baklavas are usually served cold, but I find them even more delicious served warm with the sprinkling of rose-water suggested by Theonie Mark in her *Greek Island Cooking.*

SWEET FRIED BOW-KNOTS OR LOVER'S KNOTS
Diples

You see these in every Athenian pastry shop—very sweet they are, so you must order tea or coffee to go with them. They're also a favourite tea-time snack with the children.

Serves 4–6
4 egg yolks, beaten until light
4 level tablespoons/5 tbs sugar
30 g/1 oz/2 tbs butter, melted
grated rind of 1 small orange
4 tablespoons/⅓ cup ouzo, brandy or orange juice
flour
pinch of salt
oil for deep-frying
TO FINISH
454 g/1 lb jar of clear honey
water
juice of 1 lemon
small stick of cinnamon
chopped walnuts, optional
powdered cinnamon, optional
coffee crystals or other coarse sugar

Mix the egg yolks, sugar, butter, orange rind and liquid together. Add enough flour, with the salt, to make a firm dough. Break off small pieces and roll them out very thinly, then using a pastry wheel, cut them into strips about 2.5 cm (1 in) wide.

Tie the strips into lover's knots or pinch them into bows, or make any other shapes you like. Deep-fry them, a few at a time, in hot oil (190°C/375°F) until golden brown. Drain on kitchen paper.

Heat the honey with half its volume of water, together with the lemon juice and cinnamon stick. Boil for 1 minute, then discard the cinnamon.

Layer the diples on to a serving dish, scattering them with walnuts and cinnamon, if you like, then the sugar. Spoon over a little of the honey syrup.

YEAST FRITTERS WITH HONEY SYRUP
Loukoumades

One of the cheapest and most delicious of European sweet dishes. In cafés and cooked food shops in Greece, you will see the huge bowl of bubbly batter waiting to be cooked to order.

Serves 6
FOR THE BATTER
packet of Harvest Gold dried yeast
250 g/8 oz/2 cups plain flour
½ teaspoon salt
250 ml/9 fl oz/scant 1¼ cups warm water
olive oil, for frying
FOR THE SYRUP
250 ml/8 fl oz/1 cup clear honey
short stick of cinnamon
teaspoon lemon juice
2–3 teaspoons brandy or red wine
1–2 tablespoons water

continued on p. 34

FILO PASTRY

Everyone likes the idea of light crisp pastry layers. In Western Europe puff pastry was invented to this end, with 729 layers (though it does not always seem like it). In the Eastern Mediterranean they use a simpler and older system of pulling the dough into transparent sheets and piling them one on top of the other with butter or oil in between. The layers are far fewer, but they make a lighter effect than badly-made puff pastry. In south-west France a similar pulled-dough pastry is used, and La Varenne, the famous 17th-century chef, gives a pie with layered dough. It makes me wonder if we ever went in for the filo system in a wider way? But we do so no longer, and I was not prepared at all for what I saw in a pastry shop in Crete.

In the cool shadows at the back of the shop there was a tall mound made almost entirely of sheets of pastry. Round it walked a young man, very relaxed, pulling and stretching each lump of dough that the proprietor flung to him. He chatted and cheeked the customers, he whistled and patted and pulled, stretching each lump at an easy pace into a huge, transparent circle. Every so often he flung a canvas sheet over the pile—to keep the pastry moist I imagine, and to act as a tally. When customers bought pastry, it was folded in polythene to help keep it soft.

Feel no shame about buying filo in packets. It comes, frozen, in 500 g (1 lb) packs. When you take the wodge of sheets from their packet have a damp tea-towel ready to cover them. Every time you remove a sheet, replace the tea-towel as filo soon turns dry and brittle.

Melted butter (ideally clarified) or olive oil can be used to brush the sheets (choice depends on the filling).

Halfway through pulling and stretching a sheet of wafer-thin filo pastry

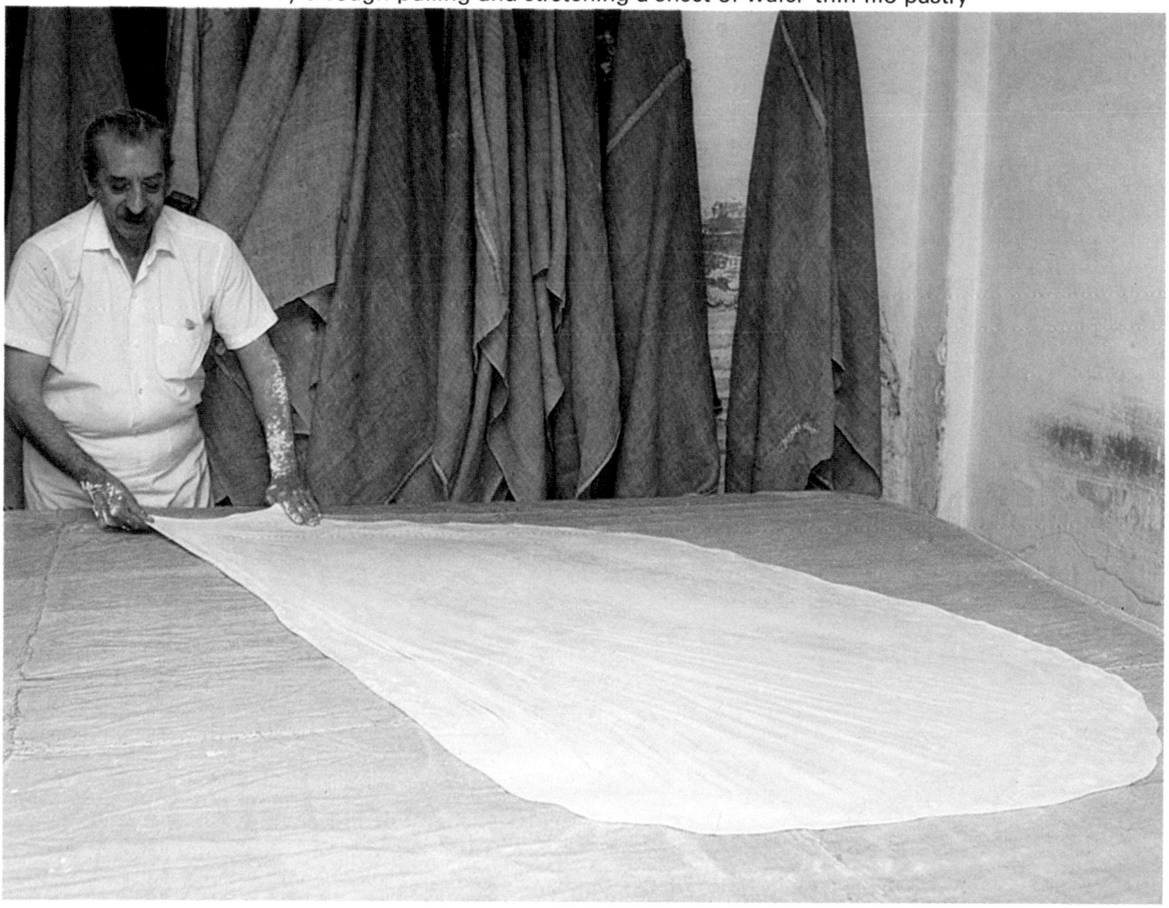

The Aristokratiko sweet shop in Athens

Mix all the batter ingredients together in a large bowl, adding the water gradually to make a very thick batter. Cover and leave in a warm place for about 2 hours, until it rises to an even bubbling level. Pinch the batter, then pull your fingers away: it should stretch like elastic. It can stand for longer in a cool place or you can stir it down and leave it to rise again.

Make the honey syrup by warming together all the ingredients; set aside.

Heat 3 cm (good inch) of oil in a large deep pan to 190°C (375°F). Drop in small amounts of dough, using 2 teaspoons. They will puff up and cook to a pale brown, more the colour of a pale bread crust than a golden fritter-brown. It is wise to make a test fritter or two, which should be crisp and hollow. If they are a little tough also, add 1 tablespoon warm water to the batter before continuing. Spoon the syrup over cooked fritters.

Note fresh or other dried yeasts can be used for the batter. Dissolve them with half the water; when they froth up, mix in with remaining ingredients.

YOGHURT CAKE
Yaourtopitta

A light cake that appears in many versions in Greek cookery books. This one comes from *The Complete Greek Cook Book* by Theresa Karos Yianilos, published in New York. She says that in the grand region of Meteora where 'gigantic rock pillars rise 1800 ft into the sky, the women of Trikkala use yoghurt made from goat's milk to enrich their cakes and breads'.

Serves 6–8
4 eggs, separated
250 g/8 oz/1 cup caster sugar
125 g/4 oz/$\frac{1}{2}$ cup butter, melted, or oil
4 tablespoons/$\frac{1}{3}$ cup whisky, optional
300 g/10 oz/2$\frac{1}{2}$ cups plain flour
3 level teaspoons baking powder
$\frac{1}{4}$ level teaspoon bicarbonate of soda
250 ml/8 fl oz/1 cup plain yoghurt or soured cream
pinch of salt
icing sugar, for dusting
23-cm/9-in mould or tube cake tin, or 28 × 18-cm/11 × 7-in oblong tin

Set oven at moderately hot, 190°C (375°F), gas 5.

Using an electric mixer if possible, beat the yolks until thick, then add the sugar, butter or oil and whisky, if used. Sift the flour with the baking powder and mix in. Blend the bicarbonate of soda with the yoghurt or cream and beat into the flour mixture. Whisk the egg whites with the salt and fold in.

Pour the mixture into the buttered mould or tin and bake in the heated oven for 35 minutes or until cooked. Let it cool for a few minutes in the mould or tin, then turn out on to a wire rack. Dust with icing sugar before serving. Or pour over a hot sugar syrup, flavoured with lemon rind and a piece of cinnamon stick. Scatter with toasted almonds, leave to cool, then serve with cream.

GREEK EASTER CAKE
Halvas

From India to Greece, halva covers many more sweet things than the rich sesame blocks that we particularly associate with the word. Even though it is modified by the grains of semolina, the sweetness of this cake means that it should be served in very small quantities, with cream if you like, and black coffee with the customary glass of water.

continued on p. 36

YOGHURT & CHEESES

To a traveller, a surprising thing about Greek food in Greece, as opposed to Greek food elsewhere, in restaurants and cookery books, is the sheep's milk. Being richer than cow's or goat's milk, it makes the most superb yoghurt, the kind found in shops in great bowls, with a crinkling rich crust on top. This yoghurt is so delicious that I do not understand why Greece and Spain are the only countries that go in for it.

To make this kind of yoghurt at home, you'll need to use sterilised milk plus cream to make something of a crust. In a saucepan heat 1200 ml (2 pt/5 cups) of milk with 150 ml ($\frac{1}{4}$ pt/$\frac{1}{2}$ cup) double cream to blood heat. Remove from the heat and stir in 2 rounded tablespoons of plain (live) yoghurt. Put a lid on the pan, wrap it in a towel or blanket (or tip the milk into a warmed vacuum flask)—and leave for 6 hours until very thick. Refrigerate and use chilled. Keep back a couple of spoonfuls to start the next batch. Every three or four batches, buy a new pot of yoghurt as a starter.

Sheep's milk is also used in making butter, in flavouring other fats, and in cheese-making. Typical Greek cheeses to watch for are:

Feta, fetta (from sheep, goats or cows) The best-known Greek cheese outside Greece, and the most easily bought. The salty, sour flavour and moist crumbliness come from the brine it is stored in.

Kasseri (from sheep) A mild, creamy firm cheese similar to the Italian provolone. Grilled or turned in flour and fried, as part of the mezedes.

Kefalotiri (from sheep or goats) The Greek equivalent to Italian pecorino and Parmesan; use with pasta, sauces.

Manouri (from sheep or goats) Another soft cheese, sometimes mixed with dill.

Mizithra (from sheep or goats) Soft cheese eaten with fruit, honey or sugar, or on its own. Italian ricotta cheese is a fine substitute. As it ages and hardens, it is grated for cooking.

Sheep's milk yoghurt has a thick, crusty top layer of cream

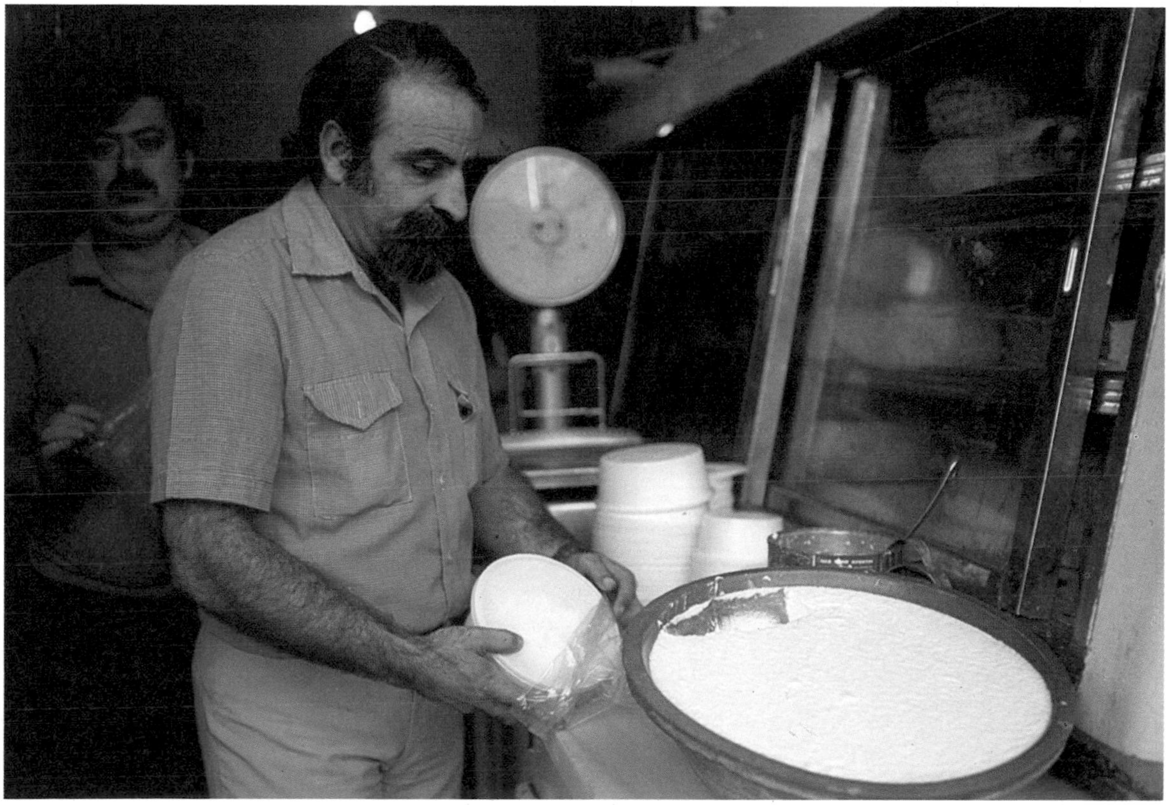

If you have an electric mixer or food processor, this is an easy cake to make by the all-in-one method.

Serves 8–10
125 g/4 oz/$\frac{1}{2}$ cup butter, softened
125 g/4 oz/$\frac{1}{2}$ cup caster sugar
grated rind of 1 orange
4 tablespoons/$\frac{1}{3}$ cup orange juice
2 large eggs
175 g/6 oz/1 cup semolina
2 level teaspoons baking powder
100 g/3$\frac{1}{2}$ oz/scant cup ground almonds
FOR THE SYRUP
375 g/12 oz/1$\frac{1}{2}$ cups caster sugar
175 ml/6 fl oz/good $\frac{2}{3}$ cup water
5 cm/2 in stick of cinnamon
4 tablespoons/$\frac{1}{3}$ cup lemon juice
150–175 ml/5–6 fl oz/good $\frac{2}{3}$ cup orange juice
2 heaped tablespoons chopped candied orange peel
1.5–1.7-litre/2$\frac{1}{2}$–3-pt/6$\frac{1}{4}$–7$\frac{1}{2}$ cup ring mould

Set oven at hot, 220°C (425°F), gas 7.

Cream the butter and sugar together until light and fluffy. Beat in the orange rind, juice and eggs, then the semolina mixed with the baking powder, and the almonds. Or mix everything electrically.

Turn the cake mixture into the lavishly-buttered ring mould. Bake in the heated oven for 10 minutes, then reduce the temperature to 180°C (350°F), gas 4, and bake 25–30 minutes longer or until the cake is done. Let it cool for a few minutes in the mould, to give it a chance to contract slightly, then ease it gently with a knife and turn out on to a warm, deep plate. The cake is very fragile while it is still warm, and if it should break at this point, just push it gently back into shape.

Meanwhile make the syrup by simmering the sugar, cinnamon and water together for 4 minutes. Take the pan off the heat, discard the cinnamon, and stir in the fruit juices and candied orange peel.

As soon as the cake is turned out, bring the syrup to a vigorous boil and spoon it over the cake so that the peel falls in an even and decorative manner. The syrup is soon soaked up, and will keep the cake moist for several days, especially if it is covered with clear film.

GREEK SHORTBREAD
Kourabiedes

A wonderful version of shortbread, made especially at Christmas, when each small diamond or crescent will have a clove struck into the top, to remind people of the spices brought by the Three Kings to Bethlehem. In village bakeries they are kept in a basket of icing sugar.

Recipes vary from house to house: some have almonds, some do not, sometimes the blanched almonds are chopped, sometimes coarsely ground; sometimes they are toasted before being chopped or ground. A variation I have taken to recently is to cook the butter until it is a nut-brown colour; if you do not want to bother with this, creaming the butter is the more usual style.

Makes 24
250 g/8 oz/1 cup lightly salted Danish butter, or unsalted butter
60 g/2 oz/$\frac{1}{4}$ cup caster sugar
large egg yolk
2 teaspoons ouzo or other aniseed-flavoured spirit, or brandy
125 g/4 oz/1 cup almonds, blanched and chopped or ground (optional)
60 g/2 oz/$\frac{1}{2}$ cup cornflour
300 g/10 oz/2$\frac{1}{2}$ cups plain flour
24 cloves, optional
rose-water or orange-flower water
plenty of icing sugar

Cream the butter thoroughly. Alternatively, cut it up and melt it in a heavy pan, then cook it until there is a golden-brown, delicious-smelling oil under a white crust, cool and strain off the oil into a bowl, and discard the sediment.

Beat the sugar, egg yolk and alcohol into the butter. Put the almonds, if you are including them, into the bowl and add the cornflour and flour. Mix to a soft but firm dough, using extra cornflour and flour if it is too soft to handle.

Set oven at 160–180°C (325–350°F), gas 3–4.

Divide the dough into about 24 equal lumps and mould them into plump crescents round a finger. Or pat the dough out and cut it into 24 diamonds. Stick a clove into each piece, if you like. Put them on to baking trays, lined with non-stick baking paper, leaving room for them to spread slightly. Bake in the heated oven for 15 minutes, then check the biscuits and lower the heat for 5–10 minutes if they seem to be colouring; they should remain pale. When cool, they should be crisp.

Pour some rose- or orange-flower water into a small bowl, and tip icing sugar into a large bowl. Put a layer of icing sugar into your biscuit tin. Dip each biscuit quickly into the flower water, then roll it in the icing sugar and put it into the biscuit tin. Put any icing sugar remaining into the tin, so the biscuits never lose their white coating. Stored this way, they will keep well.

ITALY

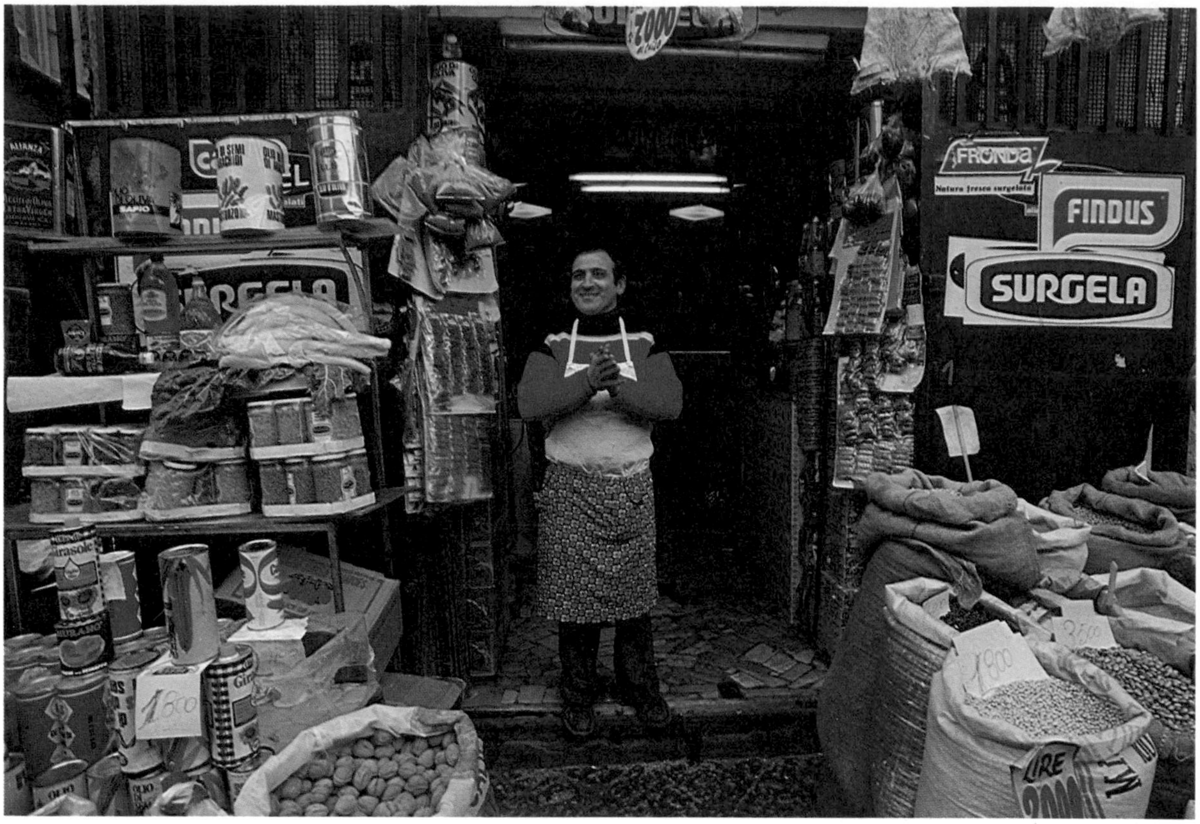

Inside, this grocery will smell of Parmesan cheese and salami

Everyone in England has some idea of Italian food, since Italian eating places in this country must be second in number only to Chinese. The boom started after the last war, with immigrants cooking for other homesick immigrants. The food was cheap, the welcome cheerful, and they seemed to be open day and night. Inevitably the natives began going to them too. Then we had the espresso coffee bar. Next came a rash of places where you couldn't rise from the table without bumping into straw-covered Chianti bottles, fishing nets, or trusses of onions. Nowadays, we have chains of pizzerie, even a pasta factory that exports pasta—wholemeal pasta—to Italy.

But the picture we get from many of our Italian restaurants today is not altogether a good one. It shows too limited and too coarse a cookery. Once you're in Italy, though, sit down in a sunny piazza for an ice, smell the unfamiliar but intriguing midday smells, see a market or two or the wonderful display of food in the columned entry of some good restaurant, and you will understand that a deep-frozen pizza has given you a poor idea of what true Italian food can be.

What, then, is 'Italian' food? Certainly, 'Italian' food existed once, at a certain level, in the Renaissance, when the high and grand city States vied with each other over dinner tables. Great families and church dignitaries demanded feasts to astonish their guests, cool buffets on the terrace of new palaces, dishes sharpened with the bitter oranges associated especially with the splendid Medici. For a while cooking diversified, refined itself, took off in this Renaissance Italy, a country of olives and grapes and gardens, of the world's most civilised people, masters of city life and villa life. Gardeners rose to the ambitions of their masters—think of the plump apples, pears and cucumbers around the edge of a Crivelli painting. Chefs produced the best food in Europe, more refined than the Rabelaisian feasts north of the Alps.

This skill passed into our general European style via France, which with the foundation of that French art, has shaped food for the last three centuries. Italian food today is different, though obviously a number of dishes survive. Food plants from the New World made a difference though not as quickly as you might expect. Maize, the grain now used for polenta, didn't start to replace the anciently cultivated millet until the early 18th century. Beans gradually invaded Tuscany, and the tomato liked Neapolitan sunshine, but surprisingly, perhaps, it did not begin to dominate Italian food until the last 50 years when tomatoes, tomato concentrates, pastes and purées, came into every household.

The truth is that, according to where they live, Italians eat Roman food, or Sicilian food, or Tuscan food, or, if they are particularly lucky, Bolognese food. That is what makes eating and shopping in Italy such fun. There is, however, one thread that runs through the national diet and that is pasta asciutta. For 1000 years it has been going strong. The futurist poet Marinetti tried to bring it down in 1930. He launched a campaign for lighter food, new combinations, 'la cucina futurista', suitable for inhabitants of the new Italy. The fun of Marinetti's ideas—'steel chicken', roast chicken stuffed with zabaglione and metal confetti, or salami smothered in coffee—had a sinister background: he felt that pasta asciutta ruined an Italian's virility, made him gross and greedy, unlikely to triumph in the struggle to come. His friend Mussolini must have agreed but thought it bad publicity to appear as an enemy of pasta ascuitta—every Italian's dream of a good meal at that time—and did not support him.

The regional nature of Italian cooking seems to—but perhaps I am wrong—be more deeply genuine than that of France. The states of the peninsula were not after all united into one country until 1861. Although grand tables looked to French skill as they did elsewhere in Europe, there was a strong set of traditions to be discovered and added to when Italians turned to the food of their native regions in a double patriotism. To an outsider there is, with every visit, something new and delicious to find which comes as a shock after years of the Casa Mia menu in our British high streets.

Dishes such as fonduta or bagna cauda, the truffle-laden menus of Norcia or Piedmont, broccoli finished in olive oil with hot chilis, puntarella (asparagus chicory) and cavolo nero (black cabbage) which seem to be almost entirely unknown in Britain and North America are the kind of happy surprises assiduous travellers may discover for themselves. How many people who go regularly on holiday to Italy have any idea of the reality of the winter olive harvest in Tuscany or the drying of tomatoes?

These days the Italians celebrate the varied and glorious culinary delights of their regions thinking of the past but making new dishes for the present. Good food shops, like Peck's in Milan, have fine displays of regional specialities, old and new. There you get an idea of the dozens of different salami and of the many kinds of ham that do not come only from Parma. As you travel about you discover that some of the best beef in Europe is found in Florence, the best pork in Umbria, the best hazelnuts in Avellino behind Vesuvius and, almost everywhere, the best watermelon you have ever tasted.

TUSCAN BEAN AND CABBAGE SOUP
Ribollita

I had never succeeded in finding a recipe for this Tuscan soup until Arabella Boxer gave one in her *Mediterranean Cookbook*. Ribollita is yesterday's minestrone heated up again with an extra ingredient added, a particular dark cabbage, cavolo nero. This isn't available in England, so use chard, spinach beet or dark green cabbage instead. If you have a favourite minestrone recipe already (there is enormous variety in the hundreds of recipes), use that instead of mine, but add the finishing items below. You have, in any case, to start a day in advance if you begin from scratch.

Serves 6–8
125 g/4 oz/scant ½ cup white beans (cannellini or small haricot)
large onion, chopped
2 large carrots, chopped
3 stalks of celery, chopped
head of fennel, chopped
250 g/8 oz/1½ cups unpeeled courgettes, chopped
250 g/8 oz/1 cup peeled tomatoes, chopped
4 tablespoons/¼ cup olive oil
2 plump cloves of garlic, finely chopped
1.25 litres/2 pts/5 cups hot chicken stock
salt and black pepper

TO FINISH
6–8 slices of dry white bread
500 g/1 lb chard, spinach beet or dark cabbage
salt
small jug of olive oil

Put the beans into a large pan and cover generously with cold water. Bring to the boil, cover and leave for 1 hour. Drain well. Stew the chopped vegetables slowly in the oil in a deep pan for 10 minutes, adding the garlic towards the end. Pour in the hot stock and the drained beans. Simmer for 1 hour or until the beans are tender: only season the soup at the end.

Next day, put a slice of bread in 6–8 soup plates. Cook the cabbage, drain and chop coarsely, adding salt. Pile on to the bread. Reheat the soup while you prepare the cabbage, so that you can ladle it on to the cabbage in the bowls straightaway. Serve at once, with the jug of oil separately.

Variation Soften a chopped medium onion and 2 cloves of garlic in 100 ml (3½ fl oz/½ cup) good olive oil. Add a carrot, a stick of celery, the white part of two leeks and a fine tomato—all shredded or sliced —and stew for 15 minutes. Add a kilo (2 lb 2 oz) of fresh beans (or 600 g (1¼ lb) dried beans, soaked overnight), a ham bone and enough water to cover. Simmer 1½ hours. Put 2 tablespoons (3 tbs) of oil in a small pan and in it cook very slowly 2 cloves of garlic, two or three sprigs of thyme and rosemary, then strain off and keep the oil. Take the bone from the soup and discard it, then remove a ladle of beans and set them aside. Sieve the soup, or put it through a Mouli-légumes, and return to the rinsed out pan. Add 300 g (10 oz) black cabbage leaves, cut into shreds, and the strained oil. Simmer until the cabbage is ready, put in salt and the ladle of beans. Simmer 10 minutes, add pepper and pour into a tureen in which are slices of dark Tuscan bread or wholemeal bread.

This recipe comes from the Italian magazine, 'Panorama', 30 March, 1981.

A tureen of minestrone and bowls of ribollita

TUSCAN BLACK FISH SOUP
Cacciucco

Whenever I make or think of this soup of the Tuscany coast, I remember my first startling experience of it in a small restaurant in Viareggio. I hid my shock at the black plateful that was put in front of me, but what a soup it was! I have never had such a fine cacciucco since, and I suppose I never shall.

Octopus waiting to be cooked in a Neapolitan pizzeria

Our choice of fish is limited, but you must have at least five kinds—one for each C in cacciucco, according to Wilma Pezzini in *The Tuscan Cookbook*. She also recommends using half saltwater fish—sole, bass, hake, swordfish, mullet and so on—the other half consisting of two-thirds squid, shrimps, prawns, crawfish or lobster and one-third clams, mussels, cockles and so on. Squid or cuttlefish is essential to make the soup black.

Serves 6–8
1.5 kg/3 lb saltwater fish, cleaned, scaled and heads reserved
1 kg/2 lb prepared squid, cuttlefish, with ink sacs, octopus and shellfish
500 g/1 lb mussels or other molluscs
salt and pepper
olive oil
medium carrot, finely chopped
2 stalks of celery, finely chopped
2 sprigs of parsley, finely chopped
2 bay leaves
sprig of thyme
2 cloves of garlic, finely chopped
2 small hot chilli peppers, seeded
1 kg/2 lb tomatoes, peeled and chopped, or 794 g/1 lb 12 oz can of tomatoes
300 ml/½ pt/1¼ cups red wine
6–8 large slices of bread, toasted or fried and cut into 2 triangles each

Slice the fish, unless very small. Put the ink sacs from the squid, cuttlefish into a bowl; chop the tentacles into pieces, discard the fine purple skin from the body sacs and slice them: put the 'debris' with the fish heads. Shellfish should if possible be uncooked: chop the lobster into pieces, or ask the fishmonger to do it for you. Scrub the mussels or other molluscs and open them in a covered pan over a very high heat—about 2 minutes. Put them into a bowl, discarding half the shells. Strain the liquor carefully through muslin. Season all the fish, sprinkle with oil.

Meanwhile, heat about 8 tablespoons olive oil (⅔ cup) in a large pan. Add the vegetables, herbs, garlic, chillies, fish heads and debris, browning them nicely. Add tomatoes and any juice. Pour a little water on to the ink sacs, crushing them so that the ink dyes the water black. Add a little more water and tip into the pan. Swill the bowl out—use 1.5 litres (2½ pts/6 cups) of water in all. Pour the mussels or other liquor into the pan, plus the wine. Simmer for 30 minutes. Rub the contents of the pan through a fine sieve into another pan, ready for reheating. Season.

Take a large glazed flameproof earthenware casserole (or a pan), put it on the stove, using a heat-diffuser with gas, and switch on. Pour 8 tablespoons (⅔ cup) olive oil into the casserole. When hot, put in the squid, cuttlefish or octopus pieces and cook 15 minutes. Then add live shellfish, if using, and saltwater fish. Cook 10 minutes. Put in cooked shellfish if using, and molluscs; cook for 2 minutes, stirring gently once or twice.

Have ready 6–8 deep soup plates, heated, or a tureen, with the bread in the bottom. Put in the fish, and pour the reheated soup over. Serve straightaway, with finger bowls for people to rinse their fingers.

SMOKED TROUT
Trota affumicata

In the grandest food shops, such as Fauchon in Paris and Peck in Milan, you are so dazzled by the elegant display of food that you sometimes do not realize how simple and how easy to copy it is.

Take the smoked trout at Peck's. The fillets have been removed from the skin and bones of the fish. They are carefully arranged like the spokes of a wheel on a plain white round china dish. At the rim end of each fillet there is a transparent slice of lemon. And over the whole thing, the very best green Tuscan olive oil. Put that on the table with good bread, and you have the perfect first course. No fuss, but great elegance and pleasure, to the eye as well as the tongue.

If you cannot afford smoked trout, try smoked buckling instead. Or smoked sprats, if you have the patience, though they are best sprinkled with white wine.

STUFFED SARDINES
Sarde a beccafico

A Sicilian dish, from Palermo, of fresh sardines stuffed with a sour and sweet mixture. Beccafico is Italian for a warbler, and refers to the way the sardines are tucked into the dish like little birds.

Small herrings can be cooked in the same way. Or you can use the stuffing for larger boned herring and mackerel, folding them back together round it in the normal way.

Serves 6
1½ kg/3 lb sardines
salt, pepper
olive oil
6 heaped tablespoons soft white breadcrumbs
125 g/4 oz/⅔ cup sultanas, soaked in water
125 g/4 oz/1 cup pine kernels
sugar
8 salted anchovies, soaked, boned, dried
6 sprigs parsley, chopped
4 bay leaves
3 level tablespoons finely chopped onion
juice of 1–2 lemons, bitter oranges or sweet oranges

Cut off the heads of the fish. Clean them and split them open down the belly. Turn them, cut side down, on to a smooth surface and press firmly down the backbone. You should feel it giving. Turn the fish over and pick out the backbones and remove any small bones with tweezers. Wash and dry.

Heat about 125 ml (4 fl oz/½ cup) olive oil and brown two-thirds of the crumbs lightly. Put into a bowl, draining off any surplus oil into a baking or gratin dish. Mix drained sultanas, pine kernels and a level teaspoon of sugar into the crumbs. Chop or pound the anchovies to a purée, and add to the stuffing. Mix with your hands, working in the parsley and onion. Taste and add seasoning if necessary. Pepper will be welcome.

Divide the stuffing between the fish, putting it on to the cut sides. Roll up from the tail, or fold the fish over to their original shape. Put the sardines into the baking dish (oil it first, if you have not done so already). Tear the bay leaves into pieces and scatter over the top, then sprinkle on the remaining crumbs and a little olive oil. Bake at 180–190°C (350–375°F), gas 4–5 until the sardines are cooked—about 30 minutes. Pour over the juice and serve.

A basket of fresh sardines

GRILLED EEL
Anguilla arrosta

Buy fine plump eel which will cut to pieces measuring 2–3 cm (1 in) in diameter. According to the rest of the meal, allow one for every two or three people. Ask the fishmonger to kill it for you, and to cut it into 8-cm (3-in) lengths.

You will also need a small bay leaf for each piece of eel. Thread them on to skewers, alternating with the eel. Make the grill or charcoal very hot and cook the skewers of eel. The skin keeps the delicate flesh moist and cooks to a crisp brown. Some people cut it off but I cannot bear to see such delicious morsels wasted.

In north-western Italy eel is served, oddly as it may seem to us, with a sweet fruit pickle flavoured with mustard. It is called mostarda di Cremona and has a long history going back to at least the 16th century. Bottles of it can be bought at Italian groceries, but you may not always be lucky. Some brands are over-sweet and nasty: look for jars which contain pieces of vegetable as well and take advice, if you feel you can trust the shopkeeper's pride rather than his desire for profit. Mostarda goes with ham and other meats that are served with fruit sauces: that is its normal role, but try a little bit at least with grilled eel.

SOLE WITH PARMESAN
Sogliole alla parmigiana

This recipe is intended for proper sole, Dover sole, but to me so good a fish is not improved by the strength of Parmesan cheese. I find the method more suitable for the second and third ranks of flat fish, where extra interest is needed to compensate for the fact that they are not Dover sole. The idea is a simple one, and can be adapted to several fish or one or two large ones.

Switch on the grill and leave it to warm up while you cook the fish. Skin and clean them if the fishmonger has not done so already. Flour them lightly and fry in butter on both sides until they are pale golden brown. Pour into the pan enough fish, shellfish or chicken stock to come 5 mm (scant $\frac{1}{4}$ in) up the sides of the pan. Complete the cooking at a steady boil, so that the stock reduces a little: do not overcook the fish which should remain slightly pink at the bone.

Scatter the fish with a layer of grated Parmesan cheese, not too thickly. Baste with stock, being careful not to dislodge the cheese. Put under the grill until the cheese melts. Baste again. Put back for the cheese to colour lightly, and baste again. Put back for the cheese to turn an appetising but pale brown. The basting will have given the cheese a juicy, shiny appearance. There will be little stock left.

PROSCIUTTO

Prosciutto is merely the Italian word for ham, but to Americans and the British it carries the special meaning of Parma or San Daniele ham, raw ham (prosciutto crudo) cut in transparently thin slices. Parma ham has a special sweetness of flavour which comes—so a friend tells me—from the pigs being fed parsnips to fatten them.

Hams of this kind can be eaten simply with bread and butter (curls of butter are often served on the plate, with the ham). Or slices can be wrapped round pieces of melon, or fresh figs, to make the perfect salty sweet lunch for a hot summer's day.

CARPACCIO AND BRESAOLA

Although Carpaccio, named after the Venetian painter, is attributed to Harry's Bar in Venice, I believe it has long been a speciality of the mountain valleys of Lombardy. It is the fresh version, as it were, of bresaola, the uncured beef eaten in the first instance by peasant farmers soon after the animal has been slaughtered, before the meat is salted and dried to make bresaola. If you have ever eaten air-dried Grisons beef from Switzerland, you will have an idea of what bresaola is like.

Carpaccio Buy a piece of topside or fillet of best quality, well hung beef (Scottish is ideal), that will give you 250 g (8 oz) when it has been thoroughly trimmed and skinned. Chill in the ice compartment of the refrigerator or the freezer until it is firm and easy to slice. Either use a slicing machine or a very sharp knife, to cut it into transparent slices. Alternatively, cut it as thinly as you can and beat it out carefully between two pieces of olive-oiled clingfilm. You should be able to see light through it.

Arrange the pieces, rosette style, on six plates. Mix an olive oil vinaigrette, with lemon juice, salt and pepper, and brush it over the meat to keep the slices moist and season them. Scatter with a little chopped parsley and chives. Make central mounds of chopped anchovy and capers, as an extra seasoning.

Bresaola Good moist bresaola is not easy to find, but it is always worth enquiring at Italian groceries. It is not part of the normal supermarket range of

Much ham is eaten, uncooked and thinly sliced, with fruit, or with butter and bread

charcuterie. Spread out the slices on a large serving plate and brush them very lightly with olive oil and lemon (no salt needed). Scatter discreetly with chopped parsley, and serve with bread and butter. With fruit, too, if you like, in the manner of prosciutto.

MEAT SAUCE
Sugo di carne

We cannot, perhaps, aspire to the finest ragù bolognese as perfected in the demanding kitchens of the gastronomic city of Bologna, but a perfectly good meat sauce can be contrived for which no apologies are required. Quantities below are enough for lasagne to serve 6–8, made with any one basic pasta or for spaghetti or tagliatelle for 8–10.

Three points—do not buy butcher's mince, do try and use an earthenware pot or casserole (with gas, you need a heat-diffuser: with electricity, put the pot on the element before switching it on), and do arrange to make the sauce when it can bubble gently for 4 hours as this is the major secret of success. The sauce can be kept for several days in the refrigerator, and it freezes well. If you have a freezer, make double quantities.

about 750 g/1½ lb feather steak, shoulder fillet or chuck steak
60 g/2 oz/3 slices unsmoked gammon or green bacon
packet/⅓ oz dried mushrooms, e.g. funghi porcini (optional)
175 g/6 oz/1½ cups chopped onion
4 tablespoons olive oil
60 g/2 oz/¼ cup butter
medium carrot, chopped
2 stalks of celery, chopped
300 ml/½ pt/1¼ cups dry white wine, or half wine, half stock
150 ml/¼ pt/⅔ cup milk, slightly less half-cream
¼ nutmeg, grated
396 g/14 oz can of plum tomatoes
dessertspoon tomato paste
salt and pepper

Cut up the beef and bacon. Chop in the processor (best) or put through a mincer. Pour very hot water over the mushrooms and leave to soak. Soften the onion in the oil and butter, and when it is yellow and transparent put in the carrot and celery. Stir about thoroughly, then put in the meat spreading it over the base and breaking up the lumps. Turn it about so that the red rawness turns opaque without the meat browning.

Raise the heat to medium and pour in the wine or wine and stock. When it has almost disappeared, add the milk or cream with the nutmeg. When that too has been absorbed, put in the tomatoes, their juice and paste—break up tomatoes with a wooden spoon as they cook. Cut up and stir in the mushrooms, with their strained liquor.

Leave the potful to burble gently for 4 hours—the occasional bubble and heave is all that's required; stir occasionally. The sauce will reduce a little and slowly, but not too much. The meat dissolves to an agreeable mealiness. Add salt and pepper at the end.

TOMATO SAUCES
Sughi di pomodoro

It is in Italy that many of us eat our first real tomatoes. Around Naples in particular you may see field after field of them, plum-shaped drops of red, blazing in the sun among wrinkled sunburnt leaves: this is the San Marzano tomato, truly a 'pomo d'oro' in that light. Here we have to buy it in cans, not at all the same in flavour but better for cooking with than the feeble tomatoes sold here. The sun-dried tomatoes now on sale in Britain and America are a useful seasoning to liven up canned or northern tomatoes, and stronger than the familiar tomato concentrate in tubes and small cans.

The three sauces following cover most situations, as far as northerners are concerned. The first is a cooked down sauce, made with fresh ordinary tomatoes or canned ones, a useful winter recipe. The second demands reasonably good firm tomatoes, and the third should only be made with superb tomatoes straight off the stalk when you are in Italy on holiday or elsewhere in the Mediterranean. The first two sauces freeze well. They all give enough for six people.

Tomato sauce I

250 g/8 oz/2 cups chopped onion
4 tablespoons/$\frac{1}{3}$ cup olive oil
125 g/4 oz/6 slices pancetta (cured belly pork) or green streaky bacon, chopped (optional)
125 g/4 oz carrot, chopped
stalk of celery, thinly sliced
150 ml/$\frac{1}{4}$ pt/$\frac{2}{3}$ cup dry white or red wine or 5 tablespoons/6 tbs sweet Marsala (optional)
1 kg/2 lb tomatoes, peeled and quartered, or 794 g/1 lb 12 oz can of tomatoes
salt and pepper
sugar
level teaspoon of dried oregano
fresh basil, chopped

Fresh pasta, often green with spinach juice, is becoming a national obsession

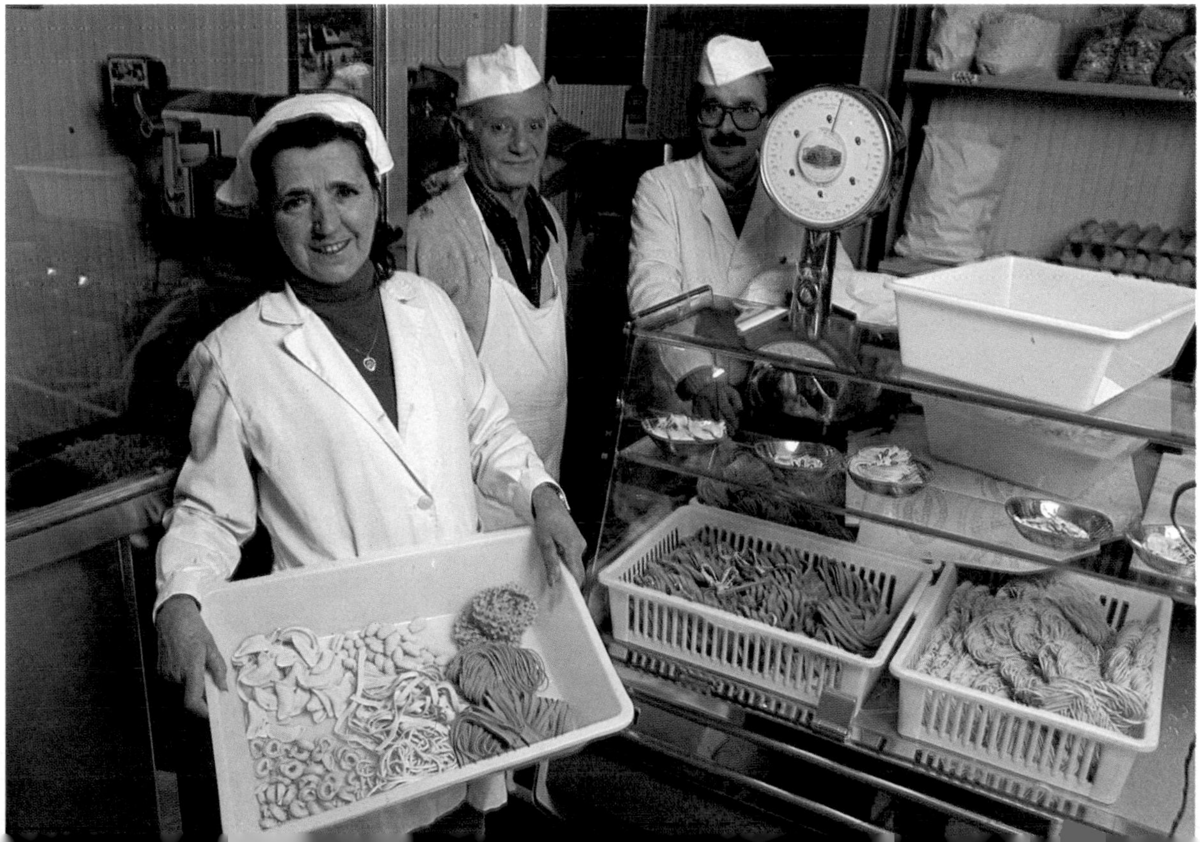

Soften the onion in the oil until yellow over a low heat. Raise the heat and add pancetta or bacon with the carrot and celery. When they begin to brown appetisingly, put in the wine if used, and boil down vigorously by half. Add the tomatoes and cook hard for 15 minutes. Put in seasoning to taste, including a pinch of sugar and the oregano.

Continue to cook vigorously, uncovered for 20–30 minutes until the wateriness has boiled away to leave a pulpy sauce. Check the seasoning. Freeze at this stage, after cooling.

For a smooth sauce, put through the coarse or medium blade of the Mouli-légumes. For a very fine sauce, useful for adding to other sauces, liquidise, process or sieve it: in this form it can rapidly be turned into soup, by adding an equal volume of appropriate stock and some cream, or mussels, or clams, with a leaf or two of basil.

Chopped fresh basil should only be added to the sauce when it has been reheated and is ready for serving.

Tomato sauce II

medium to large onion, chopped
young carrot, diced
clove of garlic, mashed with a little salt
60 g/2 oz/¼ cup butter
1 kg/2 lb good tomatoes, peeled and coarsely chopped
salt and pepper
sugar
fresh basil

In a covered frying pan, sweat the chopped onion with the diced carrot and garlic in the butter. When they are soft, put in the tomatoes. As the juices run, remove the lid, raise the heat and cook hard for 10 minutes. If the pulpy sauce is at all watery at the edges, pour it off rather than increase the cooking time.

Season with salt, pepper, a hint of sugar and plenty of torn or chopped fresh basil. A summer sauce for pasta with butter and Parmesan, or for making Parmigiana melanzane (see page 51).

Tomato sauce III

¾ kg/1½ lb tomatoes, skinned
large new young onion with a green stalk, or several spring onions
large clove garlic
salt, pepper
olive oil
chopped fresh basil or parsley

Deseed and chop the tomatoes. Add the onion, also chopped, and the garlic crushed to a paste with salt. Stir well, taste and add more salt, plenty of pepper. Cover and chill for 3–4 hours. Sprinkle with olive oil and basil or parsley. Serve ice-cold with very hot pasta.

PESTO SAUCE

An aromatic sauce for pasta made by combining basil, pine nuts, garlic, olive oil and strong cheese. Half fill a litre-measure (¾-pt/2¼-cup) with fresh basil leaves, pressing them down lightly. Put the basil into a processor or blender with 50 g (scant 2 oz/½ cup) pine nuts, 2 sliced cloves of garlic, and 4 tablespoons (⅓ cup) olive oil. Whizz until smooth, adding a further 6 tablespoons (½ cup) olive oil. Put in 30 g (1 oz/¼ cup) each freshly grated Sardinian pecorino and Parmesan cheeses. Taste and add more of one or the other cheese, or both, to your liking—another 30 g (1 oz/¼ cup) approximately. Some people add 1 tablespoon butter.

If you use other pecorino cheeses to make pesto watch out for their saltiness, and use extra Parmesan: a good tip from Marcella Hazan in her *Classic Italian Cookbook.* As a consolation for town dwellers with a couple of weedy basil seedlings, I offer the thought that some proprietary brands of pesto are quite good.

Variation In the autumn when the fresh walnuts are about, they are often used in Liguria instead of pine kernels. Pour boiling water over them and remove the thin yellowish skin. Shell the nuts first of course, before weighing them.

PASTA

Pasta, meaning boiled dough, is an old dish of East Mediterranean eating. Forget silly stories about Marco Polo. It made its way from the eastern Roman Empire between the 6th and 11th centuries, into such parts of Italy as came under Byzantine rule. And although it has become a badge of Italian food to present-day tourists, pasta asciutta—dry pasta as opposed to pasta in soup—was by no means a universal dish in Italy until about 60 years ago.

Once they managed to master the business of eating it, foreigners took to pasta with enthusiasm. There is a recipe for macaroni in an early 15th-century cookery manuscript in the British Museum, smart and idle young men in the 18th century were called 'macaroni' in London, and the German poet

Heine dreamed of himself as a harlequin, all lazy under a weeping willow: 'The hanging sprays of the tree were macaroni, which fell, long and lovely, into my mouth, and in between, instead of the sun's rays, flowed sweet dreams of golden butter, and at last a fair white rain of powdered Parmesan.'

The business of stretching the dough makes me think of pulling transparent sheets of filo or strudel pastry, which are for quick use, turning brittle if allowed to dry. Pasta, being a little thicker and cut small, dries well and can be stored indefinitely—an early 'convenience' food, a neat way of keeping flour.

An amazing point about pasta is that despite the different varieties—and there are hundreds—they are all made basically from one simple dough. Many pasta recipes are interchangeable with regard to the sauces or fillings, but it can be confusing knowing which type of pasta to use for what.

For soup, choose tiny shapes like alphabet letters, bows, shells, or stars.

For boiling, choose flat noodles; round solid types of which spaghetti is the best known; tubular types like macaroni and rigatoni, and stuffed shapes like ravioli or tortellini.

For baking, choose lasagne, macaroni or stuffed ones like cannelloni.

Making pasta, 'all long and lovely', as an occasional family dish is simple and entertaining (daily pasta demands an electric pasta machine). No special equipment is required, and children can take it over most successfully. Ingredients present no problem—our strong white bread flour, the nearest thing to Italian durum wheat, is on sale everywhere these days. Wholemeal bread flour can, of course, be used.

Pasta can also be flavoured in a variety of ways but I have three standard mixtures.

BASIC PASTA RECIPES

Enough for 6 servings

YELLOW *(pasta gialla)*
3 eggs
about 275 g/9 oz/2¼ cups strong flour

PINK *(pasta rosa)*
2 eggs
2 level tablespoons/3 tbs tomato paste
about 275 g/9 oz/2¼ cups strong flour

GREEN *(pasta verde)*
2 eggs and 1 egg yolk
an 'egg-shape' of cooked, chopped, squeezed spinach (about 250 g/8 oz fresh)
about 250 g/8 oz/2 cups strong flour

Put the eggs and flavouring, if used, into a mixer bowl or processor. Switch on at top speed, and after a few seconds, begin adding the flour, slowly. When you have a soft, coherent unsticky dough, stop adding flour. Knead the dough on a slab until it is smooth and silky looking. Divide into two, three or four pieces and leave to rest under an upturned bowl.

Roll out on a lightly-floured surface, moving the piece by a quarter turn every so often until the dough is like a piece of cloth. Every so often, roll it round the pin at the far end and pull or push it to stretch the dough. An illustration in Bartolomeo Scappi's *Opera* (first published in 1570) shows the pasta table in a kitchen with one person pulling the dough, while another on the other side of the table holds it down with a rolling pin. You will discover the thickness of dough you prefer by taste and experience—thin narrow strips for butter and cheese, thicker wider strips for meat sauces and so on. Cut to the required shape.

COOKING PASTA Freshly made egg pasta cooks much more quickly than dried pasta. Allow 75–100 g (3–4 oz) pasta per person. Allow 5 minutes for fresh flat pasta, and about 7–10 minutes for stuffed pasta, depending on its size. Start timing immediately after the water (salted) or liquid into which the pasta has been dropped returns to the boil. Stir with a wooden spoon after putting it in or the pasta may stick together.

LASAGNE AL FORNO

My best memories of this dish are of a Venetian rosticceria where an immense lasagne was baked in a vast tin. Customers indicated how much they would like, it was put on to a plate and then weighed to see what it cost. An admirable system. Lasagne al forno is not a Venetian dish by origin: it comes from the next province down, Romagna, at least in its classic form. Everyone in Italy makes it these days, with many variations. The pasta can be yellow or pink, but green looks and tastes best with the meat and sauce. Note that it is not necessary to boil the pasta first. The moisture of the sauces is enough, particularly in the case of home made lasagne which are especially tender. On boxes of bought lasagne you will sometimes see a sentence or two about this; even if you do not, boiling is unnecessary.

It is really an assembly job. Have ready the following items:

Serves 6
500 ml/generous ¾ pt/scant 2 cups meat sauce (see page 44)
béchamel sauce made with 60 g/2 oz/¼ cup each butter and flour, and 600 ml/1 pt/2½ cups milk. Simmer down to about 500 ml/generous ¾ pt/scant 2 cups
1 tablespoon butter, melted
1 basic quantity of fresh green pasta (see page 47), cut into 4–6 sheets to fit the tin or dish you intend to use, or bought lasagne
60 g/2 oz/½ cup grated Parmesan cheese
5-cm/2-in deep tin, with a capacity of 1.5 litres/2¾ pts/7 cups

Set oven at hot, 230°C (450°F), gas 8. Heat the meat sauce through, and the béchamel. Brush the tin or dish with melted butter and put in a sheet of pasta. Dab it with meat sauce, bearing in mind the number of layers to follow. Spoon béchamel over it and sprinkle with cheese. Repeat until the items are used up, ending with béchamel and grated cheese. Drip the rest of the butter over the top.

Put into the heated oven and leave for 15–20 minutes, until the sides are bubbling and the top is patched with colour. If you use bought pasta reduce the heat after 15 minutes and give it another 10 or 15 minutes to make sure the pasta is cooked through.

POLENTA

Serves 8–10
The first thing we ever knew about Italy as children was polenta. My father had been there in the First World War, and would recall vividly his surprise at the first midday meal he shared with a peasant farmer and his family. By the fire a woman endlessly stirred a great pot, then without a word she turned and tipped out a grainy yellow mass directly on to the wooden table. Not on to a board, or a plate, or a cloth, but straight on to a grimy table. The men devoured it in enormous quantity. My father hesitated, but came in time to like it. Eaten like this, I cannot pretend to enjoy it very much: sliced and fried, it is absolutely delicious.

As with many other cereal dishes, measure the yellow corn meal by volume after measuring the water. Put four mugs of water into a heavy pan, and as it comes to simmering point, measure out two mugs of cornmeal. Trickle it into the water from your hand, stirring all the time with a wooden spoon. Keep the heat low, or it will burst in plopping spurts and burn your hands.

Once all the meal is in the water, keep the heat down so that the polenta just boils and stir. Stir quite slowly but regularly, for 20–30 minutes. After 15 minutes, add a good tablespoon of butter – unorthodox, but it helps to make a coherent mass that comes away from the side of the pan. Add salt. When you stir the bottom and you can make clear trails the polenta is ready. Tip it out, scraping the sides, on to a buttered dish.

The polenta can be eaten immediately, with hare or beef stews, or on its own with butter and cheese.

If you keep it until it is quite cold and firm, it can be sliced neatly and fried. The crispness is something quite special to polenta, succulent and grainy with a light crunch.

GNOCCHI

Gnocchi, meaning dumplings and idiots, appear in several forms in Italian cookery. Potato or spinach gnocchi are boiled in the conventional way, or rather simmered, but these semolina gnocchi are baked and crisp at the edges. A most appetising dish, either for a first course, or after soup in the evening.

600 ml/1 pt/2½ cups milk
salt, pepper, nutmeg
150 g/5 oz/scant cup coarse semolina, or 175 g/6 oz/1 cup fine semolina
2 large egg yolks
60–90 g/2–3 oz/½–¾ cup grated Parmesan or pecorino
90 g/3 oz/¾ cup butter

Bring milk and seasoning to boiling point. Tip in the semolina all at once, stirring with a wooden spoon. And cook, still stirring, until the mixture is stiff enough to hold the spoon more or less upright. About 10 minutes. Remove the pan from the heat, beat in the egg yolks, then half the cheese and about a third of the butter. These additions turn the grainy dough into a coherent shiny ball, clinging to the spoon and leaving the sides and base of the pan more or less clean. Add a shade more butter if you like.

Rinse a baking tray and your hands. Turn the dough on to the tray and pat it out until it is a little less than a centimetre (¼ in) thick. Pat it as smoothly as you can. Leave to cool completely and set in the refrigerator. After about 20 minutes, you can turn the whole thing over if you like and press it gently, so that you end up with two smooth sides.

Cut out small circles of dough with a scone cutter and arrange them in mounting circles, or overlapping lines. Squeeze the offcuts together, pat them out and cut more circles. Melt the remaining butter. Sprinkle the gnocchi with the remaining cheese and pour on the butter. Bake for about 30 minutes at 190°C (375°F) gas 5, until the gnocchi are caught with golden brown. Serve with more Parmesan or pecorino, or with tomato sauce.

Gnocchi freeze very well indeed.

NEAPOLITAN PIZZA

The variety of pizza and their toppings is enormous, but pizza alla napoletana is the classic pizza of Naples. Pizza should be baked on the brick floor of an old-fashioned bread oven, when the ashes of the fire have been swept away. The remarkable thing is that in Italy there are many ovens of this kind still in the pizzerie (in Genoa such ovens are also used to bake farinata, a batter of chickpea meal that turns crisp in the heat).

The business of getting a pizza on to the floor of the oven is taken care of by a long-handled metal peel (the baker's shovel)—you slide it in, give a twist and the pizza flips neatly into its place. At least that is what happens if you are an expert. In his *Grains, Pasta and Pulses* (Time-Life Books/*The Good Cook* series) Richard Olney suggests putting quarry tiles on your oven rack to simulate the old oven floor. A good idea, except that flipping a well-garnished pizza on to the tiles from a metal baking sheet takes practice. Even if you succeed, the pizza will lack the right woody flavour, and the characteristic bits of charcoal underneath. But it's worth a try.

The simplest way of making a pizza is to remove the amount of dough required after the first rising, when you are baking bread.

Serves 4–6
500 g/1 lb bread dough
750 g/1½ lb tomatoes, peeled and sliced
salt and pepper
oregano
50 g/2 oz can of anchovy fillets in oil, drained, or 1.5 kg/3 lb mussels, scraped and opened
about 250 g/8 oz mozzarella, fontina or Bel Paese cheese

Set oven at hot, 220°C (425°F), gas 7. Roll out the dough as thinly as you can—which means that it will be just about 5 mm (¼ in) thick. Put it on to a well-oiled baking tray. Put the tomatoes on top, leaving a small border, season them well, and add oregano to taste. Split the anchovy fillets and distribute them over the tomatoes, or remove the mussels from their shells and dot them about. Cut the cheese* into large slivers on the cucumber blade of a grater and put them between the anchovy fillets or mussels. Sprinkle with olive oil and the oil from the anchovies if used. Bake in the heated oven for 20 minutes, check and give the pizza another 5–10 minutes if it is not nicely browned underneath and sizzling on top. Remove and eat.

* If you are using Bel Paese, put it on to the pizza when you check it, and give it about 5 minutes more or a little longer. Too long and it turns to leather.

MOZZARELLA IN A CARRIAGE
Mozzarella in carrozza

An elegant version, and lighter tasting, of those fried cheese sandwiches which used to be called 'cheese dreams' when I was a child. Of course, any firm cheese can be used, but the right one is mozzarella. There is a Danish imitation but it does not do; better to use Bel Paese instead. Mild, milky-tasting Italian cheeses are not to everyone's taste

continued on p. 51

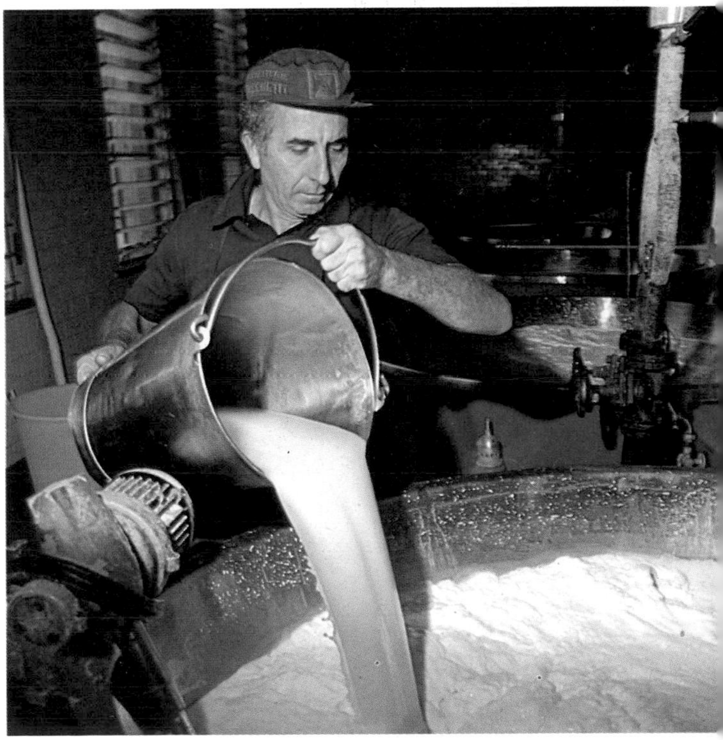

In the early stages of cheesemaking

Making pizza in the old-fashioned style at the pizzeria Port Alba, Naples

here; when making up these sandwiches, I put a little salt and pepper with the cheese and season the beaten egg.

Serves 3–4
Slice 250 g (8 oz) mozzarella neatly, and season the pieces. Cut enough slices of bread for sandwiching each piece of cheese: the bread should be just a shade larger than the cheese.

Beat 2 large or 3 small eggs in a wide dish. Season with salt. Turn the sandwiches in the egg, pressing the edges closely together, round the cheese. Leave in the egg for about 20 minutes, turning once.

Heat about 1 cm (¼ in) olive oil in a frying pan. Cook the sandwiches quickly until they are golden on both sides. Drain on kitchen paper. Serve as a first course or with drinks.

MOZZARELLA OR FONTINA SALAD

Mild cheese salads make a good first course if you do not intend to serve cheese later in the meal, or a simple lunch dish after some soup. The important thing is the quality of the cheese: a dripping mozzarella from a good Italian store should be used, not a Danish imitation. Good fontina is easier to find.

Serves 8
Mozzarella Slice a couple of Italian mozzarella cheeses. Arrange the pieces in concentric rings on a serving dish, with a slice of tomato and a piece of anchovy fillet between each one, plus a basil leaf. The anchovy fillets should be drained, cut in two lengthways and each long piece cut across in two. Dress with an olive oil vinaigrette, and grind black pepper over the rings.

Fontina Cut 375 g (12 oz) fontina cheese into dice, and mix with strips of grilled, skinned yellow peppers (6 large ones) and 18 halved and stoned green olives. Whisk 4 tablespoons (⅓ cup) of double cream and add 6 tablespoons (½ cup) of olive oil vinaigrette, well seasoned.

BAKED AUBERGINE AND CHEESE
Parmigiana di melanzane

A favourite dish, simple and good to make if you can find the right cheeses—Parmesan which gives the dish its name, and Italian mozzarella (if the latter is unobtainable you can substitute Bel Paese, fontina or even Port Salut).

In preparing this dish, Italians deep-fry the slices of aubergine. I find it better to shallow-fry them in a little olive oil and on one side only. If you like the slightly tough black skin aubergines, there is no need to peel them; or you could peel them in stripes.

Serves 6
1.5 kg/3 lb aubergines, peeled and sliced
1 tablespoon salt
flour
olive oil
generous 500 ml/¾–1 pt/2–2½ cups tomato sauce I or II (see page 45)
250 g/8 oz mozzarella cheese, thinly sliced
60–90 g/2–3 oz/½ cup grated Parmesan cheese

Put the aubergine slices in a colander and sprinkle them with 1 tablespoon of salt. Wedge them down with a plate and leave for an hour. This process makes them less bitter, and less absorbent of oil. Drain, rinse and dry the slices. Flour them lightly and fry on one side in olive oil. Drain on kitchen paper. Set the oven at moderate 160–180°C (325–350°F), gas 3–4.

Into a shallow ovenproof dish or tin, put a layer of aubergine slices, fried side down. Cover with a layer of tomato sauce topped with mozzarella cheese and a sprinkling of Parmesan. Repeat until the aubergines are finished, making a top layer. You may have a little tomato sauce over—it depends on how thickly you spread it—but see that all the mozzarella is used up.

Scatter the remaining Parmesan over the top and trickle olive oil over it, not too generously. Bake in the heated oven for 45–60 minutes until the cheese has turned to a golden crust on top and the sides are bubbling.

SHIN OF VEAL WITH RISOTTO
Ossi buchi con risotto alla milanese

Years ago in Milan, in a steamy little cafe full of workers, I had ossi buchi put in front of me with the most delicious saffron rice that I had ever eaten, plump Italian rice of a kind I had never come across before. These days Italian rice has become a supermarket commonplace, but a better quality still can be found in Italian groceries, labelled 'arborio', where it can also be bought loose. Only this rice has the proper qualities—creaminess and firmness—for a risotto.

Ask the butcher for slices of veal shin cut across the bone, 5 cm (2 in) thick. During the cooking, see that the slices remain upright so that the bone marrow is not lost.

Serves 6

FOR THE VEAL

6 slices of veal shin
seasoned flour
butter
large onion and carrot, chopped
stalk of celery, thinly sliced
200 ml/7 fl oz/¾ cup dry white wine
500 g/1 lb tomatoes, peeled and chopped
beef or veal stock
salt and pepper
small bunch of parsley, finely chopped
large clove of garlic, finely chopped
finely grated rind of lemon

FOR THE RISOTTO

3 shallots, or a medium onion, chopped
60 g/2 oz/¼ cup butter
500 g/1 lb Italian rice
about 1.25 litres/2¼ pts/5⅔ cups chicken stock or water
200 ml/7 fl oz/¾ cup dry white wine
generous pinch of saffron
extra butter, for serving
grated Parmesan cheese

Turn the veal in the flour and brown in butter on both sides in a deep sauté pan. Lower the heat and put in the onion, carrot and celery. Give them 10 minutes, so that they soften slightly, without browning very much. Raise the heat and pour in the wine. Deglaze the pan, scraping underneath the slices to dislodge any bits and pieces into the liquid. Add the tomatoes and, as they settle down, pour in enough stock to come level with the top of the veal. Cover and simmer for 1 hour.

Remove the lid, turn the veal pieces over and leave for a further 30 minutes, uncovered, so that the sauce can reduce. When the meat parts easily from the bone, it is done. Allow yourself 2 hours cooking time in all, as the meat will come to no harm if it is kept warm for a while. Season well, and have ready a gremolata mixture, made by mixing together chopped parsley, the garlic and lemon rind, to scatter over just before serving.

To make the risotto, soften the shallots or onion in the butter until it is golden. Stir in the rice and keep it moving until it glistens and looks transparent. Meanwhile heat up the stock in a separate pan. Raise the heat under the rice pan and pour in the wine. When it has bubbled away and been absorbed, add about a quarter of the simmering stock. As it disappears add a similar amount. Dissolve the saffron in the remaining stock; keep it gently simmering, ready to add to the rice.

Do not stir and fuss the rice about, but keep an eye on it. You will see that the top looks very flat with holes in it, as the stock disappears. This is the signal to add more stock—the rice will absorb at least twice its volume.

Towards the end, as the rice becomes tender, add stock by the tablespoon, so the final result is not liquid, but a creamy mass of yellow grains. In all about 20 minutes cooking time.

To serve, stir in a good tablespoon or two of butter, and some Parmesan cheese. Put a bowl of grated Parmesan on the table with the veal and the rice. Serve hot on very hot plates.

Variation A risotto is often served on its own as a first course, like pasta. It is particularly successful flavoured with shellfish.

Use the shellfish debris, or in the case of mussels their liquid, to make or improve fish stock which should take the place of chicken stock in the recipe above. Cook or reheat the shellfish in butter with a little chopped parsley, and stir it into the completed risotto, with the butter and Parmesan. As with any risotto, serve very hot.

A good cheap risotto can be made with a small can of anchovies, which should be softened and chopped in their own oil. Use fish stock from the freezer if you have it, or make some from an assortment of bones, heads and skins from a fishmonger.

Risotto with green peas (Risi e bisi) A Venetian risotto for the early summer, when there are young and tender peas about. Cook half the quantity of the risotto above, without the saffron. Cook 500 g (1 lb) shelled peas separately and stir them in at the end. By adding more stock, you can turn this risotto into a soup.

Fried rice and cheese balls (Supplì al telefono) The best way of using up left-over risotto, a good dish and great fun. Supposing you have about half the risotto left, beat 2 small eggs and add them gradually to the rice. Stop when you have a mould-able consistency, before the egg makes the rice sloppy. Put a tablespoon of rice in the palm of one wet hand. Place a piece of mozzarella (or Bel Paese or fontina) cheese in the middle, with a little slice of ham, if you like. Put another tablespoon of rice on top, and mould into a ball, the size of a small Scotch egg. Repeat until the rice is used up. Roll gently in fine white breadcrumbs and fry in plenty of sun-flower oil—better still, deep-fry—until golden. As

Sitting in an outdoor café is a main pleasure of holidays—or living—in Italy

you bite into the supplì, the cheese pulls away in long strings, like telephone wires.

SALTIMBOCCA

A quick appetising dish—the name means 'leap into the mouth'—which should not be kept hanging about. With veal the price it is, Italians are beginning to use sliced turkey breast for dishes of this kind. But be careful, turkey is a much drier meat than veal and should be cooked more briefly. Chill it thoroughly in the ice-making compartment of the refrigerator, so that you can cut paper-thin slices on the slant.

For 4–5 people you will need 500 g (1 lb) turkey slices, or 4–5 escalopes of veal, which need to be beaten out between greaseproof paper or clear film. You also need 125 g (4 oz) prosciutto crudo and enough small fresh sage leaves to give you one for each saltimbocca—18 to be on the safe side.

Spread out the turkey slices, or cut the flattened escalopes into 2–3 pieces each, and spread them out. On each put a piece of prosciutto cut to fit, and a sage leaf. Roll up the little pieces and secure them with a wooden cocktail stick or toothpick. (In some versions, the sage leaves are put between veal and ham, and the pieces are not rolled up: this shortens the cooking time to 4 minutes.)

Brown the little rolls on both sides in butter. Pour in 90 ml (3 fl oz/$\frac{1}{2}$ cup) Marsala, cover and simmer for a further 3–5 minutes, turning the rolls once. Serve immediately with the pan sauce.

Note if you replace the sage with batons of Gruyère cheese, the dish is known as bocconcini (little mouthfuls).

VEAL WITH TUNNY MAYONNAISE
Vitello tonnato

A dish of summer meals in Italy, a delicate combination of veal and tunny that seems odd to us. If you have roast or braised veal, or a fricandeau, you can make this dish next day by slicing the meat thin and arranging it on a large plate and pouring over it the tunny sauce given below. If you are making it from scratch for a buffet party, you should braise the veal first:

Serves 8–10
1½ kg/3 lb veal cut neatly from one of the leg muscles
½ tin anchovy fillets, or 6 salted anchovies, soaked
3 or 4 pickled gherkins
large carrot, chopped
large onion, chopped
3 sticks celery, chopped
2 rashers green bacon, chopped
175 ml/6 fl oz/¾ cup dry white wine
100 ml/3½ fl oz/scant ½ cup olive oil
FOR THE SAUCE
4 egg yolks
½ litre/¾ pt/scant 2 cups light olive oil, or mixed sunflower and stronger olive oil
200 g/7 oz tunny, canned in oil, or cooked fresh tunny, skinned, boned
5 anchovy fillets, chopped
lemon juice
capers, gherkins, lemon slices to decorate

Make holes in the veal and stick in bits of anchovy fillet and strips of gherkin. Tie into shape. Put the chopped vegetables and bacon in the bottom of a deep dish into which the veal fits closely. Put the veal on top and pour over the wine and oil. Bring to simmering point, cover and cook gently until the veal is tender, turning it occasionally. Allow 1½ hours.

Put the veal on a plate and strain the juices over it. When cold, skim off the fat from the juices, taste them and reduce them a little if they are on the weak side. Set aside while you make a mayonnaise in the usual way with the yolks and oil. Crush the tunny and anchovy together, and add to the mayonnaise. Thin with the juices from the veal, and with lemon juice.

Slice the meat and arrange on a plate, spoon over the sauce and decorate with capers, slices of gherkin and lemon.

ABBRUZZI LAMB WITH OLIVES
Agnello con olive all'abruzzese

In the mountains of the Abruzzi on the Adriatic side of Rome, lamb is a fine and prized meat. This is one of the best ways I know for cooking well-flavoured lamb, being succulent and piquant at the same time. My version is based on Waverley Root's recipe in his *Best of Italian Cooking*, which, sadly, is now out of print.

Serves 6
1 kg/2 lb boned leg of lamb cut into 6 steaks
flour
olive oil
salt
250 g/8 oz/1⅓ cups black olives, stoned and chopped
½ level teaspoon oregano
2 small green peppers, chopped
juice of 1 lemon

Turn the lamb slices in flour, shake off the surplus and brown them briskly in a little olive oil, on both sides, allowing 5 minutes. Salt the lamb and pour off any surplus fat. Add the olives, oregano and green pepper, with two-thirds of the lemon juice. Cook for a minute or two, stirring the olives and peppers about, until the lamb is just pink in the centre. Arrange on a hot serving dish.

Taste the olive mixture and add the rest of the lemon juice if it seems a good idea. Arrange round and over the lamb. You don't need any vegetable with this—just bread and white wine.

BEEF FILLET WITH GENTLEMAN'S SAUCE
Filetto al sugo signore

A Tuscan version of the north Italian way of cooking meat and poultry in milk. You can adapt the recipe to loin of pork or chicken by leaving out the rosemary and vinegar, and using 600 ml (1 pt/2½ cups) milk. Milk and cream, or milk, reduced, takes on a slightly caramelised flavour that goes well with meat. If the lumpiness bothers you, sieve or process the sauce finally.

Serves 6
large onion, chopped small
large clove of garlic, chopped to a mash
large sprig of rosemary
olive oil
1 kg/2 lb fillet of beef, trimmed
4 tablespoons/5 tbs wine vinegar
250 ml/9 fl oz/generous 1⅓ cups each whipping cream and milk, or 500 ml/18 fl oz/generous 2⅔ cups single cream
salt and pepper

Stew the onion, garlic and rosemary in just enough oil to cover the base of a frying pan. When the onion is soft and yellow, transfer with a slotted spoon to a pot that will just take the beef. Remove the rosemary (it doesn't matter if a few leaves are left

OLIVE OIL

For centuries, the green oils of Tuscany have been regarded as the best—'smooth, light and pleasant on the tongue,' said John Evelyn, 'such as the genuine omphacine and native Lucca olives afford'. If you know olive oil only from the chemist or the standardised products of big firms, you have a high pleasure in store. Small enterprising food companies are beginning to import the fine oil of Tuscan producers. Like wine, olive oils vary from farm to farm, from year to year, from variety to variety (incidentally, olives for eating come from varieties that grow plump fruit; oil olives are smaller).

Harvest begins about the middle of November, lasting for one to three months according to the size of the crop. I suspect we are ignorant of good oil because we are never in Italy at the right time. We never see how olives absorb whole communities for weeks on end. 'The countryside is dotted with people up olive trees, people carrying sacks of olives, tractors pulling loads of olives. The lovely warm olive oily smell in the presses is unforgettable,' says Mrs Zyw, one of Tuscany's liveliest oil producers. And so is the taste of new oil running out, when you dip bread into it, or toasted bread rubbed first with garlic—a favourite snack which is known as bruschetta.

First the olives are ground, stones and all, to a knubbly paste, and then spread on to coconut fibre mats. These are stacked one above the other on a spiked base which goes into a hydraulic press. As the mixture of oil and water runs down, it is channelled through a separator. This is cold pressing, the best oil pours out, greenish gold. Residues from the press go to factories for hot water treatment and a second pressing. The result is blended with other olive oils to produce the rather tasteless stuff sold under big brand names—it is the plonk of the olive oil business.

Buckets of olives and other pickles

Oil is classified according to acidity. The best is Cold Pressed Extra Virgin, Extra Virgin means less than 1% acidity, and Sopraffino, Fine Virgin and Virgin have increasing acidity up to 4%. Olive oil is best during its first year: store it away from extremes of temperature and light.

behind). Set the oven at moderate, 180°C (350°F), gas 4.

Raise the heat under the remaining fat and quickly brown the piece of fillet. Put on top of the onion. Pour off any oil remaining in the pan, put in the vinegar and boil it down as you deglaze the pan. Add cream and milk which will promptly curdle. Bring to the boil, pour over the beef and cook—the pot covered—in the heated oven for 50 minutes.

Remove the beef to a hot serving dish and inspect the sauce. Boil it down if it's on the copious side and season it. Slice the beef 1 cm ($\frac{1}{2}$ in) thick, salt the slices lightly and arrange neatly on a heated serving dish.

Pour the sauce down the centre. Surround with fennel or celery, blanched 7 minutes and finished in butter. Diced, fried potatoes can be served as well, if you like.

CARLINO'S TIMBALE
Timballo di spinaci ed animelle

For family birthdays and celebrations, this is a favourite dish. It may look and sound complicated, but it is really quite easy: the spinach ring, which seems rather grand, is a pushover for anyone who has ever baked a custard.

Do not worry about sweetbreads, if your butcher never has them. Use scallops, prawns or soft roes instead, binding them after they have been lightly fried with a little of the sauce. Make some fish stock with fish bones and heads or the prawn shells for the sauce, instead of using veal or chicken stock (although chicken stock boiled up with prawn shells can also be used very successfully).

Serves 6
750 g/1½ lb prepared, cooked sweetbreads
generous 500 ml/¾ pt/2 cups stock, reserved from cooking sweetbreads
FOR THE SPINACH RING
100 g/3½ oz sliced ham, cooked on the bone, and cut into strips
3 large eggs
1.5 kg/3 lb spinach, cooked, chopped
salt and pepper
grated nutmeg
30 g/1 oz/¼ cup each grated Parmesan and Cheddar cheeses, mixed together
butter
FOR THE SAUCE
60 g/2 oz/¼ cup butter
heaped tablespoon flour
300 ml/½ pt/1¼ cups sweetbread stock
150 ml/¼ pt/⅔ cup milk
4–6 tablespoons double cream
lemon juice
salt and pepper
30 g/1 oz/¼ cup each grated Parmesan and Cheddar cheeses
1.25-litre/2-pt/5-cup ring mould

Put cooked sweetbreads between two plates; refrigerate until required.

Set the oven at very hot, 240°C (475°F), gas 9.

Reduce the ham to a purée with the eggs, in a processor or liquidiser then add the spinach. Season with salt, pepper and nutmeg. Stir in the cheeses. Butter the ring mould generously and put in the spinach mixture, smoothing the top. Cover tightly with a piece of buttered foil.

Place the mould on a trivet in a roasting tin half-filled with very hot water and put into the heated oven. Cook for 15 minutes, then turn the heat down to 200°C (400°F), gas 6, and leave 10 minutes. Switch off heat and leave in oven, keeping the door shut, until the sauce and sweetbreads are finished.

Start the sauce just before you put the spinach ring into the oven. Melt the butter, stir in the flour and cook for 2 minutes. Moisten with 300 ml (½ pt/1¼ cups) of the sweetbread stock, the milk and the cream. When smooth, leave to simmer gently while the spinach ring cooks and you complete the sweetbreads. Stir to prevent sticking.

Slice the sweetbreads, which will be slightly jellied, into convenient pieces for eating. Fry them to a nice golden brown in butter (just enough to cover the base of the pan when melted). Pour off any surplus. Stir in the wine and the sweetbread stock. Raise the heat so that you end up with a spoonful of syrupy juice. Keep turning the sweetbreads, so that they are coated in the juice. Taste and season.

Finish the sauce by stirring in the cheeses, and a drop or two of lemon juice. Add salt and pepper to taste. Keep hot, without allowing the sauce to boil again.

Remove the spinach ring from its water bath. Take off the foil. Ease the sides and centre with a slim, pointed knife, and turn out on to a warm serving dish. Don't worry if it doesn't turn out perfectly: smooth it with a knife and disguise blemishes with a little sauce. Put the sweetbreads in the centre of the ring. Pour some sauce over, serve the rest separately.

TRIPE IN THE STYLE OF FLORENCE
Trippa alla fiorentina

When I was a student in Florence, the three cheapest things on the menus of the cheapest restaurants were eggs baked in olive oil in battered little pans, spaghetti with an egg broken into it, served with butter and Parmesan, and trippa alla fiorentina. They were all delicious. The tripe surprisingly so, since the only time I had ever eaten it in England was with onions, all white and slithery, quite different from the bubbling savoury dish that was put in front of me in Florence.

The trouble about reproducing any of the famous European tripe dishes in England, is that English tripe is so blanched—I believe in lime baths—to insipidity and flop. It has lost entirely its proper pale fawn meaty look, and its proper meaty taste which makes tripe in Madrid or Caen or Florence so much worth eating. However, tripe is so cheap that it is worth knowing a recipe or two for cheering it up.

For six people, buy 1½ kg (3 lb) tripe. Check with the butcher on the time it will need to complete the cooking—about 40 minutes usually.

In a large pot, bring aromatic vegetables and herbs to boiling point with 2 pig's trotters or a pig's hock or a calf's foot and plenty of water. Simmer until the meat is nearly done, then put in the tripe and finish the cooking. Meanwhile make tomato sauce I which is on page 45.

When the tripe is cooked, cut it quickly into neat strips together with the pig's or calf's meat. Mix them all with the sauce and divide between six pots. Scatter the tops with grated Parmesan cheese, a little oregano and melted butter, and heat through in a hot oven until bubbling and lightly browned. Put on the table with extra Parmesan cheese, bread and a bottle of red wine.

ITALIAN VEGETABLES

Artichokes English shops do not stock the long tender little artichokes of Italy that are eaten raw, or fried into crisp open flowers (carciofi alla giudia). The lavish supply of artichokes in Venice, for instance, means you can buy the trimmed bases alone, from people who sit on the quays cutting off leaves and stalks and chucking them into the canal, while the greenish white saucer at the bottom slips into a pail of vinegared water: these are for fricassées and mixed vegetable stews.

Aubergine has two particularly good recipes. One—melanzane a funghetti—for hot or cold eating. Peel down the aubergine in strips, dice and put in a colander with salt and a plate on top. Leave an hour, rinse and dry. Fry gently in olive oil until almost done, then raise the heat and add 4 chopped cloves of garlic for each kg (2 lb): stir 3 minutes, then mix in plenty of chopped parsley. The result looks like a dish of cèpes, with something of the same texture.

The second recipe is even better. Peel as above, slice thinly and salt. Pat dry. Flour lightly and fry in plain oil until the slices curl and colour into brown crisp leaves. Do not overbrown them. Good with drinks, fish, sweetbreads, chicken.

Cauliflower and broccoli when steamed or boiled to crisp tenderness, are improved by a final cooking in olive oil flavoured with a small red-hot chilli or two, split so that the seeds emerge. This is a favourite Roman dish. A little chopped sweet red pepper can be added as an extra garnish to this broccoli al peperoncino.

Radicchio, rossa di Verona, rossa di Treviso may be floppy and red like a large relaxed Brussels sprout, or red and cream splashed like a tulip (use in salads, or cooked); or it may be forced so that the heads are tight and firm like the English white Belgian witloof chicory, but a deep red—cook it in the same way.

Spinach Especially a Florentine vegetable. Ham, poached eggs or fillets of fish, on a bed of spinach with a blanket of cheese sauce browned off in the oven, or under the grill, are known as Florentine—jambon à la florentine, oeufs pochés, sole and so on à la florentine. Young raw spinach leaves come as a salad, sometimes with fine slivers of peeled Jerusalem artichoke.

A profusion of Italian vegetables on sale at the Campo del Fiori market, Rome

PEPERONATA

Choose red, yellow or green peppers, or a mixture (red and yellow is the combination I like best). To every 2 peppers, allow 5 tomatoes, rather less if they are good quality tomatoes, but peppers should predominate. You'll also need a large onion, chopped, 1 or 2 large cloves of garlic, crushed with a knife blade, olive oil, salt and pepper. For 6 people you will need 1 kg (2 lb) peppers and $\frac{1}{2}$ kg (1 lb) of tomatoes or more if the tomatoes are watery.

Method I Cut the peppers into strips, discarding the stalks and seeds. Peel and chop the tomatoes coarsely. Soften the onions in 3 tablespoons olive oil, add the garlic, then the peppers. Cover and simmer 15 minutes. Add the tomatoes and boil steadily, uncovered, until the pepper lies in a rich sauce. Season.

Method II Grill or bake the peppers in a very hot oven, 240°C (475°F) gas 9, until the skins are blistered all round. Under a cold tap, rub off the skins. Discard the stalk and seeds, and cut into strips. Cook the onion as above, add the garlic and the peeled, chopped tomatoes. Cook vigorously and, as the tomato reduces, put in the pepper and cook another 5 minutes. Season to taste.

Serve peperonata chilled, with chopped parsley and black olives, or hot with grilled or roast meat, or topped with poached or soft-boiled eggs.

ZABAGLIONE

My favourite pudding, very nearly, the only snag being that it needs to be made between courses as it is best eaten warm. It can of course be served cold, and cold or hot it is sometimes served as a sauce with fruit (in which case use half quantities).

For 6 people, put 5 large egg yolks into a large heatproof bowl, with 5 level tablespoons caster sugar and 10 tablespoons ($\frac{3}{4}$ cup) Marsala. Other wines can be used, but increase the sugar, if they are dry. Beat thoroughly together, using a spoon whisk or a hand electric beater. Have 6 tall glasses ready.

Set the bowl over a pan of steadily simmering water and whisk until you have a bulky foam of enormous quantity compared with the original mixture. Divide between the glasses and serve. Sponge finger biscuits, or not too sweet almond biscuits, or thin shortbread should be served as well.

MONTE BIANCO

This pudding is supposed to resemble the snow-clad slopes of Mont Blanc, hence its name. Use dried chestnuts for this pudding, and you will have no problems. The flavour will be a little weaker than if you had used fresh chestnuts, but still good.

For 6 people, pour plenty of boiling water over 250 g (8 oz) dried chestnuts. Leave overnight. Put into a pan with fresh water, bring to the boil and simmer about 20 minutes until the chestnuts are bitable but not soft; drain. Or nick, boil and peel 500 g (1 lb) fresh chestnuts.

Cover the chestnuts with milk and bring them slowly to simmering point. Leave them to cook until the milk disappears and the chestnuts are reasonably soft. Crush them to a rough purée with, say, a potato masher. Flavour with sugar and a tablespoon or two of rum. Mix thoroughly then push through a colander or the coarse plate of a Mouli-légumes, letting the ropes of purée fall to make a mountain.

Now whisk 300 ml ($\frac{1}{2}$ pt/$1\frac{1}{3}$ cups) double cream and 125 ml (4 fl oz/scant $\frac{2}{3}$ cup) whipping cream, with sugar to taste, and heap it on and around the chestnut mountain.

ZUCCOTTO

Stories about this Florentine pudding are on the wild side. The word means skullcap, which describes its shape exactly—its construction, too, since the liqueur-soaked cake caps and conceals a filling. It is one of those gastronomic surprises that Italians in particular seem to enjoy. Marcella Hazan wonders if the zuccotto was not some pastrycook's emulation of Brunelleschi's dome, the fame of the city, with brown-edged slices imitating its ribs. Another writer pulls out the tale that Buontalenti, the 16th century architect of the Boboli Garden grotto, invented the skullcap style, with ice-cream—during one of the frequent military episodes of the time, he and some soldiers stored their food in snow deep in a cave. One day some wine spilled and froze. Buontalenti liked the accidental sherbet and had everyone making more engaging mixtures to freeze in their protective metal skullcaps.

We first ate zuccotto years ago at the Otello

The mechanised grape harvest still needs hand pickers

restaurant in Florence. It was filled with raspberries and cream, and, I think, some chocolate chippings. Two more fillings are given below. Or you could fill the cake skullcap with separately made ice-cream, one or two flavours. Any pound cake can be used for the zuccotto, so long as it is baked in a wide slab.

scant kg/2 lb Madeira or pound cake
125 ml/4 fl oz/½ cup brandy
60 ml/2 fl oz/¼ cup Aurum or Cointreau
60 ml/2 fl oz/¼ cup Maraschino or kirsch or sweet Marsala

Cut the cake into slices just over ½ cm (¼ in) thick, then halve them diagonally to make long triangles. Take a hemispherical bowl of 1½ litres (2¾ pt/scant 7 cup) capacity and cut a piece of butter muslin which will line the bowl and hang slightly over the edge. Mix the alcohols, dip in the muslin, squeeze it out and put it in place in the bowl.

Working as neatly as you can, dip a triangle of cake into the alcohol, then put it into the bowl, narrow point towards the centre. Dip a second piece and put it into the bowl in the same way overlapping the brown edge of the first piece with the long side of the triangle. Continue until the bowl is lined, and all the long brown edges hidden. Patch any holes with left-over cake.

Make one of the fillings below and put it into the cake. Make a lid with the remaining cake. Flip over the muslin, cover with film and leave overnight at least. Two days, or even three will be all right in the refrigerator.

To turn out, remove the film, flip back the muslin and invert a plate over the bowl. Turn the whole thing over quickly, remove the bowl and the muslin, and you will find the zuccotto beautifully ribbed with the long brown edges, though not as regularly as Brunelleschi's dome.

Note be prepared to make up more of the alcoholic mixture, if you run out. However, avoid making the cake too sodden.

Ricotta filling Break up and mix 300 g (10 oz/1¼ cups) ricotta cheese with caster sugar to taste. Chop 125 g (4 oz) toasted hazelnuts or almonds or a mixture of both, 125 g (4 oz/⅔ cup) candied peel and fruit, and 30 g (1 oz) dark chocolate, grated. Fold into the ricotta, then whip 300 ml (½ pt/1¼ cups) double cream and fold it in. Fill and cover the liqueur-soaked skullcap.

Raspberry filling Sprinkle 375 g (12 oz) raspberries with 100 g (3½ oz/scant ½ cup) caster sugar. Leave several hours, then drain off the syrup and mix with 4 tablespoons (⅓ cup) Aurum or Cointreau or Maraschino or kirsch. Use this to moisten the cake. Whip 300 ml (10 fl oz/1¼ cups) double cream with 6 tablespoons (½ cup) single cream. Fold in the raspberries, and if you like, add 30 g (1 oz) chocolate coarsely grated.

Marcella Hazan's filling Toast 60 g (2 oz/½ cup) hazelnuts, rubbing off the dry skins afterwards. Blanch and dry off 60 g (2 oz/½ cup) almonds in the oven for a minute or two. Chop coarsely and also chop 100 g (3½ oz) dark dessert chocolate. Whip 600 ml (1 pt/2½ cups) double cream with 125 g (4 oz/½ cup) caster sugar. Add nuts and chocolate. Spoon half into the cake-lined bowl, smoothing it over to make an inner lining. Melt 50 g (scant 2 oz) dark chocolate and fold into the remaining cream and nuts. Use to fill the cavity. Cover with a cake lid, and finish as above.

If you use two ice-creams, this is the method to follow. You need to soften the consistency so that it is spreadable but not melting. The inner layer can be done first, and then put back into the freezer to firm up a little before you pack in the central ice.

GRANITE

Granite are halfway between a sherbet and a solid water ice. As the name suggests, the texture is grainy: little flecks of flavoured ice, delicious and dissolving; a sharp chill, softened in the case of a bitter-sweet coffee granita by a soft cloud of cream.

The mixtures are simplicity itself, the texture is the problem. To achieve the elegant slush, you need to be on call every 15 minutes or so to stir it up: moreover you need to have a fairly firm idea of when you will be serving it. No wonder most Italians prefer to leave granite to the professionals. All they have to do is to saunter down to an outdoor cafe in their favourite square, sit back and enjoy the prospect until their granita is brought to them, exactly right, perfectly delicious. We tend to regard ices as a handy storage item in the freezer, a fallback. Alas, when fine fruit is involved, or black coffee, such an ice should be eaten the day it is made or else it will lose the fine delicacy of its flavour.

Note the recipes below are enough for 4–6 people. If you use an ice-making machine, follow the manufacturer's freezing instructions rather than mine, which are intended for a freezer or refrigerator with a large ice-making compartment.

Coffee granita with whipped cream. Make 1 litre (1¾ pt/5 cups) of espresso coffee with a filter, better still with an espresso machine if you have one. Use 10 rounded tablespoons of the finely ground coffee. Sweeten it mildly while warm, then leave to cool. Pour it into two ice-trays and freeze at the lowest possible temperature.

After 20 minutes, if the sides and bottom are frozen, stir the crystals into the liquid. Continue doing this at regular intervals. Serve when it is not quite solid, in tall glasses, with a swirl of whipped cream on top, lightly sweetened if you like but you may find you prefer it plain.

Orange granita Take the peel thinly from 1 lemon and 2 oranges, and use it to flavour a syrup made with 500 ml ($\frac{3}{4}$ pt/2 cups) water and 125 g (4 oz/$\frac{1}{2}$ cup) sugar. Squeeze the juice of the lemon into a measuring jug. Add enough orange juice to bring it up to 400 ml (about 13 fl oz/$1\frac{1}{2}$ cups). Stir in the cooled strained syrup to taste. Freeze as above.

Strawberry or melon granita Make a fruit purée by processing, liquidising or sieving 500 g (1 lb) strawberries or melon pulp. Take the peel thinly from 1 lemon and 1 orange and use to flavour a syrup made with 300 g (10 oz/$1\frac{1}{3}$ cups) sugar and 150 ml ($\frac{1}{4}$ pt/$\frac{2}{3}$ cup) water. Strain and add gradually to the fruit purée, using the juice of the lemon and the orange to enhance the flavour. Freeze as above.

This can easily be turned into ice-cream, by adding 300 ml ($\frac{1}{2}$ pt/$1\frac{1}{3}$ cups) cream, whipped, into the almost frozen ice.

A selection of splendid ice-creams, including a 'spaghetti' concoction

SICILIAN CANNOLI

When you see cannoli in the window of a Palermo cake shop, there's no hint of the way they are made. The two major surprises are wine in the pastry, and deep-frying as the method of cooking.

Depending on the size of the pan you use for deep-frying, you will need 4–6 cannoli tubes, or pieces of aluminium tube, 2 cm ($\frac{3}{4}$ in) in diameter and 15 cm (6 in) long. If you can get stainless steel, so much the better. I started by asking an ironmonger, and ended up in an electrician's.

Makes 16–18

FOR THE PASTRY

175 g/6 oz/$1\frac{1}{4}$ cups plain flour
pinch of salt
3 level tablespoons caster sugar
60 g/2 oz/$\frac{1}{4}$ cup lightly salted or unsalted butter
a standard egg
Marsala or white wine to mix

FOR THE FILLING

375 g/12 oz ricotta cheese
175 g/6 oz/$1\frac{1}{3}$ cups icing sugar
tablespoon orange-flower water
60 g/2 oz/$\frac{1}{3}$ cup chopped candied orange peel or glacé fruits
30 g/1 oz grated bitter chocolate

TO FINISH

icing sugar

To make the pastry, mix the dry ingredients, rub in the butter and mix to a soft, unsticky dough first with the egg, then with as much of the wine as necessary. Knead until smooth and elastic. Roll out thinly and cut out 16–18 squares, about 8 cm (3 in) a side. Flour the tubes and wrap a square of pastry round each one diagonally, pressing to seal.

Deep fry in olive oil for preference, or in groundnut or sunflower oil, at 180°C (375°F), until golden, crisp and slightly puffy. Drain on kitchen paper. When tepid, turn the tubes carefully to loosen them, draw them out and cook the next batch.

Mix all the filling ingredients thoroughly together. When the pastry tubes are cool, spoon or pipe the filling in. Pile them on to a dish and sprinkle with icing sugar. Serve the same day.

CHEESES

Parmesan The major grana, i.e. grainy, cheese of Italy. There are others, but the large dark-skinned drums of cheese stamped Parmigiano Reggiano are the ones to look out for (avoid grated 'Parmesan'—it can come from Latin America). Like the other grana cheeses, Parmesan is delicious to eat on its own with a good red wine. It seems expensive, but it is matured for at least two years; its flavour is so concentrated that a tablespoon or two will flavour a sauce or soufflé: to get a similar intensity from farmhouse Cheddar, you need a much greater weight and have to cope with the disadvantage of extra fattiness.

Pecorino Another group of hard, grating cheeses, made as you may gather from the name, from sheep's milk. Sardinian pecorino can be recognised from its attractive, basket-moulded, deep brown skin. It is essential to pesto, the Ligurian basil sauce (recipe on page 46), that is so delicious with pasta, soups, fish or chicken.

Gorgonzola One of the three most famous blue cheeses, the others being Stilton and Roquefort. Unlike the other two, Gorgonzola is left to turn blue naturally, a process which is speeded up by aerating the cheese with copper wires. It is a cow's milk cheese, from Lombardy, and old, with tales of varying plausibility to account for its origin.

Mozzarella, Provatura, Provolone These are—or were—buffalo cheeses of southern Italy (nowadays cow's milk is mixed in with or substituted for buffalo milk). For us their consistency can be an acquired taste, since the kneaded curd has a rubbery blandness quite unlike the texture of English cheeses and the commoner French ones. When you bite into a cooked slice, it pulls away in quite thick elastic strings which can be embarrassing if you are not prepared for it: once you know, a dish of fried rice and cheese balls (supplì al telefono) for instance (recipe on page 52), becomes fun and enjoyable.

These cheeses are quickly spotted in an Italian grocery. Mozzarella, in little soft-looking white handfuls, sits in a bath of whey, loosely enclosed in its wrapping paper (it should, for perfection, be eaten the day after it's made). Use it for appetising first courses, crisp, soft, piquant and melting, and for salads. The others hang from ceiling hooks in a variety of shapes—eggs, sausages, melons—suspended by dark strings that may press into the

Some magnificent, craggy Parmesan on the counter with a stamped cheese, uncut, on the right

The mozzarella is made from the milk of these buffaloes, at Battipaglia, near Salerno

cheese to form its bulges and curves. One cheese, burrino, has a knob of butter in the centre. Taste varies: mild (dolce), sharpish (piccante), smoked (affumicato), and as the texture firms up with age, it becomes suitable for grating.

Ricotta Made from the whey of mozzarella, provolone and other cheeses, in other words a recooked cheese, Its milky mildness makes it the perfect cheese for desserts (see the recipe for Sicilian cannoli on page 60), or eating with fruit and cream. It may be mixed with spinach as a ravioli filling, or turned into gnocchi.

Although you are most likely to see ricotta in the form of a white cake with sloping sides, and evenly blobbed from the draining holes of the mould, tasting very pure and mild, it is sometimes salted—so it's prudent to taste or ask. And sometimes it is smoked.

Fontina A buttery, firm-soft cheese from the Val d'Aosta high in the Alps, with a few holes in its supple texture that might make you think of a miniature Gruyère. And indeed it is the cheese for fonduta piemontese, just as Gruyère is the cheese for Swiss fondue, but it comes from the Val d'Aosta, not Switzerland. (At this point I should add that there are Italian imitations of Gruyère marketed as groviera.) Fonduta piemontese is a mixture of eggs and cheese which is covered with fine slices of white truffle. Unfortunately, this truffle is only obtainable in Italy and so it is virtually impossible to make this dish elsewhere. Unlike the black truffle the white truffle is not cooked in with food though sometimes it is warmed through. It has a powerful smell. A friend on business in northern Italy bought a white truffle from Alba, the great centre for such things where the truffle hounds are trained; to get it safely home he swaddled the package in socks, shirts and handkerchiefs. When his wife opened the case a few hours later, the smell burst out as the lid was raised in unmistakeable glory. If you have a chance to do the same thing, melt 300 g (10 oz/good $1\frac{1}{2}$ cups) cubed fontina in half a tumbler of milk in a water bath or over a double saucepan. When it is creamy put in 3 egg yolks beaten with 30 g (1 oz/2 tbs) of melted butter and a little hot milk. When the mixture is smooth divide it between six warmed bowls and grate white truffle over the top. Eat immediately, with plenty of bread.

Bel Paese The trade name given to a firm-soft, Lombardy cheese, of a mild flavour that I find a little boring. However, one should be thankful for the marketing energy of the firm that makes it—Galbani—since it is easy to find in England, and a reasonable substitute for mozzarella and fontina.

Part of the genius lies in the name, Bel Paese, and its associations. If you look at the label, you see the head of a genial priest, Antonio Stoppani. In 1875 he published a geography book for children on the recently unified country of Italy. It was well written and exciting, with a knowledgeable uncle being questioned about his travels by nephews and nieces. To parents and teachers buying the book the title summed up the passion of recent history, since it came from a brief, perfect description of Petrarch's, 'il bel paese—ch'Appenin parte e'l mar circonda e l'Alpe'. And there on the label, too, you see a map of the new, beautiful country, divided by the Appenines, and encircled by sea and Alps.

SPAIN

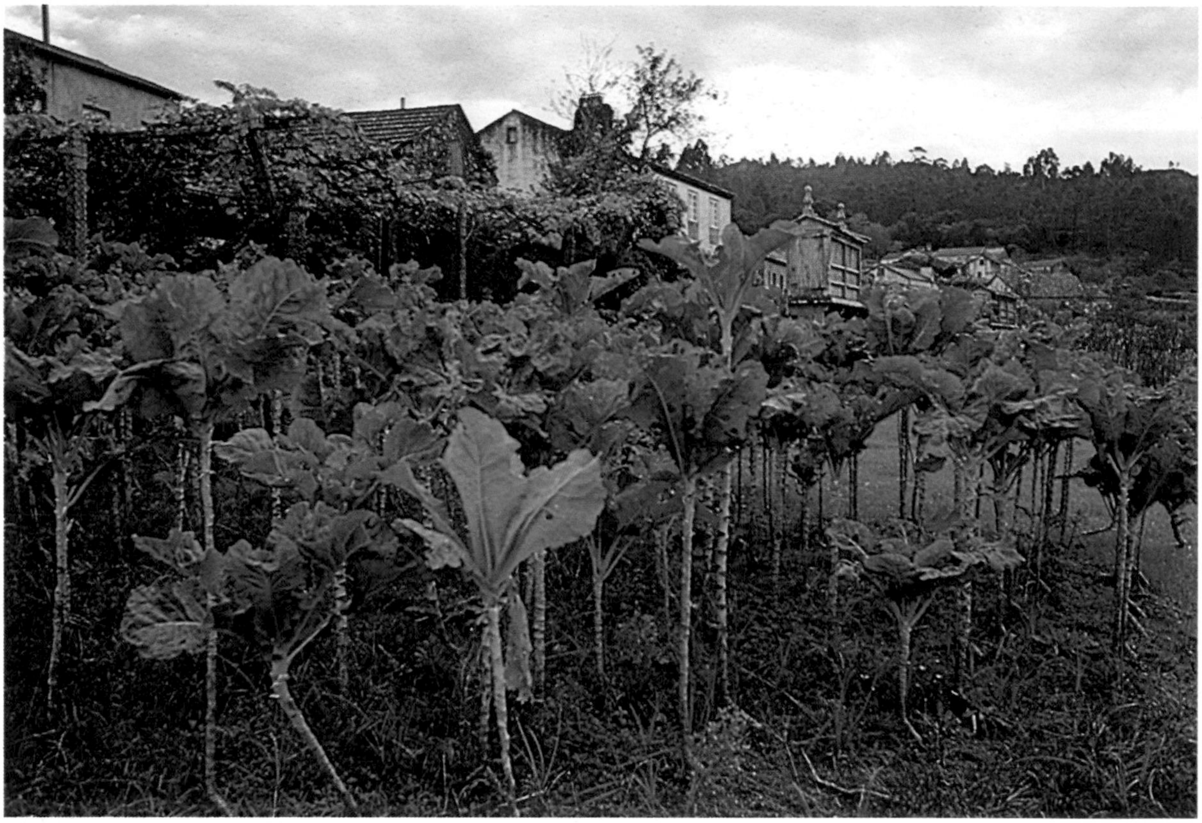

Leggy long-stemmed cabbages, typical of the wet north-western Atlantic corner of Spain

The merits of Spanish eating are indicated by a thousand sights in Spain. There are the great corn plains endlessly green in spring, endlessly ochre in autumn, which speak of the marvellous hard-crusted bread; then in the north-west, in Galicia, the long-legged, blue-green cabbages alongside every house (for the famous cabbage soup, caldo gallego—see page 67—not at all to be despised) and alongside the horreos, the little buildings on stilts, holding the maize that will feed the chickens (Galilians are so fond of the characteristic horreos that jewellers sell models of them in silver). And in such a town as Lugo, in the north-west, inside its extraordinary and complete Roman walls, by all the coloured fish and shellfish, red and scarlet, black, silver and orange, which fill every restaurant window.

In this great big country, where they make countless kinds of the red and piquant chorizo sausage, a waiter will unhook another ham from the clustered rows above him. You will see that it has a greyish-brown hairy shank and hoof like the pigs in a medieval miniature. The ham will cut into a deep pinkish-red meat lined with fat streaks, the jamón serrano from Huelva, in the south, the best of Spanish hams.

Again in the south, around Malaga, grapes dry to the best raisins in the world, and around Valencia the pink-flowering almonds produce the best Jordan almonds, and the rice paddies yield the basic fat grain of paella. Olives, some of the best and biggest in the world, come especially from the red-earthed plain around Seville. Seville is also hot enough to grow avocado pears, as well as being the first place in Europe where potatoes are known to have been grown and eaten (though I would not say much for the potatoes served up in Spanish restaurants).

Everything—and every region—is reflected in Madrid where the better cooking, or at any rate the most appetising plates, combine simply prepared meat or fish or seafood with red and green peppers. Madrid, too, is the city for eating in bars, eating tapas (snacks) of everything on the counter from prawn fritters, tiny eels and pies to toasted sandwiches, squid, tripe, chicken, omelettes and salads, with the occasional strange delicacy of rabbit guts strung in a skein between two twigs.

Tapas can be washed down in Madrid and the south by a favourite non-alcoholic drink, horchata—the perfect hot-weather drink. It is milky-looking, made from pounded chufas (tiger nuts) which are grown especially around Valencia. Horchata can be bought in bottles, even in long-life cartons, but the best is made in the bars. Any visitor who falls for horchata can try making his own back in Britain (recipe on page 82). Chufas are on sale as tiger nuts in our health food shops.

My general feeling about the way Spaniards eat is that it remains rather medieval. By that I mean that if you order the excellent lamb of Burgos in northern Spain, you get an intimidating plateful of large pieces separately roasted, served without any sauce and without vegetables (unless you happen to order them separately). Tunny the Spaniards have been eating for thousands of years. We once caught a glimpse in a northern port of girls in tight dresses and overalls dragging tight-skinned tunny across the floor of a fish processing factory—it was on our way to the Pindal cave near the lighthouse of St Emeterius to see the Old Stone Age engraving of a tunny fish on the rocky wall.

Bread, meat, fish and wine are the thing. But in the centre and north, anyway, you can finish a heavy meal very lightly and pleasantly by ordering chilled 'cuajada', a little earthenware pot of curded sheep's milk, not sharp like yoghurt but bland like some Italian ricotta. Of all the many Spanish custards, it is surprising to come across the crema catalana in a Barcelona restaurant, with a crisp sugar top slightly thinner than those of our burnt creams.

If I have to choose among the markets to visit, it would be the Barcelona market for fruit and vegetables, and the market at Salamanca—that stunning honey-coloured city rising from the endless cornlands—for sucking pig, mountain rabbit and seafood.

One mystery is how fresh Atlantic seafood is sold in such ebullient quantity and quality so far from the sea: which reminds me to mention that those who know about elvers from the Severn and have never tasted them should look out for angulas in Spain, cooked with garlic and chilli-flavoured olive oil in small earthenware pots and eaten with wooden forks. They are sold even out of season, thanks to refrigeration. They are caught by the million in the great rias, the wide estuarine rivers of the north.

On the subject of seafood, don't forget that St James of Compostela, the Patron Saint of Spain, the Hammer of the Moors, has the scallop shell as his badge. Sadly I must say that the scallops we had in the elegant restaurant alongside his stupendous cathedral in Santiago de Compostela were very overcooked. Spanish restaurant food isn't always to be relied on: it is often overmuch, overcooked and over-liquid. A comment that must also include the cooking of some of the splendid state-run hotels, the paradors converted from castles, monasteries and aristocratic houses. But in most of them the atmosphere is conducive to a total enjoyment of a meal unique in Europe. As a French traveller observed, 'In a way Don Quixote was right. He saw every inn as a castle—nowadays every castle is an inn.'

GAZPACHO

A cold soup from Andalusia originally, now widely made throughout Europe, and especially popular among cooks with a processor or blender. The meaning of the name is obscure—it may come from a wooden bowl, a kaz in Spanish Arabic, or from a Spanish word meaning stuffed from eating too much and suffering in consequence.

The first time I ate gazpacho in Spain was at Seville. A party of us were being taken out to lunch. We were driven through a depressing shanty town and ended up in a busy yard full of barrels of olives. No sign of lunch. Then we were taken through an inconspicuous door and stepped into a paradise of a garden, completely enclosed in the Arab style, a hortus conclusus from some medieval illumination, with huge blue pots of basil on the steps, palm trees, trailing and climbing flowers, and fountains. In November it was so warm we sat outside for lunch, and the first course was gazpacho, but a rather refined version. This is the recipe I prefer.

Serves 6–8
750 g/1½ lb ripe tomatoes, peeled and roughly chopped
cucumber, peeled or half peeled, and roughly chopped
2 green peppers, seeded, cut in strips
3 cloves of garlic, sliced
250 g/8 oz/4 cups fresh wholemeal breadcrumbs
5 tablespoons/6 tbs red or white wine vinegar
5–8 tablespoons/6 tbs/⅔ cup olive oil
2 heaped teaspoons salt
tablespoon tomato paste (optional)
500–750 ml/1–1½ pts/2½–3¾ cups water
FOR THE GARNISHES
small croûtons, fried in olive oil
hard-boiled eggs, crumbled
3 spring onions, chopped
½ cucumber, peeled and chopped

Mix all the soup ingredients, except the water, in a large bowl. Purée them in batches in a processor or blender, using the water to produce a smooth thickness. Tip the purée into a bowl as you work, and chill for 2 hours at least. Add ice cubes and some extra water if you like, before serving. Put the garnishes in little bowls, on a tray, so that they can be passed round.

Ingredients can, of course, be adjusted to your taste. It is difficult to be precise when the strength of tomatoes can vary so much—use the paste to accent the flavour only if absolutely necessary.

CHILLED GRAPE SOUP
Sopa de uvas blancas malaguena

I was talking to some Spaniards about food one evening in a restaurant in Palencia in Old Castile. I mentioned how popular gazpacho had become in England. The waiter paused to observe that an exquisite white gazpacho was also made in the south—did I know it? I hunted through books and found this recipe of Maite Manjón's in *Flavours of Spain*, attributed to Malaga which is famous for its muscat raisins. Here grapes are used with almonds, another local speciality, and garlic, to flavour breadcrumbs and water. A delicate soup, lovely to taste and look at, making one think of country picnics in summertime (try taking it in a chilled wide-mouthed vacuum flask).

Serves 6
30 whole almonds, blanched
4 fat cloves of garlic, peeled and halved
tablespoon olive oil
tablespoon white wine vinegar
90 g/3 oz crustless white bread
900 ml/1½ pts/2¾ cups water
salt
375 g/12 oz muscat grapes, peeled, halved and pips removed

Set the liquidiser or processor whizzing at top speed, and put in the almonds, garlic, oil and vinegar. Add a little of the bread, then a little of the water. Go on doing this until both are absorbed and you have a white liquid. Put in a little more oil and vinegar to make it smoother and more piquant, if you like, and season with salt. Pour into a bowl, and stir in the grapes. Cover the bowl with clear film and chill. Serve with an ice cube in each bowl.

CORNMEAL SOUP
Sopa de maíz

Most of the corn that is stored in the horreos of Galicia and Asturias goes to feed chickens, some ends up as yellow cornmeal, which is sometimes made into polenta of a porridge consistency; but I prefer it made into this comforting soup from Aragon. Salt cod was taken all over Spain in the past by an efficient 'tribe' of carriers, the Maragatos of Leon, in the north. If you go and look at the cathedral of Astorga a little further south, you will see a figure of one of them in his special clothes. Indeed you will see signs of them all over the town. Their advantage was their trustworthiness and reliability: you could give them gold to take from Bayona to Seville or Barcelona, and be sure it would

Maize cobs are stored in picturesque hórreos, buildings raised on stilts, in Galacia

get there. Their main, and less romantic, trade was in salt cod, rice, dried vegetables, olive oil and wine, all virtually imperishable goods which, through the Maragatos, set their mark on all Spanish cooking.

If you cannot get salt cod, use smoked haddock, ideally a good Finnan haddock: it will not taste quite the same, but will be very good. Do not soak it.

Serves 6
250 g/8 oz salt cod, soaked in cold water for at least 24 hours
125 g/4 oz/1 cup chopped onions
60 g/2 oz diced white turnip
bay leaf
grated nutmeg
1 litre/1¾ pts/scant 4½ cups water
100 g/3½ oz/⅔ cup yellow cornmeal
2 cloves of garlic, sliced
4 tablespoons/⅓ cup oil
60 g/2 oz bread, cut in cubes
strong meat stock or jelly
salt and pepper
chopped parsley

Drain the cod and put it into a pan with fresh cold water. Bring slowly to simmering point; keep it there until the fish can be flaked easily from the skin and bone, which should be discarded.

Cut the cod up into small pieces. Put into a pan with the vegetables, bay leaf and a good grating of nutmeg plus a litre of water. Bring to simmering point, mix the cornmeal with a little water, then tip it into the soup, stirring well. Cook for 30 minutes on a low heat. Meanwhile, fry the garlic in the oil, putting the pieces of garlic into the soup when they are light brown. Fry the bread, adding extra oil if necessary to serve with the soup.

To improve the flavour add strong meat stock or jelly, season and sprinkle with chopped parsley.

GALICIAN SOUP
Caldo gallego

The ingredients may sound unpromising, but this soup is delicate to eat and beautiful to look at. There are many versions, but essential items are beans, potatoes, some kind of ham flavouring and cabbage or kale as dark green as you can find it. The leggy cabbage of Galicia in north-west Spain and of northern Portugal (where a similar but at the same time different soup is made) is unfamiliar to us here. It is one of several surprising things that you see in green Galicia, which is a land for discovery.

Serves 6–8
250 g/8 oz/generous cup dried haricot beans, soaked
2 litres/3½ pts/8¾ cups ham stock, or bacon hock and water, or bacon pieces and water, or gammon trimmings and light beef stock
500 g/1 lb/2⅔ cups potatoes, peeled and diced
750 g/1½ lb/9 cups dark cabbage or kale, shredded
salt and pepper
3 tablespoons lard, or pork fat, or bacon fat

Drain, rinse and simmer the beans for 1½ hours in the stock or bacon and water, etc. Ten minutes before the meal, remove any bone, bacon or gammon pieces, and put the diced potatoes into the simmering soup. When they are just tender, add the shredded cabbage or kale. When the shreds begin to wilt but still retain a little crunchiness, pour the soup into a warmed tureen, season, stir in fat. Serve with wholemeal bread and butter.

SAUSAGES

Chorizo The most familiar Spanish sausage to us at delicatessen counters because of its reddish appearance. In Spain there are a number of versions: pork, cut finer or coarser, the sausages made longer or smaller. All of them can be sliced for eating like salame, with bread, or used to spice a stew or soup, an empanada (see page 76) or an egg dish. The redness comes from paprika, and does not necessarily indicate heat although some chorizos are slightly hot. Always enquire if the chorizos you are buying come from Spain: if not, they will be on the bland side and inferior.

Morcilla Black pudding, which is rather solid like Lancashire black pudding, but in this case the blood and onions are solidified with rice. It is added to dishes such as olla podrida (recipe on page 75), tripe in the Madrid style, even in soups; or it may be sliced and fried.

Jamón serrano Ham made from the dark, bristling long-legged pig of eastern Spain which is closer to the pig of medieval illuminations than to our animals today. The ham is dark, too, and served in thin slices, sometimes with fruit, like Parma ham. If unobtainable, substitute Bayonne ham in recipes.

Tocino Cured pork fat, which is often needed to start off a stew or soup, when it is usually chopped and fried with onion. German speck from a delicatessen is a good substitute.

Other sausages found in Spain include *salchicón* which is something like an Italian salame and eaten in the same way. *Sobresada* a soft pinky-orange sausage coloured with cayenne and paprika can be added to sauces or spread on bits of bread. *Butifara* and *butifarones*, black and white, flavoured with pine kernels, cinnamon and cumin, are added to soups, vegetables and stews.

The name *longaniza* covers a number of sausages that need cooking, some of them not unlike our fresh sausages: you will find different versions in different parts of Spain. *Lomo* is unlike our general idea of a sausage, since the pork is not cut small, but enclosed whole in the casing: loin is the piece used.

Jamón serrano, cured with the hoof

FRIED AUBERGINE AND CHORIZO SANDWICH

Berenjenas empanadas de chorizo

A recipe of writer Maite Manjón's which I like very much, although I have not come across it in Spain.

Serves 4–6
4 aubergines, peeled, sliced across and salted
125 g/4 oz thinly sliced chorizo
2 level tablespoons flour
tablespoon water
½ tablespoon vinegar
beaten egg
salt
olive oil

Sandwich the chorizo between drained and dried aubergine slices. Press the aubergine slices together round the chorizo. Make a batter with the flour, water, vinegar, egg and salt and coat the sandwiches. Deep-fry in hot oil.

If you like, fix the sandwiches together with wooden toothpicks. Then you could coat them in egg and breadcrumbs instead of batter, if you prefer, before frying them.

HOT AND COLD HORS D'OEUVRE

At the Casa Ojeda restaurant in Burgos, in the north, I was intrigued by the hot and cold hors d'oeuvre dish on the menu. I was presented with two separate plates containing quite enough for a meal. One plate was very hot, with very hot things on it, the other very cold with chilled food—everything, arranged pointing inwards.

Starting at midnight and continuing clockwise, the hot plate contained:

rings of fried squid
10–12-cm/4–5-in chorizo sausages, fried, and arranged pointed inwards
1 large slice of black pudding, fried
2 small creamy croquettes
1 slice of another black pudding, fried

The cold plate contained:

half a hard-boiled egg
salade russe
crumbled tuna, mixed with red pepper strips, with oil
1 fat stalk of asparagus, right across the plate
1 thin slice of serrano ham
1 smaller slice of another cured ham
1 slice of beautiful boiled ham

It was great fun, a way of giving people a tasting of the varied charcuterie of Spain. And an idea that could easily be adapted to your own circumstances. The hot plate involves deep-frying: the croquettes first, the chorizo second, then the black pudding and last of all the squid.

ESCALIVADA

Escalivada is a mellow dish, to be made with summer and autumn vegetables rather than pale winter hothouse imports.

For six servings you will need to place in a hot oven 200 or 220°C (400 or 425°F), gas 6 or 7 a rack set on a baking sheet with an aubergine, a large green pepper, a large red pepper, 2 or 3 onions in their skins, 2 large firm tomatoes of the Marmande or beef kind. As the skins frizzle and the vegetables become tender remove them from the oven. Peel off the skins (running them under the cold tap helps), and cut the vegetables into strips, putting each kind into a separate bowl. Season with salt and pour on olive oil. Leave to marinade for a few hours. Either place the vegetables on 6 individual plates, arranging them in separate bands beside each other. Or mix all the vegetables up together and serve them from a bowl. In either case serve chilled.

PIPERRADA

A Basque dish of cheerful colour and flavour, and an ideal summer lunch especially if you grow your own tomatoes. The tomato and pepper sauce (sofrito—see page 71) can be prepared in advance, but the eggs and ham must be dealt with at the very last moment.

Serves 6
750 g/$1\frac{1}{2}$ lb red or green peppers, or both mixed
375 g/12 oz/3 cups chopped onion
150 ml/$\frac{1}{4}$ pt/$\frac{2}{3}$ cup olive oil
3 cloves of garlic, crushed and chopped
750 g/$1\frac{1}{2}$ lb tomatoes, peeled and chopped
good pinch of thyme
salt and pepper
sugar, to taste
6 slices of Bayonne or Parma ham, or thin gammon
6 eggs, beaten

Grill, or bake the peppers in a hot oven (230°C, 450°F, gas 8), or turn them over a gas flame, until the skin turns black and blistered. Rub it away under the cold tap; seed and slice the peppers.

Make a sofrito in a shallow earthenware pot (use a heat-diffuser for gas) by cooking the onion slowly in about two-thirds of the olive oil, then adding the garlic as the onion begins to look transparent. When the onion is soft and yellow, add the tomatoes. Stir them about and when they are cooking away, put in the pepper strips, thyme and seasoning, adding sugar if the tomatoes are not as well-flavoured as they should be. Keep the mixture bubbling so that all wateriness disappears.

In the rest of the oil, heat the slices of ham briefly. Stir the eggs into the vegetable mixture. Take the pot off the heat straightaway as egg cooks rapidly and it should not be allowed to harden. Tuck the ham round the edge or place it on top. Serve immediately.

TORTILLA
Tortilla de patatas y cebolla

A maddening dish that can be perfect one minute, and disgusting two minutes later. The problem is the eggs—they should be crisp and brown at the edges, moist and almost liquid in the centre when hot, cooling to a light firmness. Resist the temptation to make tortilla a dustbin for left-overs. Think of the Arab gardeners who introduced aubergine, spinach and artichokes—I imagine that this kind of omelette which has so long been popular came originally from the Arab world—and respect the quality of the vegetables.

The word tortilla has a special meaning for us: to Spaniards it means any kind of omelette, folded or thick. The advantage of this thick kind, studded with potatoes or some other vegetable, is that it can be eaten tepid or cold.

Serves 4
½ kg/1 lb potatoes, peeled and cut into centimetre dice
250 g/8 oz onion, sliced
olive oil
salt, pepper
6 eggs

Mix the potatoes and onion together with your hands. Heat up enough olive oil to cover the bottom of a 20-cm (8-in) pan, and fry the vegetables in it slowly taking half an hour and turning them over occasionally. They should brown lightly. Season them. Beat the eggs in a large bowl, and add salt and pepper, then stir in the warm potatoes and onion.

If the oil in the pan looks clean and appetising as it should, tip the mixture in and leave to cook on the base and sides. If not, clean the pan and put in fresh oil before cooking the tortilla. After 2 minutes, free the sides with a knife and look to see if they are nicely browned. If they are, slide the pan under a preheated grill and cook the top for about 2 minutes. Keep taking the pan out, so that you can make sure the tortilla doesn't overcook. Serve in the cooking pan or leave it in to half-cool, then ease it again and turn it out on to a plate.

BAKED BREAM
Besugo al horno

A favourite way of cooking bream in Spain, more of a style than a recipe since the variations are many. Other fish can be used: one or two large ones, or several small individual fish, red or grey mullet, bass, or a piece of fish such as a tailpiece.

Clean and scale the fish. Make three slashes at right angles to the bone, and slip into each one a thin wedge of lemon (the best way to cut a wedge is to halve the lemon longways and cut each piece in half, then slice at an angle).

Brush oil over a baking dish. On it you can lay a flat bed of par-boiled potato slices. Put in the fish, lemon slices up. Set the oven at hot, 220°C (425°F), gas 7.

For each 3 people, heat 150 ml (¼ pt/⅔ cup) olive oil in a frying pan and fry a couple of sliced garlic cloves until they are a pale brown. Cool the oil and strain it on to 2 heaped tablespoons fresh breadcrumbs, mixed with a good chopping of parsley. Pour over the fish. Bake it in the heated oven (the thinner the fish the hotter the oven can be) until just cooked, basting from time to time with the oil in the dish.

SANTIAGO SCALLOPS

In France we live on a branch of the medieval route to Santiago de Compostela where, according to legend, the body of St James the Apostle, Spain's patron saint is buried. We look down to the painted church of Saint Jacques by a ford where pilgrims crossed the Loir wearing the wide-brimmed hat with the scallop shell badge of St James pinned to the brim. At night we can see the Milky Way which people took to be the millions of pilgrims crowding towards the sanctuary of Compostela. At last, on the tour for this book, we got there ourselves. The cathedral and its squares, the arcaded street were even grander theatre than we had imagined, with St James in his pilgrim clothes, with his scallop shell, on a high pinnacle on the western facade.

For a first course, buy 2 large scallops for each person, 3 for a main course. Extra ingredients for 6 people are:

6 deep scallop shells, scrubbed
125–150 g/4–5 oz/1 cup chopped onion
olive oil
3 cloves of garlic, finely chopped
small bunch of parsley, leaves chopped
salt and pepper
powdered cloves and grated nutmeg to taste
6 level tablespoons/7 tbs fine white breadcrumbs

Put the shells on to a baking tray, propping them steady with crumpled foil. Sweat the onion in a little oil until half cooked. Put into a basin with the garlic and parsley. Set the oven at hot, 220°C (425°F), gas 7.

Rinse, trim and dice the white part of the scallops. Discard the black tips from the corals and put them aside. Season the mixture in the basin, adding spices to taste, and put in the diced scallop. Divide the mixture between the shells, putting the corals on top in the centre of each one. Sprinkle with breadcrumbs and drip a tablespoon of oil over each shellful of scallops.

Bake the scallops in the heated oven for 10–15 minutes until lightly browned. Check them after 10 minutes: if necessary, remove the shells, even if they are still pale, rather than overcook them.

CATALAN COD
Esqueixada

Catalan cooking has a high reputation in Spain, and certainly one of the best meals I had was in a Catalan restaurant. I was given this piquant and rather unusual dish to start the meal with. You can use canned tunny in oil instead of salt cod, but cod is correct.

For 4 people, soak a thick piece of salt cod—weighing about 200 g (7 oz) and ideally from the part towards the head—for at least 24 hours or until it has plumped up. Drain, and cut away any skin and bone, then tear it into small shreds. Chop a medium onion and a large firm-skinned tomato and put into a bowl along with the shredded cod.

Grill or bake a red or green pepper and remove its skin and seeds; cut it into strips, then into little squares. Mix with the cod. Season with olive oil, wine vinegar, salt and pepper, and a little cayenne. Stir well. Put on to a flat dish and garnish with black and green olives.

SALSA VERDE

Salsa verde may or may not contain peas, but must have parsley to give the right colour. It is cooked in with eel or hake, not separately, and you must keep the earthenware pot shaking gently over the heat to get the right creamy consistency.

Although you start off with oil, the fish does not

SAUCES

Sofrito means something lightly fried and is the basis of many Spanish dishes and sauces. It consists of chopped onion sweated slowly in olive oil, with garlic. As it turns soft and golden, chopped parsley and tomato are added, or just tomato. The whole mixture is cooked to a thick, unwatery purée. The garlic should be crushed with the blade of a knife, skinned, and then finely chopped so that it can melt away into the sofrito. Quantities of each ingredient vary with individual recipes.

Majado Meaning something pounded, is based on nuts and adds consistency to sauces and dishes. It is especially popular in Catalonia and Mediterranean Spain where almonds, hazelnuts and pine kernels grow.

Española (Spanish) This is the great sauce not only of Spanish but also of French—and so of European—classic cookery: in other words brown sauce. In the best kitchens it took two days to make, with the best ingredients, one of which was the superb ham from Montanchez in Extremadura. As every basic cookery book will have at least one domesticated version. I do not give one here. It can be added to a number of dishes or served with red meats and game.

Romesco Is the great Catalan sauce of a thousand versions, made with hot red romesco peppers grown in the region, hazelnuts, almonds, garlic and pimentón (Spanish paprika). True romesco peppers need to be bought in Spain; the substitutes suggested below do not really give the correct taste. It can be very hot, and should be used in dabs like mustard, or mixed with allioli sauce, or more generally on its own, with perhaps sliced cold lobster and sliced roast chicken breast arranged together on a dish. It can also be added to sauces and stews. It goes with all shellfish, fish, grilled meat as well as rabbit and poultry. Romesco and allioli sauces are the Spanish equivalents of the rouille and aïoli sauces of southern France.

The recipe following comes from *Cocina Catalana*, by Maria Dolores Camps Cardona (Editorial Ramos-Majos, Barcelona, 1979). On a greased baking sheet put 2 tomatoes (weighing 200 g (7 oz) in all), 4 large cloves of garlic—more, if you like, up to a whole head—10 blanched almonds and 10 hazelnuts. Bake in a hot oven, 220–230°C (425–450°F), gas 7–8 for 10–15 minutes. Meanwhile, tear up a dried romesco pepper or a dried hot chilli pepper, having first removed their seeds, and fry briefly in a little olive oil. Put into a blender or processor. Peel the tomatoes, quarter them and remove the seeds; skin the garlic, and rub off the hazelnut skins, then put them all, with the almonds, into the blender or processor. Purée them, then gradually add 150 ml ($\frac{1}{4}$ pt/$\frac{2}{3}$ cup) of olive oil, then 100 ml ($\frac{1}{2}$ fl oz/$\frac{1}{3}$ cup) vinegar gradually to taste. Season with salt. More almonds or hazelnuts can be added.

Allioli Is tricky to make as it can separate. Have some cubes of white bread ready to add, if it begins to turn oily. Put 6 large cloves of peeled garlic into a blender or processor; plus $\frac{1}{4}$ teaspoon salt. Whizz at top speed, adding up to 250 ml (about 8 fl oz/1 cup) olive oil slowly. Taste and add more salt. Serve cold with fish and vegetables, or with roast or grilled meats.

Wild mushrooms are much appreciated in Spain

fry in the accepted sense. Put the eel, cut up, or the slices of hake into a wide dish plus enough olive oil to make $\frac{1}{2}$ cm (scant $\frac{1}{4}$ in), 2 or 3 crushed and chopped cloves of garlic, 2 good tablespoons chopped parsley and a mug of shelled peas. Set on the stove, switch to a moderate heat (use a heat-diffuser with gas) and shake the dish to and fro without lifting it until the fish is cooked and the sauce is a creamy consistency.

Turn the fish occasionally. A mashed hard-boiled egg can be stirred up with some of the sauce and added at the end. Peas can be omitted. Stock or white wine and water can be added to augment the fish juices.

This technique may seem strange, but it is fascinating to watch the gradual formation of the sauce as the fish juices and the olive oil shake together as a cream.

SQUID BASQUE STYLE
Chipirones en su tinta

This best of all squid dishes should be made with tiny tender ones, with body sacs no more than a finger's length. These are not easy to come by in England, so my recipe is adapted to larger specimens with sacs about 15 cm (6 in) long. If you get hold of the tiny squid, allow six per person and reduce the cooking time.

Serves 6
6 squid
4 tablespoons/$\frac{1}{3}$ cup olive oil
4 medium onions, chopped
3–4 cloves of garlic, finely chopped
60 g/2 oz serrano ham or smoked bacon, chopped
90 g/3 oz/1$\frac{1}{2}$ cups fresh breadcrumbs, soaked in a little milk or dry white wine, then squeezed out to a paste
plenty of chopped parsley
salt and pepper
large tomato, peeled and chopped
fried bread triangles

Pull the heads gently away from the bodies of the squid being careful not to damage the soft inside part containing the silvery ink sac. Remove the sacs gently with a sharp knife and put into a basin. Crush them with a little water, using a wooden spoon, so that the ink flows out, then set aside.

Chop the squid tentacles, then discard the rest of the head. Remove the thin purple skin from the body sacs, and take out the transparent-looking pen or backbone from inside.

In the oil, soften the onions with the garlic until golden. Set half aside for the sauce. Raise the heat slightly and add the ham or bacon and chopped tentacles. When they begin to brown, put in the breadcrumbs. When everything is well blended and mellow, add plenty of parsley and seasoning to taste. Cool a little, then stuff the squid with this mixture, filling them half full; close them with a wooden cocktail stick (or sew with thread).

Put the squid in a flameproof serving dish (glazed earthenware is ideal), together with the reserved onions and tomato. Cover and leave to cook gently for 30–45 minutes until tender. Barely allow the sauce to simmer or the squid will break. Add a little water if necessary. Just 5 minutes before serving, add the ink, sieved to keep back the skins of the sacs. If you like a smooth texture, sieve the whole sauce. Serve with triangles of fried bread.

PAELLA

Paella can worry people who like the certainty of exact recipes, because there are so many variations. Every Spanish family has a different version from its neighbours, sometimes more than one version according to their finances or what was on sale at the fishmarket that day.

But take courage—there are only four essential elements to a paella as far as I can discover: after that fantasy takes over. You need a sofrito of onion, tomato and garlic (see page 71), then Spanish or Italian (risotto) rice, saffron essential for flavour as well as for colour, and squid. Squid alone seems to give the right savoury sweetness: if your fishmonger has it rarely, buy extra when you can, then make stock with the extra and the debris of the rest to store in the freezer. Another good flavouring—easier to find here—is mussels or cockles. But because there is so little uncooked shellfish in this country, it is difficult to get the right freshness in paella. Cooked prawns, for instance, that have been deep-frozen are second best, and can easily be ruined by careless reheating.

This recipe may seem long and complex, but the idea of a paella is simple. You first prepare the flavouring meat, fish and vegetables, well in advance or just before the main cooking, if you like. You then cook the rice and, when it is half-cooked or tender, add the flavouring ingredients. In Spain, in fact, paella picnics are popular. Everything is prepared as far as possible at home, then the final cooking and assembly is done over a fire of driftwood at the beach.

The right pan, the paellera, is wide with shallow, sloping sides, and has two handles. It goes from fire to table. For a party of 6 you need one of 35-cm (14-in) diameter, but you can make an equally good paella for 6 people in a large 27-cm ($10\frac{1}{2}$-in) sauté pan: just handle it carefully so that the paella doesn't overflow. For paella, as for risotto, measure the rice by volume, since you need twice its *volume* in liquid, or slightly more.

Fresh prawns (or shrimps in America) are often an ingredient of paella

Serves 6–8

FOR THE MEAT

small roasting chicken
olive oil
250 g/8 oz pork sparerib or leg, cubed
6–10 tiny sausages (optional)

FOR THE FISH

250 g/8 oz medium-sized squid
500 g/1 lb white fish fillets, optional
small lobster, optional
1 kg/2 lb cooked prawns in their shells
1 kg/2 lb large mussels, or 500 g/1 lb small mussels or cockles

TO FINISH

olive oil
large onion, finely chopped
250 g/8 oz tomatoes, peeled and chopped
heaped teaspoon paprika
3 large cloves of garlic, finely chopped
salt and pepper
tomato paste or sugar
500 ml/$\frac{3}{4}$ pt Spanish/Italian rice
generous pinch of saffron
150–175 g/5–6 oz/1 cup shelled young peas
4–6 cooked artichoke hearts
large grilled red pepper, skinned, seeded and sliced in strips

TO PREPARE THE MEAT Cut breast meat from the chicken, dividing each side into 3 or 4 pieces. Remove wings and cut off the legs. Put drumsticks with the wings, and cut meat from the thigh bones. Cut away the oysters from underneath the chicken carcase. Put thigh bones plus carcase with giblets, minus the liver, into a large pan. Cover generously with water, bring to simmering point, and leave to bubble gently, covered.

Brown the chicken pieces quickly in olive oil, then transfer to a plate. Stir the pork into the oil, raising the heat a little, and add the sausages. When both are browned, add to the chicken. If the oil is reasonably clear, leave it in the pan. Otherwise pour it away and clean the pan with kitchen paper.

TO PREPARE THE FISH Clean the squid if not already done. Discard everything except the tentacles, which should be chopped, and the white body sacs, which should be sliced. Fry them in olive oil until lightly browned and half cooked. Put on a plate. In the remaining oil, fry the white fish fillets, cut into squares, until lightly browned and half-cooked. Add to the squid plate, in a separate heap.

Remove the lobster's large claws, if using, and divide them at the joint. Put small claws, plus body shell into the simmering chicken stock pan. Cut the body meat into pieces and set aside, together with the large claws, the soft tomalley (liver) and any roe.

Set aside some prawns for decoration. Shell the rest, adding the shells to the chicken stock pan. Cut up large prawns into 2 or 3 pieces.

Scrub and open the mussels or cockles in the usual way. Leave enough in their shells to make a decoration at the end, but shell the rest; set them all aside. Strain their cooking liquor carefully into a large measuring jug, through double muslin.

Season all the fish and meat.

Next, attend to the stock, which should have quite a robust flavour. Strain it into the mussel stock in the measuring jug: you should aim to have a generous litre (2 pts/5 cups). If you have too much, boil it down in a shallow pan: if you have too little, add water or extra chicken or fish stock. Bring to the boil, when the sofrito is nearly ready, see next paragraph.

PREPARE THE SOFRITO (see page 71) using olive oil, the onion, tomatoes, paprika and garlic. Season it well with salt, pepper, and tomato purée or sugar. At first it will seem milky, then the oil will separate.

THE FINAL ASSEMBLY Tip in the well-rinsed rice, having pushed the sofrito to one side of the pan. The rice will colour slightly but should not brown to any extent. Add two-thirds of the boiling stock. Dissolve the saffron in the remaining very hot stock. Leave the rice to bubble gently without stirring it. Just give the pan a shake occasionally.

When the rice is half-cooked, put in the reserved chicken and pork, burying them well so that only the chicken bones stick out conspicuously with a little of the meat. Pour in the remaining stock. After 5 minutes, put in the squid. In another 5 minutes put in the peas, artichokes, pepper strips, sausages, fish, lobster and prawns. Just before serving, add the mussels or cockles, together with those in their shells. Taste for seasoning. Serve with lemon wedges.

CATALAN FISH STEW
Zarzuela

A zarzuela is an operetta, a musical entertainment, very gay and brightly coloured, frivolous—a good name for this splendid Catalan fish stew with its different tones of red and white, touched with saffron yellow. As with paella, you may find it difficult to make because of the lack of fine fresh shellfish. Of course cooked and even frozen shellfish can be used, but the dish loses something of its pell-mell sweet intensity of flavour. As far as the plainer fish are concerned, squid and monkfish are essential as they have a hint of shellfish texture and flavour, after them come hake, sole or John Dory. In Spain, grouper (mero) is important to zarzuela, but this is not a common fish. Substitutions can be made of course, so long as you have a variety of textures and tastes. Use the ingredient list as a guide only. Even if the result is not authentically Spanish, it may be just as delicious in its own way.

Serves 10–14

2 kg/4 lb mixed fish, monkfish, hake, sole, John Dory, halibut, weever
$\frac{1}{2}$ kg/1 lb prawns in their shells, or shrimp, mixed kinds and sizes, uncooked if possible
1 kg/2 lb lobster, cut into 10 pieces by the fishmonger or $2\frac{3}{4}$ kg/$1\frac{1}{2}$ lb lobsters, cut up into 14 pieces
6 cloves garlic, peeled, sliced thin
olive oil
$\frac{3}{4}$ kg/$1\frac{1}{2}$ lb tomatoes, peeled, deseeded, chopped
leaves of a handful of parsley
large pinch saffron dissolved in 125 ml/4 fl oz/scant $\frac{2}{3}$ cup hot water
150 ml/$\frac{1}{4}$ pt/$\frac{2}{3}$ cup dry white wine
salt, pepper

Prepare, sort and slice the fish. Put all trimmings, tentacles, heads, bones and shells of cooked shellfish (apart from a few left whole to garnish) into a large pan. Cover with water, and boil for 30 minutes to make some stock. Aim to end up with $\frac{1}{4}$ litre (8–9 oz/1 cup).

From the next four ingredients, make a sofrito (see sauce box on page 71). When it is mellow add, saffron and its water, wine and stock, with seasoning. When boiling hard, add the firmest fish and uncooked large shellfish. Simmer 5 minutes, then add softer fish and smaller shellfish and lobster pieces. Bring back to simmering point and simmer for 5 more minutes. Add cooked shellfish, give it 2 more minutes. Pour into a hot tureen and serve.

Olla podrida of mixed meats, sausage, chickpeas and broth, is a classic of Spanish cookery

OLLA PODRIDA

The great boiled meat dish of the Iberian peninsula, from which the cocidos of Spain and the cozidos of Portugal derive. This enormous dish (the name means Rotten Stew) has to be made on the grand scale, preferably in two huge earthenware pots though most of us have to use metal ones. Its fame is ancient, Don Quixote lived on a poor version of it, and from the 17th century onwards it seems to have been the dish of grand courtly living from England across to Austria. Often it looked better than it tasted (overcooking and hanging about ruins it).

The most precise description, the one on which this recipe is based, is Richard Ford's in his *Gatherings from Spain*, of 1846. His food chapter is essential reading for anyone interested in Spanish food. He sees that in the olla 'the whole culinary genius of Spain is condensed, as the mighty Jinn was into a gallipot, according to the Arabian Night Tales', and comments on the oriental style of Spanish cooking, principally the stewing which is the method of countries short on fuel.

Serves 12

FOR THE MEATS

500 g/1 lb/2¼ cups chickpeas, soaked 24 hours or more
boiling fowl, cleaned, giblets removed
500–750 g/1–1½ lb brisket or boiling beef
1 beef bone (optional)
500 g/1 lb piece of smoked streaky bacon
2 pig's trotters or hocks, or ½ pig's head
250 g/8 oz pork belly, diced

FOR THE SAUSAGES

medium to large chorizo
a loop of black pudding

FOR THE VEGETABLES

375 g/12 oz/3 cups thickly sliced onion
2 large carrots
4 trimmed leeks
small hard cabbage
1 whole bulb of garlic
2 hot red chillies, fresh or dried
3 turnips
3 stalks of celery, or ½ celeriac

Drain, rinse and put the chickpeas into a huge pan

with all the meats. Cover well with water. Bring to boiling point, and skim until no more scum rises, then reduce the heat so that the water simmers with an occasional burp. Cook for 2 hours, then add the sausages and cook for a further hour. Keep an eye on the chicken and beef, so that they do not overcook. If there is danger of this, reduce the heat still further.

Prepare the vegetables, putting them into another large pan as you go. First the onion, then scrape and cut the carrots into 1 cm (about $\frac{1}{4}$ in) batons, about 5 cm (2 in) long. Cut the leeks into fat slices, shred the cabbage coarsely. Remove the loose papery skin from the garlic, but leave it whole. Split one of the chillies so that the seeds are exposed. Peel and quarter the turnips. Slice the celery, or peel and cut the celeriac into wedges. Cover with water, bring to the boil and leave to simmer for the last hour of the meats' cooking.

TO ASSEMBLE Arrange the meat on a large hot serving dish, together with the chickpeas, drained from the broth with a slotted spoon. Drain the vegetable water into the meat pot, then put the vegetables round the meat on the dish. Keep warm while you serve the reheated broth, with fried bread croûtons. Then serve the platter of meats and vegetables.

MEAT IN CHILINDRON SAUCE

Another of Spain's blazing red dishes, this time from Aragon. Any tender meat can be used: boned best end of neck of lamb, cut into neat thick slices, or veal cutlets, or a young rabbit or large chicken, jointed into 6–8 pieces, or kid if you can get it.

Serves 6
3 tablespoons/scant $\frac{1}{4}$ cup olive oil
250 g/8 oz/2 cups chopped onion
500 g/1 lb tomatoes, peeled and chopped, or 396 g/14 oz can tomatoes, drained and roughly chopped, juice reserved
3 cloves of garlic, crushed and chopped
salt and pepper, level teaspoon sugar
100 g/3$\frac{1}{2}$ oz tocino (salted pork fat), or fat salt pork belly, diced
1.5 kg/3 lb meat or 2–2.5 kg/4–5 lb oven-ready chicken
5 red peppers, seeded and sliced
chopped parsley

Make a sofrito (see page 71) with the first four ingredients in a large earthenware pot over a low to moderate flame (use a heat-diffuser with gas). Season, adding the sugar as well.

Remove the sofrito with a slotted spoon, or push it to one side if the pot is large enough. Raise the heat and brown the tocino or belly of pork, together with the meat or chicken. Mix with the sofrito, put in the peppers and reserved tomato juice. Cover and simmer for up to 1 hour, depending on the meat. Do not overcook it.

If, as can happen, the pepper takes longest to soften, remove the cooked meat to a dish, and leave the sauce to bubble steadily. Another way round this problem is to grill and skin the peppers before adding them to the dish.

Before serving, put the meat back into the sauce, and arrange things so that it looks nicely disposed. Scatter with parsley and serve in the cooking pot. Provide bread to sop up the juices.

GALICIAN PIE
Empanada gallega

In Galicia, bakers make great golden pies of romanesque simplicity and grandeur with rolled edges like an old-fashioned mattress. As the yeast dough is on the solid side, fillings are piquant with chorizo, peppers and jamón serrano. One evening at Bayona, inside the castellated fort that is now a

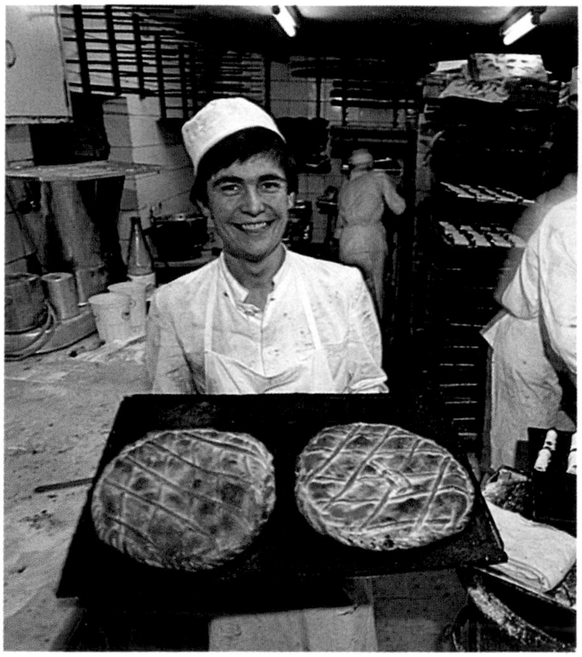

Empanada gallega in a Galician bakery

parador, we had a slice of an empanada filled with veal, chorizo, peppers and onion. I prefer the chicken filling below, and make the crust thinner so that it becomes crisp in the baking. (Bayona incidentally was the first place in Spain to hear of Columbus's arrival in America: you would not guess at the bustle and excitement of the place in those times from its peacefulness now.)

Serves 6–8

FOR THE DOUGH

300 g/10 oz/2½ cups strong white bread flour
packet Harvest Gold dried yeast
1½ level teaspoons salt
125 ml/4 fl oz/½ cup milk and water mixed, tepid
tablespoon olive oil

FOR THE FILLING

1.5 kg/3 lb chicken, jointed
3 tablespoons/scant ¼ cup olive oil
stock or water
125 g/4 oz/1 cup chopped onion
clove of garlic, finely chopped
396 g/14 oz can tomatoes, drained
red pepper, grilled, skinned, deseeded and diced
red chilli pepper, fresh or dried, chopped or split
60 g/2 oz serrano or Bayonne ham, chopped
10–12-cm/4–5-in piece of chorizo, skinned and diced
salt, pepper, cayenne
chopped parsley
beaten egg, to glaze

Make a bread dough in the usual way, and leave it to rise in its bowl, tied into a plastic bag, for 1 hour.

Brown the chicken lightly in the oil. Put into a saucepan, cover with stock or water and simmer for 15 minutes. Remove the breast pieces, and simmer another 10–15 minutes until the leg joints are almost cooked but still pink. Cut the meat from the bone into neat pieces (bones and liquid can be turned into stock for another dish).

In the chicken frying pan, make a sofrito (see page 71) with the onion, garlic, tomatoes, and pepper. Put the chilli into the pan (with the seeds if you like extra fire). As the sauce reduces, put in the meats. Season and remove from the heat. Stir in enough parsley to give a green speckled effect.

Divide the dough into two lumps, one slightly larger than the other. Roll this large one out to a 27 cm (10½ in) circle. Put it on to a greased baking sheet, or into a 25-cm (10-in) tart tin. Brush a wide border with beaten egg. Put the filling inside it. Set the oven at moderately hot, 190°C (375°F), gas 5.

Roll out the second piece of dough and cut a circle about the same size as the mound of filling. Put it on top, brush it with egg and make a large centre hole. Roll the edge of the bottom piece of dough up and over the pastry lid, pressing it and rolling it to make a seam. Take the trimmings and roll them out. With a sharp knife, cut out a wide, curve-armed cross, large enough to touch the rolled edge at all four points. It should look like a primitive Celtic cross. Put it on to the pie, make a hole in the centre and brush it with egg. Or you can make different decorations if you like.

Prove for 30 minutes, then bake in the heated oven for about 50 minutes or until golden brown and crisp.

YOUNG ROAST LAMB
Ternasco asado

In Madrid, squashed in with parties of Americans who had come to see a special bull fight, I once tried to eat massive pieces of young lamb, piled high on a plate. But how should you begin, where should you first put the fork in? Even with excellent bread and wine, it was too much, but the flavour made me want to try it at home.

For 6 people, buy a whole best end of neck, from a young lamb. Ask the butcher to chop it into two racks down the backbone, but stop him before he chops the long bones. He should then chine the backbone.

At home, remove the outer skin and any excess of fat. Rub over the meat vigorously with salt, then with a cut clove of garlic. Put the pieces in a roasting pan, skin side up. Pour over a little olive oil or melted lard, and 250 ml (8–9 fl oz) dry white wine.

Cook in a hot oven 230°C (450°F), gas 8 for 10 minutes. Baste with the juices, and lower the heat to 190°C, (375°F), gas 5. Leave for 20–35 minutes, according to the size of the pieces and how pink you like lamb to be.

Transfer the meat to a hot serving dish and keep warm. Skim fat from the pan juices and pour round the meat. Serve with potatoes, roast or fried, and aubergines or peppers.

POULTRY, RABBIT OR PARTRIDGE WITH ALMOND SAUCE
Capirotada

In the east and southern Spain—and in the Canaries—sauces are oftened thickened with nuts—an idea which survives from Arab cooking. I suppose the romesco sauce is the most celebrated example (see below and page 71). Such sauces need

continued on p. 79

SAFFRON

Saffron, essential to many dishes in Spanish cookery, consists of the dried stigmas of a cultivated species of crocus (*Crocus sativus*).

It is expensive, because it takes some 70,000 flowers to make a half kilo (1 lb) of saffron. The flowers have to be picked by hand; then, thread by thread, the stigmas-cum-styles have to be extracted. Luckily, saffron is so powerful in colour and flavour that you need to buy it only in minute quantities.

Saffron was traditionally considered an essence of sunlight and cheerfulness (sheets were dyed yellow with saffron to improve love-making and fertility), and it is from Spain, and Spanish sunshine, that we get most of our supplies today. In Spain the use of saffron no doubt derived from Arabic kitchens (along with the name, from the Arabic za'faran, which filtered down to us through medieval French).

The saffron crocus used to be grown quite successfully around Saffron Walden in Essex and at Stratton in Cornwall (hence Cornish saffron cake and saffron buns?). But really it does best with the sun, and seems by origin to have been a plant of the eastern Mediterranean, one of those very anciently domesticated plants which exist now only in cultivation.

If you want to see the saffron harvest, fields purple with the flowers, go to Consuegra, south of Toledo in central Spain. There is a grand saffron festival, when a Saffron Queen is chosen, with competitions to see who can pick the most stamens from the flowers, and one can eat barbecued meat flavoured with saffron.

Always buy saffron in its original, bright dark-red threads, and dissolve them in a little hot liquid from the dish being made. Some people strain out the filaments before adding the yellow liquid, but I like to see them there. Also some cookery books suggest substituting turmeric for saffron: the colour may be bright, but the flavour is wrong.

SAFFRON SAUCE

This beautiful sauce for fish was given me by Tom Hearne when he was at the Hole in the Wall restaurant in Bath. It is for steaks of pike, hake, turbot, halibut or bass, baked in the oven with a little fish stock.

Serves 4
generous pinch of saffron
600 ml/1 pt fish stock, heated
125 g/4 oz/$\frac{1}{2}$ cup butter
60 g/2 oz/$\frac{1}{2}$ cup flour
small red and small green pepper, seeded and cut into strips
clove of garlic, crushed and chopped
150 ml/$\frac{1}{4}$ pt/$\frac{2}{3}$ cup cream
2 tablespoons/3 tbs Madeira
lemon juice

Dissolve the saffron in the stock (this should be made with some dry white wine and a splash of vinegar). Make a roux with half the butter and the flour; moisten it with the stock. Cook down to the consistency of double cream.

Meanwhile, soften the peppers with the garlic in the remaining butter over a low heat. When they are soft, add this mixture to the sauce and simmer for 10 minutes. Pour in the cream, Madeira and lemon juice to taste. Add the juices, much reduced, from cooking the fish.

Arrange the fish on a serving plate, or individual plates. Carefully pour the sauce round it, and arrange the pepper strips on top.

Picking saffron crocus at Consuegra

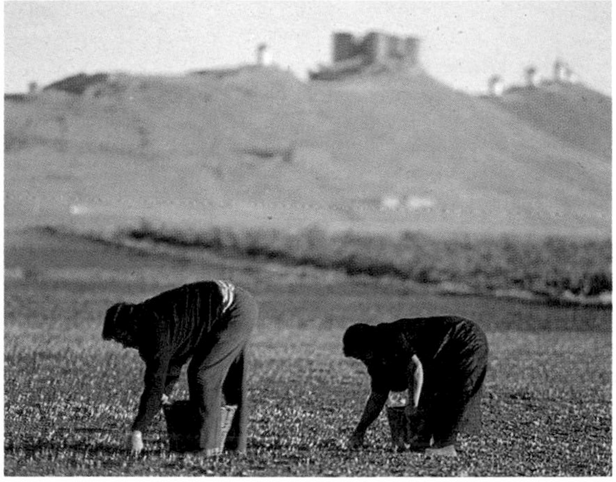

The orange stamens are dried for saffron

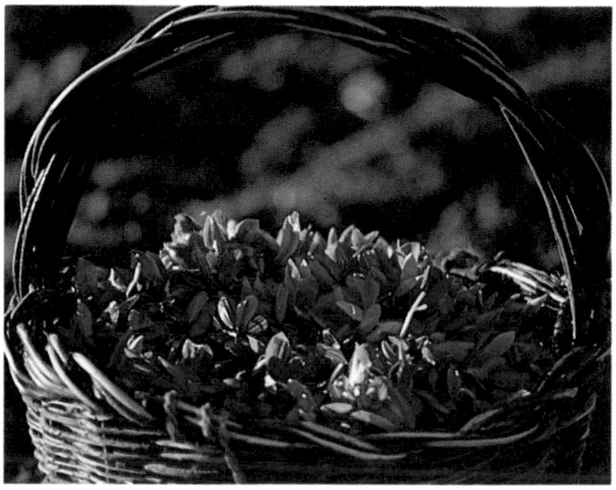

to be pounded, or put through a vigorous blender or processor. Experts say that pounding is better, but I never have time for this and could not make such things without machinery.

A variety of poultry can be used, chicken or guineafowl being the best. Wild or domestic rabbit and partridges do well. The point is not to overcook them in the first stage, or the dish becomes dry. Spanish cooks use water, but with our tasteless chickens I think chicken stock works better.

Serves 6
1 large chicken or 2 guineafowl or partridges or 1 rabbit
bouquet of parsley, thyme, tarragon, bay
about 125 g/4 oz chopped onion
1 litre/1¾ pts/scant 4½ cups stock or water
5 slices of white bread, crusts removed
lard
150 g/5 oz almonds, blanched
small stick cinnamon or 1–2 level teaspoons ground cinnamon
salt, pepper

Put poultry, game or rabbit into a close-fitting pan. Add bouquet, onion and liquid just to cover (though, with a chicken, it would be wise to leave the breast free and cover it with a butter paper). Bring to simmering point and simmer—never boil—until the meat is barely cooked, still slightly pink. Remove from the pan, cool slightly and cut meat from the bone (keep bones and skin to make stock for another dish).

Meanwhile, fry the bread in lard. Cut three slices into four triangles each and set aside to keep warm. Cut up the other two and put into a blender or processor with the almonds and 300 ml (½ pt/1¼ cups) of the cooking liquid if it seems necessary. Put the sauce in a pan, add cinnamon, salt and pepper and simmer gently for about 15 minutes. Stir and add extra stock as required: it should end up thick. Quickly fry the meat in the lard pan (if the lard is still clean—if not, replace it) until golden. Serve encircled by bread triangles and covered with sauce; pour any remaining sauce into a separate bowl. Fried potatoes go well with this dish and a salad to follow.

DUCK WITH OLIVES
Pato con aceitunas

Driving across country outside Seville is an endless experience of red soil and neat silver olive trees. Just as it begins to seem boring, a low white-washed castle of a building appears, with a few openings in the brilliant thick walls. This happens over and over again.

If you drive in under the gate, you will most likely see a courtyard with a fountain in the middle, in November a working place with an ordered huddle of baskets of olives, and a few pickers wandering about with their special bags and knives. You may be invited through the next courtyard to the house, and eventually to a secret garden courtyard with running water, many plants and shady trees, sweet-smelling flowers. There will be cool dry sherry and olives, stuffed perhaps with anchovies or almonds or the familiar red pepper strips, and perhaps a dish like this duck with olives served very late, outside, in the darkness.

Serves 4–6
large duck or 2 smaller ones
30 g/1 oz/2 tbs butter
2 tablespoons/3 tbs olive oil
2 medium onions cut in half
125 g/4 oz peeled carrot, cut in batons
20 g/⅔ oz/3 tbs flour
½ litre/generous ¾ pt/scant 2 cups giblet or poultry stock
125 ml/4 fl oz/scant ⅔ cup dry or medium dry sherry or Madeira
60 g/2 oz tomato concentrate or paste
salt, pepper, parsley
48 green olives, stoned

Brown duck all over in butter and oil, with the onion and carrot. Turn it carefully, so that the skin does not break. Allow 25 minutes. Put the duck and vegetables into a deep pot. Pour off the fat in the pan, leaving a tablespoonful (keep the fat for frying potatoes). Stir in the flour and brown it, then stir in stock, sherry or Madeira and tomato. Scrape in any nice brown bits, and when boiling and smooth, tip over the duck. Put the lid on at a slight tilt, so that the sauce reduces slightly as the duck cooks. Turn it from time to time, allowing 45–55 minutes cooking time, according to size and how pink you like duck to be.

Remove the duck to a hot serving dish, making sure that all the juices inside are tipped back into the sauce. Pour and spoon off the fat from the sauce, then season it with salt, pepper and some parsley.

Meanwhile, simmer the olives for 5 minutes in enough water to cover them. Put them round the duck. Pour on the sauce and serve with potatoes, if you like, and a salad.

PARTRIDGES/PIGEONS IN BILBAO SAUCE

Perdices or palomas en salsa a la bilbaina

The use of chocolate to accent certain game sauces in Spanish—and Italian—cookery is no more odd than to use anchovy essence in pork pies or oysters with steak and kidney as we have done in the past and in places still do. The purpose is the same—cooks use whatever intensity they have to hand in the kitchen, and chocolate, unsweetened or bitter, or at least very dark, is an old ingredient in Spain.

Partridges are more common in Spain than they are here: you will need 4 small tender ones for the best result, or two older ones with a longer cooking time and more liquid. Good stews of hare or rabbit can be made by adapting this recipe. And you may think it worth larding stewing partridges or woodpigeons to make them tender.

Serves 4
375 g/12 oz/3 cups chopped onion
3 medium carrots, diced
2–4 partridges or 4 woodpigeons
6 tablespoons/½ cup olive oil
2 rashers of bacon, chopped
2 cloves of garlic, chopped
tablespoon white wine vinegar
150 ml/¼ pt/⅔ cup dry white wine
250 g/8 oz peeled, chopped tomato
beef, poultry or game stock
salt and pepper
grated nutmeg
about 15 g/½ oz grated chocolate

Put the onion and carrots in a flameproof casserole which will hold the birds closely, breast down. In a deep pan, brown the birds lightly in the oil with the bacon, then transfer everything to the casserole. Add the garlic, vinegar, wine and tomato. No stock is necessary for young birds, but for stewing birds, add enough stock to cover them. Put on the lid and cook gently until the birds are tender. Allow about 40 minutes for young birds, and 40 minutes–1½ hours for pigeons. Check from time to time: if you did not add stock to start with, the sauce may become dry and need a little.

Remove the birds, cut them in half and put on a serving plate (with pigeons, serve the breast only). Sieve the sauce, reduce it if necessary, season with salt, pepper and nutmeg to taste and add chocolate, bit by bit, to bring out the flavour. Pour over the birds.

CHURROS

These are long doughnuts made from flour and boiling water or, as in the recipe below, from a butterless choux pastry. The mixture is pushed into very hot oil through a forcing bag, fitted with a fluted nozzle so that it comes out as a ribbed chipolata sausage. Sometimes the shapes are nipped off at about 10 cm (4 in), sometimes they are bent round into a loop or an S-shape, a figure of eight or a coil. When they are golden brown, they are removed from the pan and rolled in caster sugar. They are best eaten straightaway, dipped into milky coffee or chocolate at breakfast time as the Spanish do. Reheating is not successful: they are slightly chewy when hot, and can be tough when cold.

Serves 4
275 ml/9 fl oz/good cup water
200 g/7 oz/1¾ cups flour, sieved
¼ teaspoon salt
large egg
olive or sunflower oil, for deep frying
caster sugar

Bring the water to a vigorous boil, and tip in the flour all at once with the salt. Stir until the dough makes a coherent mass round the spoon and leaves the sides of the pan free. Remove from the heat and beat in the egg. Keep stirring until the mixture becomes smooth.

Put the paste into a forcing bag or icing syringe, fitted with a fluted nozzle, or into a biscuit maker, and pipe into the oil heated to 170°C (340°F). Fry till golden brown, then lift out with a draining spoon on to kitchen paper to absorb excess oil. Then turn in the sugar and serve at once.

Note different brands of flour absorb different amounts of water. If your paste is too firm to squeeze through a tube or bag, add a very little extra water to soften it. Be sure to push the paste firmly down into the piping implement, so that there are no air pockets. Take care not to overheat the oil or overload the pan (the oil can spatter when the paste is added). As with all deep-frying, keep children away and stand back yourself.

GYPSY'S ARM

Brazo de gitano

I remember reading that sponge cake came from Spain—pan de Spagna—Spagna turning into sponge. Not true. With a passion for eggs almost equal to Portugal's, Spain does produce a number

Draining a great coil of churros, crisp and brown, in a shop in Seville

of sponge cakes, so it seemed sensible to include one of them here, brazo de gitano. It is longer and thinner than a Swiss roll but is made in the same way. Some shops make a grand spectacle of these cakes, decorating them with butter-cream and coloured icing. Mine is the domestic version: you can choose your own filling, but the coffee one is good.

Serves 8

FOR THE CAKE

4 eggs
100 g/3½ oz/scant ½ cup caster sugar
50 g/generous 2½ oz/⅔ cup self-raising flour, sifted
melted butter, for greasing baking tray
extra sifted flour, for flouring baking tray
extra sugar
chopped, toasted almonds to decorate, or icing sugar

FOR THE FILLING

250 ml/8 fl oz/1 cup milk
vanilla pod
instant coffee
2 large egg yolks
100 g/3½ oz/scant ½ cup caster sugar
30 g/1 oz/¼ cup sifted flour
2–3 tablespoons/3–4 tbs rum
37 × 27-cm (14½ × 10½-in) baking tray

Make the filling first. Slowly bring the milk, with the vanilla pod, to boiling point. Mix in coffee to taste—the flavour should be on the strong side. Whisk the egg yolks with the mixed sugar and flour, then beat in the hot milk gradually. Stir over a low to moderate heat until the cream thickens but keep *below* boiling point. Remove and cool; take out the vanilla pod and add rum to taste.

For the cake, set the oven at moderately hot, 190°C (375°F), gas 5. Beat the eggs and sugar until thick and foamy (use an electric blender, if possible) and fold in the self-raising flour. Spread the cake mixture evenly over the baking tray, lined with greased and lightly floured non-stick baking paper. Bake in the heated oven for 15 minutes.

Put a sheet of greaseproof paper, sprinkled evenly with caster sugar, on your work surface. Turn the tin upside down on to it, lift off the tin and carefully peel away the paper. Trim the sides of the cake, put another piece of greaseproof on top and roll up the sponge, starting with one of the long sides, like a Swiss roll. Leave to cool for a few minutes, then unwind the roll; spread it with the cold filling and carefully roll it up again. Sprinkle with some chopped toasted almonds, if you like, or icing sugar. Serve as a pudding, with lightly cooked fruit, or on its own.

Note if you do not have an electric blender, whisk yolks and sugar, then whisk the whites and fold them in, before folding in the flour.

TOASTED WALNUTS WITH CREAM
Nueces con nata

This sweet blend of cream, dotted with dark toasted walnuts, is just right after a heavy main course.

For 6 people, allow 175g (6oz) good quality walnut pieces. Chop them slightly—think of dividing each half walnut in quarters, to get an idea of the size. Spread them on a baking sheet and toast in a cool oven, 150°C (300°F), gas 2, for 10–15 minutes. They should be a pale brown all through, but a deeper brown where there is skin, and with that unmistakable 'burnt-nut' taste. Which is not the same as saying they should taste burned.

Whisk together 300ml ($\frac{1}{2}$pt/1$\frac{1}{4}$ cups) double cream, 60–100ml (2–3$\frac{1}{2}$fl oz/scant $\frac{1}{4}$–$\frac{1}{2}$ cup) whipping cream and a rounded tablespoon icing or caster sugar. Do this over ice to get the maximum volume and lightness. Taste occasionally, adding more sugar to taste. The cream should be sweet enough to set off the walnuts, but not sickly. Put into wide, stemmed glasses and chill. Just before serving, scatter the cream with cooled nuts.

BURNT CREAM
Crema quemada

I wonder if this Catalan dish was the origin of our English burnt cream, which first made its appearance here in cookery books of the late 17th century?

Serves 6
500ml/18fl oz/2$\frac{1}{4}$ cups milk
cinnamon stick
thinly cut strips of peel from 1 lemon
6 large egg yolks
300g/10oz/1$\frac{1}{3}$ cups caster sugar
30g/1oz/$\frac{1}{4}$ cup cornflour

Bring the milk slowly to the boil with the cinnamon and lemon peel. Beat the yolks with half the sugar and all of the cornflour. Pour on some of the hot milk, whisking, then tip back into the pan. Stir over a low to moderate heat until the custard thickens. Strain into 6 little pots and leave to cool. The custard should come nearly up to the rim.

Cover the custards with the remaining sugar, which should come more or less level with the rim. The Catalan way of caramelising it is to heat the blade of a wooden-handled palette knife and press it lightly on the sugar to melt it. This is tricky, I cheat by cooking the sugar with a little water to a caramel, and pouring it thinly over the custards. If you stand the pots on a layer of ice or ice cubes in a grill pan, you can brown them under a very hot grill: this is tricky, too, as the sugar layer should be thinner than for our burnt cream, and you run the risk of the custard boiling.

TIGER NUT MILK
Horchata de chufas

The great refresher in Spanish heat is horchata, a milky-looking drink made from tiger nuts (*chufas*). There is in fact no milk in it, the opaque colour coming from the liquidized nuts, which are creamy inside with a brown wrinkled skin. Horchata is the same word as our orgeat, normally an almond drink of ancient style, and a survivor of medieval cookery when chefs needed a substitute for cow's milk during Lent and for fast days. In Italy you can buy almond milk—*latte di mandorla*—made in the same way, but it is not as popular as horchata in Spain. Supermarkets sell it in long-life cartons, but for the best horchata you need to go to bars where they make it themselves and put notices on the door to say so.

Chufas or tiger nuts grow in the ground and can be bought quite reasonably at health food shops. Soak them overnight, then tip them into a sieve and rinse them free of earth. Put them into a processor or blender with 500ml (18fl oz/2$\frac{1}{4}$ cups) hot water and whizz them at top speed to make a milky, grainy pinkish liquid. Pour off the liquid from the sediment, when it has settled, then add the same amount of water again, and repeat. And again. Finally press all the moisture from the nuts in a double muslin. Sweeten the liquid—about 1.25 litres (2$\frac{1}{4}$pts/5$\frac{1}{2}$ cups)—to taste, and add the finely grated zest of half a lemon and a small stick of cinnamon. Cover and chill thoroughly.

PORTUGAL

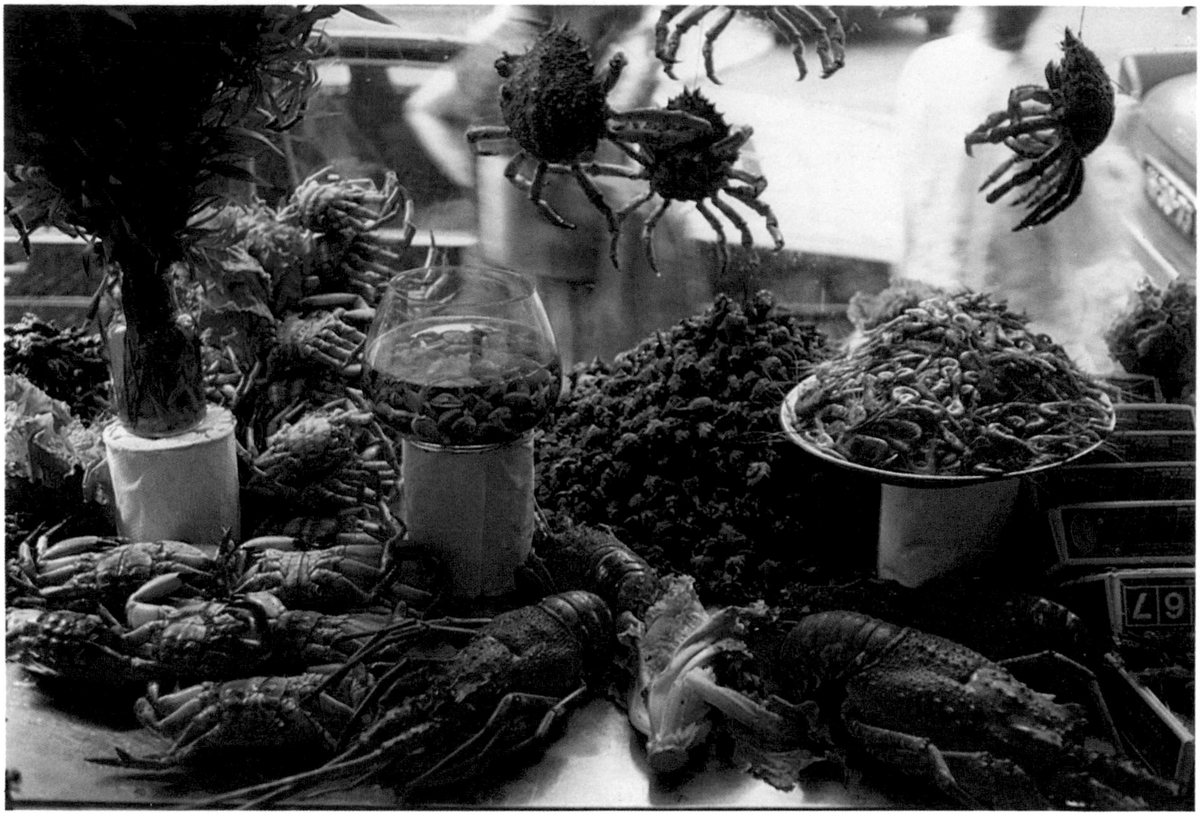

Spider crabs and other shellfish in the window of a Lisbon fishmonger's shop

'Portuguese food? Ah yes, sardines!' is what most people say, whether or not they have ever spent a holiday in Portugal. From childhood we are familiar with Portuguese sardines-on-toast. As sun-seeking holiday-makers on the Algarve coast, the aroma of sardines grilled over charcoal becomes one of our most nostalgic memories, and certainly sardines are a great Portuguese fish. Not just in the Algarve, but along the coast up to such picturesque ports as Nazaré, north of Lisbon, where yet another image shapes our idea of Portugal—that of black-clothed women helping to haul gaily-coloured boats up a sandy beach.

So our idea may be right, but it is far too limited. For Portuguese food is, in part, the food of an outward-looking people tucked away in a sea corner of Europe, with cod brought home from Newfoundland for salting and drying, with hake and seafood landed from nearer waters. Cumin and oranges are both witness to the voyaging past. Green coriander as a main flavouring herb has an exotic air—unjustifiably so, since it is native to southern Europe. Then, too, Portuguese food is the food of a country which, like its large neighbour, Spain, to the east, grows grapes, peppers, melons, quinces and apples to perfection, as well as maize and much wheat.

In case the nature of Portugal sounds routinely southern in style, I must add that it has a strangeness, and an unfamiliarity too. Such as the surprising sight of triangular fields of maize, bordered all round with a vine walk as though they were gardens, or the extraordinary deployment of hen-batteries—in a distant landscape you may see them in a setting of pine and eucalyptus forest, olive trees and vines. In market places enclosed by flat-windowed houses, with coloured walls and curvy ornamentation, a favoured mode of carrying the shopping is on the head. And, tawny pottery decorated with fish, maize and chickens in a stylised sort of antique shorthand is laid out on the ground for sale. In the north and centre, at least, Portugal must be to us the strangest of the countries of Europe.

And as I cooked the dishes, I soon realised that apart from two—quince paste and a cake, orange delight—every single one was new to me. That, in my cook's tour, this was the only country of whose food I had had no experience. For the other European countries, we all have a taste or two in our mouths—all clichés, perhaps, but little buttons that we can press for an image, however insensitive, of another country's food. Yet who can conjure up or even define açorda or bacalhau à Brás?

Partly this is because the best food in Portugal is found in the less tourist-minded parts of the country, and partly because the food itself is not always at its best in restaurants. Where public food in Portugal scores, where its fantasy and skill become apparent, is in the pastry shops, and in the tea rooms attached to them. In Britain tea rooms have almost disappeared; in Portugal, especially in Lisbon, they flourish. People in jeans or fur coats go there for tea, coffee and chocolate as well as for wine. With their drinks, they may eat a crisp and creamy rissole or two, or a few angel's breasts, golden and feathery, accompanied by Dom Rodrigos—both egg yolk desserts—another type of dish strange to us, which depends on the skilful cooking of strands of egg yolk poured into hot sugar syrup through a sieve. These brilliant little yellow creations are about the size of petits fours, rich and sweet and like nothing else I have ever met with at a pastrycook's shop. Another strange sight is the sponge cake, almost mushroom-shaped and sold in the big folded papers it was baked in. You take it home, carrying it carefully like an enormous paper-wrapped bouquet of flowers.

Fish and yellow cakes may seem from this to be the main food of Portugal, but few other countries have such a repertoire of pork dishes. Fresh pork is used mostly since the excellent charcuterie seems to concentrate on ham (presunto, which is not dissimilar from Italian prosciutto), pork and red pepper sausages (chouriços) and black pudding (morcela).

In the great agricultural province of the Alentejo, north of the Algarve, every town seems to have its own pork dish, but I think the difference between the Portuguese way with pork and ours struck me most at Mealhada, north of Coimbra, where we stopped to eat sucking pig. The district was full of places selling sucking pig, which for all inhabitants of the Iberian peninsula is the special meat of celebration. It is tricky to manage well, size apart, and our experience of it in restaurants varied. The crisp brown skin is the best part, underneath the meat can be so soft as to be nasty. Obviously around Mealhada it is done well, judging by the many restaurant signs as we started climbing the road to Guarda. Higher up kiosks at every steep bend were selling ham.

My one regret about food in Portugal was missing the lampreys of springtime along the Minho River. And I also had hoped to visit Elvas, famous for its Christmas plums. I left, though, with the feeling that the Portuguese are certainly proud of their food (and their wines, especially the young vinho verde) and that making its acquaintance had been a high point of the tour, for new experiences of taste.

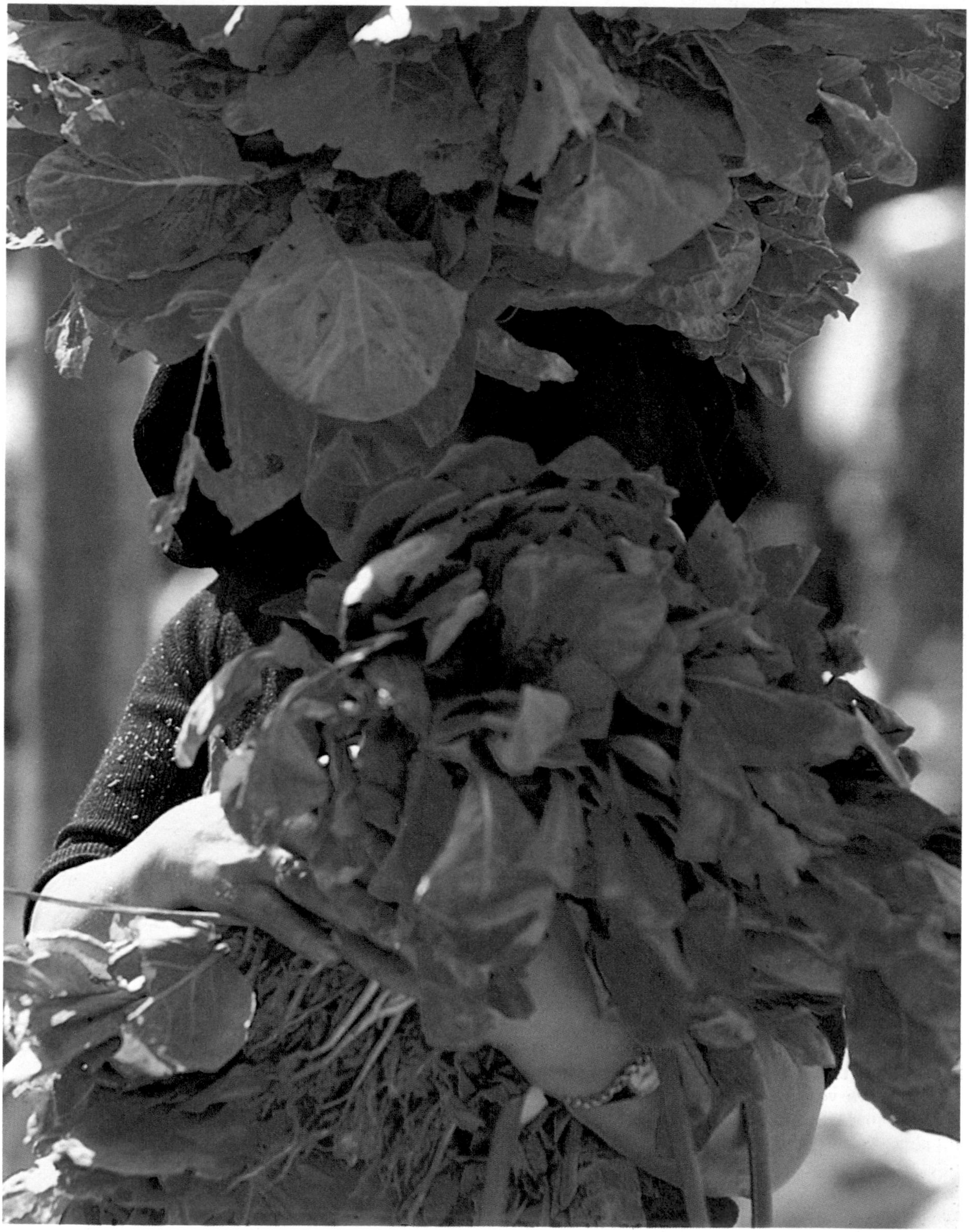

Taking home cabbages from Barcelos market

GREEN CABBAGE SOUP
Caldo verde

The Thursday market at Barcelos, in the northern province of Minho, is divided into four big squares—one for pottery, baskets and red-painted cockerels (a local emblem), one for farm and wine-making equipment, one for clothes and household goods, and one for vegetables, fruit, poultry and bread.

The crowd includes a number of 'wandering cabbages' over six feet high—in fact, women, balancing a stack of cabbages on their head, cabbages in their arms, buying more cabbages. Mostly middle-aged and older women, in black, but I did see a couple of young girls in jeans swaying their load along, threading through the crowd with skill, never hurrying, never lurching or putting even a touch to their cabbages as they bought bread, or a bag of chestnuts, or stopped to talk to another cabbage-load.

The soup I had for lunch afterwards was light and graceful, too, and it came with cornmeal bread in local pots. Between this soup and cabbage soups of northern Europe there was no resemblance whatsoever. Partly because of the cabbage itself, the deep blueish-green couve, as it is called, which grows long-legged in every northern Portuguese garden; partly because of the way it is shredded so finely by special cutters, and partly because it is barely cooked at all. In England, we must use kale or similar dark cabbage, or—as Maite Manjón suggests in *The Home Book of Portuguese Cookery*—turnip tops. You can use chicken stock instead of water, and add cream, or cut-up chouriço or morcela sausage, but I like the simple style best of all.

Serves 6
750 g/1½ lb potatoes
salt and pepper
375–500 g/12–16 oz trimmed cabbage leaves
medium onion, chopped
6 generous tablespoons/½ cup olive oil

Peel and cook the potatoes in salted water to cover, then sieve, liquidise or process. Reheat with enough water to give you a medium to thin consistency. Season well. Meanwhile, roll up the cabbage leaves and shred them as finely as you can with a sharp knife. Add, with the onion to the soup, 5–15 minutes before serving. Cook without a lid—to keep the colour—until the cabbage is a consistency you find agreeable. Different kinds need different lengths of cooking, but it should remain slightly crisp and look a little like seaweed in the white soup. Distribute between bowls, then put in the olive oil so that it is clearly visible. Serve with cornmeal bread (see recipe this page).

BREAD SOUP
Açorda

The bread soups of Portugal and Spain I find delightful. The texture is novel, and conveys perfectly the flavourings that may be added. This is the simplest of all the recipes. Good bread is a prime requisite. I find that a dough made with wheatmeal and white bread flour mixed gives a good result, though a Portuguese from the Algarve or the Alentejo might not agree with me.

Serves 6–8
250 g/8 oz stale bread
1 tablespoon chopped coriander
1 tablespoon chopped parsley
6 cloves of garlic
salt
4–5 tablespoons/5–6 tbs olive oil
1 litre/good 2 pts/5 cups boiling water

Remove the toughest or most burnt part of the crust, then cut the bread into cubes the size of lump sugar.

Crush the herbs and garlic to a paste with a little salt and some water. Put into a warm tureen, with the olive oil and the bread cubes. Pour on the boiling water and stir until the bread softens to a jellied pap. It should be lumpier and more undulating than our bread sauce: do not stir it too vigorously. Add more water if you like, as it should not be too thick.

This can be served with grilled sardines, or poached eggs can be added to the soup just as it is served.

Note the herb and garlic paste can be made in a processor with some of the boiling water, but do not process the bread, or it will be too smooth.

CORNMEAL BREAD
Pão de broa

Yellow cornmeal—not to be confused with cornflour—can be bought at health food shops and many delicatessens. It makes a sweetish, golden bread which goes well with many other soups than caldo verde, and with vegetable dishes like Broad Beans Portuguese Style (see page 88).

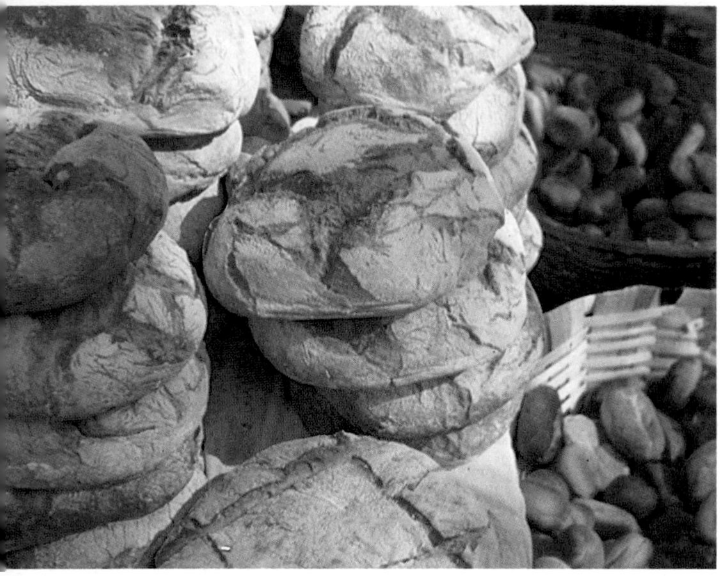

Portugese bread with a typical crust

Makes 1–2 loaves
200 g/7 oz/1⅓ cups cornmeal
2 teaspoons salt
tablespoon olive oil
about 500 ml/generous ¾ pt/2 cups boiling water
400 g/14 oz/6½ cups half wheatmeal and half white bread flour, or unbleached white bread flour
packet of Harvest Gold dried yeast

Mix the cornmeal, salt and oil in a large bowl. Pour on the boiling water (add a little more if necessary) until the meal turns to a soft yellow mass of dough. When it is tepid, knead in the flour which has been mixed with the yeast. Add a very little extra water if the dough seems dry, but be cautious: with kneading, a dry-looking mixture soon becomes coherent, especially if you use an electric dough hook.

Tie the bowl into a large polythene bag and leave the dough to rise for 1–1½ hours. Punch it down, knead it lightly and shape into one or two round loaves. Set the oven at hot, 200°C (400°F), gas 6.

Prove the dough on a greased baking sheet, again tied into a polythene bag, for 30–40 minutes. Bake in the heated oven for 30 minutes. The bread should sound hollow when tapped underneath.

Note the recipe is easily adapted to other dried or fresh yeasts. The important thing is to turn the meal into a dough first, with the boiling water.

BROAD BEANS PORTUGUESE STYLE
Favas à Portuguêsa

In Portugal, broad beans are a popular vegetable, with green coriander leaves rather than northern savory as their bitter herb. I am sure that few cooks shell the beans of their close white skins after cooking—or before—but it is well worth the trouble. Even if you only do the largest beans, you will taste the difference. The following recipes all serve 6 people and peas can be used instead of broad beans.

Broad bean purée Boil 1 kg (2 lb) shelled weight of broad beans with half a small lettuce and very little water. Drain the beans, keeping the liquid. Cool and skin them, then process or liquidise with the lettuce. Make a refogado (see page 92) with a large chopped onion, olive oil and a chopped stalk and sprig of coriander. When golden add the bean purée, with some of the reserved cooking liquor, if moisture is needed. Stir for a few minutes to heat the purée through and serve, either on its own, or with poached or mollet eggs on top.

Broad beans with ham Make a refogado (see page 92) with 60 g (2 oz) chopped belly of pork, or with lard, a large chopped onion, 90 g (3 oz) prosciutto or raw gammon, cut in strips, a crushed clove of garlic, a large sprig of coriander and 1 teaspoon paprika. When golden, put in 1 kg (2 lb) shelled weight of broad beans (skin the largest, at least) and about 150 ml (¼ pt/⅓ cup) dry white wine. Cover tightly and cook gently until the beans are tender. No other liquid than the wine should be needed, though a little veal or beef stock can be added: reduce the liquid at the end with the lid off the pan when the beans are tender. Serve on its own, or with poached or mollet eggs on top.

Broad beans with chouriço Follow the ham version, adding 90 g (3 oz) sliced chouriço.

PORTUGUESE FISH STEW
Caldeirada

There is no one right recipe for caldeirada, which is more of a stew than a soup, but as many variations as there are cooks. The one thing that matters is that the fish should be fresh: tired fish, all too common in Britain, is no good for anything. Vary fish according to local resources, but try and include squid and at least one kind of shellfish. If your family has a neurosis about fish bones, fillet the fish first, though this makes overcooking it all too easy.

Serves 6–8

FOR THE STOCK

1.5 kg/3 lb fish bones, heads and trimmings
onion, stuck with 3 cloves
teaspoon peppercorns
2 cloves of garlic
3 tablespoons/scant ¼ cup wine vinegar
large bay leaf

FOR THE REFOGADO

2 large onions, chopped
olive oil
3 cloves of garlic, split
level tablespoon paprika
500 g/1 lb chopped tomatoes or 396 g/14 oz can tomatoes, optional
salt and pepper

FOR THE FISH

250 g/8 oz red mullet
250 g/8 oz gurnard or grey mullet
500 g/1 lb monkfish
500 g/1 lb hake or cod
500 g/1 lb squid
500 g–1 kg/1–2 lb shellfish (mussels, clams or cockles)
2–4 sprigs of coriander leaves
salt and pepper
lemon juice

Put the stock ingredients into a large pan, covering them generously with cold water. Bring to simmering point and simmer for 30–40 minutes, skimming from time to time. Strain off, taste and season.

At the same time make the refogado (recipe on page 92) in a deep pan. Season when it is golden and tender, or when it is well reduced if you include the tomatoes.

Meanwhile, prepare the fish, cutting off the heads and putting them into the stock pot as you go. Cut fish into slices or large pieces. Pull tentacles of the squid away from the body, chop them, and cut the rinsed-out bag into rings; discard the rest. Season. Take some stock from the pot and use for opening shellfish. Strain and keep the liquor.

FINAL ASSEMBLY Lay the fish on top of the hot refogado, and pour on enough stock barely to cover them. Tuck in 2 sprigs of coriander and lay the opened shellfish on top. Bring to the boil and simmer for about 10 minutes until the fish are just tender. Taste for seasoning, adding lemon juice if it seems a good idea. Sprinkle with chopped coriander to your liking, or omit it. Serve with boiled potatoes or fried bread.

RISSOLES
Rissóis

Don't shrink from this recipe, when you see the title. The true rissole, of respectable European ancestry, is a couple of bites of crispness, enclosing a creamy filling flavoured with shrimps, flakes of salt cod, brains, chicken, or veal and herbs—anything small, tasty and expensive that you want to make the most of.

If you stand in a Portuguese pastrycook's round about mid-day, you have to look out for boys rushing in from the back with hot trays of rissóis, and for customers hurrying in from the street to buy them. They make a good light lunch with some salad, or a small appetiser to serve with drinks. Because they are deep-fried, the pastry needs little fat and is made on the choux principle. Rissóis can be made in advance and stored in the freezer or more briefly in the refrigerator, but never cook them until you intend to eat them as they quickly lose their charm.

Serves 6–8

FOR THE PASTRY

500 ml/generous ¾ pt/2 cups water
60 g/2 oz/¼ cup butter
300 g/10 oz/2½ cups flour
level teaspoon salt

FOR THE FILLING

60 g/2 oz/¼ cup butter
100 g/3½ oz/good 1½ cups flour
500 ml/generous ¾ pt/2 cups milk
250 g/8 oz shrimps, cooked fish or salt cod, or meat
salt and pepper
lemon juice
chopped parsley

TO FINISH

2 eggs beaten
plenty of breadcrumbs
oil, for deep frying

To make the pastry, bring the water and butter to the boil. Tip in the flour and salt in one go, and stir vigorously with a wooden spoon until you have a slightly translucent-looking lump of dough. It should come away cleanly from the sides, but will be raggy at first. Go on stirring, but be careful it does not catch. After 3–4 minutes, it will be slightly less raggy. Turn it on to a floured plate, and pat it into a smooth ball. Leave it to cool.

For the filling, melt the butter, stir in the flour and cook for 2 minutes; then moisten with the milk. Stir until you have a thick sauce, then continue to stir until all trace of flouriness has disappeared from the taste. Mix in the flavouring item—one of my most successful ideas was a mixture of shrimps and brains—and add salt, pepper, lemon juice, parsley or whatever else is appropriate to bring out the flavour. With plain cooked fish, a little anchovy can be good. Leave the filling to cool.

Roll out the pastry fairly thin: it should be almost transparent, but not so thin that it tears easily. Cut out circles with a large scone cutter, and roll them a little larger and thinner until they are 10 cm (4 in) across. Put large teaspoons of the cold filling in the centre of each but slightly to one side. Brush one edge of the pastry with beaten egg, then fold over the rest of the dough to form half-moon pasties. Press the edges together. Refrigerate them at this stage, if you like.

The last stage but one is to dip the pasties in beaten egg and roll them in breadcrumbs. It is essential to refrigerate them at this point, to give them a chance to firm up.

Finally, deep-fry the pasties until they are golden brown, and serve them straightaway.

BAKED GIANT PRAWNS
Camarão no forno

A bonus from writing about food is that it's an easy way of making friends. Last summer I took a cab in Paris and soon discovered that the driver was Portuguese. I asked her what dishes made her feel homesick. We were still talking—or rather she was still talking—when I arrived at my destination, and she would not let me go until she made sure I understood how to make this recipe and the variation of Alentejo pork on page 96.

'I make this dish, Madame, when we have something to celebrate. Or just when I want to think about home. Sometimes I can only afford one prawn each, but the oil is so good, Madame, that nobody minds!' Back at home, I made it with the huge prawns now on sale at good fishmongers; I thought it the best thing I had eaten for months. The oil is indeed delicious, so provide plenty of bread.

For each person
2–3 huge prawns (the Mediterranean type)
tiny red chilli
small clove of juicy garlic, sliced
olive oil
salt and pepper
about 10 × 2½ cm deep/4 × 2½ in deep ramekin per person

Set the oven at very hot, 230°C (450°F), gas 8. Fit the prawns—you need to push them into place—into each ramekin. Tuck in the chilli and the garlic. Pour over oil to come level with the top of the prawns. Sprinkle with plenty of salt. You can leave

SARDINES

Clean small sardines by pushing the tip of a small knife blade into the cavity via the gills. Hoick out the guts, and run cold water through. You may like to push in a small branch of mint. Arrange the sardines in a double metal fish grill, brushing the bars first with oil; the double grill enables you to turn them over without damage. Cook under, or over, a very fierce fire so that the edges catch slightly by the time the sardines are cooked. It is this fast cooking, too, that produces the wonderful summer smell of barbecued sardines.

Larger fish can be split down the back and boned. Spread the cut sides with a paste of butter, paprika, chopped parsley and a little lemon. The fire need not be quite so fierce, but the cooking should be fast.

In this country sprats and small herring can be treated in the same way, and give almost as delicious a result. Only the nostalgia is missing.

Serve with açorda (recipe on page 87), or plenty of bread or boiled potatoes.

A pavement seller grilling sardines

Wind as well as sun is needed for drying fish on the seafront of the fishing port of Nazaré

them to marinate for several hours in the refrigerator, if this suits you.

Stand the ramekins on a baking sheet and put them into the heated oven for 10 minutes. By this time the oil should be boiling ferociously, and the top of the prawn shells lightly browned. Let the dishes stand for a minute or two, then serve with plenty of bread to mop up the oil. A mixture of wheatmeal and strong plain white flour gives a good loaf for this kind of food. Put finger bowls on the table as well.

Note do not let anyone swallow the chilli, unless they have leather throats. The garlic can be eaten, and serve sprigs of parsley afterwards if people are worried about breathing over their neighbours.

MAIA HAKE
Pescada à Maiata

The top Portuguese fish are hake and salt cod. The snag about the hake is that in restaurants it is often spoiled by overcooking. Only when I returned home did I begin to appreciate this Portuguese preference, especially when I came across Maia hake in Carol Wright's *Portuguese Food*. It was certainly one of my luckiest finds.

Glancing through the list of ingredients, you may regard the dish as a version of fish and chips, but it's the differences which count, above all the use of mayonnaise as a hot gratin sauce. We think of it as a cold sauce for cold food: the Portuguese are uninhibited about using it for baked fish. Use a mixture of olive and sunflower oil, half and half, choosing a robust Greek oil if Portuguese oil is not available, or a Tuscan oil for a finer effect.

If you cannot buy hake, large fillets of whiting do very well instead.

Serves 6
750 g/1½ lb hake fillets
juice of ½ lemon
salt and pepper
mayonnaise, made with 4 egg yolks, 340–400 ml/12–14 fl oz/1½–1¾ cups oil, lemon juice or white wine vinegar, salt and pepper to taste
750 g/1½ lb potatoes, scrubbed
extra olive and sunflower oil
small onion, finely chopped, optional

Arrange the fillets in a large dish, leaving room round them to take the potato eventually. Sprinkle with lemon juice and seasoning. Make the mayonnaise in the usual way. Set the oven at moderate, 180°C (350°F), gas 4.

Meanwhile, boil the potatoes, then peel and cut them into dice. Fry them in oil quickly and lightly until they are golden brown, but not much coloured or crisp. Arrange them round and between the pieces of fish. Spoon the mayonnaise mainly over the fish in an even layer, but also a little on the potatoes. Sprinkle the potatoes, if you like, with onion.

Bake in the heated oven for 20–30 minutes. The fish should be just cooked, and the mayonnaise set but spongy-looking and lightly browned.

SALT COD TART
Torta de bacalhau

This tart makes a good introduction to salt cod, as it is not dissimilar from familiar Mediterranean pizze and pissaladières. Like them, it too becomes heavy when cold, so eat it hot or warm. What I like about this particular tart is the special texture that the gelatinous juice of the salt cod gives to the refogado. To get the best effect from this combination, sieve the refogado to a smooth purée, and put a chilli or some cayenne pepper into the mixture as it cooks to give it a little heat.

For 6–8 people, prepare 500 g (1 lb) salt cod and the refogado above. Then line a large 28-cm (11-in) tart tin with shortcrust pastry. Put in half the refogado and lay the cod in nice flakes on top. Cover with the rest of the refogado. Dot the top with 24 black olives and bake at 200°C (400°F), gas 6, for about 30 minutes or until the pastry is cooked and the top edges of the cod are tinged brown.

Meanwhile, hard-boil and shell 3 eggs. Cut them into quarters or slices. Chop a generous tablespoon of parsley. Arrange the eggs and parsley on top of the tart just before serving it, together with bread and a green salad.

SALT COD FRITTERS
Bolinhos de bacalhau

A great favourite with the Portuguese and another good way of introducing people to salt cod. Mrs Maria Cândida Holden who gave me her particular recipe—there are many variations—sometimes uses bacon instead of salt cod and makes very small *bolinhos de bacon* to serve cold with drinks. She points out that differences occur in the proportion of salt cod to potato, some people using the same quantity of each, others double the quantity of potato. As you will see from the recipe she uses about one and a half times as much potato:

Soak and cook $\frac{1}{2}$ kg (1 lb) salt cod. Remove skin and bones, then mince. Boil, peel and sieve 750 g ($1\frac{1}{2}$ lb) potatoes, using a Mouli-légumes or ricer. Mix the two together. Add a medium onion finely chopped, and plenty of chopped parsley. Gradually add four eggs, one at a time. Break a fifth egg into a bowl and beat it. Add just enough of this egg to make a smooth dough that is not too soft. If you are doubtful about the consistency, deep-fry a test

REFOGADO

A refogado is a thick onion purée and the basis of so many Portuguese dishes that it has become a common term in their cookery books. Relative quantities of the ingredients may vary, but the method is always the same. The two essential items are onion and olive oil. Tomatoes and garlic often go in as well, then seasonings appropriate to the main ingredient of the dish.

The system is more like making a matelote than a stew—you get the sauce right first, cooking it slowly, and then add the principal ingredient of the dish.

To make, finely chop 2 large onions. Heat enough olive oil to cover the base of a heavy frying pan thinly and stir in the onion. Cover and cook gently until the onion softens to a transparent juiciness. Remove the lid, add garlic at this point—a couple of cloves or 'teeth', as the Portuguese call them, is about right—leaving it whole or halved. Continue cooking until the onion is a golden purée. Take this as slowly as you like.

Some recipes require you to cook the refogado to a deep golden brown. This does not mean a dark and light speckled mixture, but a purée coloured through to an even mellow richness.

Tomato is often put in at this point—1 kg (2 lb) will do nicely. Do not peel or seed the tomatoes before chopping them. if you are going to sieve the mixture to a smooth purée. If you want a pulpy sauce, peel, seed and chop the tomatoes coarsely. Add a bay leaf, pepper and a chilli, whole or split according to the heat you prefer. With glasshouse tomatoes, 1 teaspoon sugar is required as well.

Continue cooking slowly until the tomato has subsided into harmony with the onion, and all wateriness has disappeared. You may need to raise the heat. Remove the bay leaf, chilli and, if you like, the garlic, then add salt. Sieve the refogado if necessary, then taste for seasoning again.

bolinho and see how it holds together. Then you can add more egg. Season to taste, going carefully with the salt. Form the mixture into balls with two spoons, and deep-fry at about 170°C, 325°F, until golden brown.

Drain well on kitchen paper and serve hot with, if you like, a mayonnaise mixed with chopped herbs, gherkins, capers and so on.

SALT COD ZE MARIA

Gratins of salt cod with mayonnaise and potato are served in many Portuguese hotels. I ate bacalhau Zé Maria at the Grão Vasco, in Viseu, the provincial capital of the Beiras, one stormy autumn night.

Serves 6–8
butter
500 g/1 lb prepared salt cod
250 g/8 oz carrots, sliced and cooked
6 hard-boiled eggs, sliced
mayonnaise, made with 2 large egg yolks and 250 ml/generous 8 fl oz/¾ cup mixed olive and sunflower oil
1 kg/2 lb potato, mashed with butter and milk
1.25–1.75-litre/2–3-pt/5–7-cup gratin dish

Butter the warmed gratin dish, and cover the base with flaked salt cod. Scatter over it the carrot and egg slices. Spread over the mayonnaise, then the potato. Heat through in a moderately hot to hot oven, 200–200°C (400–425°F), gas 6–7, then brown under the grill.

If you make up the dish with hot cod and potato, the gratin can be put straight under a moderate grill. Make sure everything has warmed through properly by the time the top is a nice golden brown.

SALT COD PALACE STYLE

The magnificent Palace Hotel at Buçaco is not far from Viseu. Their gratin is made of similar ingredients, but the effect is richer. Follow the quantities above.

Mash the potatoes with butter and 4 egg yolks, then spread in the base of a buttered gratin dish. Put the salt cod on top, and dot it with hard-boiled egg slices, capers and chopped olives (about 4 rounded tablespoons). Spread with the mayonnaise, and put into a hot oven until the mayonnaise is set and lightly coloured.

LOBSTER IN THE PORTUGUESE STYLE
Lagosta à portuguesa

The Portuguese eat lobster cold with mayonnaise like every other European; the only difference there is likely to be is a flavouring of green chopped coriander and chopped parsley in the mayonnaise.

Hot lobster will be more piquant altogether. For six people, you need three boiled lobsters, each one

SALT COD

Before Columbus set sail, fishermen from Atlantic coasts of Europe were drying salted cod on Newfoundland shores and spits of sand. Much cod comes from the same waters today. Pay a visit to the coastal Beira province, and you will see cod drying in the summer sun around Aveiro, for instance, where the lagoon landscape is dotted with white cones of salt. Reduced to flat, triangular boards of yellowish-grey, salt cod can be stored without refrigeration, hanging from hooks and rods in grocery shops. It is not cheap, and is hard to come by in Britain, but it has over three times the food value of the same weight of fresh fish.

In their passion for bacalhau, the Portuguese claim to have a recipe for it for every day of the year, plus one for leap years: I would judge that the normal repertoire is covered by a booklet I brought back with me called *100 Ways of Cooking Salt Cod*.

To prepare salt cod, cut off the tail, fins and large bones (keep them for soup). Divide the rest of the piece into 8 cm (3 in) pieces. Put the lot into a bucket and threequarters fill it with water. Cover and leave for 24 hours, changing the water two or three times (in the old days, salt cod was often left under a dripping fountain or spring, so that the salt gradually dissolved away).

Drain the pieces, put into a pot and cover with fresh water. Heat slowly for 2 hours, keeping the water bearably hot to the hand. This process can be shortened, by bringing the cod more rapidly to just under boiling point, and maintaining it there until the fish can be flaked easily—about 20 minutes. The first way produces plumper cod. Cool and drain.

In some shops, especially those catering for West Indians, it is possible to buy plastic packages of salt cod that is much less dry and board-like than the pieces you see hanging up in fishmongers shops. Allow for the fact that it is already quite plump, and buy a larger quantity than the recipe states to take account of this.

Salt cod gratin at the Palace Hotel, Buçaco

weighing 500–750 g (1–1½ lb). Remove and crack the claws to extract the meat; cut it up and put into a bowl. Split each lobster in half as neatly as possible. Scrape the tomalley (the deep greenish-grey part) and any eggs into the bowl. Remove and cut up the tail meat, and put with the rest of the lobster.

Cut out and discard the debris of gills, black intestinal canal and sac of grit, so that you are left with six fairly clean shells. Arrange them in a grill pan, steadying them with crumpled foil.

Mix the lobster with the refogado (see recipe page 92). If you have any béchamel, you can add it to smooth out the vigour of the sauce, but I think the dish is better without it. Fill the shells with this mixture.

Top with grated cheese; if you do not have Portuguese Serra cheese, use Italian pecorino instead, or Parmesan. Place under a hot grill, until the top is brown and the contents of the shells very hot. Serve with bread and a salad.

Note crab can be prepared in the same way.

BACALHAU A BRAS

One of the best loved and most successful of Portuguese dishes.

Serves 8
1 kg/2 lb salt cod, well soaked
1 kg/2 lb potatoes
sunflower or corn oil, for deep-frying
500 g/1 lb onions, sliced
4 tablespoons/⅓ cup olive oil
175 g/6 oz/¾ cup butter
large or 2 small cloves of garlic, sliced
salt and pepper
12 large eggs, beaten
small bunch of parsley, chopped
24 black olives

Flake and cut the cod into rough strips. Peel and cut the potatoes into matchsticks, then deep-fry until lightly coloured, but soft, rather than crisp like chips. Drain on kitchen paper.

Cook the onions gently in olive oil and one-third of the butter. As it softens, add the garlic and raise the heat slightly so that it browns mildly. Add the fish and fry together for 5–6 minutes. Add seasoning. Remove the fish mixture to a bowl and add the potatoes. Taste and adjust seasoning.

For the final operation, you need a very large pan—a wok is ideal—or two pans and two people. Another solution is to cook and serve half the ingredients, then cook and serve the rest as second helpings. The point is that the egg should not overcook—think of this dish as a vast omelette.

Having decided which course to follow, melt the rest of the butter and put in the fish and potato, stirring it about to heat through. Pour in the egg, and continue to stir—this time turning with a fish slice rather than a spoon—until the whole thing is bound together lightly. Turn on to a warm dish, sprinkle with parsley, garnish with black olives and serve.

SUCKING PIG BEIRA STYLE
Leitão assado à Bairrada

At Mealhada, north of Coimbra, at the Pedro dos Leitões restaurant, dishes of sucking pig are put down on plain tables, with a basket of excellent bread and a bottle of the local fizzy wine, very cold. Business goes on day and night almost. Two people may drop in for a quick snack. Ten may sit down to an evening's feast. On some tables, brown paper parcels of unmistakable shape indicate that similar celebrations are planned at home.

The main point of sucking pig is the skin, which cooks to a golden brown sheet of light crispness. Underneath the meat is very tender. Big London food stores can supply frozen sucking pig, and a good butcher outside London should be able to order one for you. The weight range is 5–7 kg (10–14 lb), which is enough for 10–15 people. If the pig you buy is too long to fit into your oven, cut off the head or head and forequarters and roast the two pieces together. It's advisable to pierce the skull with a skewer in one or two places or else the build-up of steam inside can cause it to explode and make an appalling mess in the oven.

PREPARING THE PIG First season some lard: chop finely or process a small bunch of parsley, 2–3 halved cloves of garlic, and a large bay leaf, and mix with 250 g (8 oz/1 cup) lard, 2 rounded teaspoons of salt and plenty of pepper. Rub this mixture lavishly inside the pig's body cavity and then outside, all over the skin. Place the pig on a trivet in a roasting tin, sliding pieces of foil into the tin at each end so that the juices can run off the pig down into the tin instead of on to the oven floor. Protect the snout and ears with more foil. Pierce the skull.

TO ROAST Set the oven at hot, 220°C (425°F), gas 7. Put in the pig and cook for 15 minutes, then turn the heat down to 190°C (375°F), gas 5. After another 15 minutes baste the pig with some white wine—have 500 ml ($\frac{3}{4}$ pt/2 cups) set aside for this purpose. Baste every 20 minutes or so, each time straining all but a little of the liquid in the tin back into the remaining wine. If you have a bulb-baster, syphon off the liquid instead. The point is to baste the pig, while reducing the basting liquor and juices, without creating too much steam which can spoil the crackling.

When basting the pig, you will notice that the chopped herbs on the skin turn dark brown after a while. Swill them down into the juices, with the wine and a knife or spoon, so that they do not make too dark a speckled effect. Be prepared to lower the heat after 1 hour, to 160°C (325°F), gas 3.

Total cooking time should be 2 hours for a large pig, $1\frac{1}{2}$–$1\frac{3}{4}$ hours for smaller ones. Check the leg

In the kitchen of Pedro dos Leitões, Mealhada, Portugal's famous sucking pig restaurant

Mixing the garlic, lard and salt which will be rubbed over the sucking pig's skin

meat with a skewer, and tap it lightly on the back of your hand. If it is hot, the meat is done. Turn off the oven, leave the door to, not closed, and allow the pig to rest while you eat a first course.

Before you start serving, pour off all the juices through a sieve into a pan and taste them. Boil down further if necessary, after skimming off as much fat as you can. It should have a strong mouth-watering taste.

TO SERVE Put the pig on a large platter, and if it is in two pieces add a wreath of bay leaves to conceal the join. Serve bread, rice or potatoes and a green salad at the same time, with the juices in a jug. Carving is not difficult, it's more a question of cutting up into pieces. Remove the legs first, then take off the back crackling in a sheet and divide it with scissors. Cut down the backbone, and divide the two sides into four or more pieces each. The head meat is by way of being a delicacy, though not everyone will be in a hurry to claim it. Some at least should be regarded as cook's perks, like the parson's nose on a turkey.

LOIN OF PORK ALENTEJO STYLE
Lombo de porco à Alentejana

The second recipe from my Portuguese lady taxi-driver is, like the next recipe, only one of many versions of pork Alentejo. She said, I think, that it comes from the town of Estrémoz.

A disadvantage of translating the recipe to England is that English pork is reared so lean that it becomes tough if sliced and fried, which is what the recipe requires. My answer is to roast the pork in a piece; alternatively you could use pork tenderloin which only needs brief cooking and is reliably tender.

Second problem is the green pepper: the ones obtainable in England often come from Holland and are tasteless and watery; you need to use more of them and cook the juices down at the end. Should you be making the dish in southern Europe, half a pepper will be enough; and should you be in Portugal itself, you may be able to get hold of the green pepper paste to mix with the oil, garlic and wine, or even the marinaded pork itself, all ready to cook.

The three elements can be prepared several hours in advance: leave the cooking until the end. And if you serve the dish in a meal of several courses, finish cooking the brains and egg immediately before you serve the pork; people may have to wait a little, but that is better than hard scrambled eggs.

Serves 6
1 kg/2 lb pork loin, or 2 tenderloins
250 g/8 oz green pepper, deseeded
rounded tablespoon chopped onion
level teaspoon ground ginger
tablespoon olive oil
2 fat cloves of garlic
5 tablespoons/6 tbs dry white wine
salt and pepper
375–500 g/12–16 oz brains
tablespoon lemon juice or vinegar
8 eggs
clove of garlic, halved
butter
orange, cut into 6 wedges
bones

Remove bone, rind and fat from the pork loin, leaving a thin layer of white round the meat (use these trimmings, with trotters, in tripe Oporto style, page 98). Or trim and cut tenderloins into diagonal slices a generous 1 cm ($\frac{1}{2}$ in) thick. Process or liquidise the next six ingredients and season the resulting paste.

Spread the cut side of the loin with this paste, tie it up, then spread paste over the outside. With tenderloin, spread half the paste on a plate, put the slices on top, and cover with the remaining paste. Leave for at least 1 hour, covered, in a cool place.

Stand the brains in salted water to cover, for 1 hour. Remove as much of the membrane as you can. Poach them in water to cover with lemon or vinegar and salt. Drain and cool the brains, weighted down with a plate. Discard the cooking liquor. Beat the eggs with the halved garlic clove and seasoning, leave for at least 1 hour.

FINAL ASSEMBLY Scrape the lumpiest of the pepper mixture from the pork and reserve. Roast the loin in the usual way. When it is done, cut it into slices and put them round a hot serving dish. Pour off the fat from the pork roasting tin, then tip in the reserved green pepper marinade and stir about to reduce without burning. Spread over the pork, and keep warm. With tenderloin slices, scrape off the paste and set aside; fry them in butter, (4 minutes a side should be ample), but the meat should not be underdone. Put them round a hot serving dish and reduce the marinade in the same way as above. Tuck the orange wedges between the pork slices.

Dice and fry the brains in butter to heat them through and make them juicy and succulent. Strain the beaten eggs over and scramble them together; keep the mixture on the liquid side, as it will continue to cook and firm up as you spoon it into the middle of the pork and put it on the table.

Note this dish can be separated into two: the pork with green pepper paste, to which you can add fried potatoes, and small ramekins of brains and egg (put the buttery diced brains into the pots, break the eggs on top, and bake or cook in a bain marie). Serve the brains as a starter, the pork as a main course, but not necessarily at the same meal.

PORK WITH CLAMS
Carne de porco à Alentejana

The most famous of the Alentejo pork variations, and—if you can get the pork right, see page 96—the most delicious for its combination of pork and shellfish. The best substitute for tiny Portuguese clams are cockles or small mussels: do not use large clams. To cook clams, there is a special pan called a cataplana. It is like a couple of curve-sided sauté pans hinged together, and fastened; this means it

A cataplana opened to show the Alentejo dish of pork and, in this case, mussels

can be turned upside down, which is useful for even cooking when it is full. This recipe, though, with its small quantity of shellfish can perfectly well be cooked in an ordinary sauté pan. Again, it is an assembly job, but the elements should not be prepared in advance.

Serves 6
750 g/1½ lb cockles or small mussels
500 g/1 lb/8 cups chopped onion
olive oil
375 g/12 oz tomatoes, peeled, seeded, chopped
rounded teaspoon paprika
bay leaf
salt and pepper
750 g/1½ lb tender pork, cut into small dice
lard or bacon fat

Scrub the shellfish, discarding any that remain open. Remove barnacles and dark beards from the mussels. Put a single layer into a wide shallow pan over a high heat, with a lid on top. After 2 minutes, look to see if they are open; remove any that are. Repeat until all the shellfish are opened but not ovesooked: this is the point of looking often and doing them in batches, if need be. Strain off the juice through kitchen paper and keep it. Set the shellfish, still in their shells, aside.

Make a refogado (see page 92) with the onion, oil, tomatoes and seasonings, adding the reserved shellfish liquor with the tomatoes. Aim for a moist sauce rather than a soup, which may mean hard boiling at the end.

Cook the diced pork fast and briefly in the fat until lightly browned. Remove with a slotted spoon to the refogado, put in the shellfish and stir about for a minute or two. Remove a few mussel shells, if you like. Serve immediately.

KID OR LAMB IN RED WINE
Chanfana

This brew of kid or lamb and red wine is a speciality of Coimbra and the country roundabout, and is traditionally cooked in a bread oven. The wine reduces to a pungent yet delicious liquid, and although the meat looks overcooked, it eats rich and tender.

Unless you live near a West Indian community shopping centre or have friends who keep goats and need to dispose of a male kid from time to time, you will have to use lamb. After such strong treatment, only a bone expert could tell the difference between the two anyway.

Serves 6–8
½ best end of neck of lamb, cut in 3, and a piece of loin, with bone, weighing about 2.5 kg/5 lb, and chopped into 6–8 large pieces
1 bottle good red wine
3 bay leaves
medium onion, sliced
3 cloves
rounded tablespoon paprika
tablespoon chopped parsley
salt
TO FINISH
mashed potato, with plenty of egg yolks

Strip off all the fat you can. Put the pieces of meat in an ovenproof pottery casserole, fitting them tightly together. Pour on the wine, and add the bay leaves, onion, cloves, paprika, parsley, and a little salt. If the wine does not cover the meat, turn it over from time to time. Cover and leave to marinate for 24 hours in a cool place.

Set the oven at hot, 230°C (450°F), gas 8. Cover the casserole with its lid or some foil, but not too tightly because the liquid must cook down. After 1 hour, turn the meat over and reduce the heat to 160°C (325°F), gas 3. Cook for 1½ hours more, then pour most of the liquid into a measuring jug—there should be about 300 ml (½ pt/1¼ cups) or a little less—return the meat to the oven and turn it down again to 140–150°C (275–300°F), gas 1–2.

Stand the jug of juices in a bowl of water, with ice cubes; stir an ice cube or two into the juices. The fat will soon solidify. Remove it, as its taste spoils the chanfana. Taste the juices and add salt, if necessary. Pour it over the meat and leave in the switched-off oven.

Put the mashed potatoes in a border round a hot serving dish. Cut up the meat into helpful serving pieces, but not too small, and put them in the centre. Pour on the sauce. The meat is dark-looking and, as it cools a little, it tastes sweet at the bone, with a piquant richness that is quite unknown in our cookery.

TRIPE OPORTO STYLE
Tripas à moda do Porto

In Portugal, port is for drinking. Although the big firms put out leaflets of new dishes to persuade people to use it in the kitchen, you will not find it in this local speciality.

Oporto itself is a canyon city. Precipitous streets and much traffic terrify a car driving foreigner. Eventually you may arrive at the bottom, at the

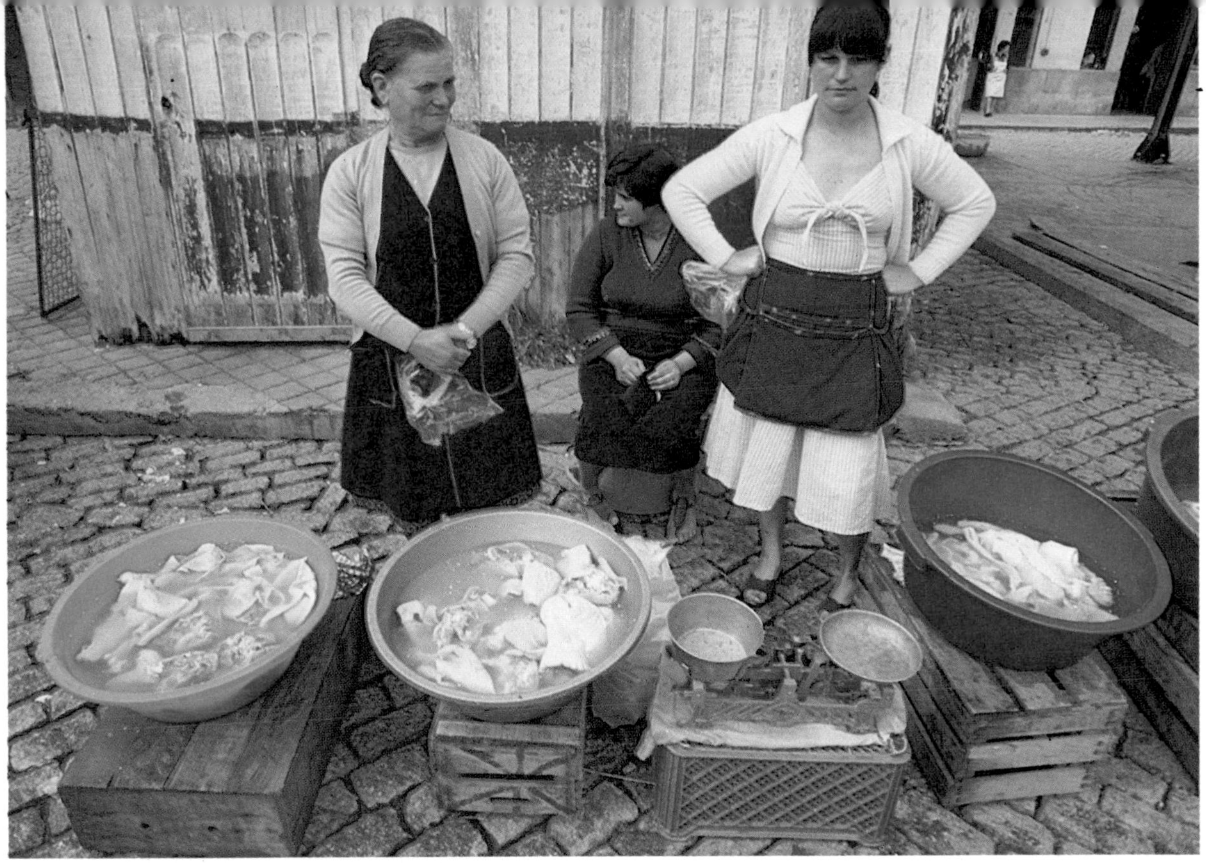

Tripe sellers: in Oporto tripe is usually cooked with beans, chicken, chouriço and cumin

quays by the Douro, where there is a market, a bar or two and restaurants, and the kind of grim pullulating many-storied intensity that I had not seen since before the war in ports of the north-east of England. Everywhere is evidence of washing, the fight back against dirt and cramping closeness: women with plastic bowls and scrubbing brushes, lines of washing strung across shabby windows, a pair of white pants strung on a line at the stall where a girl sold me some apples. Everyone, it seems, has to climb up on somebody else's shoulder, beginning with the furniture makers in the deep cellars behind the quay walls. The scene has a sombre glory, as you look up to the high bridges, the black-walled port wine depots with English names painted on their roofs, the tree-lined squares at the top, all grown up from this lowest level of all.

Oporto tripe is a noble and enormous mixture, flavoured finally with cumin as a reminder of Portugal's exotic trade with the East in the past. It is almost a curried tripe, and a very good party dish, a way of introducing people to tripe because it is embedded in so many other things that everyone likes.

The jellied lip-sticking texture of the liquid should come from a calf's foot, but pig's trotters do well instead—two if they are cut to include part of the hock, four if they are short. Pork skin and bones can go in as well. The chicken should be a boiler: if you can only buy a roasting bird, remove it after an hour's cooking, then put it back for the final reheating, and use chicken stock instead of part or all of the water.

The three elements of this dish can be made in advance. Or you can complete the dish and reheat it another day.

Serves 8–10
250 g/8 oz/good cup haricot or butter beans
calf's foot or trotters
1 kg/2 lb tripe, well washed
2 leg joints from a boiling fowl
250 g/8 oz piece of smoked gammon or streaky bacon
water or chicken stock
onion, stuck with 3 cloves
bay leaf
125 g/4 oz pork belly, chopped, or hard back fat, or 2 heaped tablespoons lard
500 g/1 lb chopped onion
250 g/8 oz sliced chouriço or chorizo
375 g/12 oz sliced carrots
3 teaspoons cumin, ground
salt and pepper

CORIANDER

Coriander, leaf and seed, is one of the most widely-used flavouring plants in the world. Yet although it is native to southern Europe, only Portugal uses the fresh green leaves in quantity.

The name derives from the Greek koris, meaning bed bug, on account of the smell of the leaves. They may look like parsley—coriander is often called Chinese parsley on account of its popularity in that country—but they taste flat and bitter. Coriander becomes a passion very easily, but at first it should be chopped into food with restraint, just a breath of flavour coming through the other ingredients from a couple of sprigs (the stalks are as pungent as the leaves).

Coriander seeds, with their hint of orange, used by the handful in Indian cookery and lavishly in Middle Eastern dishes, do not seem to have the same appeal for Portuguese cooks as the leaves, which go into vegetable dishes, soups and stews of fish in particular.

The Romans introduced coriander into Britain, where it flourishes without difficulty in the English climate, unlike basil. Buy seeds from a busy spice counter—busy, because a good turnover means fresh seeds—and plant them out. Chinese shops and some greengrocers sell great bunches of green coriander. If you cannot get to such shops very often, buy several bundles, trim off the dirty root end and rinse them. Then process or liquidise stalks and leaves to a green sludge. Freeze it in plastic egg boxes, and store the frozen lumps in a plastic bag.

Twisting off the coriander roots for a customer

Pour boiling water over the beans. Leave to soak for 1 hour.

Put the calf's foot or trotters, tripe and fowl joints into a huge flameproof pot. Cut a few slices from the gammon or bacon and set aside for the refogado; put the rest into the pot. Cover with water or stock—no seasoning—put on the lid and simmer for 2–3 hours or until the meats are done. Keep an eye on the chicken particularly to avoid overcooking and remove it when it seems tender.

Meanwhile, strain the beans. Cook them in fresh water (no salt) with the onion and bay leaf. Drain when they are just tender, before they collapse.

For the refogado, chop the gammon or bacon slices, and put them into a heavy pan with the pork belly, fat or lard. When enough fat has melted to cover the base of the pan, put in the chopped onion and complete the refogado with the remaining ingredients. It should have a golden, appetising look. Pour off surplus fat and season.

Remove, cut up and season the meats, discarding the bones. As you do this, boil down the cooking liquor to concentrate the flavour; remove and reserve about 250 ml (8 fl oz/1 cup). Put the meats back, add the beans and the refogado. Taste and add seasoning, if necessary. Pour in some of the reserved stock if it seems dry. Simmer the meat mixture for 30 minutes, then serve with rice. The flavour of cumin should be there, but not overpowering.

CHICKEN BEIRA STYLE
Frango à moda da Beira

The Beira provinces spread across the country south of Oporto and up to the eastern border, centering on a number of delightful towns. At Aveiro you have palm trees, salt, salt cod and ovos moles (recipe on page 103); at Viseu, egg cakes, red wine stews of goat or lamb (see chanfana recipe on page 98); and cream cheeses are specialities of the university town of Coimbra, with hams and sausages and firmer cheeses to be found all through the forests rising towards Spain.

The second time I had this dish, I made it with an old-fashioned chicken which had run free in a neighbour's garden. The firm yet tender flesh, full of flavour, was not overwhelmed by the strong-tasting ham or sharp cheese. Thinking back to the first time, I concluded that the quality of the bird is the key to success—go for a capon or a fattened young cockerel.

Serves 6
2 kg/4 lb chicken, dressed weight
100 g/3½ oz/7 tbs butter
250 g/8 oz/1 cup curd cheese
125 g/4 fl oz/½ cup soured or whipping cream
salt and pepper
2 large, thin slices of presunto or Bayonne ham
about 125 ml/4 fl oz/½ cup wine, stock or water

Stuff the bird with a good tablespoon of the butter, mashed with the curd cheese, cream, salt and pepper. Then spread the whole bird with the remaining butter. Raise the skin from the breast and thighs of the bird and slip in the ham. Roast in the usual way.

When the chicken is cooked, put it on a warm serving plate. Pour off the fat from the juices and deglaze with wine, stock or water, boiling it down to make a little strong sauce. Serve with game chips (crisps), or lattice or straw potatoes.

FOLAR

A great speciality of Trás-os-Montes, in the northern part of Portugal beyond the mountains, is the immense pasty of brioche filled with chicken and smoked peppery sausage and known as folar. Variations on the theme are many, each family thinking that theirs is the best. This recipe comes from a reader whose father was a native of Chaves: she makes it at Christmas time. I suggest that you halve or even quarter the quantity of brioche the first time you make it, reducing the filling quantities by slightly less.

Rabbit can be used instead of or with the chicken. One cookery book suggests veal. The liveliness depends on peppery Portuguese charcuterie and piri-piri. If you cannot find such things locally, use Spanish chorizo and a good mixture of smoked German and Polish sausage. Streaky bacon works well instead of toucinho. Tabasco or chopped hot chili can stand in for piri-piri (to make your own, chop and crush the fleshy part of hot red chilis and submerge them in olive oil; close and leave to macerate in a cool place for 10 weeks).

Another way of constructing the layers of folar, is to roll out circles of the dough and layer them with the filling into a huge Christmas cake tin. This bakes into a huge golden pie, not unlike an old-fashioned pork pie.

FILLING
2–2½ kg/4–5 lb chicken leg joints or whole chicken
medium onion, finely chopped
olive oil
3 cloves garlic, chopped
salt, pepper, lemon juice
paprika, piri-piri
bouquet garni
175 ml/6 fl oz/¾ cup dry white wine
150 g/5 oz presunto or Bayonne ham, chopped
100 g/3½ oz toucinho, or streaky bacon, chopped
2 chouriços, sliced
2 salpicões, sliced
small handful of parsley, chopped
DOUGH
12 standard eggs
30 g/1 oz/1 cake compressed yeast
250 g/8 oz/1 cup butter
150 ml/¼ pt/½ cup plus 2 tablespoons olive oil
1 kg/2 lb/8 cups flour, plain or bread flour
egg yolk to glaze

First prepare the filling, as it should be at room temperature when you spread it on the dough: this means that you can make it well in advance. Cut the chicken legs or the chicken into separate joints. Soften the onion in enough olive oil to cover the base of a large frying or sauté pan, over a low heat, then add the garlic and the chicken. Raise heat so that the chicken is sealed. Season with salt, pepper and a little lemon juice, then put in paprika—a level tablespoonful—and ½ level teaspoon of piri-piri. Tuck in the bouquet, pour in the wine and lower the heat so that the chicken cooks more gently. When it is almost done, put in the charcuterie and stir it up well. Simmer 5 minutes, and add the parsley. Cool to tepid or cold, as convenient, then bone the chicken and cut the pieces of meat into chunks.

For the dough, put the unbroken eggs into a bowl and pour over enough warm water to cover them. Dissolve the yeast in a little warm water. Melt the butter, add the oil and keep warm. Put the flour in a large, warmed bowl and make a well in the centre. Pour in the foaming yeast. Drain the eggs, break them into a bowl and beat them together.

With your hands, start working the yeast into the flour, adding the eggs bit by bit, then the fats, until the dough comes clean off your hands. Dust lightly with extra flour, cover with plastic film and keep in a warm place until the dough doubles in size and has a lacy look. This can take 2 hours or more, depending on the warmth of the kitchen.

Divide the dough into two equal parts. Grease a baking tray and cover with half the dough, rolling it out or using your hands to spread it. Put the filling on top, covering the dough all over (when the folar is cooked, it looks as if it has less meat than it really has). Roll out and cover with the second lot of dough, sealing the edges together well. Lift the bottom layer up and over the top so that the folar now occupies half the tray. Let it rise again for at least half an hour. Brush with egg yolk, and bake at 190°C (375°F), gas 5 for 1–1¼ hours. Check after half an hour and lower the heat to 180°C (350°F), gas 4, protecting the top with paper if it is browning too fast. Serve hot, warm, or cold (hot or warm are best).

TEA CREAM
Pudim de chá

Like most Portuguese desserts and cakes, tea cream is very sweet, which means that it goes a long way. I like it with the non-Portuguese accompaniment of double cream, preferably a good one from a farm. If you want to reduce the quantities below, for a smaller party, always keep the whole egg as the white is important to the texture, and bake it in little custard pots or else it will *look* meagre when you bring it in.

Use a good Indian or Ceylon tea, or a blend such as Twining's Nectar, and make a brew of normal strength.

Serves 10–12
500 ml/scant ¾ pt/scant 2 cups strained tea
rounded tablespoon flour
1 (size 2) egg, plus 2 yolks from 2 (size 2) eggs
500 g/1 lb/2 cups sugar
1.25-litre/2-pt/5-cup ring mould

Use a little of the tea to mix the flour to a smooth paste in a large basin. Then add the rest of the tea gradually, and beat in the eggs thoroughly. Set oven at moderate, 160°C (325°F), gas 3.

Swill round the ring mould with a very thick syrup, made by boiling 3 tablespoons (scant ¼ cup) from the sugar with a little water until it is transparent and pearly. This syrup can be omitted—and is unnecessary if making small pots of the cream—but it gives the finished cream a shiny gleam.

Beat the rest of the sugar into the tea mixture and pour it into the mould. Stand it on a low rack in a roasting tin, filled with enough boiling water to come half way up the sides. Cook in the heated oven for 1 hour, then test; it should be almost firm. If it seems a little tremulous, give it another 15–30 minutes. Then remove from the tin and oven and leave the cream to cool down. Chill, and turn out no more than an hour before it is required; leave the mould in place until the cream is served, to keep the shape.

PUDIM MOLOKOV

When the European cook's tour came out in the *Observer* magazine, Portugal was the country which provoked the liveliest response. I am not surprised, as for me at any rate it had been the great discovery of our journeyings. One reader asked me—politely—why I had not included Pudim Molokov, since everyone in Portugal served it. Another reader, who comes from Portugal, Mrs Holden, provided me with a recipe. And I remembered that a couple of years earlier, when she was writing her *Book of Puddings, Desserts and Savouries*, Josceline Dimbleby had asked me if I knew where a favourite recipe of her grandmother's—called Entremet Molokov—had come from. I didn't know then, but I do now and marvel again at the way bits of food information drop into place sometimes with a satisfying click. But I still do not understand the Molokov part.

Serves 4–6
125 g/4 oz/½ cup granulated sugar
3 large egg whites
60 g/2 oz/¼ cup caster sugar
up to 60 g/2 oz/½ cup blanched, slivered, toasted almonds

Dimbleby version Melt the granulated sugar with 4 tablespoons water. Bring to the boil and cook to a rich brown caramel. Remove from the heat and stir in 2 tablespoons of hot water—stand back, it can spit—then one more tablespoon. If the mixture remains lumpy, put the pan back on to a low heat and stir until smooth.

Whisk the egg whites electrically to a stiff meringue. Add caster sugar and whisk again until silky and voluminous. Keep the beater going, reheat caramel to boiling point and pour on to whites in a slow steady stream. Leave to cool down then pile decoratively into a glass dish. Serve well chilled (next day, for instance) with a rich egg yolk custard or ovos moles or cream, and scattered with a tablespoon or two of chopped toasted almonds.

Holden version Caramelise all the sugar—which can be granulated, rather than two-thirds granulated and a third caster—with 6 tablespoons water. Smooth out with 1–2 tablespoons water only to make a slightly stiffer caramel than above. Pour some into a lightly buttered $1\frac{1}{2}$-litre ($2\frac{1}{2}$-pt/$6\frac{1}{4}$-cup) ring mould. Complete the recipe as above, adding finely ground toasted nuts last of all.

Stand in a hot-water bath and put for 10–15 minutes in the oven at 180°C (350°F), gas 4. Cool slightly, then invert over a serving dish and leave: the pudding will slide down on to the dish. Chill well and serve with ovos moles, or as above.

Either version goes well with fruit such as strawberries, raspberries, mangoes or peaches.

SWEET EGG ROLL
Rolo de ovos

This simple cake is one of the best ways to discover the egg-based sweets of Portugal. You eat it in little slices—one or two per person, no more as it is so sweet—with a glass of port. Afterwards, I find a strong black coffee and a glass of water a good finish. You can eat rolo de ovos at the end of a meal, but it comes nicely in the middle of the morning or afternoon, as a snack on its own.

For 8–10 people, weigh 4 large eggs. Then weigh an equal quantity of sugar. To the sugar, add a heaped teaspoon flour and the finely grated rind of an orange. Mix them well together, then beat with the eggs, electrically if possible, to make a foamy mass. Set oven at moderate, 160°C (325°F), gas 3.

Line a Swiss roll tin, about 34 × 18 cm ($13\frac{1}{2}$ × 17in), with non-stick baking paper; brush it with melted butter. Pour in the mixture, spreading it out. Bake in the heated oven for approximately 30 minutes; the mixture will sink and develop a crisp, crackling sugar top. Underneath there will be a layer that looks uncooked and translucent, but is, in fact, set.

Spread out a clean cloth and sprinkle it with icing sugar. Turn the sheet of cake on to it, and carefully peel off the paper. Trim the sides, and roll up, like a Swiss roll. Cool, then slice.

ANGEL CAKE
Bolo de anjo

A brilliant yellow cake, cutting to brilliant white. If you are brave, you can omit the flour and halve the cream of tartar, and hope to end up with a soft light floating cloud—if you like, a heavenly floating island—but you will have firmer, safer results using flour. It is served with a glorious sauce—ovos moles (meaning soft eggs). This is a Portuguese custard in which syrup is substituted for the milk of our northern dairy countries, and this use of syrup instead of milk, in a way so small a difference, opens up a whole new world of cakes and puddings.

Serves 8–10

FOR THE CAKE

200 g/7 oz/$\frac{7}{8}$ cup caster sugar
150 g/5 oz/$1\frac{1}{4}$ cups plain white flour
level teaspoon cream of tartar
$\frac{1}{4}$ teaspoon salt
8 large egg whites

FOR CUSTARD SAUCE

250 g/8 oz/1 cup sugar
3 tablespoons water
8 large egg yolks
1.5-litre/$2\frac{1}{2}$-pt/$6\frac{1}{4}$-cup ring mould

Portuguese cakes are mainly unfamiliar to foreigners

Set oven at moderate, 160°C (325°F), gas 3. For the cake, sift the dry ingredients together three times. Whisk the egg whites until stiff, and fold in the dry ingredients. Butter the ring mould well and put in the mixture. Bake in the heated oven for 50–60 minutes: it should be lightly browned and shrink a little from the sides of the tin; also when a finger is pressed briefly on to it, it should spring back.

Turn upside-down on to a deep serving plate and leave. The cake will gradually descend from the tin, which should not be removed until the cake is completely cold.

For the sauce, dissolve the sugar in the water, then cook until it is transparent and pearling. Cool. Whisk the egg yolks, electrically, in a basin until thick and yellow, then beat in the syrup.

Put the basin over a pan of gently simmering water and stir until the custard coats the back of a spoon thickly. Do not overheat or the yolks will curdle. Strain into a basin and cool, stirring from time to time. Spoon all over the cake, until it is a rich shiny yellow in a yellow pond of sauce.

ORANGE DELIGHT
Delícia de laranja

Sweet oranges came from China, and the Portuguese began growing them in Lisbon in the 1630s; soon afterwards they introduced them to the rest of Europe. An elegantly-cut orange is still one of the favourite Portuguese ways to end a meal.

This orange-flavoured cake can also be made by the all-in-one method in a processor or with an electric beater; in which case use self-raising flour plus baking powder instead of plain flour.

Serves 6
150 g/5 oz/$\frac{5}{8}$ cup butter
150 g/5 oz/$\frac{2}{3}$ cup caster sugar
3 (size 3) eggs
150 g/5 oz/$1\frac{1}{4}$ cups plain flour, sifted with $\frac{1}{2}$ level teaspoon baking powder
grated zest and juice of 1 large orange
TO FINISH
orange juice (see method)
75 g/$2\frac{1}{2}$ oz/good $\frac{1}{4}$ cup caster sugar
peeled segments, neatly cut from 1 orange
20-cm/8-in loose-bottomed cake tin

Set oven at moderate, 180°C (350°F), gas 4.

Cream together the butter and sugar. Add the eggs, one by one, then the flour mixture. Add the grated zest and half the orange juice. Turn into the buttered cake tin and bake in the heated oven for 50–60 minutes. Leave to cool in the tin for 5 minutes, then turn out on to a wire cake rack.

When nearly cool, transfer to a plate. Mix remaining orange juice with the sugar and pour over cake. Before serving decorate with orange segments.

QUINCE PASTE
Marmelada

Many countries make quince paste, but I opt for Portugal as its creator because of its name there, marmelada, from which the French and English words are derived. Marmelada itself goes back via Latin and Greek to the ancient Semitic Assyrian and Babylonian word for a quince, marmahu.

The paste sets quite firm (rather like Turkish Delight), so it is sliced rather than spooned. Other fruit pastes can be made in the same way. Judging by the colour, I guess that some commercial quince pastes are bulked out with apple, plus lemon juice and grated zest to liven the flavour. At home orange zest and juice can be added too, if you like.

Wash and rub the grey down from ripe quinces. Cut into pieces, core and all, and stew softly in just enough water to cover. When tender, sieve out the tough bits and weigh the pulp.

Rinse out the pan and put in it 3–4 tablespoons ($\frac{1}{4}$–$\frac{1}{3}$ cup) water and a weight of sugar equal to the quince pulp. Stir until dissolved, then boil for 2–3 minutes before putting in the quince pulp. Continue to cook steadily, stirring frequently, and towards the end all the time, until the paste turns dark red and the wooden spoon makes a clear trail through it along the base of the pan. Wrap your hand in a cloth to protect it from spluttering and splashes. Pour into lightly oiled tins or plastic boxes, and leave in a warm place to dry out more. Cover and store in a cool place; refrigeration is not necessary.

Serve in slices with Portuguese Serra cheese, or a mild Dutch or Danish cheese and glasses of port, as a dessert or a snack.

FRANCE

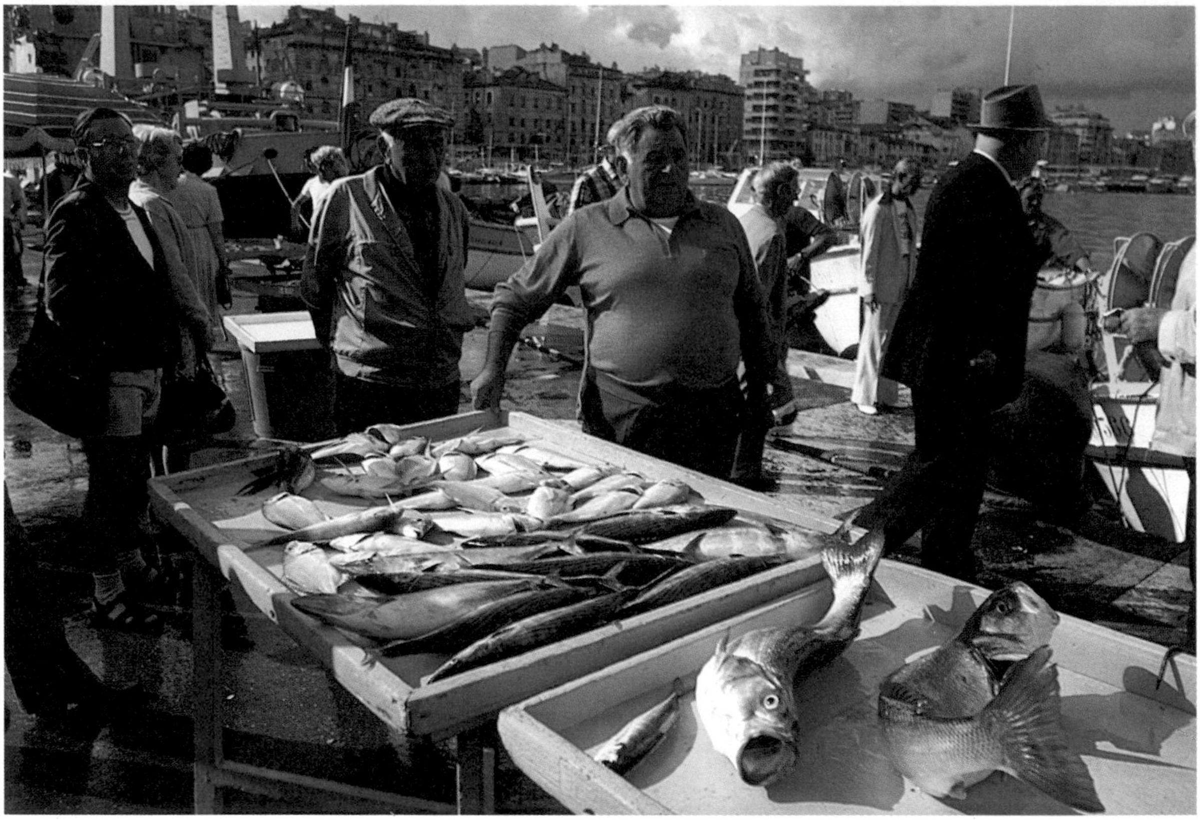

The Marseilles Old Port fish market

France has all the luck—with its toes in the Mediterranean, its head in the Channel and Atlantic, and its western elbow towards America with Nantes as its sugar and spice port. It shares borders with the two great countries, Italy and Spain, through which civilisation passed to northern Europe. How could it not be the great country for food? The heat of the Mediterranean gives it strong clear flavours and piquancy, early fruit and vegetables, set off by the green or gold smoothness of olive oil. The rain of the Atlantic side means pastures for cattle and dairying. And between north and south, on the overlapping borders, areas of great wines have been in production since the Romans. As Paul Johnson says, 'Alsace is the only major French wine region not to have Roman origins at least in part. It had to wait until about the 9th century.'

Since it took the lead from Italy in the 17th century, France has maintained its reputation for cooking. From La Varenne, the succession of famous chefs publishing famous books and training other famous chefs has not faltered. The Revolution blew them out of aristocratic kitchens, so they opened restaurants of their own or went to other countries to pass on their skills and taste. When the railways came, the chefs were down in Monte Carlo or Biarritz cooking for the rich, and making sure the trains took truffles and asparagus and fruit back to Paris. When the comfortable middle classes set off in their new cars or on bicycles in the wake of Curnonsky, who 'discovered' regional cooking, chefs were there to refine peasant dishes and invent new ones.

The secret of good French restaurants is the marketing. Suivant les

Glazed duck with fruit, masterpieces of the caterer's art in the window at Fauchon's, Paris

marchés. No slavish sticking to a list of specialities. This keen passion rules in the top restaurants—it has to. But it also fires the two- and one-star places. And their treasury is Rungis. A marvellous—and dreadful—place, the grandest and most important market in, and for, Europe, moved and expanded from central Paris to the edge of the capital, like our Covent Garden.

After visiting so many pretty markets in Europe, I found this great market something of a shock at five on a December morning. Vast hangars fill the site, crudely built rows of retail shops, glass and concrete restaurants, everywhere cars badly parked and little trucks and large lorries lurching round corners. Luckily I had a guide, Jim Whelan, who runs one of the many foreign restaurants in Paris, La ferme irlandaise, where you may observe smart Parisians ordering tea with Irish stew and Smithwick's beer with the smoked salmon. He introduced me to his friends, jolly meat and fish merchants, rumbustious offal sellers, game suppliers with wild boar slung nonchalantly across wooden boxes, poultrymen laying out a choice of chicken, geese, guineafowl that made me cross with envy. The vegetable and fruit sheds are unexpectedly solemn, their stock crated from view. The cheesemongers tend to be jumpy with the perpetual anxiety that their cheeses maturing underground will not be shifted before they are over the top.

At intervals we drank beautiful coffee and watched men in bloodstained aprons tucking into five-course dinners at dawn. I learnt that the strength of Rungis is that dealers are not just concerned with the big buyers, they

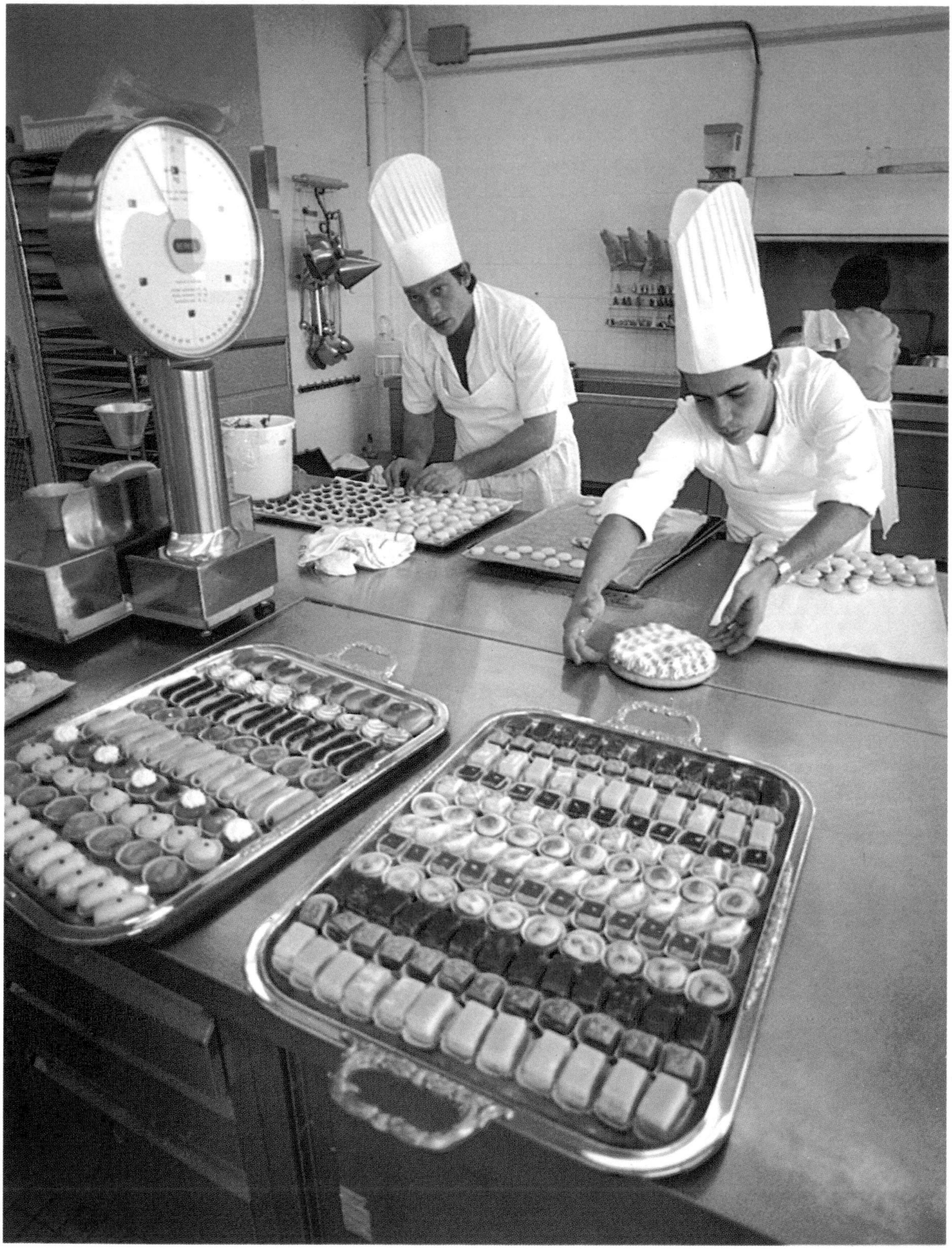

cherish the small restaurateur as well. We saw the results over the next few days. Purple-brown spiked sea-urchins were on sale at Rungis, and on the menu of the Bernardin there they were, opened and deep orange, hot, with a deep orange sauce. At the Monde aux chimères on the Île St Louis a spinach dish was suggested, as it was particularly good in the markets. We talke dd this over with Jean-Pierre Clément at the Dodin Bouffant, where we ate oysters—what oysters!—kept fresh in the great seawater tanks in the basement, crayfish, monkfish and scallops, the last two in a ragoût of pig's trotters. 'No sole,' said Jean-Pierre Clément the patron. 'We have to offer top quality at a price people expect. If something is too dear, I choose another fish instead.'

Domestic gastronomy has its temple at Fauchon's in the Place Madeleine, a small place but crammed with quality and excitement. Push open the door into the greengrocery and you breathe paradisal wafts of passion fruits, guava and pineapple. Outside on the pavement people stop to admire the windows of cooked food and charcuterie, the glazed and decorated ducks, quails with grapes across their breasts, the intarsia of the fish pâtés. At Christmas there was a great cone of Burgundy snail shells filled with green garlic butter to admire, and a beautiful graduation of black truffles set off by green leaves.

These days people wonder anxiously whether modern commerce will ruin France's passion for good food. There is more than one hamburger joint, after all, in the Champs Elysées. I remember, 25 years ago, a grocery magazine describing France as a desert waiting for supermarkets to bloom. And they have bloomed, but in ways characteristic of the country. They do not contain vast cabinets of frozen, water-bloated chickens. They stock local products. There is talk and advice. They are useful.

But many French tables are supplied still from vegetable gardens of exquisite order, edged with neat espalier trees of fat pears and bright apples (this is one source of the special charm of Michel Guérard's food at Eugénie-les-Bains—its elegance being well based on supplies from the surrounding countryside). Eggs and poultry, milk, cream and fresh cheese are brought home from a nearby farm in the evening. The one subject that makes friends, pulls everyone together, is food. Ask a question at market and you will hear many answers. There is an understanding of skill and a willingness to save up for it to celebrate an occasion. In a fine provincial restaurant, you see people who are by no means grand but who are perfectly at home. The English idea that to eat in a restaurant you should wear a tie, a jacket, a skirt rather than trousers, and not be under 16 years old, seems unknown in France.

And in value for money the French menu is unbeatable. In our travels round Europe, I had hoped that some other country would surpass France, would be a new discovery. This did not happen. Instead I came home more grateful than ever for the appropriateness of the various French styles—haute cuisine, bourgeois, peasant, regional styles; for the small bar where you can take your own food to eat; for this enormous fount of ideas which provides a dish for every occasion and an understanding that good eating starts with good ingredients, respectfully and lovingly used.

Two pâtissiers with a selection of their varied and mouthwatering confections—France is famous for its pâtisserie

PUMPKIN SOUP
Velouté au potiron

Pumpkin soups in France are often very simple indeed—a slice of pumpkin cooked and sieved, then diluted with milk and water, plus cream and either salt, pepper and nutmeg or sugar. White wine is drunk with it, and little cubes of golden fried bread set off its creamy orange colour. Here is a general vegetable soup with pumpkin predominating, from the Franche-Comté. If you have no pumpkin, substitute little gem squash, courgettes or Jerusalem artichokes.

Serves 4–6
150 g/5 oz peeled, chopped tomato
60 g/2 oz/$\frac{1}{2}$ cup chopped onion
250 g/8 oz peeled, diced potatoes
200 g/7 oz peeled and seeded pumpkin
90 g/3 oz/$\frac{1}{3}$ cup butter
1 litre/1$\frac{3}{4}$ pts/4$\frac{1}{2}$ cups water
60 g/2 oz/$\frac{1}{3}$ cup tapioca
3 egg yolks
500 ml/$\frac{3}{4}$ pt/2 cups whipping cream
teaspoon wine vinegar
salt and pepper
cayenne
pinch of sugar

Stew the vegetables in the butter in a heavy pan for 5–10 minutes, stirring them occasionally and making sure they do not brown. Pour in the water and simmer until the vegetables are tender. Process or put through a Mouli-légumes into a clean pan. Reheat, stir in the tapioca and simmer for about 20 minutes.

Meanwhile, beat the egg yolks and cream together. Pour in some of the soup, then tip it back into the pan and heat through for a minute or two without boiling. Add the vinegar gradually to sharpen the flavour, and seasonings (the vinegar is to compensate for the blandness of English cream and tomato, but you may not need it, or the sugar).

Serve with toasted bread, covered with thin slices of Comté or Gruyère cheese melted under the grill.

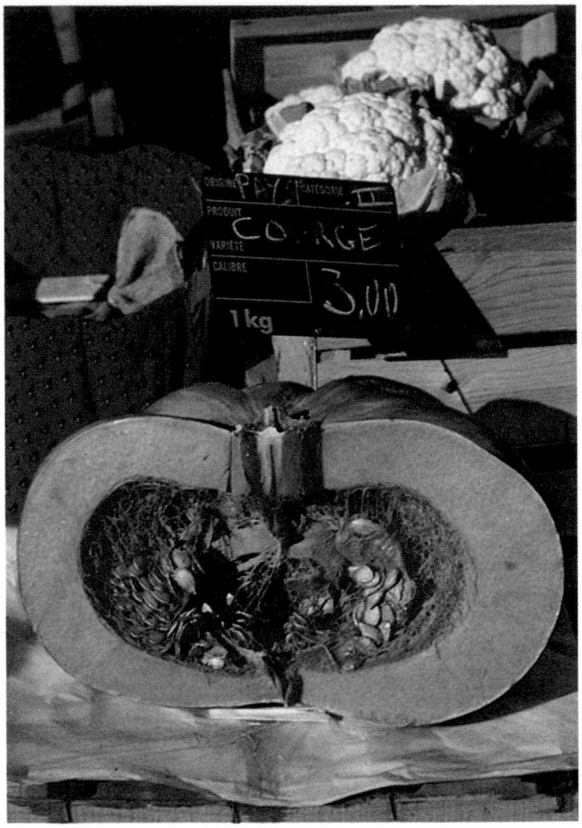

One can buy pumpkin for winter soups by the slice

FISH SOUP
Soupe de poisson

As there is no point in attempting a bouillabaisse since we do not have the right fish, here is another Mediterranean fish soup from France which we can make successfully. The vital ingredient is saffron, followed by fennel and a dried strip of orange peel—things we can get hold of here. Be sure to buy fish with heads on, and ask the fishmonger if he can give you a collection of sole or turbot bones, skin and heads from filleting white fish (they increase the flavour, improve the texture and cost nothing).

generous kg/2–2$\frac{1}{2}$ lb fish, monkfish, conger, mullet red or grey, gurnard or rascasse
bones and skin
large leek, trimmed, sliced
large onion, quartered
medium carrot, sliced
3 large cloves garlic, sliced
outer layer trimmed from a fennel bulb, or 2 fennel stalks or 2 level teaspoons fennel seed
olive oil
bouquet garni
strip dried orange peel
salt, pepper, cayenne, sugar
large pinch saffron
dash white wine vinegar (optional)
125 ml/4 fl oz/good $\frac{1}{2}$ cup white wine, reduced by half (optional)
90 g/3 oz vermicelli or other soup pasta

Clean and cut up fish; chop bones into convenient pieces. Put vegetables, garlic and fennel into a huge pan with enough oil to cover the base. Stew with an occasional stir for about 15 minutes, until the onion is soft and yellowing. Put in fish bones, skin and fish. Bring 2 litres (3½ pt/8¾ cups) water to the boil and pour it into the pan. Bring rapidly to the boil and boil hard for 15 minutes. Tip into a sieve laid across a large pan. Extract the more recalcitrant objects, bones, peel, bouquet, hard bits of fennel. Push through as much of the debris as you feel inclined, to give texture to the soup. Season to taste, adding a pinch of sugar if the flavour needs enhancing. A dash of vinegar or wine can be added with the same idea.

Bring soup to the boil, tip in the pasta and simmer until it is just cooked. Serve the soup with toasted or baked bread and rouille (see page 112), either to spread on the bread or stir into the soup.

BRIOCHE WITH BACON PIECES
La pompe aux grattons

In the Bourbonnais, they serve wine with this brioche—la pompe—flavoured with scraps left over from melting down lard, hence grattons (they have other names elsewhere in France, which can be most confusing). I have bought pompes baked in rough circles, village style, and one spectacular brioche-shaped pompe at St Pourçain-sur-Sioule which we ate for our picnic. Like most brioche, pompes toast beautifully and can be served with soup (for fine pâtés, plain brioche is better).

The following mixture is enough to make a pompe for six people, plus a *pain brioché*.

500 g/1 lb/4 cups plain flour or bread flour
packet Harvest Gold dried yeast
2 level teaspoons salt
3 eggs
100 g/3½ oz/scant ½ cup butter, melted
150 ml/¼ pt/⅔ cup milk
300–375 g/10–12 oz piece fat, smoked streaky bacon
beaten egg to glaze

Mix flour, yeast and salt. With an electric dough hook or processor (family size) or beater, mix together eggs, butter and half the milk in a warmed bowl. Tip in the flour and work up into a dough, using the extra milk if you need it. The dough should be soft, slightly waxy, and yellowish: if it is slightly tacky do not worry. Tie the bowl into a plastic bag and leave to rise in a warm place for 1½–2 hours or until it has doubled its volume or more.

Meanwhile, dice the bacon and fry it in its own fat until nicely browned, but not hard or crisp. Drain and cool.

Punch down the dough, put one half into a warmed, buttered loaf tin. Mix the bacon pieces into the other half, kneading them well in. Put into another loaf tin, or a brioche tin, or make into a ring and put on a baking sheet if the dough is not too soft. Tie back into plastic bags and leave 30–40 minutes to prove. Bake at 190–200°C (375–400°F), gas 5–6 for up to 40 minutes. Check after 25 minutes and brush the tops with beaten egg. Put back for another 5 minutes at least, out of the tins, to give the sides a chance to bake crisp. Serve the same day.

GOUGERE

Cheese-flavoured choux puffs are sometimes served hot from the oven in Burgundy with a glass of red wine. A similar dish across the River Loire in the Sancerrois is discs of the tiny round goat cheeses, crottins de Chavignol, baked with a dab of butter and a pinch of wild thyme in circles of puff pastry. Such things show off wine well. They also make a good supper dish, after some soup, or with the soup.

If you bake the puffs in a ring, you can fill the centre with a cheese (mornay) sauce, or creamed mushrooms, ham or shellfish—an excellent idea for a first course for a party.

Serves 4
250 ml/9 fl oz/good cup water
100 g/3½ oz/scant ½ cup butter
pinch of salt
150 g/5 oz/1¼ cups sifted flour
4 eggs, beaten
60 g/2 oz/½ cup grated Gruyère cheese
45 g/1½ oz/⅓ cup slivers or tiny cubes of Gruyère cheese
pepper
grated nutmeg

Set oven at hot, 220°C (425°F), gas 7.

Bring the water, butter and salt to the boil. Remove the pan immediately from the stove, tip in all the flour at once and stir until the mixture leaves the side of the pan. Put back for a moment or two, and stir. Off the heat, beat in the eggs, bit by bit. You may not need all the egg—remember that the dough should be coherent enough to keep its shape.

Beat in the grated cheese first, then the slivers or cubes. Season with pepper and nutmeg to taste. Put tablespoons of the mixture well apart on a baking sheet, lined with non-stick baking paper and brushed with melted butter. Put into the heated oven until brown and risen—about 30 minutes; check after 20 minutes keeping the door firmly shut until then. Serve immediately as they are, or filled with mornay sauce.

To bake in a ring, line a 25-cm/10-in tart tin, with non-stick baking paper, and brush with butter. Put in tablespoons of the mixture round the edge, a little apart. They spread together in baking, to make a ring. Allow 30–35 minutes.

CRUDITES AND AILLOLI GARNI

Crudités and ailloli garni are, above all, dishes for the gardener, or for someone who is particularly lucky in their local market. Both consist of nicely cut raw vegetables and a bowl of sauce, and ailloli has a bowl of hot rouille sauce (see below) as well.

To the crudités vegetables, hard-boiled eggs, or lightly cooked, still crunchy beans and cauliflower may be added, as well as cooked, sliced artichoke bases, a pickle or two, or olives. Serve with mayonnaise (see below) or soft cheese, flavoured in various ways.

Ailloli is a bigger, more enthusiastic business altogether: the vegetables, plus cooked salt cod or other fish, new potatoes, and eggs, are piled up round the central bowl or bowls of sauce (ailloli and rouille). If you grow cardoons, Florentine fennel or celery, this is the dish for showing them off. It is a whole meal, whereas crudités make a first course. Soak and poach the salt cod, or steam fresh fish, with appropriate herbs. Drain and serve tepid.

Mayonnaise Put 4 egg yolks in a warmed bowl, with salt and pepper, and beat with a spoon whisk. Mix 150 ml ($\frac{1}{4}$ pt/$\frac{2}{3}$ cup) sunflower oil with 150 ml ($\frac{1}{4}$ pt/$\frac{2}{3}$ cup) good olive oil, and warm them very slightly to take the chill off. Gradually add to the yolks, drop by drop, then in a very thin stream as the mayonnaise thickens. Add wine vinegar or lemon juice to sharpen, and salt, pepper, chopped green herbs, to season.

Ailloli Soak a 2 cm ($\frac{3}{4}$ in) slice of white, crust-free bread in 4 tablespoons ($\frac{1}{3}$ cup) milk, then squeeze out. Pound 6 peeled cloves of garlic, add the bread, then 300 ml ($\frac{1}{2}$ pt/$1\frac{1}{4}$ cups) olive oil gradually. A tricky sauce, which can turn; if so, whisk 2 egg yolks in a basin, and gradually beat in the turned ailloli. Or prevent it happening by crushing the garlic with 2 egg yolks at the start, then add the oil as when making mayonnaise. Sharpen ailloli to taste with lemon juice and wine vinegar.

Rouille is a sauce of varying hotness, which is made from red chilli peppers. It is a sauce to be eaten in small quantities, like mustard. Pound 2 large red dried chillies, seeds and all, with 2 large peeled cloves of garlic, and—if you like—a sweet deseeded red pepper cut in strips. Soak a thick slice of bread, crusts removed, in water, squeeze dry, and add to the garlic mixture, followed by 250–300 ml (8–10 fl oz/1–$1\frac{1}{4}$ cups) olive oil or half olive and half plain oil.

Aillade A nut sauce, that goes particularly well with fish or grilled chicken. Grill 8 large shelled hazelnuts or toast them and rub away their skins. Pour boiling water over 8 whole shelled walnuts (16 halves) and skin them. Crush with 3–6 cloves garlic and 2 egg yolks. Add gradually, as for mayonnaise, up to 300 ml ($\frac{1}{2}$ pt/$1\frac{1}{4}$ cups) oil—use half walnut or hazelnut oil with sunflower oil, or half olive and sunflower oil.

GLOBE ARTICHOKES
Artichauts

From misericords in Tréguier cathedral, not far from Roscoff, and from a book of hours painted for Anne of Brittany in the same period, we know that artichokes were already being grown in Brittany by about 1505. The trade did not take off until the 1830s oddly enough, considering that there had been a vigorous trade in onions for some time, but, by 1845, boats took artichokes to Le Havre for Paris, to London, Dover, Plymouth, even to St Petersburg. Outside this regular trade, boys would take fishing boats across the Channel at night to get rid of the family's surplus artichokes and cauliflowers in English markets.

Preparation You need do little to artichokes. The one thing to remember is always to smear any cuts you make with lemon or vinegar to prevent discoloration. Have ready a huge pan half full of salted boiling water, with 2 tablespoons (3 tbs) vinegar (malt will do) to each litre (2 pts/5 cups) water. When it is boiling, quickly slice off the artichoke stalks, and put the artichokes into the pan, base down if they have to be closely fitted together. After 25 minutes steady simmering, try tugging out a leaf at the base of an artichoke. If it comes away fairly easily, and the little nugget of flesh at the base is tender, the artichokes are done. Remove and drain them.

Serve them hot with hollandaise or béarnaise

sauce (recipes on page 114). Serve cold with vinaigrette, a lemon-flavoured mayonnaise (recipe on page 112), or clotted cream seasoned with lemon juice, salt and pepper.

To eat artichokes, pull away the outer leaves, one by one, dipping them in the sauce or dressing. The inner cap of leaves does not offer much, so pull it away. Then pull away the hairy choke in the centre: you are then left with the best part—the base (the fond or cul d'artichaut).

Artichoke cups Trim off the stalk and lower rows of leaves to neaten the base. Slice the top off the artichoke, leaving it flat. Cook as above. Cool slightly, then pull out the centre leaves and scoop out the hairy choke. You now have a cup which can be reheated in a steamer and filled with hot vegetable purées (peeled broad beans or peas, puréed with butter and cream, or spinach treated in the same way plus Parmesan cheese), shellfish with hollandaise sauce, cooked mixtures of brains and sweetbreads with mushrooms and bacon. The cups can also be filled with a light breadcrumb stuffing, with bits of crisp bacon and mushrooms, and then baked.

Artichoke base Cook artichokes in the usual way. Pull off all the leaves and serve them for a family supper, or else patiently scrape the bases of the leaves and use the mixture, sieved, to build up the nest shape of the base. In it serve very young new peas (artichauts Clamart), as a first course, or with lamb. Or else mussels and cockles with a béarnaise sauce flavoured with the shellfish liquor much reduced (artichauts Grosse Horloge), as a fish course. The bases will look more elegant if you pare away the lower rows of leaves before the artichokes are boiled, but you will have more waste.

Note artichokes have a strong effect on one's ability to taste other things, especially wine. Serve them with plenty of bread, and keep following courses clear in taste rather than delicate and creamy.

Artichokes have been grown around Roscoff in Brittany for over four centuries

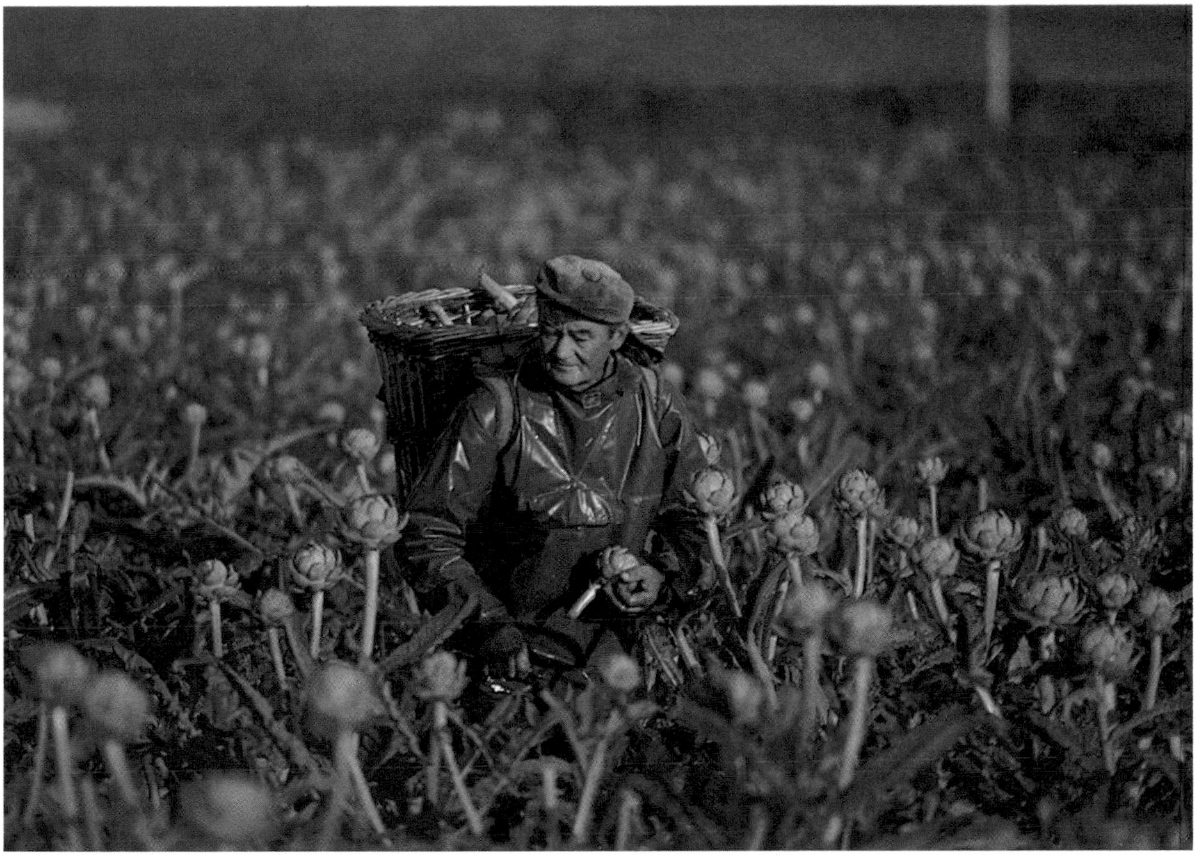

SAUCES

Since civilisation began, cooks have embellished their main ingredients, increased their variety, complemented their good points and corrected their faults, by means of sauces. In modern times, since the 17th century, the French have been supreme in Europe in this art. The basis of many sauces is a good stock, made by the slow cooking together of bones, certain meats and vegetables—what might seem the debris of the kitchen—in water. If you resolve never to throw away another chicken carcase or set of giblets, you can always have to hand a little stock to give your sauces their special character. Stock cubes can be used, of course, but they are boring; a bit of a stock cube added to a homely collection of ingredients is another matter, but think of such things as seasonings rather than substitutes.

The opportunity that most of us miss is the making of fish stock. Most fishmongers will give you a kilo or two (2–4 lb) of bones, skin and heads from filleting, which in 30 minutes will make a quality stock costing no more than a few pot-herbs and a basic bouquet garni (bay leaf, sprig each of parsley and thyme).

Today, many chefs have turned against the classic sauces on account of the flour required to make them. Instead they concentrate on pan sauces: they deglaze the pan in which the main item has cooked with an appropriate stock and alcohol, reduce it, and then thicken and enrich it with little cubes of butter, stirred or swirled in, or a few tablespoons of cream. Nonetheless, it is well worth learning a few classic sauces.

Béchamel Melt 30 g (1 oz/2 tbs) butter and into it stir 30 g (1 oz/¼ cup) flour. Cook for 2 minutes. Gradually add 500 ml (¾ pt/scant 2 cups) hot milk, whisking all the time, with a wire hand whisk, to make it smooth. Simmer it down to the consistency you require. The milk may be first flavoured with carrot, onion and bay leaf, then strained. The sauce may be finished with a few tablespoons of cream, or half the milk may be replaced by cream to give a cream sauce. Use for binding meat or fish mixtures, as a base for other sauces (see below), or serve with meat, fish or vegetables.

Mornay Flavour the béchamel sauce to taste with half grated Parmesan and half grated Gruyère cheeses, a little grated nutmeg, and occasionally some Dijon mustard, depending on the food it is to accompany. The sauce can be made richer with the addition of a large egg yolk or cream. Serve with eggs, vegetables, fish.

Velouté Make as for béchamel sauce, but use stock, instead of milk, to moisten the sauce. The stock can be poultry, game, veal or fish, according to what you are serving it with, and often 30–60 g (1–2 oz) chopped mushroom stalks are cooked in it as well.

Bigarade A velouté sauce flavoured with bitter orange (bigarade in French) juice and peel, or with sweet orange mixed with lemon juice. To give the sauce a rich brown colour, cook the butter to the noisette stage, i.e. a golden brown and smelling of nuts cooking. Stir in the flour, to make a pale brown roux, then duck stock. Finish with orange juice, a little sugar and a knob of butter. Shreds of blanched orange peel are stirred in at the last moment. Serve with duck or cooked ham.

Suprême Boil down 250 ml (8 fl oz/1 cup) each of velouté sauce and stock till reduced by half. Add 125 g (4 fl oz/scant ⅔ cup) cream and 60 g (2 oz/¼ cup) butter, in little bits. Serve with brains, chicken breasts, or sweetbreads.

Hollandaise Beat 3 large egg yolks in a bowl with 2 tablespoons (3 tbs) water or strong stock from the dish it is to be served with, season; melt 200 g (7 oz/scant cup) butter and pour it through muslin into a warm jug. Set the bowl of eggs over a pan of barely simmering water, and beat in the warm butter gradually. Do *not* overheat or it will curdle. Gradually you get an emulsion, like a hot mayonnaise. Sharpen with lemon juice and correct seasoning. It is tricky to keep hollandaise warm without curdling it. Either make it at the last moment, or set aside and reheat over water at the last moment. It should be warm rather than hot when served.

Béarnaise Boil together 3 tablespoons (scant ¼ cup) each dry white wine and white wine vinegar with 3 chopped shallots and 6 sprigs of tarragon, chopped. When you have a moist purée, cool it to tepid, then beat in the egg yolks as for hollandaise sauce, and then the warm clarified butter. Flavour, finally, with chopped tarragon and parsley, salt, pepper and cayenne. Serve with steaks, noisettes of lamb, or with eggs.

Beurre blanc The Loire sauce served with river fish, like shad or pike, also with sea fish. Beurre blanc is like a béarnaise sauce without the egg yolks, and the trick consists in not overheating it. Very much a last-minute sauce. The first time you make it, have a bowl of ice cubes handy for quickly cooling the base of the pan. Make a reduction of wine, vinegar and shallots as for the béarnaise sauce above. Cut up 280 g (8 oz/1 cup) butter, chilled till firm, into cubes. Whisk in the butter, bit by bit, keeping the heat very low; it should melt to a cream—raise the pan from the stove to make sure it does not get too hot. Season to taste.

Vin blanc Cook 3 chopped shallots gently in butter until very soft. Put in 125 ml (4 fl oz/ scant ⅔ cup) each dry white wine and fish stock, and boil hard to reduce to 3–4 tablespoons (¼–⅓ cup). Stir in 2 level tablespoons (3 tbs) double cream and a squeeze of lemon juice. Then, on and off the heat, whisk in 200 g (7 oz/scant cup) chilled butter, cut into little bits, as for beurre blanc. Serve with fish.

RATATOUILLE

Ratatouille used to be a sign of the right-thinking table when I was young: it was often disgusting, because we did not in those untravelled days realize the difference between Mediterranean and northern vegetables, tomatoes in particular. The difference can be summed up in two words, water and sun. Southern tomatoes grown in fields are vast and firm-fleshed, with a small amount of juice and seeds. If you try removing the seeds from a supermarket tomato, almost nothing is left. Ratatouille is for holidays—or for people who grow the right tomatoes in a sunny corner or who can buy them. If you do not belong to this blessed group, try the boumiano recipe instead, at the end.

Slice or dice equal weights of onions, courgettes, peppers, aubergines and tomatoes. Put courgette and aubergine pieces in a colander, sprinkle with a little salt and leave to drain for 1–2 hours; then pat them dry.

Soften the onion in a large sauté pan, with enough olive oil to cover the base. As it turns yellow, put in aubergines, courgettes and peppers. Cover and give them 20 minutes, stirring occasionally. Do not cook too fast. Put in the tomatoes and cook, without a lid, until you have a moist, unwatery stew, with discernible but melting pieces of vegetable. From 20–50 minutes. Stir from time to time, and keep the heat low enough to prevent sticking. Season.

Five minutes before serving, add a tablespoon of crushed coriander seeds, or a handful of black olives (the small Nice olives are best, if you can find them). Serve, hot, warm, cold, reheated, alone or with grilled or roast meat, or in pastry cases. Sprinkled with basil or parsley.

Boumiano Makes a stew on the ratatouille principle with an equal weight of tomatoes and aubergines, plus a large clove of garlic. Mix in a little bowl a heaped teaspoon flour, 8 chopped anchovy fillets, 2 tablespoons milk. Stir into the cooked, moist stew. Taste and correct seasoning. Pile into a gratin dish, scatter with breadcrumbs and chopped parsley, drip on some olive oil and bake until lightly golden, or grill. Boumiano is the Vaucluse word for bohémienne, meaning a gypsy girl—vegetables in the gypsy style.

EGGS EN COCOTTE
Oeufs en cocotte

One of those simple, classic dishes of French cooking that anyone can make. The most inexperienced cook can get it right: the most skilful cook can ruin it by a minute's inattention. The secret is to keep your eye on the eggs and to use a kitchen timer if there is the least chance of your being distracted.

Assemble enough eggs, the best and freshest you can buy, to give each person two. Then set out a small pot ramekin, soufflé dish, for each person large enough to take two eggs comfortably.

Butter them generously with plain butter, then put in a tablespoon of cream, or strips of smoked fish, or asparagus tips, or little brown bits of bacon, or lightly cooked wild mushrooms such as girolles or inky caps or sliced cèpes.

Alternatively use a flavoured butter—anchovy, parsley, prawn, paprika butters are all suitable.

Put the pots on a rack in a roasting pan, and pour in enough hot water to cover the rack and come a little way up the pots. Keep over a low heat to melt the butter slightly, then put in the eggs.

In Dehillerin's kitchen shop, Les Halles, Paris

Have the oven preheated to 190°C (375°F), gas 5, and put in the pan. After 4 minutes, check the eggs—if the yolks have a white skin and the whites are just milky but not hard and obdurate, they are done. If there is much transparent white left, which is likely, give them another minute or two. Put a pinch of parsley on top of the cooked eggs, and a dusting of cayenne if appropriate. Serve immediately.

Eggs en cocotte can be steamed on top of the stove. Cover each pot, and then the whole pan with foil, ballooning it up, and keep the water at simmering point. Check as above.

SPINACH ROULADE WITH TOMATO SAUCE

Roulade aux épinards, sauce tomate

A roulade sounds showy—and it does look attractive—but it is no more than a soufflé mixture baked like a Swiss roll sponge. The flavouring can be varied by using a purée of leeks or artichokes, either globe or Jerusalem, or by making a plain cheese soufflé mixture with béchamel sauce instead of a purée. Spinach, though, is particularly successful, especially with the curd cheese filling and lightly cooked crisp onion: if this does not appeal to you, make a seafood filling instead.

FOR THE ROULADE
175–200 g/6–7 oz drained, chopped cooked spinach
tablespoon béchamel sauce (see filling below)
4 egg yolks
level tablespoon grated Gruyère
level tablespoon grated Parmesan
salt, pepper, grated nutmeg
4 egg whites

FOR THE FILLING
30 g/1 oz/2 tbs butter and 30 g/1 oz/¼ cup flour
about 300 ml/½ pt/1¼ cups milk
125 g/4 oz/1 cup finely chopped onion
175 g/6 oz/¾ cup fromage frais, quark or curd cheese
salt, pepper

FOR THE SAUCE
medium onion, chopped
60 g/2 oz/¼ cup butter
clove garlic, crushed, chopped
625 g/1¼ lb tomatoes, skinned, chopped
salt, pepper, hint of sugar

First attend to the filling. Make a thick but not gluey béchamel sauce from butter, flour and milk. Remove a rounded tablespoon for the roulade. Add chopped onion and cook for 3 minutes, stirring all the time. Add soft cheese and cook a further 3 minutes, stirring. Season. The onion remains crisp.

Now, the roulade. Bllend or liquidize the spinach with the tablespoon of sauce, egg yolks and cheese. Season vigorously to taste. Whisk whites until stiff and fold into the spinach. Spread out on a baking tray 33 × 23 cm (13 × 9 in), lined with Bakewell paper and brushed with melted butter and sprinkled with flour. Bake 15 minutes at 190°C (375°F), gas 5. Remove from the oven, turn upside down on to a clean cloth and leave 5 minutes. Then lift tray, peel off paper and trim edges. Reheat the filling, spread over the spinach and roll up using the cloth as an aid. Flip it on to a dish and keep warm, until ready to serve.

Make the tomato sauce while the spinach was cooking. Melt the butter in a wide pan and add the onion. Cook until soft. Add tomatoes and cook hard and briefly to make a fresh-tasting, light sauce. Pour round the roulade and over any blemishes. Serve hot.

CRAB TART

Tarte au crabe

A great pleasure of French eating is the crab, especially spider crabs, many of which come from British waters (the official view is that the British housewife refuses to buy them). You go into some ordinary little port cafe in Brittany, and these spendid creatures will be brought to your table, often in a heap of shellfish bedded on ice and seaweed, with a bowl of mayonnaise. An ideal way of eating, since it takes a long time to eat quite a small amount.

For this tart you can use either kind of crab, or prepared crab meat so long as it contains no cereal filler to bulk it out (inquire firmly). Other shellfish can be used, too.

Serves 6–8
1 kg/2 lb crab, boiled, or 250 g/8 oz crab meat
salt and pepper
cayenne
3 eggs
250 ml/8 fl oz/good cup cream
tablespoon Parmesan cheese
tablespoon Gruyère cheese
23–25 cm/9–10 in shortcrust pastry case, baked blind for 10 minutes

Set oven at moderately hot, 190°C (375°F), gas 5.

Pick the meat from the boiled crab, discarding

the dead man's fingers; the shell can be used as a flavouring for fish stock. Season the crab meat, then beat in 1 whole egg and 2 yolks, then the cream and cheeses.

Whip the 2 egg whites until really stiff, then fold them into the crab mixture and spread in the cooled pastry case.

Bake in the heated oven for about 40 minutes. The mixture will puff up and turn golden brown in light patches; the final test is the centre, which should just have lost its liquid wobbliness under the crust (it will be creamy, however, not solid). Serve straightaway with brown bread and butter.

Quiche lorraine If you put a baking sheet into the preheated oven a few moments before cooking the quiche, there is no need to bake the pastry case blind. For a 22–25 cm (9–10 in) tart, cut 9 rashers of smoked streaky bacon into little strips and fry them briefly in a minimum of butter to make them slightly brown. Scatter them over the base of the tart. You can also add a couple of onions, sliced and sweated in butter with chopped green herbs, if you want a more substantial dish. Beat together 300 ml ($\frac{1}{2}$ pt/1$\frac{1}{4}$ cups) cream with 2 large eggs and 2 egg yolks, season and pour over the bacon. Dot with 30 g (1 oz/2 tbs) butter, cut in little bits. Bake at 200°C (400°F), gas 6 for 20 minutes, then lower the heat to 180°C (350°F), gas 4 for a further 15 minutes, or until the tart is puffed up and browned. Serve warm, rather than very hot or cold.

Quiche tourangelle Scatter the pastry base with 150 g (5 oz) rillettes, then with a couple of rillons cut into neat little slices, and a chopping of green herbs or just parsley. Beat 250 g (8 fl oz/1 cup) cream with 2 large eggs, season with pepper, salt and nutmeg. Cook as above. In France this is served as a first course, but most of us would find it a meal in itself, if served with a salad, some bread and a glass of Vouvray.

Tarte aux oignons verts et au fromage blanc A tart that is made in Poitou and Vendée when the young onions with their thick green stems first come in. You could use large spring onions instead, or a nice thick layer of chopped chives and green herbs. Trim the tough-looking stalk from a good bundle of young onions, slice them and soften them in a little butter: alternatively use two bundles of spring onions. Scatter them on the pastry. Beat together 200–250 g (7–8 oz/1 cup) fromage frais Jockey or Quark with 4 egg yolks, salt and pepper. Fold in the stiffly beaten egg whites, and put into the tart. Bake as for *tarte au crabe.*

CHICKEN LIVER PATE WITH ONION CHUTNEY

Terrine aux foies de volaille avec confiture d'oignons

What I like about nouvelle cuisine is the way chefs look again at familiar dishes and give them a little push in a new direction. I found this recipe in Michel Guérard's *Cuisine Gourmande*—the secret of the pâté is plenty of alcohol, and the best sausages you can find.

The chutney is served cold with the pâté, but it can also be heated through and served instead of the usual sweet-sour sauces or red currant jelly with meats or game.

When you buy your ingredients, ask the butcher for a slab of pork fat, cut away from a loin piece. Some supermarkets sell thick pieces of pork fat, too, which are worth storing in the freezer for larding and pâtés. Chill the fat slightly and then shave off pieces with the sharpest knife you have. They can be neatened up afterwards, with the most regular strips being kept for the top of the pâté, the rest for lining the dish.

Serves 8

2 tubs or 500 g/1 lb chicken livers, cut up in large pieces
200 g/7 oz belly of pork slices, 1 cm/$\frac{1}{4}$ in diced
200 g/7 oz good sausages, skinned and crumbled
strips of pork fat
4 bay leaves
4 sprigs of fresh thyme

FOR THE MARINADE

7 tablespoons/$\frac{2}{3}$ cup Armagnac or brandy
3 tablespoons/scant $\frac{1}{4}$ cup port
3 tablespoons/scant $\frac{1}{4}$ cup sherry
4 fat cloves of garlic, finely chopped
20 g/$\frac{2}{3}$ oz/$\frac{1}{2}$ cup chopped parsley
level teaspoon dried thyme
$\frac{1}{4}$ teaspoon freshly grated nutmeg
level teaspoon caster sugar
2 rounded teaspoons salt
12 turns of the pepper mill

FOR ONION CHUTNEY

750 g/1$\frac{1}{2}$ lb onions, thinly sliced
120 g/4 oz/$\frac{1}{2}$ cup butter
1$\frac{1}{2}$ teaspoons salt
heaped teaspoon pepper
160 g/5$\frac{1}{2}$ oz/good $\frac{2}{3}$ cup caster sugar
7 tablespoons/$\frac{2}{3}$ cup sherry vinegar
2 tablespoons/3 tbs grenadine or pomegranate syrup, or cassis or blackcurrant cordial
250 ml/8 fl oz/1 cup red wine
20 × 11 × 8-cm/8 × 4$\frac{1}{2}$ × 3-in terrine

A characteristic display with ham and quails

Put the chicken livers, diced pork and sausages into a bowl, with all the marinade ingredients. Cover and refrigerate until next day.

Set oven at hot, 220°C (425°F), gas 7.

Line the terrine with strips of pork fat, setting aside enough for the top. Stir up the pâté mixture and pack it in; there will probably be some left over, so put it into a small deep pot as a taster. Cover the top neatly with the remaining fat strips and place bay leaves and thyme sprigs on top.

Stand the terrine (and pot) on a rack in a bain-marie, and put into the heated oven. Cook for $1\frac{1}{2}$ hours, taking out the smaller pâté once it shrinks from the sides in clear, bubbling fat. Cool for 2–3 hours at room temperature, then put a sheet of non-stick baking paper over the top, weight it lightly and refrigerate.

Put the onions into a large pan in which you have cooked the butter to the noisette, golden-brown stage. Stir in the salt, pepper and sugar. Cover the pan and cook very gently for minutes, stirring occasionally; the onions should soften and turn to a moist brown. Add vinegar, syrup or cordial and the wine. Cook, uncovered, for a further 30 minutes, stirring regularly. The result is less jammy than a chutney, but the relationship is obvious.

After 3–4 hours, remove the weights and leave the pâté for at least 24 hours. Then serve it with onion chutney, gherkins, pickled onions and, of course, bread.

FISH TERRINE
Terrine de poisson

Making fish terrines—or pâtés, as they are often called—is one of the most entertaining exercises of French cookery. It gives you a chance to make something beautiful and delicious that is completely your own. Seeing the works of art in Fauchon's in Paris first gave me the hint of what could be done: some terrines are simple layers of two or three mixtures, interspersed with an occasional layer of finely chopped herbs or mushrooms; others look like pink marble, studded with strips of sole or eel. At home it is wise to eschew the fussier effects of a professional caterer's kitchen, but that is no reason not to enjoy the fun.

Loaf tins can be used if you intend to turn the terrine out before slicing it. I prefer an oblong earthenware dish and serve the terrine from it; the slices hang together far better this way. When making your choice of decorative centre ingredients, reflect on whether they are likely to shrink in cooking, and give up much liquid: if they are, it is wise to cook them lightly and cool them down before layering them into place.

A mousseline should be what its name implies: very fine and smooth. This used to be achieved by pounding and sieving, and more sieving. Today, we have blenders and processors, which account for the return of this kind of dish to our tables.

Serves 8–10

500 g/1 lb whiting, sole, salmon, eel, or red mullet, etc, weighed after boning

2 large egg whites 300 ml/$\frac{1}{2}$ pt/$1\frac{1}{3}$ cups whipping or double cream

salt, pepper, cayenne

lemon juice

FOR THE FILLING

salt, pepper, lemon

250–375 g/8–12 oz fillets of fish (sole or salmon), or scallops with shellfish (shrimps, prawns, crab), or mussels, weighed without shells, or mixed smoked fish, cut in strips

chopped parsley, chives and tarragon

fish stock or white wine, for scallops, if using

PREPARATION Cut the fish into pieces and drop them on to the whirling blades of a blender or processor and reduce them to a purée. This purée will now go easily through a sieve into a bowl set over ice. With an electric beater, mix in the egg whites then the cream, bit by bit, salt and pepper, until it becomes a bulky lightness. Taste and add extra seasoning and lemon juice.

For the filling, first season the fish fillets then cut them neatly, bearing in mind that they will be set longways through the terrine, so that each cut slice will contain a piece. Roll the fish pieces in the herbs. If you use scallops, which do shrink, slice the cleaned white discs across, horizontally, into two; cut off any black bits from the corals. Steam or poach them in a little fish stock or white wine. Cool and season them.

If the terrine is to be served cold, brush the dish or tin out with a tasteless oil. If it is to be turned out, cut a long strip of non-stick baking paper the narrow width of the base of the dish or tin, and run it down one end, along the base and up the other end. Brush it with oil. Put in another oiled strip, cut to fit widthways.

If the terrine is to be served hot or warm, line it in the same way and brush with butter instead of oil.

Beginning and ending with mousseline, layer in the mixtures. Cut a butter paper to fit on top, then cover with double foil. The preparation so far can be completed earlier in the day, and chilled until required, if you wish to serve the terrine hot or warm for dinner.

TO COOK Set oven at moderate, 180°C (350°F), gas 4. Stand the terrine on a rack in a roasting tin, pour hot water round to come about half way up the sides, bring to the boil on top of the stove. Transfer to the heated oven and cook for 30 minutes.

Inspect the terrine; if it seems firm and if a skewer or larding needle pushed into the centre feels hot on the back of your hand, it is done. Remember that it will continue to cook a little as it cools.

Serve hot with beurre blanc or vin blanc sauces (recipes on page 114), or cold with mayonnaise (recipe on page 112), flavoured with an appropriate herb, or coloured and flavoured pink with tomato, or green with spinach juice or the juice of a bouquet of green herbs and watercress, blanched and squeezed in muslin.

SNAILS WITH GARLIC BUTTER, BURGUNDY STYLE
Escargots farcis à la bourguignonne

The Escargot in Paris, on a corner of the rue Montorgueil, is easy to spot from the great golden snail on the wall outside. You can have snails stuffed with Roquefort, garlic, fennel, mint or curry butter—or le colimaçon, which is a mixture of all five (the reckless can have little pots of snails with

A plate of stuffed snails and little ports of snails at the Escargot restaurant, Paris

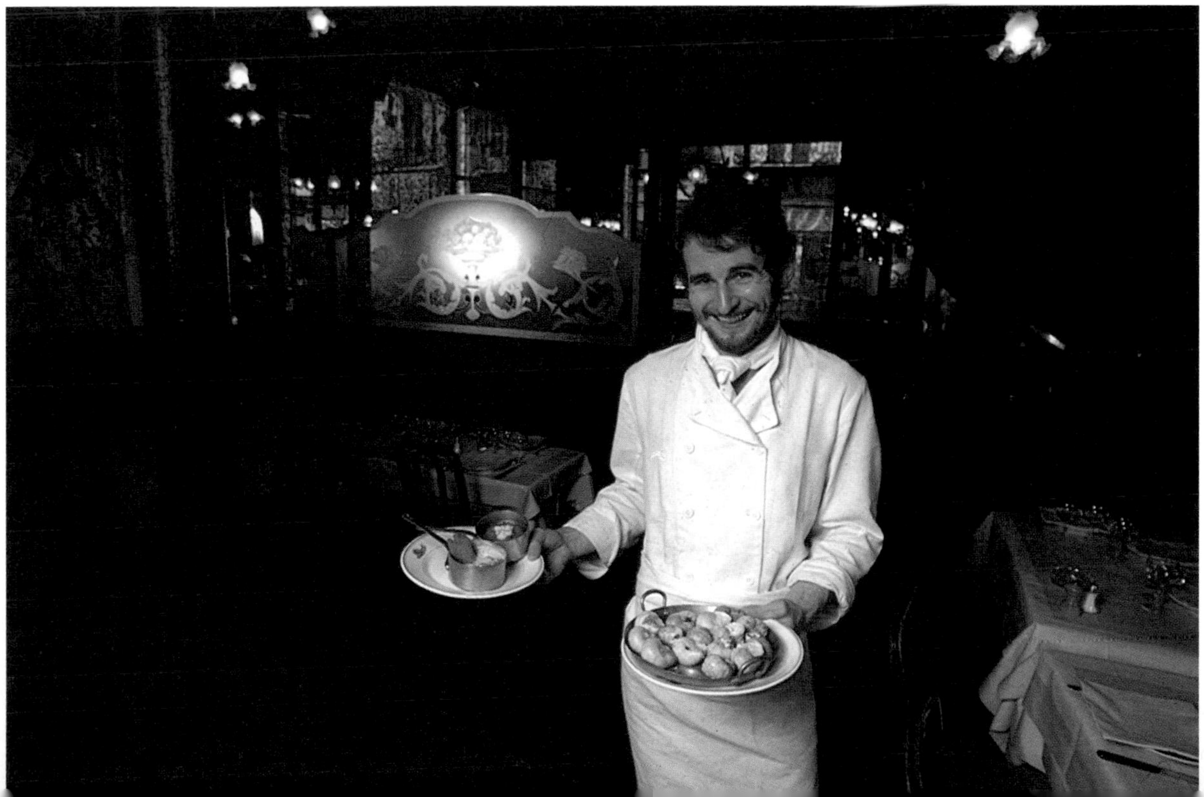

Chablis sauce or caviare). I still like garlic butter best, though fennel came close (it had, I suspect, pernod in it as well as chopped fennel leaves).

Deep-frozen stuffed Burgundy snails are quite good, but you can make a better garlic butter yourself at home with a blender or processor. If you do this, buy canned snails with their attendant pack of shells, or hunt your own. The big Burgundy snail is rare in Britain, but the smaller garden snail is abundant. Instructions for preparing them can be found either in my *Good Things* (Penguin) or Susan Campbell's *English Cookery. New and Old* (Consumer's Association, 1981).

There's no need to buy special snail plates. Instead, cut discs of bread from a round loaf to fit into buttered ovenproof plates, and cut holes in them with a tiny pastry cutter or apple corer. The juices that bubble over make this bread worth eating. No need for snail tongs either: provide pins stuck into corks, also cloth napkins and small finger bowls of water with a slice of lemon floating in each one.

Whizz together in a blender or processor the leaves of a large bunch of parsley, 5 large cloves of garlic, skinned and split in half, 60 g (2 oz/½ cup) peeled shallot or onion, 4-level teaspoons salt, and 2 level teaspoons ground black pepper, until they are well chopped. Gradually add 500 g (1 lb/2 cups) fairly soft unsalted butter. Taste and put in extra salt if you think it needs it. This is enough for 4–6 dozen snails, according to their size.

Set oven at hot, 220°C (425°F), gas 7.

Remove the cooked snails from their shells with a pin, put a dab of garlic butter in each, replace the snail, then cover to the rim with more butter. Place the stuffed snails on their plates or bread discs, so that the openings are flat on top. Scatter lightly with fine crumbs. Bake in the heated oven until bubbling and browned—about 10 minutes, but go by appearance rather than the clock. Or bake at a lower temperature, then brown under the grill. Serve sizzling, straight away.

Grilled stuffed mussels (moules farcies grillées) Allow 12 large mussels per person, plus extra ones for duds and a couple of tasters. Scrub and scrape them, remove the beards. Throw away any broken mussels or ones that refuse to close when tapped. Put a single layer, with a little water, into a wide heavy pan; cover and set over a high heat. Check after 30 seconds, and remove any that are open. Check again after 10 more seconds—the point is to catch them the moment after they open, to avoid over-cooking. Repeat with the rest of the mussels.

Throw away one half shell from each mussel. Free the mussel from the other shell, then put it back and cover with garlic butter and breadcrumbs. Arrange on oyster plates or bread discs, or on a bed of coarse salt. Put not too close to a preheated grill; then as the mussels begin to bubble, put them closer to the heat to brown them. Or bake them (called gratinées) as for snails.

Grilled stuffed oysters (huîtres farcies grillées) Allow 6–12 oysters per person. Open, drain liquor and discard the flatter shell. Ease out oyster, and finish as for mussels, allowing a slightly longer cooking time as they start off raw. Or bake as for snails.

SCALLOPS IN A SHELL
Feuilleté de Saint-Jacques

Based on a dish we ate years ago at Rouen, at La Couronne, by the market place where Joan of Arc was burned. The gin sounds unlikely, but works well.

500 g/1 lb weight puff pastry
18–24 scallops
seasoned flour
4 tablespoons butter
4 tablespoons oil
6 tablespoons/½ cup gin
200 ml/7 fl oz/good ¾ cup double cream
chopped parsley
salt, pepper, lemon juice
extra butter

Scrub well and dry six deep scallop shells, then rub them over with a butter paper or a little oil *on the back side.* Cut the pastry into six pieces, and roll them out one by one, fitting each piece on to the scallop shells. Trim to shape, prick lightly and bake at 220–230°C (400–425°F), gas 7–8, until risen and lightly browned. This can be done well in advance. Alternatively cut six oblongs of pastry, turn them upside down on a baking sheet and score them lightly with a pattern, brush with egg and bake: when cooked and slightly cooled, split them in half horizontally, to make a sandwich with the scallop filling.

Slice the cleaned white discs of scallop across horizontally into two. Trim any black bits from the corals. Turn all the pieces in the flour. Cook them lightly in the butter and oil. Warm the gin, set it on fire and pour it over the scallops, turning them in the flames. When they die down, pour in the cream. When the scallops are done, remove them to a warm dish, and boil down the sauce vigorously. Season with salt, pepper and lemon juice, and—off the heat—swirl or stir in a tablespoon of butter, in little bits. Put back the scallops for a moment, then divide between the pastry shells or *feuilletés*.

SOLE MEUNIERE

Chefs make endless variations on the theme of sole; delightful as many of them are, this simple way is the one I always come back to. It is the ideal method to show off a fine, fresh fish, which was invented, so the story goes, at Royat, near Clermont Ferrand, at the mill which is now an hotel, La Belle Meunière.

Sole meunière is not the dish for a large party, as it needs last minute attention; keep it as a special treat for 2 or 4 people. Ask the fishmonger to skin the sole.

First, clarify 125 g (4 oz/½ cup) butter, cut into dice; bring slowly to the boil and, when a white crust has formed, pour off the yellow oil through muslin into your frying pan(s). Turn the sole in seasoned flour, and shake off any surplus. Fry them in clarified butter until golden, turning them once. Remove to a hot serving dish and tuck in a sprig or two of parsley and lemon wedges.

Clean out the pan with kitchen paper. Heat the pan, put in 100 g (3½ oz/scant ½ cup) unsalted butter, chopped up, stirring it round. When it is beginning to brown and smell deliciously of hazelnuts, pour it over the fish and serve at once, with bread, or a few new, small potatoes.

RED MULLET WITH FENNEL
Rougets au fenouil

Kitchen shops sometimes sell bundles of dried fennel stalks intended primarily for the Provençal dish of red mullet grilled on a bed of fennel. But unless you are cooking out-of-doors, you will do better with this more reflective way of combining the two flavours.

When you buy the mullet, make sure the fishmonger leaves the liver inside (it's the great delicacy), and removes the large and uncomfortable scales; otherwise it is a beautiful pinkish-red fish, with a delightful flavour.

Serves 6
6 red mullet, with their livers
salt and pepper
3 fennel bulbs
4 level tablespoons fine white breadcrumbs
rounded tablespoon butter, softened
2 tablespoons/3 tbs olive oil
extra butter

Remove the livers from the fish, season both. Remove the tough outer layers of the fennel, cutting off any fine green leaves carefully and chopping them into a bowl. Quarter the fennel bulbs, and simmer in salted water until almost tender. Remove them and keep the water. Set oven at moderately hot, 190°C (375°F), gas 5.

Chop 4 fennel quarters and add to the bowl of fennel leaves. Slice the rest of the fennel and spread in a layer over the base of a buttered gratin dish that will hold the mullet in a single layer. Add the crumbs, softened butter and just over 1 tablespoon oil to the chopped fennel, moistening the mixture with a little of the fennel cooking liquor. Season and add the chopped livers; stuff the fish with this mixture. Any leftover can go with the sliced fennel.

Put mullet into the dish. Dribble remaining oil over; season. Bake in the heated oven for 15 minutes or until cooked.

MACKEREL IN WHITE WINE
(Maquereaux au vin blanc)

This is so popular a dish in France that I wonder we do not see cans of it in England and America as well in every supermarket. It is simple to make at home, and good. (Be careful not to get the juice on your clothes as it leaves a searching smell that takes some getting rid of.)

For 6 people—or for 12, if you are serving a mixed hors d'oeuvre or buffet meal—buy 6 fresh, medium-sized mackerel. Ask the fishmonger to cut off the heads and clean them.

Put them into a pan in one or two layers, and pour on water to cover generously. Then tip the water into a measuring jug and note the quantity. You will need half that amount in white wine—Muscadet is the ideal—and half in white wine vinegar. Throw the water away.

Put the wine and vinegar into another pan, with 6 neat slices of carrot, and the rest of a large carrot cut into bits. Add 2–3 cloves, a tiny hot chilli, 1 teaspoon black peppercorns, lightly crushed, and a bouquet garni (bay, thyme, parsley, tarragon, and a small sprig of rosemary). Simmer for 10 minutes. Meanwhile, tuck a large sliced onion and a sliced lemon between the mackerel.

When the wine liquor is ready, bring it to a rolling boil and pour over the mackerel. Put them on the heat and when the liquor returns to the boil, give it a bubble or two, then cover and put aside to cool.

Transfer the mackerel to a serving dish, with the neat carrot slices, and 2–3 lemon slices, plus the chilli, the bay leaf from the bouquet garni, and a few fragments of onion if they are not too tatty. Add fresh peppercorns. Cover and leave to marinate in the refrigerator for 2–4 days. Serve with bread, butter and Muscadet, or whichever wine you used, to drink.

VEAL OR VENISON CHOPS FROM THE ARDENNES
Côtes de veau ou chevreuil à l'ardennaise

The best introduction to French cooking is Elizabeth David's *French Provincial Cooking*. This is one of my favourite recipes from it. Ask for venison double chops, cut across the saddle. With veal, ask for boned loin chops, weighing at least 125 g (4 oz) each.

Serves 6
6 veal or venison chops
18 juniper berries, crushed
1½ level teaspoons dried marjoram or thyme
salt and pepper
juice of 1 lemon
60 g/2 oz butter
medium onion, chopped
2 medium carrots, diced
125 ml/4 fl oz/scant ⅔ cup dry white wine
125 ml/4 fl oz/scant ⅔ cup water
6 dessertspoons chopped cooked ham
100 g/3½ oz breadcrumbs
3 tablespoons chopped parsley
extra butter
level tablespoon red currant jelly and the juice of a bitter orange (for venison)

Put the meat in a single layer in a dish. Mix together the juniper berries, herb, salt and pepper. Pour the lemon juice over the meat, then turn it and rub on juniper mixture. Cover; leave 1–2 hours.

In the butter brown the onion and carrots lightly, then add meat to brown. Pour in the wine and reduce by half. Transfer to an ovenproof serving dish to accommodate meat in one layer. Set oven at cool, 150°C (300°F), gas 2.

Deglaze the pan with the water. Pour round the meat. On top put the ham, then scatter with the breadcrumbs and parsley, mixed. Put a dab of butter on top, and bake in the heated oven for 1¼ hours (for veal), or 1¾ hours (for venison).

For venison, pour off the juices into a pan and whisk in the jelly and orange juice (when Sevilles are not in season I use a little bitter marmalade instead). When smooth, pour round the meat.

Serve the veal with potatoes, and venison with a purée of potato and celeriac, or chestnuts, or with dark green lentils and parsley butter.

PORK WITH PRUNES, TOURS STYLE
Noisettes de porc aux pruneaux de Tours

I use noisettes cut from the tenderloin for this dish (when I have had loin chops in a local Touraine restaurant they are often dry and almost tough).

Prunes used to be dried from plums grown around Tours, but today they come from further south, or California.

Serves 6
18 prunes
½ bottle Vouvray or other dry white wine
2 pork tenderloins
seasoned flour
60 g/2 oz/¼ cup butter
level tablespoon redcurrant jelly
500 ml/¾ pt/2 cups whipping cream
lemon juice
salt and pepper

Bring the prunes and wine slowly to the boil. Switch off, cover and leave for 1 hour. Then simmer until the prunes are tender, stone them and put on a warm dish. Reserve the liquor.

Meanwhile, cut the thin ends from the tenderloins (keep them for another dish). Slice the tenderloins into thick noisettes, about 18 of them: the end slices may look a little meagre, but shape them as best you can. Turn them in seasoned flour and fry in butter until just tender. Arrange them on the serving dish and keep warm.

Pour off any surplus fat and deglaze the pan with the prune liquor. Reduce to a syrupy consistency over a high heat. Whisk in the cream, and when the sauce is thick, season with lemon juice, salt and pepper. Serve at once.

PIG'S EARS WITH LENTILS
Oreilles de porc aux lentilles

A good cheap family dish, in England at least. In France pig's ears are quite expensive, since they are rightly regarded as a delicacy. In England you may well be given them for nothing. If you cannot get ears, use pig's tails or trotters, giving them 30 minutes' preliminary cooking, before the lentils go in.

For 6 people, cut 6 pig's ears in two, lengthways;

FATS

A thing that is difficult for us to realize is the way different fats characterize the cooking of the different regions of France. We can buy any fat we want at any supermarket in the country, and choose whichever kind a particular dish seems to require. Of course this is partly true in France these days: you can buy olive oil in the north and butter in the south, but people are still faithful to the fat appropriate to their region and climate.

Butter Very much the northern fat and the basic fat of high class and bourgeois French cookery. Usually unsalted. The highest qualities come from Isigny on the Normandy coast, from the Charentes, and from Brittany where butter is mainly salted. European butters are made differently from ours, since the cream is ripened first: for butter sauces choose French or Danish butter.

Lard North of the olive line, used particularly where the charcuterie is a matter of local pride. The French for lard is *saindoux*; *lard* means what we should call streaky bacon. When the fatty parts of the pig are boiled down for lard, the little bits strained out are carefully treasured, either for eating as a rough pâté, or for adding to bread and brioche dough (see pompe aux grattons page 111).

Goose fat The prized cooking fat of the foie gras districts of south-west France and Alsace-Lorraine. Mixed with blanched and pounded garlic, it is known as Gascony butter and stirred into cassoulets and soups. Duck fat is used in the same ways. Goose or duck fat, along with olive oil, make the best fried potatoes in the world.

Olive oil The northern limit of the olive—above which the trees will grow but will not fruit successfully—includes much of southern France between the Pyrenees and the Alps and below the Massif Central with a north-pointing finger up the Rhône valley. Different oils vary as wines do, the qualities are defined in the same way as they are in Italy.

Although olive oil seems expensive, you need very little with a salad of tomatoes or cooked vegetables to make a very fine dish indeed. Whereas if you used one of the tasteless oils, you would feel obliged to liven the salad with extra ingredients.

The choice of olives in France is bewildering. Markets as far north as ours in Touraine will have 10 or 11 different wooden buckets of them, from the bruised looking mauve olives large and pulpy to the tiny little niçois olives, and the Greek-style olives from North Africa, wrinkled and slightly dry.

Walnut, hazelnut, almond oils Walnut oil was once much used in France, and is now enjoying a return of popularity for salads and breadmaking, or as a final flavouring for mayonnaise, particularly when it is to be eaten with fish. Often some of the chopped nut is mixed in as well. Hazelnut oil has a fine toasted smell, and can be used in baking, as can almond oil: these two are ideal for brushing out moulds for creams of various kinds, and almond oil is the best treatment for ivory-handled knives which begin to dry and crack.

Groundnut oil The most popular and pleasant to use of the tasteless oils in France. Whenever you see the word 'oil'—*huile*—in a French recipe, arachide (groundnut) oil is intended, though maize (mais) or sunflower (tournesol) can be used instead. Many people prefer mayonnaise made with groundnut oil, or with groundnut oil flavoured lightly with olive or nut oil, to an entirely olive oil based mayonnaise. Egg yolks seem to have a coarsening effect on the taste of olive oil, unless it is very delicate.

put them into a flameproof pot with 500 g (1 lb) dark green lentils. Add 2 medium carrots, neatly diced, 2 chopped onions and 2 chopped cloves of garlic, plus a large onion stuck with 2 cloves, a bouquet garni and a 200–250 g (7–8 oz) piece of smoked bacon. Cover generously with water. Simmer until the meat and lentils are tender, adding extra water from time to time if need be. Add salt at the end of the cooking time (about $1\frac{1}{2}$ hours).

Drain off remaining stock. Discard the whole onion and bouquet garni. Mix plenty of butter with the lentils, and arrange with the ears and bacon on a hot dish. Sprinkle with chopped parsley. A vinaigrette sauce with chopped herbs and capers can be served as well.

HAM IN PARSLEY JELLY
Jambon persillé de Bourgogne

This beautiful Easter dish from Burgundy, a contrast of pink ham and bright green-flecked jelly, is ideal for a party of people. No need to turn it out, if you set it in an attractive bowl. The desirable wine is Meursault, and the desirable ham is locally cured, but you can do very well instead with a reasonably dry white wine and unsmoked gammon. The veal knuckle, etc, is important to give the jelly a good set and flavour; the meat is not needed in the final assembly, but provides a lunch dish to be served with a vinaigrette with plenty of green herbs.

Serves 8–12
1½–2 kg/3–4 lb boned unsmoked ham or gammon
knuckle of veal, cut in 3–4 pieces
calf's foot or 2 pig's trotters
pieces of pork skin, cut in squares (optional)
large bay leaf
2 good sprigs each of parsley and thyme
3 sprigs each of chervil and tarragon, optional
12 lightly-crushed peppercorns
1½ bottles dry white wine
about 2 tablespoons tarragon wine vinegar
large bunch of parsley, finely chopped
2 shallots, finely chopped

Soak ham or gammon as necessary (ask when you buy it). Put all the meat items into a large pan, cover with cold water, bring to simmering point and cook for 30 minutes, then drain. Pour off the water. Take out the ham or gammon, remove skin and discard, then cut it into large pieces, having a measurement of 5–8 cm (2–3 in) in your mind as a guide. Put these back into the pan.

Tie the herbs and peppercorns into a piece of muslin and put into the pan. Pour on enough white wine to cover the meat completely. Bring to simmering point, covered, and keep there until the ham or gammon is very tender—between 2–3 hours. Make sure the liquid never boils in the true sense, or your jelly will be murky, and you will have to clarify it.

When the ham or gammon is ready, remove the pieces to a board and crush them slightly. Strain off the liquor through muslin and add up to 2 tablespoons (3 tbs) wine vinegar to taste, plus other seasonings should they be necessary. Put into the refrigerator and when it is of egg-white consistency, stir in enough chopped parsley to make it heavily green, but not solidly so. Stir in the shallots. Mix with the ham or gammon, holding back enough of the parsley jelly to make a top layer, and put into the bowl. Put into the refrigerator to set and when almost but not quite firm, run the last of the jelly—softened over a little hot water, if necessary—over the top.

Note it is prudent to test the set of the jelly, which can be too firm. When you have added the vinegar, parsley and shallots, put a little into a small bowl in the coldest part of the refrigerator. If it sets too firmly for pleasant eating—though it should be firm enough to cut cleanly—add a little hot water to soften it.

SCHNITZEN AU LARD

Arthur Young, the agriculturist, gave an agreeable picture of travelling in Alsace in 1789: 'The moment you are out of a great town all in this country is German; the inns have one common large room, many tables and cloths ready spread, where every company dines; gentry at some, and the poor at others. Cookery also German: schnitz is a dish of bacon and dried pears; has the appearance of a mess for the devil; but I was surprised, on tasting, to find it better than passable.' Yes, indeed it is delicious, a Monday dish in Alsace perhaps, but a good midday meal any day, after some soup.

Serves 6
150 g/5 oz each dried apple rings and pears
60 g/2 oz/¼ cup sugar
300 g/10 oz German streaky bacon, Fetterspeck or Geraüchter Bauchspeck, in a piece
750 g/1½ lb potatoes, peeled and quartered
250 ml/9fl oz/scant 1¼ cups beef stock
salt, pepper

Either soak the dried fruit overnight, or pour boiling water over it and leave for an hour or so until plumped up. Drain. Caramelize the sugar with 3 tablespoons (scant ¼ cup) of water in a saucepan and stir the fruit about in it. Put the piece of bacon under the fruit and add half the stock, stirring to deglaze the base of the pan from any lumps of caramel. Cover and simmer for 45–60 minutes, until the fruit is almost tender. Add the potatoes, salt and pepper, plus extra stock if the mixture seems to be drying out too much. Cover and cook until the potatoes are done, about an hour.

Just before serving, slice the bacon and discard the rind. Stir up the fruit and potatoes and put on to a hot dish. Arrange the slices of bacon on top.

Note a large smoked sausage can also be cooked in this dish. Put it in with the potatoes.

IVORY CHICKEN
Poulet ivoire

The aim of this simple dish is to keep chicken and sauce a beautiful ivory colour; not even the lightest brown should be visible on the skin. Serve it on a dish of clear colour to show off its delicacy, and keep vegetable accompaniments to a discreet quantity.

I first came across the recipe in a cookery magazine of the 1890s, *Pot-au-feu*, which was, I think, revolutionary for the careful step-by-step explanation of recipes: the woman responsible later produced an enormous, exact book, *La Cuisine de Madame Saint Ange*, which I recommend to anyone who wants to start cooking the French way properly. My copy is a 1958 Flammarion reprint of the 1927 original.

This version of the recipe is made without a butter and flour roux, which makes it a little lighter.

Serves 6
2–2.5 kg/4–5 lb free-range chicken
$\frac{1}{2}$ lemon
salt and pepper
piece of pork back fat
10 cm/4 in square of pork skin
100 g/3$\frac{1}{2}$ oz peeled carrot, cut up
75 g/2$\frac{1}{2}$ oz/good $\frac{1}{2}$ cup sliced onion
250 ml/9 fl oz/good cup dry white wine
500 ml/18 fl oz/good 2 cups chicken stock
200 ml/7 fl oz/1 cup whipping cream
level tablespoon butter

Remove chicken giblets, setting the liver aside for another dish. Rub the bird over with the lemon, then season it. Tie the pork fat over the breast. Put it with the giblets, pork skin and vegetables into a deep flameproof pot so it fits fairly snugly. Set over a low heat for 10 minutes—the vegetables and so on must not brown. Pour in the wine and stock. Simmer, covered, until the chicken is cooked, turning it over from time to time ($1\frac{1}{4}$–$1\frac{1}{2}$ hours). When the legs can be wiggled easily and the juices run clear the chicken is done.

Pour off the juices into a pan, leaving the chicken to keep warm in the pot. Skim off all the fat from the juices, then strain them through muslin into a wide pan; boil down vigorously until strong-flavoured. Whisk in the cream gradually, then the butter and season with lemon juice, salt and pepper.

While the juices are reducing, carve the chicken and put on to a hot dish. Pour over some of the sauce, and serve the rest separately.

Note put a bunch of tarragon into the chicken for a marvellous summer dish, and then a sprig or two into the juices as they boil down.

Bresse chickens with their characteristic feather ruff

DUCK STEAK
Magret

The word 'magret' comes from South-West France: it is the name given to the breast of a duck which has been fattened for foie gras. However, the breast of an ordinary duck, even a deep-frozen duck from the supermarket, can be removed and treated in exactly the same way with success.

The first thing to do is to remove the duck's collar bone, cutting it away to free the meat. Then cut through the skin of the breast bone, and slide the knife down each side of the bone and down over the ribs, to free the breast meat on either side. You now have two large oval pieces of meat. Turn them skin side down and remove the small fillets of meat for another dish, see below.

You now have two options. You can skin the breasts, brush them all over with sunflower oil and grill them like a beef steak, keeping them rare to medium rare. Your guests will be puzzled, if you have not told them what they are eating. It looks like steak, yet it is more tender and hasn't the same flavour—but what is it?

My own preferred way is to leave the skin in place and follow Michel Guérard's method of pan-frying. Heat up a heavy iron pan over a moderate flame. Put in the magrets skin side down. Leave 10 minutes. The fattiness of the skin prevents sticking. Turn the steaks over and cook for 3 minutes only on the lean meat side. Put them on to a warm plate and invert another warm plate on top. Leave to relax for 10 minutes in the plate-warming oven, or a very low oven with the door just ajar. Transfer to a very hot dish for serving with little bunches of watercress, or with one or other of the following suggestions:

Anton Mosimann's duck steak Nossi-Bé (Nossi-Bé is a mountain in Madagascar where green peppercorns come from) Grill the steaks without their skins, and have ready caramelized apple pieces. To make them, peel, core and slice three well-flavoured eating apples into 8 pieces each. Cook 30 g (1 oz/2 tbs) butter with 45 g (1½ oz/scant ¼ cup) sugar until they begin to turn brown. Put in the apple pieces, turning them in the caramel, and add 5 tablespoons (6 tbs) dry white wine. Simmer 2–3 minutes. Arrange with the duck steaks on the serving dish, plus a little watercress. Meanwhile, heat 30 g (1 oz) drained green peppercorns in the apple pan juices. Scatter them over the steaks and serve.

Sauce cassis Prepare the steaks with their skins on, and slice them neatly, each slice with its bit of skin. Have the sauce ready up to the reheating stage at the end. Deep-frozen black currants can quite well be used for this sauce, which can also be served with plain roast duck (pour the fat from the pan juices and add the meaty part to the sauce).

300 g/10 oz black currants
level tablespoon caster sugar
5 tablespoons/6 tbs wine vinegar
rounded tablespoon red currant jelly or black currant jelly or jam
2 tablespoons crême de cassis or gin
250 ml/8 fl oz/1 cup duck stock made from giblets and carcase
90 g/3 oz/scant ⅓ cup unsalted butter, cubed
salt, pepper, extra sugar

Cook a heaped tablespoon of the black currants in a little water. Remove them with a perforated spoon and set aside for the final garnish. Put the rest of the black currants into the pan with the sugar, cover and simmer until tender. Meanwhile, reduce vinegar and jelly or sieved jam to a caramelized syrup in a small pan. Deglaze with the alcohol and half the stock. Pour into the black currant pan with the rest of the stock and simmer a further 20 minutes, covered. Sieve into a wide pan, pressing the juices through and just enough of the black currants to make a sauce the consistency of single cream. Taste and season it. Bring to boiling point, bubble vigorously for a minute or two, then whisk in the butter off the heat. Check the seasoning again, adding a very little sugar if necessary, though the sauce should not be very sweet.

CONFIT OF DUCK LEGS

Confit of goose or duck is a speciality of South-West France, where poultry is fattened for foie gras. The rest of the bird—apart from the magrets which are often salted and smoked as tiny 'hams'—is spiced and cooked and preserved in its own fat. A piece will be used from time to time to enrich a cassoulet; or as a treat several bits will be fried and served with mashed potatoes and apple as a main course. Here is a practical version of this country preserve for small households:

6 whole duck legs
1 clove garlic, peeled
3 level teaspoons sea salt
rounded teaspoon freshly ground black pepper
¼ teaspoon grated nutmeg
bay leaf cut in thin strips
2 sprigs thyme or ½ teaspoon dried thyme
1 kg/2 lb goose fat or lard
extra bay leaf
extra thyme

Rub duck legs all over with the cut side of the garlic clove. Crush the salt and mix it with the pepper and nutmeg and rub it into the duck too. Put the legs into a bowl and scatter with the bay leaf strips and the leaves from the thyme sprigs or the dried thyme. Cover and leave for 8–10 hours in a cool place, turning the pieces occasionally.

To cook, wipe the duck legs free of bits and pieces and the salt. Put into a flame-proof pan. Melt the fat and pour it over. Put in the extra bay leaf and another 2 sprigs thyme or ½ teaspoon dried thyme. Bring to the boil, cover and lower the heat to a bare simmer. In 1½ hours the meat should be very tender.

Strain some of the fat into a deep china or glass container that will hold the legs, or into two or three smaller containers. Put to set in the refrigerator or freezer. Put the legs on top, then pour over enough of the fat to cover them. If you need more, melt extra goose fat or lard. Tap the containers to make sure there are no air holes. Put them to set firm in the refrigerator. Cover closely with cling film, pressed down on to the fat, and leave for a week.

Either stand the container in hot water, or put it over a low heat to melt the fat. Extract the pieces of duck. Use them in a cassoulet. Or brown them in some of their fat, and serve them with mashed potatoes and fried apple slices. Alternatively, leave them to cool and eat them with a salad.

NORMANDY-STYLE COOKING

The Normandy style means cooking poultry, game or pork with Calvados (apple brandy) and cream, sometimes with apples as well. Occasionally the dish will be labelled pays d'Auge or vallée d'Auge, since that part of Normandy is strong in those three ingredients. It's an attractive land of timbered manor houses, dovecots, farms and orchards, and includes the village of Camembert.

For the simplest poulet vallée d'Auge, gently fry a plump young chicken in 150 g (5 oz/$\frac{2}{3}$ cup) butter, turning it over from time to time, until it is tender. Flame with 100 ml (3 fl oz/$\frac{1}{2}$ cup) Calvados (whisky is the best substitute), deglaze with a very little stock, then stir in 500 ml ($\frac{3}{4}$ pt/scant 2 cups) cream. Give the chicken a moment or two longer, then cut it up, put on a hot dish and pour over the sauce. Serve with rice, and mushrooms or apple slices (use Cox's orange pippins or a similar eating apple), fried in butter.

Serves 4
750 g/1$\frac{1}{2}$ lb Cox's orange pippins apples, peeled, cored and sliced (reserve 3 for the garnish)
butter
level teaspoon powdered cinnamon
sugar
brace of pheasant or guineafowl, or large chicken, or 1 kg/2 lb boned, rolled loin of pork
100 ml/3$\frac{1}{2}$ fl oz/good $\frac{1}{2}$ cup Calvados or whisky
250 ml/9 fl oz/1 cup appropriate stock
150 ml/$\frac{1}{4}$ pt/$\frac{2}{3}$ cup each whipping and double cream
salt and pepper
lemon juice

You need enough apple slices to make a layer in the bottom of an ovenproof pot which will hold the game, poultry or pork closely.

Set oven at moderate, 180°C (350°F), gas 4.

Fry apple slices in butter, then as they soften, sprinkle with cinnamon and 1 tablespoon sugar, turning them over in the juices. Put into the pot. In the frying pan, brown the birds or meat and flame with Calvados or whisky. Put the birds, breast down, or the meat on top of the apples. Deglaze the pan with stock, pour into the pot and add the whipping cream. Cover and cook in the heated oven, turning once, for about 45 minutes for the game birds, to 1$\frac{3}{4}$ hours for the chicken or pork.

Meanwhile, peel, core and slice the remaining apples, and fry them in butter, caramelising them with sugar towards the end.

When birds or meat are done, carve and put on to a hot dish, with the caramelised apple slices. Skim fat from the sauce and sieve, taste for seasoning and heat through. Stir in the double cream and a squeeze of lemon juice. Pour some of the sauce over the meat, and serve the rest separately.

A rice pilaff is the usual accompaniment, with perhaps a few sprigs of watercress tucked round the dish with the apple.

BEEF BURGUNDY STYLE
Boeuf à la bourguignonne

Here is the basic recipe for many kinds of French stew. Alter the beef to chicken, and you have a version of coq au vin; use hare and you have a civet, oxtail and you have a hochepot. Use veal with white wine, and finish with cream and egg yolks, and you have a blanquette, or a coq au Riesling if you choose a young cockerel and the appropriate wine.

Serves 8–12
1.5 kg/3 lb braising or stewing beef, cubed
FOR THE MARINADE
500–750 ml/$\frac{3}{4}$ pt–1$\frac{1}{2}$ pt/scant 2–4 cups red wine
5 tablespoons/6 tbs brandy
large onion, quartered
bouquet garni
sprig of rosemary, optional
12 peppercorns, lightly crushed
level teaspoon salt
FOR THE SAUCE
60 g/2 oz/$\frac{1}{4}$ cup beef dripping, bacon fat or butter
200–250 g/7–8 oz piece of green bacon, diced
2 large onions, chopped
2 large carrots, chopped
3 cloves of garlic, crushed
beef, veal or poultry stock
salt, pepper, sugar
TO FINISH
500 g/1 lb small or pickling onions, peeled
2 level tablespoons sugar
1 tablespoon butter
salt and pepper
250–375 g/8–12 oz small, closed mushrooms, fried
3 slices of bread, cut in triangles, fried
chopped parsley

Leave the meat in the marinade ingredients overnight. The next day, remove and dry the meat. Keep marinade.

In the fat, brown the bacon, then the vegetables and put into a casserole. Then brown the beef and add to the vegetables with the garlic. Pour off fat. Deglaze with the marinade minus onion and pour on to the meat. Add stock to cover. Put on the lid and simmer until the meat is tender—about 2–3 hours. If the sauce is on the copious side, strain it into a wide pan and boil it down hard. Add salt and pepper and a very little sugar. Pour back over the meat, leave to cook for 10 minutes.

While the meat is cooking, caramelise the onions. Put them into a pan in a single layer. Cover with cold water, add the sugar and butter. Boil, without a lid, until the water has evaporated, and the sugar has caramelised to a glossy brown juice. Turn the onions in this, and season.

Arrange the onions and mushrooms on top of the stew, tuck the bread round the side and scatter with parsley.

LEG OF LAMB WITH A GARLIC CROWN
Gigot d'agneau à la couronne d'ail

At lunch with a friend last summer, near Le Mans, I had a leg of pré-salé lamb from Normandy's salt meadows with a great bowl of cooked garlic—1 kg 400 g/2$\frac{3}{4}$ lb before peeling.

Handfuls of garlic surround the pot-roasted gigot

I asked her why she cooked them separately rather than together in the traditional style. She said that this kept the flavours clearer and lighter: I think she was right. All you do is melt enough lard to make a thin layer in a heavy pan. Then pile in the garlic and jam the lid on with foil. Leave on the lowest possible heat, or in a cool oven, 150°C (300°F), gas 2, for 3 hours. Shake the pan occasionally. The garlic should be meltingly soft. Season it well and serve round the lamb, roasted pink.

I reflect that the French have a sparer attitude to their food than we do: the good things come one after another, on their own, rather than in a muddle together on a piled plate. I should add that after lunch, no one breathed garlic or had the slightest touch of indigestion. Here, though, is the richer, Périgord style of combining lamb and garlic. A large chicken, better still a capon, can be cooked in the same way.

Serves 8
2 kg/4 lb leg of lamb
2 tablespoons/3 tbs poultry fat
50–60 cloves of garlic, peeled
3 tablespoons/scant $\frac{1}{4}$ cup brandy
150–300 ml/$\frac{1}{4}$–$\frac{1}{2}$ pt/$\frac{2}{3}$–1$\frac{1}{4}$ cups Sauternes or Montbazillac
salt and pepper

Brown the lamb all over in the fat. Put into a deep pot (flameproof if cooking on top of stove) with the garlic. Warm the brandy, set it alight and pour over the lamb. Add the wine and seasoning. Cover closely and cook as slowly as possible for 3 hours, turning the lamb occasionally. If you can manage a very low and regular heat, allow 5 hours.

Put the meat on a hot dish, surrounded by its crown of garlic. Remove any fat from the juices, season them if necessary and pour them round the meat. Serve with a salad of endive or dandelion.

FRUIT DESSERTS

French cooking at home is simple compared with ours: this is partly because their basic ingredients are so good (meals finish with cheese and fruit every day except Sunday), and partly because their ready-prepared charcuterie, pâtisserie and salads are of a quality we cannot begin to imagine.

In summer, a favourite dessert is a peach skinned and sectioned into a glass, with wine poured over it. Each person prepares their own, especially if it is a lazy meal out-of-doors on a sunny day. And if you are lucky enough to be the guest of a château, you

FROMAGE FRAIS

Every French supermarket in the north at least has a choice of fromage frais at varying fat contents up to 42%. This is a soft, moist cheese, much softer and nearer to a yoghurt consistency than our cottage and curd cheeses with a similar range of fat content. It is this softness and delicacy of flavour that makes it so useful to have always in the refrigerator. Serve it with puddings instead of cream (add a little cream if you like), substitute it for a part of the cream in ices, sauces and the fillings for tarts and quiches. With chopped toasted nuts and glacé fruit or fresh fruit mixed in, it makes a dessert on its own, or just put a bowl of it on the table with plenty of chopped herbs mixed in as a first course. Drained in muslin and mixed with whipped cream, it can be put into heart-shaped moulds to make coeurs à la crème. Our supermarkets now stock Gervais Jockey fromage frais, as well as quark, the German equivalent.

Petits Suisses and Gervais squares are richer and drier forms of fromage frais, and most delicious. These can be stuffed into game birds or guineafowl, plus herbs or some appropriate fruit, before roasting, but usually they are served on their own as a dessert, with cream and sugar, and strawberries or raspberries when they are in season. There are many local forms of these cheeses, made sometimes with goat's milk, and then you may well find them offered along with other cheeses on a cheese board: this is usually a sign that they are of particularly fine quality.

may be handed a crystal bowl of peaches in Champagne, with a dash of raspberry eau de vie. If you make this at home with a less costly sparkling wine, don't soak peaches too long in the wine or else they go soft.

Another simple idea is to put buttered bread or brioche on to a baking sheet, buttered side down. A little butter on top, then wedges of peach, apricot, apple or pear, a dusting of sugar and into a hot oven. When the bread is crisp and brown, the fruit slightly caught and melting, the croûtes aux pêches, apricots, pommes or poires are ready. They can be served plain, with cream, or with a bowl of fromage frais, enriched with a little cream and made bulky and light with a couple of stiffly beaten egg whites—this last mixture is popular, too, with Pithiviers (see below) and fruit tarts.

APPLE TART
Tarte aux pommes

The reason why French apple tarts taste particularly good in the autumn and winter is that they are made with firm eating apples, for example, a reinette variety or Belle de Boskoop. In late spring and early summer Golden Delicious will be used, which by that time has melted in flavour. I read that the Golden Delicious is the world's most successful commercial variety, accounting for 75 per cent of all apples produced: perhaps we should be thankful it is not worse. People making tarts at home will use windfalls and follow a recipe of the kind I give below. Pastrycooks simply fill their tarts with slices of apple, beautifully arranged, which you might prefer to do if you are prepared to buy 1½ kilos (3 lb) Cox's or similarly rich-flavoured eating apples. Eating apples do produce a particularly harmonious flavour which makes one understand why the French do not serve cream—it simply is not necessary as it is with cookers which remain sharp even when sweetened.

Serves 6–8
1 kg/2 lb Cox's or similar eating apples
2 huge cookers, or 1 huge cooker and 1 large quince, or the equivalent in windfalls
sugar
3 tablespoons apricot jam, or quince or apple jelly
PASTRY
300 g/9 oz/2¼ cups flour
200 g/6 oz/¾ cup butter
100 g/3 oz/scant ½ cup caster sugar
pinch salt
iced water or egg to mix

Set aside 4 of the best eating apples. Cut up all the rest of the fruit, core, peel and all, except of course for blemishes and bruises. Run a thin layer of water over the base of a large pan, tip in the fruit and cook, covered, until the juices flow. Then stir up the fruit and cook without the lid until it is tender. Sieve. Return to the rinsed out pan to boil down a little if the purée is watery. Add sugar to taste and cool.

Make the pastry in the usual way. Chill for at least 30 minutes. Roll out and line a 25–28-cm (10–11-inch) tart tin. Prick the base lightly. Return to the refrigerator.

Finally peel and core the 4 eating apples set aside.

Cut in halves and slice thinly into a bowl of water, very lightly salted or acidulated with a tablespoon of lemon juice.

Spread the cold purée over the pastry case, filling it no more than halfway. Drain and dry the apple slices. Arrange them in overlapping concentric circles, so that the straight side of each semi-circular slice is concealed. The outer circle should lie one way, the next circle the other way. And so on. Keep a nice slice or two to make a central rosette. Sprinkle with sugar.

Bake at 200°C (400°F), gas 6, for 15 minutes, then lower the heat to 175°C (350°F) gas 4 and bake until the slices are tender and the pastry nicely brown at the edges—about 15 minutes more. Be guided entirely by appearance and the feel of the slices when tested.

Melt the jam or jelly with 3 tablespoons of water, then sieve if lumpy. Brush over the hot tart, including the pastry edges. Serve warm for the best flavour.

LEMON TART
Tarte au citron

Of the numerous lemon tart recipes, this is my favourite. It is rich and refreshing. The pastry is a slightly unorthodox pâte sucrée.

Serves 6
250 g/8 oz/2 cups plain flour
½ teaspoon salt
60 g/2 oz/¼ cup caster sugar
2 egg yolks, beaten
125 g/4 oz/½ cup butter, softened
FOR THE FILLING
2 large eggs
100 g/3½ oz/7 tbs caster sugar
150 g/5 oz/1¼ cups ground almonds
100 ml/3½ fl oz/good ⅓ cup whipping cream
6 lemons
200 g/7 oz/scant cup granulated sugar
100 ml/3½ fl oz/good ½ cup water
23-cm/9-in loose-bottomed flan tin

For the pastry mix the first four ingredients to a sandy texture, then beat in the butter to make a dough. Chill for an hour, then use to line the flan tin. Set oven at moderate to moderately hot, 180–190°C (350–375°F), gas 4–5.

For the filling, beat together the first four ingredients, then grate in the rind of 4 lemons, and add the juice of 2 only. This leaves you with 2 whole lemons and 2 minus their outer zest. Put the filling into the pastry. Bake in the heated oven for 25 minutes or so until nicely browned.

Meanwhile, slice the whole lemons thinly, discarding the end pieces and the pips. Put the slices into a pan, cover with water and simmer them gently. Remove the pith from the remaining 2 lemons and slice them thinly as well. When the peel of the first lot of slices begins to soften, add the second lot of slices, and continue simmering until tender. Drain well.

Make a syrup by dissolving the sugar in the water in a shallow pan. When the syrup is clear, bring it to boiling point, then simmer gently for 2–3 minutes or until thick. Slip in the lemon slices and cook them for 15 minutes or until candied and soft.

Arrange the slices on the lemon tart, the ones with the peel outside, the rest in the centre. Brush the syrup over the lemon slices. Serve hot, warm or cold, with extra cream if you like.

PITHIVIERS ALMOND CAKE
Gâteau de Pithiviers feuilleté

The French always buy their Pithiviers cakes from the pastrycook at great expense. This surprises me, as it is one of the simplest cakes in the world and looks sensational. If you are good at puff pastry, here is a chance to show off your skill. But even if you have to buy pastry from a local confectioner who makes it with butter, or the ready-made frozen type, then you will have a delightful cake just the same.

Serves 8
500 g/1 lb weight puff pastry
beaten egg, to glaze
icing sugar
FOR THE FILLING
125 g/4 oz/1 cup almonds
125 g/4 oz/½ cup caster sugar
60 g/2 oz/¼ cup melted butter
2 large egg yolks
2 generous tablespoons/3 tbs double cream
2–3 tablespoons/3–4 tbs rum, brandy or malt whisky
2–3 macaroons, crushed (optional)

Roll out the pastry. Cut a circle about 24 cm (9½ in) in diameter, and another about 25 cm (10 in). Put the smaller one on a moistened baking sheet or into a shallow pie plate. Mix the filling ingredients in the order given, grinding the almonds first—you need not blanch them, but wash the dustiness off the skin.

Brush a wide border with beaten egg on the

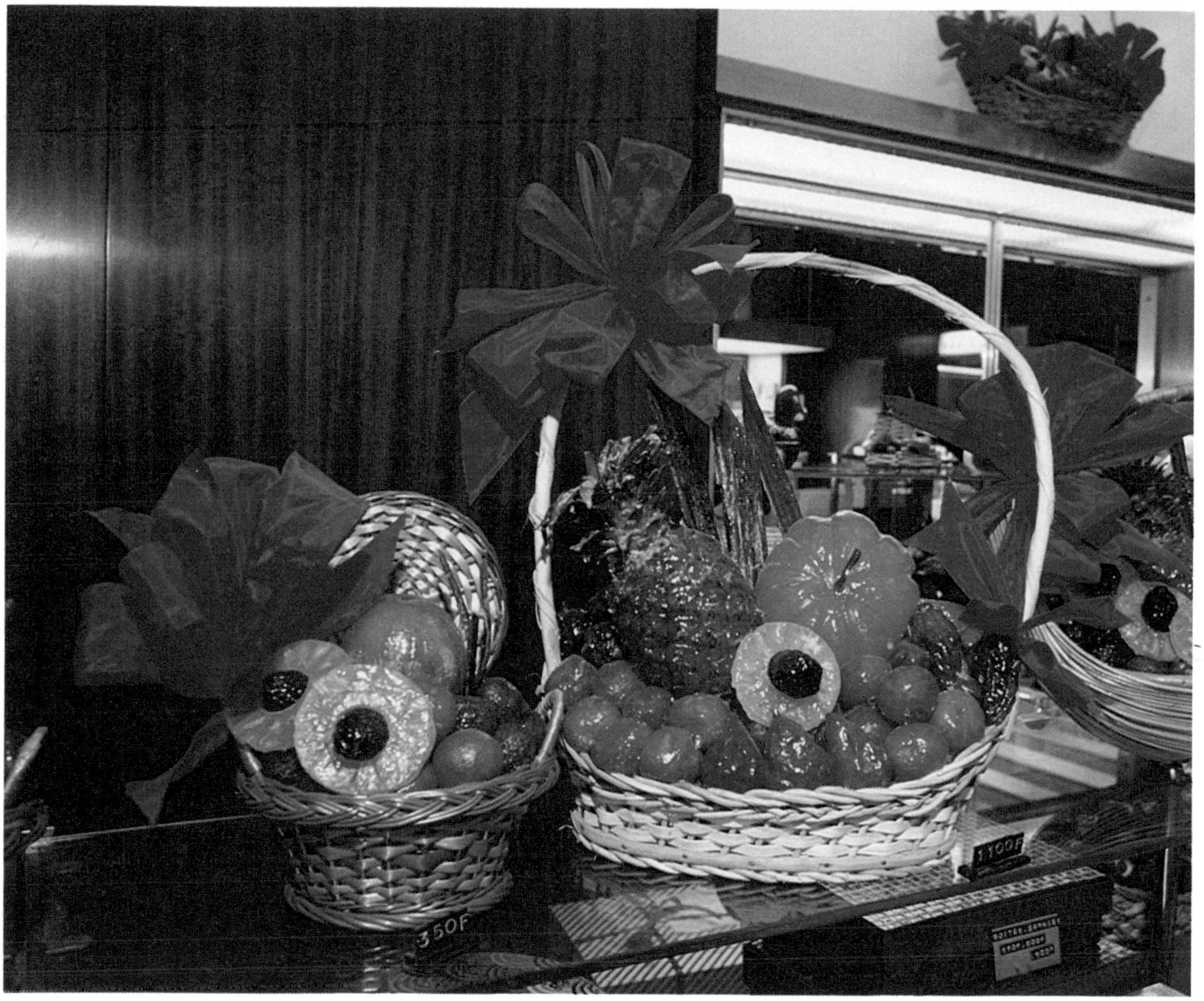

Opulent glacé fruit comes from Clermont-Ferrand in central France, and from Apt in Provence

smaller pastry circle, and pile the filling in the middle. Put the larger circle on top, gently pressing it down round the edge to seal. Make a central hole, brush with beaten egg and leave 5 minutes. Set oven at hot, 230°C (450°F), gas 8.

Now for the decoration, which is what distinguishes a Pithiviers from the many other pastry and almond cream cakes in the French repertoire. Knock up the pastry edges, then make two nicks opposite each other, then two more so that the cake edge is quartered. Use this as a guide to make 4–8 more, equally placed nicks if you like. Push up the pastry with your thumbs at each nick to scallop the edge into petals. With the point of a small sharp knife and working from the centre, score the top in curves like the petals of a flower, taking care not to cut through the pastry.

Bake in the heated oven for 15 minutes then check the pastry: if it is only lightly coloured, leave at same temperature for another 15 minutes. Otherwise lower the heat to 200°C (400°F), gas 6 and leave for about 20 minutes. Be guided entirely by eye.

When the cake is a beautiful brown and well risen, remove from the oven and place the baking sheet or plate on a newspaper. Dredge the top evenly and not too heavily with icing sugar. Raise the oven temperature to 230°C (450°F), gas 8. Slip the Pithiviers on to the top shelf, close the door and leave for a few minutes until the sugar melts to a deep brown glaze. Keep looking—within reason (you do not want to lower the temperature too

CREME FRAICHE

French cream has a slightly acid tang because it is treated at the dairy with a starter culture, after pasteurisation. So, too, is our soured cream, but the two are not the same: crème fraîche has a butter-fat content of 35% (equivalent to our whipping cream), whereas soured cream has a butter-fat content of 18% (like single cream). However, you can use soured cream, or better still, buttermilk, to make crème fraîche.

Mix 2 parts double cream with 1 part soured cream in a pan. Bring slowly to just under blood heat, 32°C (80°F), pour into a pot, cover and leave to ripen for 8 hours at 25°C (75°F). Stir up and store, covered, in the refrigerator for up to 10 days. This is a splendid cream with fruit or for sauces.

In my French recipes, I have usually indicated whipping or double cream with lemon juice, where a French cook would use crème fraîche. This is a quick alternative, but you will do better making your own crème fraîche.

It is fair to say that many French chefs and housewives envy us our choice of creams, and consider that our unpasteurised cream from Jersey herds is superior to even the best crème fraîche from Normandy.

much). Alternatively do this under a hot grill.

Serve warm, rather than hot, with cream, immediately after baking.

MALAKOFF/CHESTNUT CHARLOTTE
Charlotte Malakoff/St Clément

Why Malakoff? The pudding does have the look of a bulgy stockade. I imagine it was first made and named in the 1850s after the Malakoff tower at Sebastopol that the French took in the Crimean War. Many generals were killed, making it a victory glorious enough to celebrate. The French being given to la gloire, have an odd way of naming dishes after battles: chicken Marengo, navarin of lamb.

Why St Clément? Not oranges and lemons for the French, but chestnuts, since he was the name saint of Clément Faugier, of Privas in the Ardèche. When the silk trade slumped in the 19th century, he began to commercialize a local delicacy, marrons glacés, to give people work. The firm produces chestnut purées as well, and prospers.

CHARLOTTE
2 packets boudoir biscuits
6 tablespoons/⅓ cup rum or kirsch
24 lumps sugar

MALAKOFF
200 g/7 oz/1¾ cups almonds
250 g/8 oz/1 cup sugar
250 g/8 oz/1 cup unsalted French butter
pinch salt
3–4 tablespoons rum or kirsch
250 ml/8 fl oz/1 cup double cream

CLÉMENT
500-g/1-lb can sweetened chestnut purée
100 g/3½ oz/scant ½ cup unsalted butter
3–4 tablespoons/¼–⅓ cup rum or kirsch
300 ml/½ pt/1¼ cups double cream
bits of broken marrons glacés to decorate

Take a large pudding basin for the Malakoff, a charlotte mould for the St Clément. Put two strips of foil into the basin or mould, then line with the biscuits. Dip the base biscuits in the alcohol mixed with an equal amount of water. Make a caramel with the 24 sugar lumps. Dip the long side of each biscuit into the caramel before placing it against the sides, so that they are all glued together. Keep the sugar side out. Mix the remaining alcohol into the filling and put in the basin, with the remaining biscuits. Cover and leave overnight in the refrigerator. Turn out, after easing the charlotte by means of the foil straps. Decorate with toasted almonds or marrons glacés.

MALAKOFF Set aside a few almonds to blanch and toast for the final decoration, grind the rest unblanched not too finely. Beat sugar and butter, add almonds, salt and alcohol. Whip cream and fold in. Taste and add more alcohol if you like.

ST CLÉMENT Cream the butter, add purée and alcohol. Dilute any caramel remaining from the biscuits with a little, very hot water, just enough to prevent it hardening, and mix with the cream. Whisk until firm. Put chestnut mixture into the biscuits first, then the cream.

CHEESES

Every European country makes cheese—some kinds become famous internationally—but no country in the world makes cheese as France does. The old cliché—was it Churchill who was responsible for it?—that it was impossible to govern a country with over 365 cheeses indicates the difference. Nowadays, I would say there must be well over 400 cheeses, so fast do new ones appear. Some are what I think of as fakes, cheese not quite of the top quality smashed up with other things, emulsified, and stuck with walnuts or fancy pepper mixtures, the definition residing in decor rather than manufacture. Such baby affairs have nothing to do with a Gaperon or a fourme d'Ambert, or with one of those squeezed handfuls of goat cheese that you buy once in a market and never find again. We bought such a cheese, wrapped in chestnut leaves, dripping whey, from a gypsy in St Girons in the Pyrenees. It was the best cheese we had ever eaten. Journeys back to St Girons have never disclosed another.

What one must also realize about French cheese is that much has been taken over by the local dairy, in other words a factory. If you buy a farm Camembert from one of the two farms making it, or which were making it when we went that way a few years ago, you see immediately and then you taste that it has nothing in common with the trite cheeses that normally go under that name. When you eat a farm Camembert you see immediately why Colette as a child in bed with a temperature demanded Camembert rather than rice pudding or breast of chicken, a story that seems odd if you only know the factory kind. It is the same with Brie. In such cheeses the difference is far greater than ever it is between, say, a farm and a factory Cheddar.

When we first went to France over twenty years ago, goat cheese was declining. Our small village of Trôo had been famous for its goat cheese (and it still is according to some inadequate reference books). By the time we arrived in 1961, all the petit Trôo cheeses sold up and down the Loire valley came from a dairy across the river in the next commune, and were made of cow's milk. Nowadays goat cheese is booming, though not alas in Trôo. All over

A flock of milking sheep on the Causses near Roquefort

the west of France, especially in Poitou and the Vendée, farm notices call your attention to it. Often the couple in charge will be two young people escaping city life and redundancy. Their cheese will be perfectly made, their goats shiny clean and affectionate—but the product will not always have the character of the less hygienic peasant farm cheese. Such cheeses have a short life, though in the south this is prolonged by storing them in olive oil with herbs to give new flavours.

Another cheese which has known a modern revival—thanks to the invention of a milking machine for sheep—is Roquefort. As you drive across the Causse country to the south of the Massif Central you are likely to see huge flocks of sheep gathering round a stone-paved dew pond, precious water in dry upland. Cheeses made from their milk, along with similar cheeses from Corsica, end up in the caves at Roquefort where the blue veining develops in a controlled humidity.

To us with our tradition of Cheddars and Cheshires, the strangest of all are the enormous discs of Emmenthal, Gruyère, Comté, Beaufort, the first with its large holes, the second with holes the size of hazelnuts and the other two with hardly any holes at all, but all having a firm close texture that in inferior copies can be rubbery. They are the cheeses of transhumance, made when cattle go up to the high flowery pastures for the summer, cheeses of the Alps where Switzerland and France meet. French versions are close to Swiss originals, though the Swiss would claim superiority of flavour. In either case, buy from the whole cheese, which will have been properly matured. Vacuum packaged cheese is young and bland. Another Swiss cheese that is taking over in France is raclette: you can buy special apparatus to hold it and melt the cut surface, which is scraped off—*raclette* means scraper—on to new potatoes.

A fat book is needed to catalogue such a perplexity and luckily there is one, by Pierre Androuet, the *Guide du fromage*, translated by John Githens. Monsieur Androuet has a famous shop near the Gare St Lazare in Paris, where well over 100 cheeses may be bought—or sampled in the restaurant upstairs, with the appropriate wines, and the rustic brown breads that the baker Poilâne has made so popular in recent years. For a glimpse into the richness of French cheesemaking, this is the place to go.

The style of both shop and restaurant is 1920s monastic, which makes for solidity and more comfort than you might imagine. We settled for a lunch of four cheese dishes, and were much entertained by our two neighbours who had come to Paris from Marseilles with the express purpose of working their way through the special Androuet cheese and wine lunch. It consists of seven courses of cheeses, grouped in families, each one served with appropriate wines. Out of the 120 cheeses offered, they sampled 40 each, making notes at first. Should you ever feel inclined to give a cheese party, take note of the contents and order of those seven courses—each one served on a huge wicker tray:

1 Triple cream cheeses, with 75% fat content, e.g. Brillat Savarin
2 Pressed curd cheeses, the mountain Emmental, Gruyère and so on
3 Camembert and Brie style
4 Cendré cheeses (ash-covered cheeses, often matured in hay or leaves, from the Orléanais and Pithiviers areas); salty cheeses such as Neufchâtel; Chaource cheese
5 Goat cheeses
6 Strong-tasting and strong-smelling cheeses, Maroilles, Munster, Langres, Epoisses
7 Blue cheeses, e.g. Roquefort, fourme d'Ambert, Bresse, and some of the robust cheeses that are not strong enough for the sixth course.

As we left, I bought a round wooden box of cheeses, Monsieur Androuet's choice for a large dinner party—a slice each of Comté and Roquefort, plus a Brillat Savarin (the richest and best of Normandy cream cheeses), a Livarot, a Saint-Maure goat cheese, a farm Camembert and an Entrammes from Mayenne. And in the introduction to his book there are many suggestions for a smaller cheese board which would fit in with shopping possibilities in other countries. My own feeling is that if choice is limited, as it can be outside large towns, you do best to go for one perfect cheese, a Vacherin for instance, or a fine goat cheese.

The French incidentally do not eat butter with bread and cheese (nor do they serve biscuits and celery in the English style). Sometimes the cheese comes along with the salad. This often happens in our regions of Touraine and Anjou where the small mild cheeses marry well with salad greens and a walnut oil vinaigrette. Some restaurants these days serve tiny goat's cheeses, the crottins from Chavignol near Sancerre very often, baked or grilled to melting point, on a bed of mixed greenery: usually this comes as a first course, in which case you do not serve a cheese course after the meat or game. The particular point of serving cheese after the main course, before the dessert, is to finish off the wine, whether it be red or white. You are then clear to serve a sweet wine with pudding or fruit. If you consider the question of wines, however humble they may be, you obviously cannot return to the main wine of the meal after a pudding, as you would have to do if you served cheese last in the English manner of the past. Today with the increase in wine drinking many people arrange their meal in the French order, leaving the dessert to run naturally into the coffee stage.

I would not want to give the impression that Androuet's is the only cheese shop in Paris. You may get cheeses every bit as good in small shops elsewhere: your choice will be more limited, that is all. A favourite place of mine is between the Bibliothèque Nationale and the Comédie Française. I could not resist a rusty-red cone of cheese I saw there one day, labelled 'suppositoire du diable'. It turned out to be a northern speciality. One of the strong-tasting cheeses, a boulette d'Avesnes. It has been given its saucy nickname by some of the actors at the Comédie Française.

GREAT BRITAIN

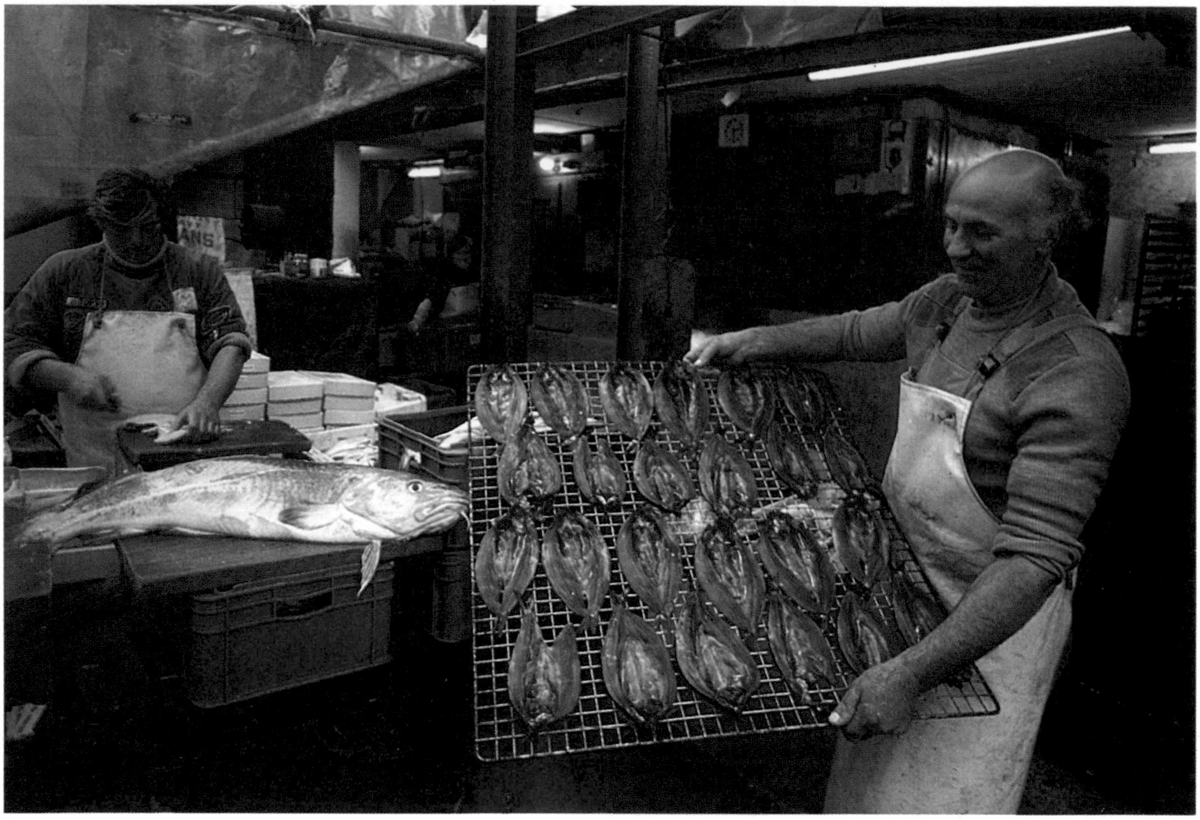

A tray of kippers cured at Newton Abbot in Devon

Round the Mediterranean they knock down the olives (and pick the grapes). In Britain our ancestors knocked down the acorns which fattened the pigs, which filled the pot, which fed the stomach (followed by a wash-down of mead made from honey and meadowsweet).

It is in that contrast that I see an inkling of some British habits of cooking and eating. One of the worst habits is tackling too much food at one go. Chefs from abroad find to their horror that what they cook is judged by bulk as much as taste—'plenty to eat' is still a favourite commendation.

How did the overloading begin? In amplitude of supply, I suspect. Great Britain was Great Larder, Great Barn. Abroad, poor soils meant more grubbing round for food, more discovery, more invention; whereas our ancestors sat down to plenty, without having to take trouble. Is this why we have some fine hams, but little charcuterie? And roast beef, roast lamb, but few good beef stews and a repetitious collection of mutton hotpot dishes? Abroad, where it was often a question of eat or starve, all sorts of mundane edible items turned out to be delicacies after all, but delicacies which our people, our ancestors, didn't need to eat.

Why don't we, for instance, eat most kinds of edible mushroom? Like cèpes, which the pigs once knocked over in their rush to the autumn woods for acorns? Or girolles, which haven't even got an English or Scottish name? How they would have enhanced skirlie in the Highlands where they grow so abundantly! Bilberries are another neglected food and marsh samphire; so too are tripe and oatmeal pancakes outside the

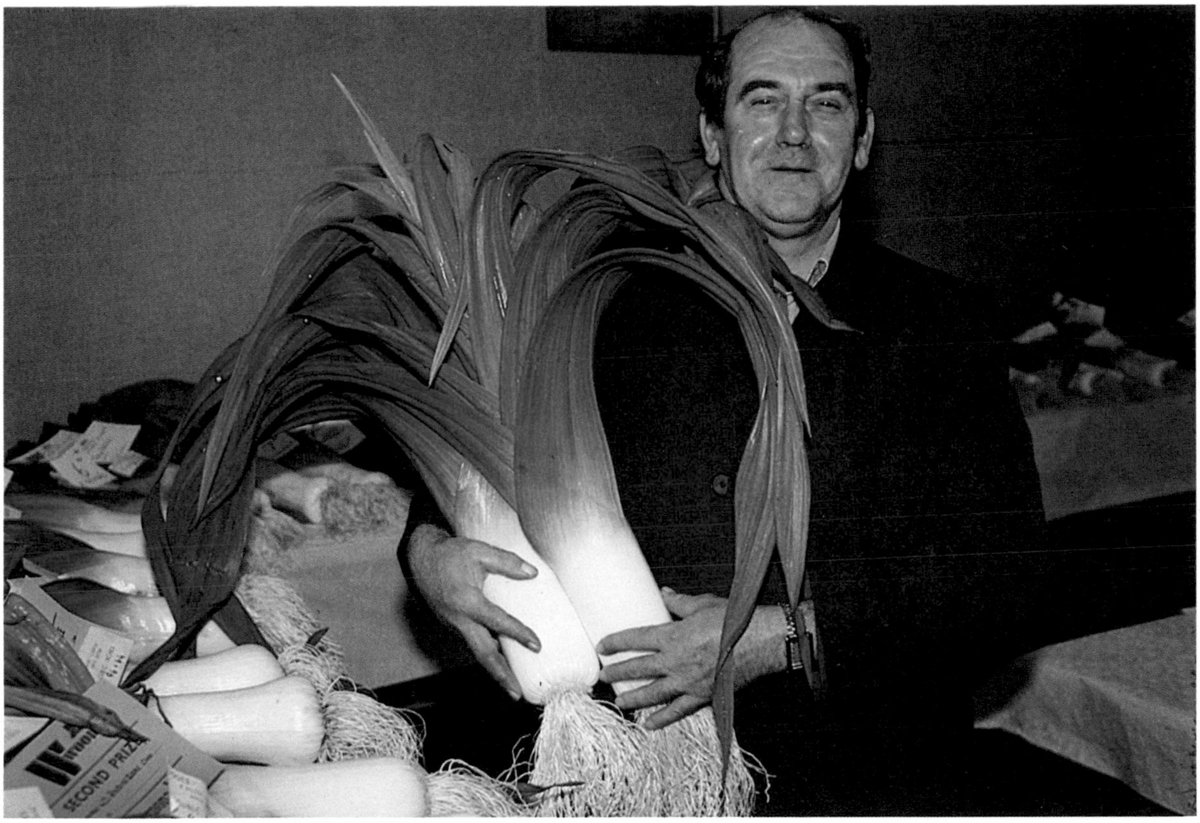

Prize leeks grown for competitions, not eating

sensible regions of the north, as well as laverbread. Even fish is neglected—choice at most fishmongers' makes a poor showing by comparison, say, with the crammed shops and restaurants of Galicia in Spain. The British do not love their good things enough to pay for them (which is why the best is sold abroad), neither do they have much curiosity about them. Few people eat seakale regularly, one of Britain's native vegetables. Peppers, avocados, aubergines, yes—seakale no, or rarely.

I imagine that this is why many restaurants in the country are run by people from other countries. Something which makes us unique. In Düsseldorf, the best places offer German food, in Lyon or Barcelona, French or Spanish food. Go to Manchester, and you have a choice of Armenian, Spanish, Nepalese, Indian, French or Chinese—five Chinese—restaurants, with only one offering food in what might be called the new English style.

It is of course thanks to immigrants that private as well as public food has become more lively in the last twenty years. Everyone complains, often rightly, and deplores the declining quality of, for instance, chickens and meat generally, commercial pork pies and sausages, but compared with public and private eating when I was young, it is miraculously improved. At least above a certain level. What does make people resentful is the impossibility of finding honest simple food as a matter of course, in surroundings that do not smell of stale oil and malt vinegar. If you are caught in a strange town, at a railway or bus station, at an airport or on the motorway, there is nowhere pleasant to sit for an hour over honest, high-quality food. I mean no more than a ham sandwich made with ham

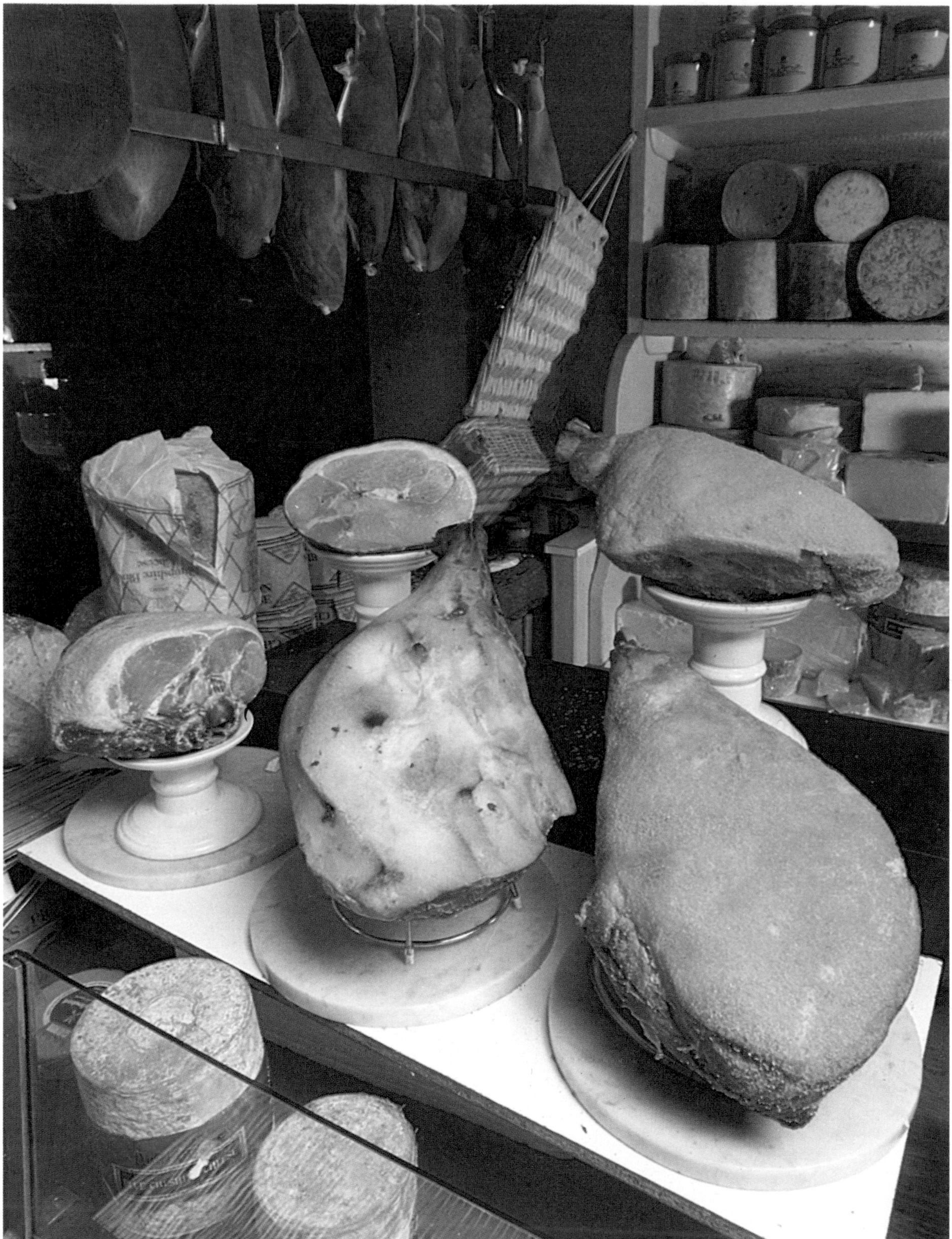

off the bone and proper bread, plus good coffee or tea or decent beer. Where pub food has improved, the place will be crowded; in any case hours are restricted and you cannot take children with you.

My other grouse is the poor supply of good basic ingredients and skilful, ready-prepared food. No one can respond to shelves packed with so much trash, cubed, sliced, bulked-out with water or air, artifically coloured and flavoured, plastic-wrapped and sweaty. If someone wants to give a dinner party, everything has to be made at home, often starting with the bread. With a few brilliant exceptions, most places outside central London do not run to a skilled charcutier to provide a special pâté, or a skilled pâtissier to make a special ice or elegant cake. Cooks elsewhere in Europe do not have to work nearly as hard to give a celebratory meal. Or a good homely one.

These problems are obvious to anyone who cares about good eating. Efforts are made to break through the blanket of sliced bread that suffocates the country. Some look back to a past when much of our food was admirable, to the hundred or so years culminating in Eliza Acton's *Modern Cookery* of 1845. The Scots base their efforts on *The Cook and Housewife's Manual* (1826), by Mistress Margaret Dods, published under Sir Walter Scott's influence, which contains a section devoted to Scottish recipes. Some people in Wales resuscitate the cookery of the fictitious Hermit of Gower, as chronicled by Lady Llanover. In Dublin, folklorists and archaeologists delve into Irish food beyond the potato, or before it.

At the same time publishers jump in with an unsatisfactory splash of books—there must be more published in London than elsewhere in Europe—that might collectively be titled, *Ye Olde Barsetshire Farmhouse Kitchen and Country House Recipes.* A sad mistake, even if they sell.

If our food has improved in recent years, foreign restaurants apart, it is where we have pegged our efforts on to Elizabeth David's books. From Mediterranean, Italian and French food, from our own food of the past, she draws conclusions that may seem obvious, but if heeded lead to revolution and a battle-royal with big commercial food interests. Insist on first-class ingredients is her message, and prepare them with respect and affection, without pretentiousness. She has made us look at the basis of good food in France or in Italy, at the underlying need for quality of product. Of course many of her recipes have become famous and figure on the menus of some of our pleasantest restaurants, but it is her concern with ingredients themselves that has been such a stimulus to food writing and interest. The nouvelle cuisine chefs of France have been best sellers in Britain: their practice has had an effect notably on top restaurants, and reinforced attainable goals that Elizabeth David had been urging for over twenty years. Whenever I come across another small, busy specialist shop, someone making sheep's milk yoghurt or curing their own hams from properly fed pigs, her influence is never far away.

It is no good trying to take refuge in spurious regionalism; we have to go on with our old magpie style—our eclectic style, if you prefer a grander name—bits from here and there, whatever takes our fancy on our travels abroad or into our own past of splendid puddings and pies. And then develop and display it in a fresher, more knowledgeable way.

The curing of black Bradenham hams with molasses and cochineal—one is shown in the centre of this display of hams, skinned for carving—ceased in 1981, soon after the photograph was taken

CURRIED PARSNIP SOUP

Parsnips are very much our taste alone. Although French cooks will put a parsnip into pot-au-feu, they regard it as cattle food. Italians fatten Parma ham pigs on parsnips. People adapting mid-European or Central American recipes for an English audience regard them as fit substitutes for Hamburg parsley or sweet potatoes (they aren't, being much too individual in flavour). We have the sense to deep-fry them as chips, mash them with cream and butter for a purée, set them to brown under beef or roast with potatoes—and now, it seems, to turn them into this soup, which I made up for an *Observer* article in 1969.

Serves 8
1 large or 2 medium parsnips, peeled and cut up
medium potato, peeled and diced
125 g/4 oz/1 cup chopped onion
90 g/3 oz/⅓ cup butter
clove of garlic, crushed
level tablespoon flour, optional
rounded teaspoon curry powder
generous litre/2 pts/5 cups hot beef stock
150 ml/¼ pt/⅔ cup cream
chopped chives and parsley

Cook the parsnips, potato and onion in the butter with the garlic for about 10 minutes, in a heavy pan. Keep the lid on and shake the contents occasionally or stir them up. Mix the flour, if used, and curry powder together and stir into the vegetables; cook for a couple of minutes, then add the stock gradually. Simmer until the parsnip is tender.

Liquidise or process the vegetables, or put through the Mouli-légumes for a rougher texture. Return to the pan. Dilute the consistency, if you like, with water—the soup should be neither thick nor strong, but delicately comforting. Correct the seasoning, adding a pinch more curry powder if it seems right (don't overdo it, though). Pour in the cream and reheat without boiling. Scatter with chives and parsley, or just chives. Serve with croûtons of bread, fried in butter.

WATERCRESS SOUP

Hampshire is the country for watercress—and trout—with its clear streams. The watercress farm is a place of cold beauty: huge springy, green cushions of leaves, confined in wide concrete basins, with stretches of fresh spring water running over gravel where watercress has recently been cut for the market. The water, of certified purity, comes from deep boreholes. Never pick watercress growing wild; you cannot see pollution in water but it is often there in the clearest streams.

A watercress farm in Hampshire, showing the shallow beds of close greenery

A tureen of cockie-leekie, floating with prunes and leeks, one of Scotland's oldest and best dishes

You can prolong the vigour of ready-cut bunches of watercress for a day or two by wrapping them in plastic bags and storing in the vegetable drawer of the refrigerator. Such stalks as have roots can sometimes be planted successfully in pots to give you a small bonus crop. If you need to store watercress for up to a week, you will do best to buy it in sealed plastic bags. It seems expensive but there's no wastage.

Watercress sandwiches seem an especially British fancy, but everywhere in Europe sprigs of watercress are served with grills and game, or with duck, or wild duck, and orange.

Serves 8
about 150 g/5–6 oz picked over watercress
250 g/8 oz/1⅓ cups peeled, diced potato
125 g/4 oz/1 cup finely chopped onion
60 g/2 oz/¼ cup butter
1 litre/2 pts/5 cups hot water
salt and pepper
grated nutmeg
up to 150 ml/¼ pt/⅔ cup cream

Follow the method for the parsnip soup, using water instead of stock.

PALESTINE SOUP

Jerusalem artichokes were first introduced into England, and grown in Hampshire, in 1617 by the young botanist John Goodyer. (He started with two tubers from a French friend, and had enough to stock the county). They came to Europe from Canada soon after 1605, and were recognised as being relations of the sunflower or girasole—hence Jerusalem artichoke, and Palestine soup.

Follow watercress soup recipe, page 140, substituting 500 g (1 lb) peeled, sliced artichokes for the watercress, and ham or bacon stock for the water, or a light poultry stock, with 3 rashers of smoked bacon added to it.

COCKIE-LEEKIE

Fynes Moryson, the traveller, visited Scotland in 1598 and described a kind of cockie-leekie. He dined in a grand house. The lower tables had broth with a bit of meat, the high table 'had a pullet with some prunes in the broth.' What makes the dish so good is the simmering together of chicken and beef or beef stock, plus the two simple embellishments, prunes and leeks. We have few recipes in which meats are cooked together, no bollito misto or olla podrida, which is, I think, a pity.

Use a chicken of good flavour. If it has to be a roaster, buy a large one and add it after the beef has simmered for at least half an hour.

Serves 8–10
boiling fowl or capon
1 kg/2 lb piece of stewing beef, e.g. shin, tied up, or 2 litres/3½ pts/8¾ cups beef stock
1.5 kg/2–3 lb leeks, trimmed
500 g/1 lb/2⅔ cups prunes, soaked if necessary
salt and pepper
chopped parsley

Fit the bird, breast down if it is a boiling fowl, into a large pot with the beef, if used. Cover with water or beef stock. Bring slowly to the boil and skim.

Slice half the leeks and set aside. Tie the rest into a bundle and put into the pot when the liquid is clear. When the meat is almost cooked, put in the prunes and add seasoning. Complete the cooking. Put in the sliced leeks and simmer 5 more minutes. Skim off the fat.

To serve, discard the bundle of leeks. Either serve the broth in bowls, with a slice each of chicken and beef, a prune or two and a few slightly crisp leeks. Or serve the broth first, sprinkled with some parsley and plenty of extra pepper, with the meats, prunes, leeks as a main course. If you choose the first way, you can make an elegant dish of it, like a Japanese soup and follow it with a different unrelated main course. Serve the rest of the chicken and beef another day.

SEAKALE

A thoroughly English vegetable that the English neglect. It has been appreciated by French chefs and one American president. Discerning English gardeners grow it, but you rarely see it on sale. It grows wild on the southern coast, where the beach meets the land—sand and pebbles blown up over the plant have the effect of blanching the stalks, which are the parts you eat. If they are the slightest bit coloured, the stalks will be bitter.

Wash the stalks well, together with the small yellow leaves. Steam or boil them, like asparagus, and serve with melted butter or hollandaise sauce (see page 114) or with an old-fashioned cream sauce:

Melt 175 g (6 oz/¾ cup) butter, diced, in a wide sauté or frying pan, then stir in 250 ml (8 fl oz/½ cup) double cream and salt, pepper and lemon juice to taste. Once the ingredients are amalgamated—it takes a few seconds only, so do not overheat—pour into a warmed sauceboat. If the sauce turns oily at the edges, stir in 2 tablespoons of cold water off the heat.

SCOTCH EGGS

The reason why most Scotch eggs are so disgusting is that they are made with poor sausagemeat and are not eaten quickly enough. Make an effort to buy free-range eggs with bright yolks, as well as good sausagemeat, and serve the Scotch eggs while they are still warm, if possible, or just cool.

Serves 6
6 hard-boiled eggs
flour
750 g/1½ lb sausages or sausagemeat
beaten egg, seasoned with salt and pepper
plenty of white breadcrumbs

When cooking the eggs, give them 7–8 minutes boiling so that they are not too hard. Shell them carefully and roll them in flour. Skin the sausages and form them into six mounds, or divide the sausagemeat into six equal mounds.

Dampen your hands and pat out the first mound of sausagemeat. Shake surplus flour from an egg, then put it on the sausage, shaping it carefully round so that the egg is completely enclosed. Repeat with the other eggs. Roll them in beaten egg, then in breadcrumbs and deep-fry 170°C (335°F), until golden brown, or shallow-fry in a good cm (½ in) clarified butter or oil. Serve whole, with one or two cut in half.

Quail eggs, treated in the same way, make a good first course, with two cut in halves and served in a lettuce nest per person.

BOXTY PANCAKES

Boxty is the Ulster name for these pancakes, after the tin box or cocoa tin that was pierced all over and used as a grater in poor households. There is also boxty bread, which contains shredded potato, but the pancakes are much more enjoyable, and are like German Kartoffelpuffer (see recipe on page 188). The Irish eat their pancakes with sugar, lemon juice, or jam. They go well, too, with bacon and meat dishes.

Serves 4–5
750 g/1½ lb potatoes, scrubbed
level teaspoon each salt and bicarbonate of soda
250 g/8 oz/2 cups flour
buttermilk, whey or milk
butter or oil, for frying

HAGGIS

People shudder at the idea of haggis. I am not sure why because it is only another sausage, and no odder in shape than, say, mortadella. Perhaps they think of it as an odd food from the wilder Highland glens. It is no more Scottish in origin than goulash. A number of recipes exist for it in English court cookery from the middle ages to the 17th century. It is tempting to see haggis as a form of the French 'hachis', meaning something chopped, but our dictionaries will not have this and maintain the origin of the word is unknown.

What the Scots have done for haggis—which is the chopped cooked pluck (liver, lights and heart) of a sheep mixed with onions, toasted oatmeal and suet—is to set it off with neeps (swede) and whisky (single malt is best, especially one of the peaty Islay whiskies). That was inspiration.

Haggis can be bought in many parts of Britain these days, and Charles Macsween & Son, the Edinburgh butchers, sell more haggis south of the border than in Scotland (they complain that Scots eat haggis on Burns Night all over the world, then more or less ignore it the rest of the year). You can buy it from them by post. They also supply especially splendid haggis for grand occasions, and dried swede so that you can eat haggis in summer—comforting on a drenching July day. The best thing is to try different brands of haggis and find the one that suits you best. Up in Carlisle, I saw haggis made in garlic sausage size and shape, for slicing; next day at my hotel I had it for breakfast with eggs, bacon and sausage as part of the standard northern breakfast.

TO BOIL A HAGGIS Cover it with tepid water and bring to simmering point. Cover and cook gently for $1\frac{1}{2}$ hours, turning it over occasionally. Peel and cube a swede—called turnip in Scotland as well as neep—and cook it in a little salted water. Drain, purée and reheat with plenty of butter and pepper. Put round the haggis on a dish. Serve very hot, with very hot plates. Make a cut and spoon out the inside. Make sure everyone has some whisky with a little water to drink with it.

If you want to see how you like haggis, make a 'pot' or 'pan' haggis yourself in a pudding basin.

250 g/8 oz sheep's liver, or 125 g/4 oz sheep's liver and a sheep's heart
125 g/4 oz whole onion
90 g/3 oz/$\frac{1}{2}$ cup pinhead oatmeal
60 g/2 oz/scant $\frac{1}{2}$ cup grated suet
salt, pepper
approx 300 ml/$\frac{1}{2}$ pt/$1\frac{1}{4}$ cups liquor from cooking liver

John MacSween and some of his finest haggis

Simmer liver or liver and heart with the onion in water to cover for 30–40 minutes. When tender, cool and mince both meat and onion, or chop them. Put oatmeal in a heavy frying pan or non-stick frying pan and stir it over a moderate to high heat until lightly browned: be careful not to burn it. Mix meat, onions, oatmeal and suet, season well and add enough liquor from the liver to make a soft dropping consistency. Turn into a well buttered basin and cover with foil. Steam for 2 hours. Serve with mashed swede, and with mashed potato or the two mixed together with butter and chives (this is known as Clapshot). Drink whisky with it.

I find that plenty of butter is required with haggis. The recipe above comes from Atholl Crescent, the famous Edinburgh domestic science college, and appeared in *The Home Book of Scottish Cookery*, by Aileen King and Fiona Dunnett.

Boil half the potatoes, then peel and weigh out 250 g (8 oz); keep them warm. Grate enough of the remaining potatoes, peel included if you like, to provide an equal weight, using the coarse side of the grater, or the julienne blade of a mandolin. Put a clean cloth into a basin. Tip in the potato shreds and wring hard so that the juice falls into the basin. Put the potato shreds into another basin, then the reserved cooked potatoes, and mash them down.

The juice in the basin will separate to leave a clear liquid on top and the starch underneath (though this does not happen with all varieties of potato). Pour off the clear liquid. Scrape the starch into the mashed potatoes. Sift the salt and soda with the flour and mix into the potatoes, adding enough of your chosen liquid to make a soft dropping consistency.

Heat a frying pan or griddle, grease well and fry spoonfuls of mixture, turning them as they brown and the whiskery edges become crisp. A frying pan permits a shallow depth of fat, which gives you crisper pancakes than the drier pancakes cooked on a griddle.

WELSH RABBIT

Not rarebit, but a kind of joke against the Welsh that they were proud to take up themselves in the end. It began as plain toasted cheese, the sort of dish that was familiar in every cheese-making district of Europe. In recent more prosperous times, the simplicities have been embellished, sometimes in a ritual (Swiss fondue, raclette, Italian fonduta and so on).

For myself, I think there is little to beat a slice of good cheese set on toast and slipped under the grill, but I am almost converted to this elegant version given by Bobby Freeman in *First Catch Your Peacock*, and make it as a first course for dinner parties. At Cirencester we are lucky to have a cheese stall at the market where one may buy single Gloucester from the man who makes it (and other fine cheeses as well). Cheshire is my second choice.

For six people, cut slivers of cheese on to the scales until you have 375 g (12 oz). Put them into a pan with an equal weight of butter cut into dice, and 3 tablespoons (4 tbs) of cream. Stir over a low heat until the mixture is smooth. Off the heat, beat in three eggs. Put into six little pots and brown under the grill. Serve with toast fingers. Ale is the appropriate drink, or white wine at a party.

THREE SAVOURIES OR FIRST COURSE DISHES

Quite apart from the work required at the wrong end of a dinner, savouries spoil the sequence of wines that you may be serving with a meal. They come much better at the beginning of the meal.

Angels on horseback Although this savoury came from France in the mid-19th century, it was soon a top English speciality. Allow three large oysters for each person. Wrap each one, after seasoning it with a drop of anchovy essence, 2–3 drops lemon juice and a tiny pinch of cayenne, in a thin strip of streaky bacon. Impale them on to wooden cocktail sticks, three rolls per stick. Have ready a piece of bread fried in butter for each stick. Fry the rolls in clarified butter, or brush them with butter and grill them under a high heat, then put on the bread. The cooking hould be brief. Sheila Hutchins points out that mussels or pieces of scallop can be used instead of oysters.

Devils on horseback Roll soaked, stoned prunes in bacon, as for angels on horseback. Fry or grill, serve on toast or fried bread, with some English mustard and a jug of cream.

Lady Jekyll's prunes on toast Soak and cook and stone the largest prunes you can find. Fill the cavities with cooked Finnan haddock, beaten up with a little cream and cayenne. Heat through in the oven and serve on pieces of bread fried in butter, allowing 2 for each person, or 3 if they are small.

ANCHOVY TOAST

An emergency recipe that I picked up from Mrs de Salis' *Savouries à la Mode*, published in the mid-1880s, and have many times been grateful for. She served it at the end of the meal, but it makes a good first course, or light supper dish after some soup.

'Cut little rounds of bread, fry them a pale colour; curl some washed and boned anchovies and place on them, and pour over either Devonshire or whipped cream.' The contrast between hot bread, salty anchovy and chilled thick cream is most successful.

OYSTER LOAVES

A favourite English dish of mine. Normally I make it when I'm in France where oysters are a sensible price. But now it begins to be a possibility again in

Britain, as oysters come more cheaply on to the market from enthusiasts like John Noble at Ardkinglas. In America the dish was popular in New Orleans: husbands who had been out late would buy a loaf hot from street vendors and take it home as a peace offering to their wives—hence the name, la médiatrice. East coast Americans at least seem never to have lost their cheap oysters and can still make this dish easily: in Britain mussels can be substituted, or a mixture of cockles and mussels, if oysters are out of the question.

Serves 6
6 brioches or soft rolls
butter, melted
36 oysters or very large mussels, scrubbed
cayenne pepper or Tabasco sauce
salt and pepper
250 ml/9 fl oz/good cup double cream
150 ml/¼ pt soured cream
lemon juice, optional
chopped parsley, optional

Set the oven at moderate to moderately hot, 180–200°C (350–400°F), gas 4–6.

Cut a lid from the brioches or rolls and scoop out the crumb to form six little cases. Brush inside and out with melted butter, or dip into melted butter, and butter the lids, too. Put into the heated oven on a baking sheet, and bake until crisp; check after 5 minutes, then after 10. Keep the cases warm.

Meanwhile, open the oysters by pushing in a stubby knife or oyster knife near the hinge, flat side up, and levering the shells apart. Tip the oysters and their juice into a pan with 3 tablespoons (4 tbs) melted butter. Put over a moderate heat until the oysters turn opaque and slightly stiff. Do not overcook them. Lift out the oysters with a perforated spoon and set aside.

Boil the juices down hard to make a concentrated essence. Flavour with cayenne or Tabasco. Put salt and pepper to taste and both creams into a wide pan; bring to simmering point and whisk in the oyster juice to taste, sharpening further if you like with a little lemon juice. Boil until thick, slip in the oysters to reheat for a few seconds, then distribute between the cases. Serve immediately. Extra sauce can be poured round the cases.

If using mussels, clean and open them in the usual way (see page 120). Cut up the mussels, if they are particularly large. Strain their liquor and use to make the sauce as above. Add a little chopped parsley to the sauce, if you like.

POTTED CRAB

Potted fish—and meat—in the past have been our equivalent to French pâtés and terrines. The difference is that the main item is cooked in advance, and then mixed with or embedded in butter, which has been so important an ingredient in English cooking.

I always pot crab from Elizabeth David's recipe. Pick all the meat from 1 or 2 boiled crab—about 300–375 g (10–12 oz), and season with salt, pepper, ground mace or grated nutmeg, cayenne and lemon juice. Pack into a round or oval stoneware pot, in layers of yellow and pinkish-white meat. Melt 250 g (8 oz/1 cup) slightly salted Lurpak butter. Pour enough over the crab just to cover it.

Put the pot into a bain marie and leave at the bottom of a cool oven, 150°C (300°F), gas 2, for 25–30 minutes. Remove, cool, then seal with a layer of clarified butter. When set, cover with foil and chill overnight at least, or for up to 48 hours. Serve with thin toast.

Potted shrimps or prawns Shell recently cooked shrimps or prawns and tip them into a measuring jug as you go. Calculate a fifth of their volume in butter; melt it with a blade of mace, cayenne and grated nutmeg to taste. When boiling stir in the shrimps or prawns and heat them through slowly without allowing them to boil. Pour into one large or several little pots. When cold, cover with clarified butter and foil as above.

HERRINGS WITH OATMEAL

This must surely be the best way of cooking herrings. You can use coarse or medium oatmeal. With the coarse, a good deal falls off the herring into the fat, which makes a slightly messy-looking dish; to my mind, the crunchiness of the oatmeal compensates for the appearance. Medium oatmeal gives a tidier result altogether. Lard or bacon fat should be used for the frying, and one or two little rolls of streaky bacon can be put into the frying pan for each herring.

Ask the fishmonger to behead and bone the herring (allow one or two per person according to the size of the herring and the capacity of the people eating them).

Dip the herrings into milk, and then into oatmeal. Press down the cut side particularly firmly. Heat up the lard or bacon fat, put in the herrings and fry about 2 minutes per side—though this depends on the thickness of the herring. At all events, do not overcook.

WHITING OR SCALLOPS WITH ORANGE SAUCE

Sweet oranges came to England in the 1660s from Portugal. Like most other citrus fruits, they came originally from the Far East, so were known as Portugals or China oranges. When the word 'orange' was used on its own, it meant a bitter orange of the Seville type. This is something to look out for if you use 17th or 18th century recipes.

The aromatic juice and peel of the orange was much appreciated with meat, fish and spinach, as a richer, alternative sharpness to the lemon. If you have a freezer, it is well worth storing Sevilles for sauces of this kind.

Serves 6
6 cleaned and filletted whiting, or 18–24 scallops, cleaned and sliced across
3 Seville oranges, or 2 sweet oranges and 1 lemon
150 ml/$\frac{1}{4}$ pt/$\frac{2}{3}$ cup dry white wine
scant tablespoon white wine vinegar
$\frac{1}{2}$ teaspoon ground mace
2 cloves
salt and pepper
cayenne pepper
3 large egg yolks, beaten
4 tablespoons/$\frac{1}{3}$ cup double cream
150 g/5 oz/$\frac{2}{3}$ cup butter
seasoned flour

For the whiting, put them in a dish. Remove enough shreds of orange peel with a zester (or peel off strips, blanch and shred them), to make a final garnish. Pour the juice of half a Seville orange over the fish, or 1 tablespoon each of sweet orange and lemon juice. Put the rest of the fruit juice into a pan with the wine, vinegar and spices, salt and peppers. Bring to simmering point and leave to infuse for about 10 minutes.

Whisk the egg yolks and cream together in a basin, then strain in the spiced wine mixture. Place the bowl over a pan of barely simmering water, and stir until thick, adding 60 g (2 oz/$\frac{1}{4}$ cup) of the butter in little bits. Remove the basin from the pan so that it does not overheat. Taste and adjust seasoning – a hint of sugar can be a good idea.

Drain the fish, pouring the juice into the hot sauce. Pat it dry and flour it, then fry gently in the remaining butter. Do not overcook it. Dish up, pour over the sauce and add the reserved peel.

For scallops, poach them lightly in the simmering wine mixture, with all the juice etc, adding a little water barely to cover. Set aside the scallops, reduce the liquor and complete as above, reheating the scallops in the sauce. Add an extra 30 g (1 oz/2 tbs) butter to the sauce when thickening and omit the seasoned flour as frying is unnecessary for scallops.

WHITEBAIT DINNERS

'The peculiar attraction of a Blackwall or Greenwich dinner consists in the trip, the locality, the fresh air, and perhaps the whitebait—for, although served at most of the leading clubs, it loses in delicacy by transportation and is seldom so well dressed as in the immediate proximity of its haunts.' A very general 19th-century opinion on the summer excursions out of London, made between May and August, when the shoals of tiny herrings and sprats—whitebait—came up the Thames. Brown bread and butter and champagne went with the whitebait. Afterwards duckling or chicken with broiled ham, or grouse in the second half of August, with ices or apple fritters to follow. An occasion for genial feasting which drew this comment from Tennyson's eccentric elder brother, Frederick:

I had a vision very late
After a dinner of whitebait.

Nowadays whitebait comes in frozen blocks, its delicacy much reduced though it is still worth eating.

Serves 4–6
500 g/1 lb whitebait
300 ml/1 pt/1$\frac{1}{4}$ cups milk
125 g/4 oz/1 cup flour
2 level teaspoons salt
level teaspoon black pepper
cayenne
lemon quarters, parsley sprigs

Thaw and spread out the whitebait on kitchen paper, as soon as you can separate them without damage. Put them into the milk for a few minutes. Drain them well. Mix the flour, salt, black pepper and a rounded teaspoon of cayenne in a large bag.

Heat a deep-frying pan half full of oil to between 180 and 190°C (350–375°F)—use an electric pan if possible. Shake the whitebait in batches in the seasoned flour, 125 g (4 oz) at a time, and deep-fry for about 2 minutes, or until they are crisp and golden brown. Put them on to a baking sheet lined with kitchen paper and keep warm in a low oven while you fry the rest of the whitebait. Divide between 4–6 plates add lemon and parsley, and serve with brown bread and butter, plus extra cayenne.

KEDGEREE

The Hindi khichri, a rice and lentil dish that could be embellished with fish or meat, was turned into the splendid kedgeree by English people living in India. Today, it is always flavoured with fish, and rice is the only grain. Although smoked Finnan haddock is—to me, at any rate— the essential item after the rice, the beauty of the dish, both in look and taste, is improved by adding a little salmon and some prawns.

Serves 6
375 g/12 oz cooked prawns, in their shells
1 smoked Finnan haddock, weighing about 400 g/14 oz
generous 600 ml/1 pt/2½ cups boiling water
250 g/8 oz fresh salmon
salt and pepper
olive oil
large onion, chopped
175 g/6 oz/scant cup Basmati or other long grain rice
teaspoon curry paste or powder
butter
3 hard-boiled eggs, sliced
chopped parsley

Shell the prawns, apart from four to make a final decoration. Put the shells into a saucepan and lay the haddock on top. Pour over boiling water to cover generously. Leave for 10 minutes over a low heat to keep very hot. Then remove the haddock and put in the salmon to poach. When it is just done, remove that as well, leaving the pan of liquid and prawn debris to bubble on.

Skin and bone the haddock and salmon, dropping the trimmings back into the pan, which should bubble on while you flake both fish and add them to the shelled prawns. Season the fish.

In a large pan, heat a thin layer of olive oil and cook the onion until golden, transparent and lightly browned in places. Stir in the rice, and after a couple of minutes as it becomes transparent, add the curry paste or powder. Strain in about 600 ml (1 pt/2½ cups) of the fish stock and cook steadily until the rice is tender and the stock absorbed. Watch the pan, adding more stock if necessary.

Mix in the flaked fish and prawns and a large piece of butter, so that the kedgeree is moist and juicy. Check the seasoning. Turn into a hot serving dish. Arrange egg slices on top, with parsley and the reserved prawns.

SKIRLIE

This simple mixture of onion, oatmeal and suet that made a poor man's dinner in Scotland, with potatoes, is used by the more prosperous to stuff game and duck. The name comes from the noise of the frying, as in the skirl of the pipes I suppose, though happily more muted. Cookery writer Katie Stewart recommended skirlie in a *Times* article several years ago, the first time I had come across it used as a stuffing; the dish itself is an old one.

Skin and chop or grate coarsely 60 g (2 oz/scant ½ cup) fresh beef suet; chop a large onion, and weigh out 175 g (6 oz/1 cup) medium oatmeal. Melt the suet in a frying pan, stir in the onion and cook until it is nicely browned, then add oatmeal, which will take up the fat and become brown and crunchy. Cool before stuffing a duck or a brace of game birds or mix the ingredients, uncooked, and stuff birds, which gives a softer, closer result.

ROAST BEEF AND YORKSHIRE PUDDING

Yorkshire pudding seems to have been invented early in the 18th century by frugal housewives who did not want to waste the delicious juices in the dripping pan under spit-roasted lamb or mutton. Nowadays, we eat it mainly with beef, though there are Yorkshire people who eat it with every kind of meat and on its own as well. Like suet pudding, it is—or was—served with gravy before the meat course. My Northumbrian grandfather liked to have his second helping of Yorkshire pudding at the dessert stage, with condensed milk; this meant that the pudding could not be cooked under the joint, which to me would be a great deprivation.

Everyone has their theories on this national dish; this is what I do, but I would not be dictatorial about it. If you can call on a skilled and rapid carver, beef on the bone—ribs for instance—is the best choice.

For six people, I buy a piece of well-hung, rolled sirloin, preferably Aberdeen Angus, weighing between 2.25–2.5 kg (4½–5 lb), plus 175 g (6 oz/¾ cup) dripping. I put the beef across a trivet that raises it well above a large oval earthenware gratin dish, measuring 35 cm (14 in) long. The dripping goes over it and in the dish. I salt the fat of the meat lightly. This goes into a hot oven, preheated to 230°C (450°F), gas 8, for 15 minutes.

Meanwhile, I mix a batter of 250 g (8 oz/2 cups) flour, pinch of salt, 3 eggs and 300 ml ($\frac{1}{2}$ pt/1$\frac{1}{4}$ cups) each milk and water. I open the oven door, quickly stir 2–3 tablespoons (3–4 tbs) very cold water into the batter, then pour it into the gratin dish. I close the door and turn the heat down to 180°C (350°F), gas 4. After an hour, I switch the oven off and leave the meat to rest for 15–20 minutes.

It is then taken to the table as it is; the meat is removed to a hot plate for carving and the trivet goes into the sink. Horseradish cream and mustard are put on the table, plus a few French beans or Brussels sprouts. In very cold weather, or when everyone is likely to be very hungry, I do roast potatoes and parsnips as well. But normally the beans are enough. No gravy is required as the juices of the beef moisten the Yorkshire pudding in the centre, and pour out when the meat is carved and served on very hot plates.

STEAK AND KIDNEY PUDDING OR PIE

The old way of preparing this dish is to flour the meat and cook it inside the crust, but this can mean a poor over- or under-cooked filling, without proper seasoning. Better—and more convenient—to cook the filling in advance and get the balance of flavours right. For the best steak and kidney pudding or pie, use well-hung Scotch beef and veal kidney. Oddly enough, it seems that this favourite national dish is not particularly old, kidney being a 19th century addition to John Bull's beefsteak pudding (though Eliza Acton does point out in 1845 that veal kidney suet makes a truly epicurean crust).

Serves 6–8

FOR THE FILLING

1 kg/2 lb rump or shoulder fillet of beef, cubed
500 g/1 lb veal or ox kidney, sliced
seasoned flour
250 g/8 oz/2 cups chopped onion
90 g/3 oz/$\frac{1}{3}$ cup butter
600 ml/1 pt/2$\frac{1}{2}$ cups red wine and beef stock, or stock
bouquet garni
grated nutmeg
salt and pepper
cayenne
250 g/8 oz mushrooms, quartered (optional)
18 oysters (optional)

FOR THE CRUST

375 g/12 oz/3 cups self-raising flour
level teaspoon baking powder
$\frac{1}{4}$ level teaspoon each salt and pepper
$\frac{1}{4}$ level teaspoon thyme
175 g/6 oz/good cup fresh suet, chopped
cold water to mix
1.75-litres/3-pt/7$\frac{1}{2}$-cup basin

Turn the meats in the flour. Soften the onion in two-thirds of the butter, then put into a flameproof casserole. Raise the heat, put in the beef and kidney and brown them. Add to the onion. Deglaze pan with the wine and stock or just stock. Pour over the meat. Put in the bouquet garni and a generous pinch of nutmeg; add other seasonings to taste. Cover and cook closely until just tender, either in a cool oven, 150°C (300°F), gas 2, or on top of the stove. Judge whether there is too much liquid left, bearing in mind the oyster juices if you intend to add them. Strain off the liquid and reduce it, if there is a lot of it. Tip back on to the meat. Fry the mushrooms, if used, in the last of the butter, and add them to the meat. Cool. Remove any fat that congeals on the top.

Mix the crust ingredients in the given order to a soft, but not sticky dough. Roll out to a circle about the size of a large dinner plate. Cut out a quarter and set aside for the pudding lid. Fold the rest over lightly, in half. Drop into the buttered basin, open it out and gently press it into place, joining the edges together so that the basin is evenly lined, the top of the dough lolling slightly over the rim.

Put in the meat mixture, together with the oysters and their juice, if using. Roll out the remaining pastry to make a lid. Moisten the edges of both the lid and basin lining. Put the pastry circle in place on top of the filling; flip over the pastry hanging over the basin, and press down gently to seal. There should be quite a gap between the top of the pudding and the rim of the basin.

Cover with a piece of foil pleated to allow for expansion and tie it over the basin with string, to make a handle for easy lifting in and out, and boil or steam for 2$\frac{1}{2}$ hours. Do not turn out to serve, but remove the foil and tie a clean napkin round the basin.

Steak and kidney pie Precook the filling as above and turn into a 1.75-litre (3-pt) pie dish. Cover with a shortcrust or puff pastry lid. Brush with beaten egg. Bake for 15 minutes in a hot oven (preheat to 220°C (425°F), gas 7), lowering the heat to 180°C (350°F), gas 4, for 45 minutes, or until the meat is tender and bubbling hot.

FORFAR BRIDIES

A lavish form of Cornish pasty made from beef topside or rump rather than skirt, and much eaten in Aberdeen Angus country in the vale of Strathmore. Forfar is the main town and Bridie was the surname of the woman who first made them, or so it is said.

The Aberdeen Angus scores because it is a heavy animal, and the meat is most concentrated above an imaginary line going from the shoulder diagonally across the animal. Moreover, the meat is flecked through with fat, which makes it tender and well-flavoured, qualities that are emphasised by proper hanging. One of the other people on a trip I joined to see the Aberdeen Angus on its home ground was Catherine Brown; here is the recipe for Forfar Bridies from her *Scottish Regional Recipes*.

Serves 4
500 g/1 lb rump steak or topside
90 g/3 oz/6 tbs fresh suet, grated
2 medium onions, finely chopped
salt and pepper
FOR THE PASTRY
400 g/14 oz/3½ cups plain flour
100 g/3½ oz/scant ½ cup
100 g/3½ oz/scant ½ cup lard
salt, 1–2 tablespoons/1–3 tbs water, to mix

First make the pastry in the usual way, making a stiff dough. Divide into four and roll into large ovals. Set the oven at moderately hot, 200°C (400°F), gas 6.

Beat out the steak and cut it into 1 cm (½ in) squares. Mix with the suet and onion, then season. Divide between the ovals, putting the filling to one side and leaving a border. Brush the edges with water, fold over the uncovered pastry and crimp the edges to seal them. Make a hole at the top. Bake in the heated oven for 45 minutes.

Cornish pasties Make in the same way, but using all lard for the pastry. The beef should be skirt or chuck, freed of skin, etc, and chopped, then mixed with 125 g (4 oz) each chopped onion and turnip and 250 g (8 oz) thinly sliced potato, with a pinch of thyme. Brush pastry with beaten egg before baking.

GUARD OF HONOUR WITH LAVERBREAD AND ORANGE SAUCE

To make a Guard of Honour, you buy a whole best end of neck of lamb and ask the butcher to split it down the backbone and chine it, but to leave the long rib bones as they are. You have to speak fast,

Guard of honour surrounded with laverbread and orange sauce, reading for serving

as most butchers trim them automatically without thinking.

Recently I was asked if it was really a British idea since a recipe for Guard of Honour appeared in a BBC booklet on French cookery. Certainly it does not figure in the English cookery books that I have. My impression is that it is a northern dish, since I had the idea from my mother.

Lamb in England is a problem in many parts, as so much of the best goes abroad. Tantalising for people round Romney Marsh, who see but never taste pré-salé lamb unless they go to France. I try to get Welsh mountain lamb, or else Shetland lamb, which is tiny and quite diferent in taste since it feeds on seaweed. Both are particularly appropriate for this dish, since the accompaniment is laverbread, which comes from both Scotland and Wales.

Serves 6–8
whole best end of neck of lamb, halved and chined
dried thyme
salt and pepper
500 g/1 lb prepared laverbread (see below)
90 g/3 oz/⅓ cup butter
juice of 2 oranges and 1 lemon
water or wine, for deglazing pan (optional)
orange, thinly sliced, to garnish

continued on p. 151

LAVERBREAD

Laverbread is a national delicacy that has clung on in spite of being ignored by most British cooks. If the nouvelle cuisine chefs had been living and working here, it would have been on every chic menu; it is excellent with marinated salmon. Nowadays, you have to go to Wales, the West of England or Scotland for it.

Laverbread is made from several seaweeds, the most common being *Porphyra umbilicalis.* You can gather it yourself and rinse it free of sand in a solution of bicarbonate of soda, which takes away the bitterness. The drained seaweed is then stewed and stewed until it is tender; the water is drained off to leave a dark mass that is a little like a spinach purée, but blacker and softer (see roast lamb with laverbread recipe on page 149). Laverbread goes well, too with lobster, or scallops with orange sauce.

Orange, lemon and butter are all good with reheated laverbread. The Welsh mix laverbread with porridge oats until it can be formed into little cakes, fish cake-sized. They are then fried with the bacon for breakfast. If you are able to make up great platters of seafood, put a bowl of laverbread, seasoned with lemon juice, on the table with the mayonnaise; a little mouthful on bread with oysters or prawns is delicious.

Laverbread can also be ordered by post, as it keeps well. The supply varies with the weather. After stormy days when people cannot go out on the rocks to pull the seaweed, you cannot expect to buy laverbread.

Carrageen (*Chondrus crispus*, and *Gigartina stellata*), also known as carrageen or Irish moss, is a purplish-red and brown seaweed, mainly collected in south Ireland. It has long been valued as a medicine—you can buy it in health food shops—but these days it is mostly used to set jellies and blancmange, especially milk jellies which allow its delicate and pleasant flavour to come through.

If you want to prepare your own carrageen, rinse it well, then spread it out on grass 'so as to get the night dews. It gradually changes from brown through beetroot to pink eventually a creamy white. It must be kept wet with fresh water during these changes. Showery weather is useful.' Carrageen is gathered, in Donegal at least, in April and May—'Directly all the colour has gone from it, it should be quickly sun dried. It can be hung up in paper bags and if well dried will keep indefinitely', according to *Irish Country Recipes by* Florence Irwin, a book now, sadly, out of print.

TO MAKE CARRAGEEN MOSS PUDDING Wash 15 g ($\frac{1}{2}$ oz) carrageen and put it into a pan with 850 ml

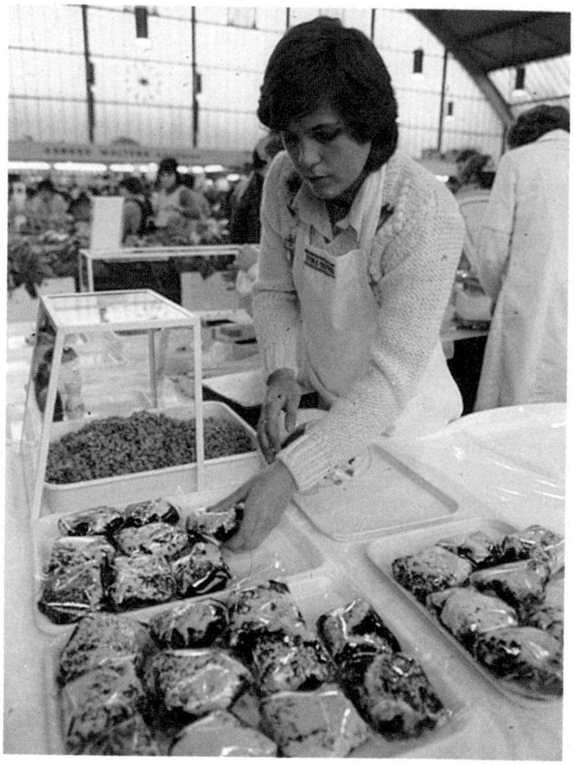

Packets of laverbread on sale in Swansea market

(1$\frac{1}{2}$ pts/3$\frac{3}{4}$ cups) milk and some wisps of lemon rind or a vanilla pod. Bring slowly to the boil and simmer slowly for 15 minutes. Strain and push through all the jelly from the swollen carrageen, then stir it till smooth. Beat together 2 level tablespoons (3 tbs) sugar and 1 egg yolk, then beat in the milk. Test for a set by putting some into a saucer and chilling it. If it is too stiff, beat in more warm milk. Finally whisk 1 egg white and fold in. Pour into a bowl.

This pudding is based on Myrtle Allen's recipe from her *Ballymaloe Cookbook*. She serves it in her hotel, with a thin layer of Irish coffee sauce on top, then whipped cream. For the sauce dissolve 125 g (4 oz/$\frac{1}{2}$ cup) of sugar in 75 ml (2$\frac{2}{3}$ fl oz/6$\frac{1}{2}$ tbs) of water, then boil to the caramel stage. Remove from the heat and add a 225 ml (8 fl oz/1 cup) of black coffee; stir over heat until smooth. Cool; add 1 tablespoon Irish whiskey.

Set the oven at hot, 220°C (425°F), gas 7. At home, cut a 4 cm ($1\frac{1}{2}$ in) strip from the top of the bones of both pieces of lamb. Then scrape the bones free of fat. Pull off the skin from the lamb, with any extra fat and discard. Score the remaining fat and rub it over with thyme, salt and pepper. Place the two joints in a roasting tin, bones up, and push the two sides together so that the bones interlock in a military-looking way. Press foil over the bones to prevent them catching. Roast in the preheated oven for 45 minutes, if you like lamb pink, for 60 minutes if you like it brown all through.

Meanwhile, complete the laverbread. Melt half the butter in a pan, stir in the fruit juices and the laverbread. Heat gently and season with salt and pepper. It does not need cooking, but should be left to simmer gotly for about 5 minutes to heat through. Just before serving beat in the remaining butter.

To serve, transfer the lamb to a hot serving dish, keeping it together, and keep warm. Remove the foil. Pour the fat off the pan juices, if there are any, and deglaze with a little water or wine. This can be poured over the meat, which does not require gravy. Arrange the laverbread round it, together with steamed minted new potatoes, if you like, then the sliced orange. Cut down between bones to serve, and put on to hot plates.

ROAST PHEASANT OR GUINEAFOWL

Always buy pheasant from an expert game butcher, and order it in advance so that it can be hung to the stage you like it. Since pheasant can be dry, take the precaution of larding it; the same applies to guineafowl. Avoid overcooking, since a thinly sliced, pink bird is better eating than a stringy tough bird that is brown all through. Don't be put off by all this, since our classic roast pheasant is one of the most delicious things it is possible to eat. And guineafowl comes a close second.

Serves 6–8

a brace of pheasants or two 1 kg/2 lb guineafowl
small block of hard back fat, for larding
125 g/4 oz fillet steak, cut in strips or butter, or skirlie (see page 147)
2 thin sheets of back fat, to cover
salt and pepper, cayenne
seasoned flour
6 tablespoons/$\frac{1}{2}$ cup port
300 ml/$\frac{1}{2}$ pt/$1\frac{1}{4}$ cups game, giblet or beef, stock
watercress

FOR BREAD SAUCE

small onion, stuck with 3 cloves
500 ml/$\frac{3}{4}$ pt/scant 2 cups milk, giblet or beef stock
90–125 g/3–4 oz/$1\frac{1}{2}$–2 cups fresh breadcrumbs
powdered mace or nutmeg
salt, cayenne
60 g/2 oz/$\frac{1}{4}$ cup butter, or 6 tablespoons/$\frac{1}{2}$ cup double cream

FOR BROWNED CRUMBS

90 g/3 oz/$1\frac{1}{2}$ cups fresh breadcrumbs
60 g/2 oz/$\frac{1}{4}$ cup butter, melted

FOR GAME CHIPS

750 g/$1\frac{1}{2}$ lb firm potatoes
fat, for deep-frying
larding needle

Set the oven at moderately hot, 190°C (375°F), gas 5. Lard the birds with little strips of fat, taking stitches in the breasts. Trim the fat to an even length of whiskers. Put the steak, butter or skirlie into the body cavities. Season and cover with the fat. Place in a tin and roast in the oven for 35 minutes; remove the larding fat, dredge lightly with the flour and return to the oven to brown and finish cooking (from 45–60 minutes in all, according to size).

When the birds are done, put them on a hot serving dish and keep warm. Skim the fat from the juices, then pour in the port and stock, scraping to deglaze the pan. Boil to reduce to a concentrated sauce, and strain into a jug. While the birds are cooking, prepare the bread sauce, crumbs and game chips (or cook earlier and reheat).

For the sauce, gently heat the onion and milk or stock together for 10 minutes. Stir in the crumbs, stopping when the sauce is fairly thick: it will thicken further as the bread and liquid blend together. Season with spices, salt and cayenne. Just before serving, stir the butter into a milk-based bread sauce, or cream into a stock-based sauce. Bread sauce should have an agreeably pulpy look.

For the browned crumbs, put them into a pan and pour over the melted butter. Set over a moderate heat and stir until browned. Drain on kitchen paper in a cool oven; serve in a bowl.

For the game chips, peel and slice the potatoes very thinly on a mandolin, into a bowl of water. If you like a gaufrette-latticed slice, use the ridge blades, turning the potato at right angles at each cut. Dry the potatoes and deep-fry in batches, at 190°C (375°F) until brown and crisp. Drain on kitchen paper; sprinkle with salt before serving.

Just before putting the birds on the table, tuck little bunches of watercress round them. Mushrooms or celery can be served as well.

BALLYMALOE BROWN BREAD

In the middle of Paris there is a most popular little Irish restaurant, La Ferme Irlandaise. At simple tables, against white walls, the French crowd together drinking tea with Irish stew, Guinness with Irish oysters, and Smithwick's ale with some of the best smoked salmon (Irish too) that it is possible to eat anywhere. The restaurant is run on behalf of a group of Irish farmers by Myrtle Allen, who already runs a famous restaurant at Ballymaloe near Cork.

Mrs Allen's bread is the best wholemeal I have ever eaten. Here is her recipe for it, based on the old favourite, the Doris Grant loaf, that requires only one rising and no kneading whatsoever. More of her recipes can be found in *The Ballymaloe Cookbook* (Eyre Methuen, p/b £3.95). You may need to add extra yeast to lighten this dough. It all depends on the wholemeal flour. You may also need to add 2–3 more tablespoons water. The dough is best baked in a long narrow bread tin or two small tins: with a large wide tin of traditional type, you get a loaf that crumbles as you cut it. A slice measuring about 8 cm (3 good ins) is the ideal.

Makes 1 loaf
500 g/1 lb wholemeal flour, preferably stone-ground
2 level teaspoons salt
1 packet instant dried Harvest Gold yeast
level tablespoon black treacle
about 350 ml/11 fl oz/good 1¼ cups warm water, at blood heat

Warm the flour and salt in a very cool oven. Stir in the yeast, then add the treacle, dissolved in half the water. Add enough of the remaining water to make a wettish dough that is just too wet to knead. Put into the greased loaf tin. Tie it into a polythene bag and leave in a warm place until the dough has risen by one-third (about 45 minutes). Set the oven at hot, 230°C (450°F), gas 8.

Bake in the heated oven until nicely browned. This takes 40 minutes. Brush the top with water and put back into the oven for 5 minutes. Remove from the tin, tap the bottom which should sound hollow; turn out to cool.

SAFFRON CAKE

Those who have grown up in Cornwall will appreciate the need for an adequate quantity of saffron to give the right brilliance and flavour to their favourite cake. In England, buy the Mancha saffron from Boots; it is expensive, but not as expensive as the same quantity elsewhere—you need two packets, which amounts to 2 level teaspoons (though this is difficult to judge exactly). Pour a little boiling water over it, 4 tablespoons (⅓ cup) for instance, and leave to infuse while you assemble the other ingredients.

Makes 1 cake
500 g/1 lb/4 cups plain flour
packet instant dried Harvest Gold yeast
pinch of salt
250 g/8 oz/1 cup butter
125 g/4 oz/½ cup sugar
250 g/8 oz/1⅓ cups mixed fruit and chopped peel
saffron liquid (see above)
about 175 ml/6 fl oz/good ⅔ cup milk, at blood heat
two 20-cm/8-in cake tins

Mix the flour, yeast and salt together. Rub in the butter. Stir in the sugar, fruit and peel. Mix to a dough with the saffron water (do not strain out the filaments) and as much milk as required to make a soft, coherent mass. Tie the bowl into an oiled polythene bag and leave in a warm place to rise; it will take 2 hours, on account of the butter in the dough.

Set the oven at moderate, 180°C (350°F), gas 4. Divide between the greased cake tins, then tie back into the polythene bag. Leave for a further hour, then bake in the heated oven for an hour, or until golden brown on top. Turn out—the base should sound hollow when tapped—and cool on a wire rack.

WALPOLE HOUSE TREACLE TART

Standard treacle tart, solidified with breadcrumbs, can be a stodgy affair. Try this recipe given in the 1969 revised edition of Lady Jekyll's *Kitchen Essays* (1922). Serve it with lightly whipped cream, and black coffee to cut the sweetness. Addicts of such things can make the tart with molasses or black treacle, but I find the flavour far too powerful.

Serves 6–8
golden syrup
30 g/1 oz/2 tbs butter
level dessertspoon caster sugar
5 tablespoons/6 tbs double cream
2 large egg yolks
150 g/6 oz quantity of shortcrust pastry
20-cm/8-in shallow cake tin

In Cornwall you can buy saffron cake and heavy cake (left), Cornish pasty and 'tea treat bun'

Put a saucepan on the weighing scales. Mark its weight and pour into it 250 g (8 oz) golden syrup. Warm with the butter and sugar. Beat the cream and egg yolks together and add to the syrup. Set the oven at moderately hot, 200°C (400°F), gas 6.

Line the cake tin (a tin that is deeper than the usual tart tin) with shortcrust pastry. Prick the bottom lightly, then pour in the syrup mixture. It should come between a half and two-thirds of the way up the pastry. Put into the heated oven. After 8 minutes check that the pastry is not rising through the syrup; if it is ballooning up, prick it and it will subside. Check after 30 minutes to see if the filling is more or less set and the pastry browned, but be prepared to give it up to 45 minutes. The syrup jellies slightly with the egg yolks, and should not be set too firmly.

FRUIT PIES

Everyone knows how to make fruit pies, but here are one or two things you may not have thought of:

1 Revive the old habit of cooking apples or pears or apricots lightly in butter, then sprinkling them with the sugar so that they are bathed in a rich juice, before putting them into a pie dish.

2 Use acid eating apples, Cox's for instance or Charles Ross, instead of cookers to make apple pie. Try a little cinnamon as a spice instead of cloves. Even a proportion of good eating apples improves the flavour.

3 In the autumn include some grated quince as a flavouring for an apple or pear pie. Later on use quince jelly and cut down on the sugar. For me, quince is the supreme flavouring for apple pie. No spice is required.

4 Use the trimmings, peel, core and so on, from the fruit to make a flavoured juice with water, and use that rather than plain water to moisten the pie. This works particularly well if you are including quince, and means that none of the precious flavour is wasted.

5 When making a soft fruit pie, mix a tablespoon of arrowroot or cornflour or even flour with the sugar and sprinkle it over each layer. This thickens the juice very slightly, without giving it the gluey consistency of canned pie fillings.

6 As a rough guide, allow 125 g (4 oz/$\frac{1}{2}$ cup) sugar to each $\frac{1}{2}$ kg (1 lb) of fruit, lessening the quantity if the fruit has a particularly good sweet flavour.

7 Another old idea was to pour a caudle into the top of the pie when it was baked and ready. It was then returned to the oven for a few moments. A caudle consists of cream and eggs: it enriches and thickens the fruit juices. The proportion of egg or egg yolk to cream depends on the quantity of juice in the pie: a useful guide is 125 ml (4 fl oz/scant $\frac{1}{2}$ cup) whipping or double cream brought to the boil and whisked into a large beaten egg yolk.

PEACH AND ALMOND TARTLETS

Another of Mrs Allen's Ballymaloe dishes that causes a sensation in Paris, at her Irish restaurant.

Mix together 100 g (3 oz/6 tbs) each soft butter and caster sugar and 100 g (3 oz/$\frac{3}{4}$ cup) ground almonds. Drop teaspoonfuls into 16–18 small tartlet tins—no need to grease them. Bake at 180°C (350°F), gas 4, for about 10 minutes, or until they have turned into little golden brown saucers. Cool slightly in the tins, then on a rack.

Just before serving, put a piece of skinned peach into each tartlet, with a blob of whipped cream on top. Other fruit can be used—raspberries, grapes (skinned and pips removed), or lightly cooked chunks of young pink rhubarb. If you are picking billberries in Ireland or the Lake District or Derbyshire, or blueberries in Maine, this is a delightful way of serving them (use them raw or lightly cooked and drained).

As a dessert, serve three tartlets per person. If you must fill the cases before the meal, put the fruit on top of the cream so the crust is not made soggy.

TRIFLE

Trifle is a fine dish of bourgeois cookery, from manor houses and comfortable rectories; it should be rich yet clean-tasting, lavishly simple, appetising and gentle on the eye.

It has three elements: a wine-soaked sponge base, a central layer of custard, and a top layer of cream, preferably in the form of a syllabub. In my experience, the less you fool about with this scheme the better. By the 18th century, cooks had worked out what was required, and there is no reason to ignore their conclusions. Cash and care should be concentrated on the essentials, i.e. decent cake instead of yellow 'trifle sponges' in a packet, and cream and egg custard rather than custard powder. If you have to economise, cut out the glacé cherries or make a whim-wham (wine-soaked sponge finger biscuits, topped with whipped cream and some toasted nuts), which is a simple kind of trifle.

Start the trifle the day—or two days—before you intend to serve it, adding the syllabub an hour or two before the meal. For the cake, use a fatless sponge from a good baker, or bake a 4-egg mixture such as is used for the Gypsy's arm (see page 80) in a 21 × 32-cm ($8\frac{1}{2} \times 12\frac{3}{4}$-in) shallow baking tin; or buy real sponge finger biscuits (packet boudoir biscuits are too dry), and cut them quite ruthlessly to fit into the base of a large glass bowl. Over it pour about 150 ml ($\frac{1}{4}$ pt/$\frac{2}{3}$ cup) sweet wine, e.g. muscat, or Marsala, Madeira or sherry, and a measure of brandy. The cake should be moist, not dry or soggy. You may need to add some more—it depends on the cake. If you are short on wine, some fruit juice or cordial does well, too. To serve 10, you will also need:

FOR THE CUSTARD

600 ml/1 pt/$2\frac{1}{2}$ cups single cream, Channel Islands milk or half cream, half milk
2 large eggs
2 large egg yolks
level tablespoon ground rice or flour
sugar
jelly or sieved jam, e.g. apricot, raspberry, strawberry

FOR THE SYLLABUB

8 tablespoons/$\frac{1}{2}$ cup wine as used to soak the sponge
2 tablespoons/3 tbs brandy
pared rind and juice of 1 lemon
60 g/2 oz/$\frac{1}{4}$ cup sugar
300 ml/$\frac{1}{2}$ pt/$1\frac{1}{4}$ cups double cream
grated nutmeg

TO DECORATE

toasted nuts or macaroon crumbs
edible silver or gold balls
pale green or lemon candied peel

For the custard, bring the cream, milk or cream and milk, to the boil. Pour on to the eggs and yolks, which have been beaten up with the rice or flour.

A proper trifle is topped with a syllabub

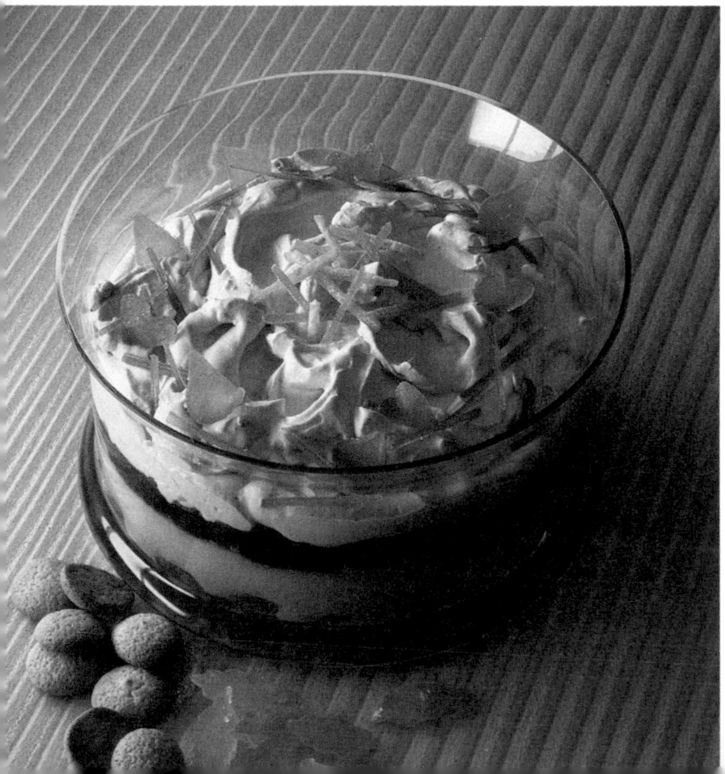

Return to the pan and stir until very thick and very hot; sweeten to taste, bearing in mind the other items. When tepid, pour over the cake. When set, spread with jam or jelly, warming it if necessary. Keep the layer thin.

For the syllabub, put the wine, brandy, rind and juice in a covered basin, and stir in the sugar until dissolved. Still stirring, pour in the cream slowly, whisking not too hard with a spoon whisk, in the other hand. Avoid an electric beater or the mixture can curdle. Whisk until the cream holds its shape.

Spread the syllabub lightly over the custard and jam. Decorate discreetly with the remaining ingredients.

FOOLS

A nice name, humorous like trifle, for a pudding that any fool could make. Indeed it is so simple that I am surprised no other European country seems to make it.

The basic idea is to mix crushed soft fruit with an equal quantity of double cream, whipped to a light bulkiness. Early on, fools were made by stirring egg yolks into a fruit purée and cooking the whole thing to a cream. Recently fools have been ruined by substituting powdered custard for cream. Half egg custard, half cream works quite well. I think, too, that the fruit should not be reduced to an even-textured purée—it tastes better if it is mashed with a fork and sugared lightly; 600 ml (1 pt/2½ cups) of a good fool is plenty for six people. Serve well chilled.

Gooseberry The classic fool. Cook gooseberries lightly with an elderflower, if possible, tucked in for flavour. Wash, top and tail the fruit and set over a low heat with no extra liquid. Add a knob of butter, then sweeten when tender. Toasted almonds or almond biscuits go well with it.

Raspberry Copy the 17th century idea of flavouring the fruit with rose-water. Buy triple strength rose-water from the grocery; chemists' rose-water is often mixed with glycerine. In Scotland, the fine raspberries of the Carse of Gowrie are mixed with cream cheese (crowdie) and cream, plus some medium oatmeal soaked with a little whisky and honey; this needs to be done with great delicacy. I prefer a raspberry fool with a little toasted oatmeal (medium) and no more.

Strawberry Mix strawberries, slightly crushed, with whipped cream. Go for a patchy effect of pink, red and white.

Boodle's Flavour 500 ml (18 fl oz/2¼ cups) double cream with the finely grated zest and juice of 3 large oranges and 1–2 lemons. Pour this over a layer of light sponge cake.

QUAKING PUDDING

This is an English pudding of a most unusual and pleasing texture. I use Elisabeth Ayrton's version, from her *Cookery of England*, which is based on a 1680 recipe. The cream custard is lightly thickened with breadcrumbs into a shape that wobbles or quakes and develops light cracks when it is turned out. Mixtures of custard and bread—queen of puddings, bread and butter pudding, and so on—are usually baked, but this one is boiled like a suet pudding. Cream is the ingredient which transforms these puddings from domestic dullness into real pleasure.

Serves 6–8

600 ml/1 pt/2½ cups double cream, or half whipping, half double cream

3 eggs

extra egg white

pinch each of powdered mace and nutmeg

125 g/4 oz/½ cup caster sugar

45 g/1½ oz/6 tbs floub

2 level tablespoons and 1 level teaspoon fine white breadcrumbs

FOR THE SAUCE

60 g/3 oz/scant ½ cup butter

30 g/1 oz/2 tbs sugar

2 glasses dry white wine

1.5-litre/2½-pt/6¼-cup pudding basin

Bring the cream slowly to the boil and boil slowly for 30 seconds. Meanwhile, whisk the eggs and egg white together, ideally with an electric beater, until thick and foamy. Cool the cream slightly, then pour on to the whisked eggs. Cool completely. Mix the remaining ingredients together and stir them in.

Put into the buttered basin, cover with foil and tie with a string, to make a handle, then stand on a trivet in a pan ⅓ full of boiling water. Adjust the heat so that the water simmers steadily, or cook in a steamer. Replenish the water with more boiling water—1 tablespoon malt vinegar or lemon juice put into the pan will prevent it discolouring. Allow 1½ hours cooking time. Remove the wrappings, then ease round with a thin knife and invert the pudding on a serving plate. If it needs to keep warm for a while, leave the basin in place to hold it together.

To make the sauce, melt the butter and sugar

continued on p. 157

CHEESES

We make some of the finest cheese in the world, but the variety is limited, and it is not easy to find the best outside specialist shops and big stores.

There is a move at the moment to give an impression of variety by smashing up slightly sub-standard hard cheeses and turning them into layer cakes, or by colouring cheeses with swirls of bright dye. Other cheeses are mixed with walnuts or peppercorns, and they can be quite pleasant, but they need choosing with care. Genuine variety can only come from different methods of cheesemaking, and I long for our increasing number of goat farmers to learn the simple French methods that produce the discs and pyramids and logs of fine goat cheese that are common in Touraine and Poitou.

Another new development is the increase in sheep dairy farming, which should lead to new and distinguished cheeses, on wider sale in a few years' time. A book that gives a true picture of cheese in Britain today, and of the many cheesemakers, is *The Great British Cheese Book* by Patrick Rance.

Caerphilly Like Wensleydale, this is a semi-hard cheese produced mainly in the south-west nowadays. It is bland, and was originally a thin skimmed milk cheese. When it came to cheese for toasting, though, the Welsh preferred Cheddar, which they could find in Somerset in exchange for their mutton and lamb.

Cheddar The lack of an appellation contrôlée system, means that Cheddar is made all over the world. This is the penalty of success, since a Somerset cheese-maker, Joseph Harding (1805–1876), was one of the first people to standardise farmhouse cheese-making. He lectured all over the country, sharing his knowledge, and taught his 13 children his methods—one of them went, like a missionary, to Australia. There are 24 farms making the best Cheddar; the milk has always to come from the same herds, feeding in the same fields; no mixing. This gives the basic quality. After that, it is a question of the skill of individual cheese-makers and correct storage. That is what you pay for with farmhouse cheese. The extra money is very little by comparison with the extra quality.

Cheshire One of the oldest English cheeses, much more crumbly than Cheddar, and with a tang that comes from the salty pastures of Cheshire. The different colours mean nothing in terms of taste; some cheeses are dyed an orange-fawn, that is all. Blue Cheshire is a rare cheese, that occurs 'more often by accident than design', according to one cheese expert, though there are two farms which specialise in it. There are 22 farms in Cheshire and Shropshire producing farmhouse cheeses.

Double and single Gloucester Close-textured cheeses, made by the Cheddar method, the double being richer than the single. If you are in the West Country, you can buy these two cheeses from Charles Martell, along with other English and French cheeses, at the markets of Cirencester, Gloucester and Ledbury. He makes them from the milk of his Old Gloucester herd, the breed that originally supplied the milk for these cheeses.

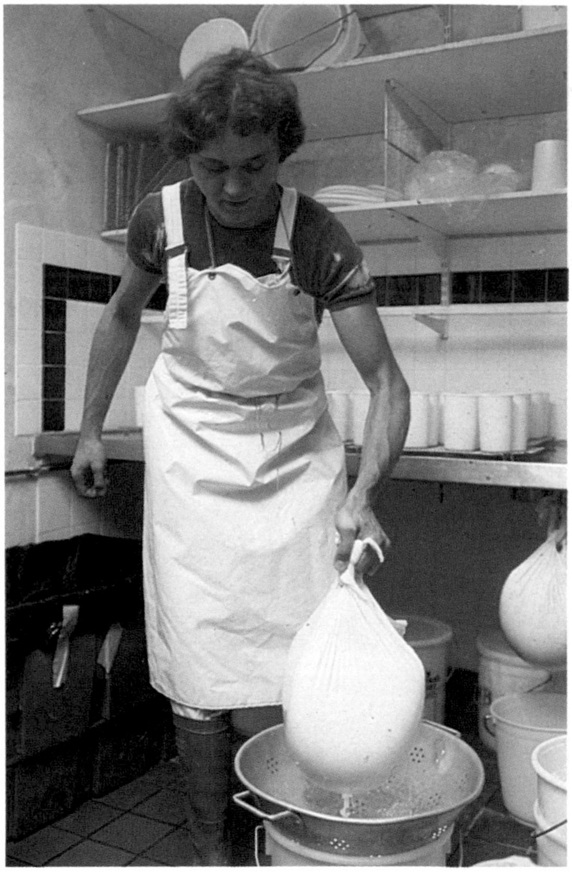

Cheese making by small goat and dairy sheep farmers is on the increase today

Dunlop A Scottish cheese that is now made in the Cheddar way, but with its own flavour.

Highland cheeses There are a number of soft Highland cheeses, from a low-fat Crowdie to the full fat Hramsa, flavoured with wild garlic leaves. Caboc, a double cream cheese rolled in oatmeal, should be bought from a shop with a rapid turnover, as it can sometimes develop an unpleasant aftertaste.

together and stir in the wine. Serve hot or warm. The pudding need only be warm, too, but the plates must be very hot; you do not want the sauce to congeal.

SUSSEX POND PUDDING

My star of English puddings. You might think, especially when you look at it, that it is heavy, meagre and dull. You would be wrong. The crust is light, the filling rich and lifted completely above the ordinary by the bitterness of a whole lemon, the surprise in the middle. Versions of this pudding without the lemon are not worth bothering about. I have successfully used a couple of limes instead, but have never yet tried an orange, which if it were a Seville orange might be even better than a lemon.

Serves 6

FOR THE CRUST

375 g/12 oz/3 cups self-raising flour
level teaspoon baking powder
$\frac{1}{4}$ level teaspoon salt
175 g/6 oz/good cup chopped fresh suet
cold water, to mix

FOR THE FILLING

about 200 g/7 oz/scant cup butter, diced
about 200 g/7 oz/scant cup granulated or demerara sugar
large lemon, well washed and pricked
1-litre/3-pt/7$\frac{1}{2}$-cup pudding basin

Mix the crust ingredients in the given order to a soft, but not sticky dough. Roll out and shape as for steak and kidney pudding, page 000. Drop into the buttered basin, open it out and gently press it into place, joining the edges together so that the basin is evenly lined, the top of the dough lolling slightly over the rim.

Put in half the butter and sugar, lay the lemon on top. Fill the gaps with the remaining butter and sugar. You may need another 50 g (2 oz/$\frac{1}{4}$ cup) of each. Roll out the remaining pastry to make a lid. Moisten the edges of both lid and basin lining. Position the pastry, seal and cover as for steak and kidney pudding. Boil or steam, allowing 3 hours. Remove the wrappings; ease round the pudding with a thin knife, then turn out on to a shallow serving dish. As you put the spoon into the pudding the brown sauce will flow out to make a pond—

Lancashire Related to Cheshire, white and crumbly, and ideal for toasting. An unmistakeable rich salty-acid taste. There are four farms making it, as well as commercial dairies.

Leicestershire Another crumbly cheese, related to Cheshire again. Dyed bright orange, but with a mild taste, and rather drier in texture than Lancashire.

Sage Derby A close-textured, Cheddar-type cheese, layered with bands of cheese, dyed green from sage leaves.

Stilton The finest of all blue cheeses—though a Frenchman or an Italian might not agree, and some Yorkshiremen will prefer a blue Wensleydale. Defoe remarked on its fame in 1727, and he, like other 18th century travellers on the Great North Road, encountered it at Stilton, in Cambridgeshire. Perhaps at the Bell Inn, which is said to be the place where it was first known. Stilton is made today in Derbyshire, Nottinghamshire and Leicestershire. The blue veining develops from *Penicillium roquefortii*, which is added to the milk at the beginning of the cheese-making process. The finished cheeses are pierced with steel needles to help the mould develop by means of contact with the air. The **Blue Vinny** that is on sale occasionally is made by the same method as Stilton. It is different, though, from the old and famous Blue Vinny, which was made from skimmed milk in Dorset.

Wensleydale A quickly made, mild cheese that goes well with apples, apple pie and fruit cake, as well as being delicious to eat on its own. It developed from a sheep's milk cheese made by the monks of Jervaulx Abbey, in Yorkshire, but now it is made of cow's milk. England had lost most of its sheep's milk cheeses by the middle of the 17th century. Happily, sheep's milk cheeses are now being made again.

Testing blue Stilton, for the Christmas market

more like a moat—and you will see the lemon inside. Give everyone a bit of lemon as you cut up the pudding and put it on the plates.

MERTON SAUCE

I treasure a copy I have of *The Women's Suffrage Cookery Book*, compiled by Mrs Aubrey Dowson, with its menus for meals for suffrage workers and Mrs Bertrand Russell's recipe for cooking and preserving a good suffrage speaker. I also treasure a piece or two I have of the special china made for the movement, which did not harm the people who produced it. It is white with a mauve and green pattern of periwinkle, gentle and elegant like the recipes in the book. Merton sauce is in fact a much older recipe than the suffragette movement, but I first came across it in their collection.

Cream 125 g (4 oz/½ cup) of butter with 175 g (6 oz/¾ cup) of caster sugar, and gradually add half a wineglass of brandy and half a wine glass of sherry. About 4 tablespoons (⅓ cup) each, but add them slowly as the butter cream may not absorb the full quantity. An electric mixer helps.

Brandy butter is made in the same way, with less sugar and more butter, plus a squeeze of lemon and brandy to taste. Rum butter demands soft brown sugar and goes particularly well with oatcakes. All these butters, or hard sauces, go with Christmas pudding, and mince pies.

TEA CREAMS

Tea, coffee and chocolate came to us in the 17th century, and altered our eating habits as well as our drinking habits. All these beverages were used in cookery, but tea gradually dropped out as a flavouring for food. Perhaps it had something to do with the packaging of blended, low quality teas that we now suffer from. Certainly you have to use pure green tea to get a delicate but truly unmistakable taste. Or, as I have recently found out, tea grated from a black Chinese tea brick: it is made from over 1 kg (2 lb) tea compressed under 60 tons into a flat, patterned tile. You have to attack it with pincers, graters and zesters to get a powder, which makes the most beautiful smooth tea, perfect for drinking without milk, good for making creams.

Tea brick cream Dissolve a packet (½ oz) powdered gelatine in 150 ml (¼ pt/⅔ cup) strong tea. Add 150 ml (¼ pt/⅔ cup) single cream. Stir in 2 level tablespoons (3 tbs) sugar, add drops of lemon juice to bring out the flavour. When it sets to an egg white consistency, fold in 300 ml (½ pt/1⅓ cups) whipped double cream. Chill until just firm, and serve with ratafias or amaretti di Saronno.

Green tea cream Put 25 g (scant oz) green (gunpowder) tea into a pan with 2 level tablespoons (3 tbs) sugar, 3 strips of lemon peel, and 450 ml (¾ pt/scant 2 cups) whipping cream. Bring slowly to the boil, tasting from time to time, and stopping when the tea flavour is pronounced enough (remember that flavours weaken as they cool). Pour through a sieve, pushing through the last greenish drops. Taste and add extra sugar, plus up to 150 ml (¼ pt/⅔ cup) more whipping cream to taste. Dissolve a packet (½ oz/2 envelopes) powdered gelatine in 6 tablespoons (½ cup) very hot water and add to the tea mixture. Brush out a decorative mould with almond or tasteless oil. Pour in the tea cream. Chill and turn out to serve. Or divide between 8 little custard pots (this rich cream goes a long way). Serve with biscuits, as above.

JUNKET

A mild form of soft cheese that takes its name from the little rush baskets the curd was drained in (Norman French jonquet, a basket made from jonques or rushes). We do not drain the curd, but leave it smooth as glass and preferably in a glass bowl. The richer the milk you use, the better the junket will be. Milk from Jersey or Devonshire or Cornish breeds is the ideal, but attainable by few, I am afraid.

Bring the milk slowly to blood heat (maximum 39°C, 100°F), allowing two bottles (1200 ml/2 pts/5 cups) for 8 people. Dissolve in it 2 level dessertspoons sugar, and add 4 tablespoons (⅓ cup) brandy, if you like. Set a large glass bowl in a warm place in the kitchen where it can stay undisturbed. Pour in the milk, then gently stir in 2 teaspoons rennet; cover with a clean cloth and leave until set.

If you use bottled rennet or tablets, follow the pack instructions.

When set, junket may be chilled. Before serving spread the surface with clotted cream; if it is too stiff to spread, mix in a little single cream. Sprinkle with grated nutmeg or powdered cinnamon. Serve with thick pouring cream and extra sugar, if you like. Fruit is often served with junket; sugared raspberries or strawberries are best.

SCANDINAVIA

Bornholm smoked Baltic herring is the best in Scandinavia

Fish and freshness, above all salmon, herrings and prawns ... dark, purple-brown reindeer meat ... smoked pork loin ... close rye bread ... sweet pale cloudberries ... sugar and spice in unexpected foods ... aquavit and unfailingly good coffee are things I have most enjoyed on Scandinavian trips. You might think that being so far north, their food and ours would be close in shared dishes and ideas. But this is not the case. They have a parallel style, using ingredients we know well, but a different style and one that is much more demanding as far as food retailers are concerned.

Few markets in this country can compare with the Saluhall in Stockholm's Ostermalms square for vitality of produce. It is a covered market, not an enormous place, but there are no dud stalls, which means a wider choice than might first appear. One woman specialises in great discs of rye bread, flat and crisp, and in bright wrappings. She sells fresh bread, too, and the soft tunbröd, baked pancake-thin in a griddle; you cut this into wedges and roll them round slices of pickled herring.

I remembered a portrait I had seen of the great Gustav Vasa, the 16th-century King of Sweden, dressed all in black with yellow slashes, like a regal insect, who encouraged his subjects to grow rye and make crisp bread. He is the Rye King of the packaged crisp breads sold in Britain. Then I caught sight of a smug, ironic reindeer head, high up, and walked over to the reindeer meat stall beneath. I bought dried reindeer, very salty, that Lapps grate into their coffee, and peppered reindeer steaks, smoked reindeer and a reindeer sausage, like a French andouille, of thinly-rolled sheets of fat and lean meat.

The great thing, though, in the Saluhall is the fish. There was even more choice than I found later in the gabled Fiskekorka at Göteborg, which iss right on a quay, with screaming seagulls. Smoked filleted eels lay long and appetising beside tubs of pickled herring in many varieties. There were tanks of fish and lobsters, piles of small Baltic herrings with spicy-pink flesh, black-streaked squid, freshwater pollan and pike.

A young fishmonger showed me the difference between pale, tapering Baltic salmon, which feeds on Baltic herring, and the brighter pink, stumpier salmon from Norwegian fish farms that are set up in the fjords. In that cold, rich water, fish farming produces admirable salmon and large pink prawns (US shrimp). Sometimes Norwegians have prawn parties, with kilos of them heaped down the centre of a table and frequent bowls of mayonnaise. Everyone helps themselves to the prawns, eats them with bread and mayonnaise, gets in a thorough mess as far as hands are concerned and has a wonderful time.

The other great Norwegian fish is cod, so good that it is eaten at Christmas feasts. Coley, one of the cod's lesser relations, goes into Bergen fish soup, right at the top of Norwegian specialities. This we cannot reproduce any more than we can fake up a convincing bouillabaisse, because most of our fishmongers are not good enough. When our Norwegian niece comes to England she snorts her way round fish shops, pitying us. Where are the fish tanks, she asks, with the *fresh* fish? Where indeed? For Bergen fish soup, you need fish that jumps into the pot, otherwise it can be dull. But it is worth having a try, and making sure that every other ingredient is as fresh as can be.

Another major Scandinavian food, especially in Denmark, is pork. Oddly enough, the Danes do not eat much bacon, they export it (to Britain). They cure it for themselves in other ways. The best as far as I am concerned is the boned, smoked loin known as hamburgerryg. In England you can buy it from most branches of Marks and Spencer and Danish Food Centres. It is packaged with cooking instructions, but the best way to eat it is chilled, thinly sliced and not cooked at all (see page 172).

Wherever you find pork, you find cheese and butter, as pigs are, or were, fed on the skim milk and whey. In England we are well used to Danish cheese. I find lightly salted Lurpak butter the best by far for cooking, and for potting fish and meat as well. It amused me to discover from a member of the Young family, the British seafood specialists, this same butter has been used since the beginning of this century for our Lancashire potted shrimps. It is also ideal for open sandwiches, where strong items of a topping need a mild creaminess between them and the rye bread base.

On a final thought of unrepentant gourmandise, may I recommend the skill of the pastrycooks of Scandinavia. If your experience of Danish pastries has been the flabby offerings of mass catering, you may think I am joking. Indeed, the fine skill and lightness, the lovely and unusual notes of aniseed, cardamom and cinnamon, the special winter festival biscuits and cakes, and swirls and curves of well-buttered dough, are as outside our experience as any product of Austria or France.

It is not just the cakes and fine breads and buns, but the places where you eat them. They have a clear, clean amiability. The food may on occasion be bland, and at the cheaper end of the scale even boring, but it is never nasty or served in squalid surroundings. The wholesome charm of vivid colours, or the neutral tones of polished wood and light woven fabrics, make the chance stop for coffee or a quick meal into a pleasant and restful experience.

APRICOT AND APPLE SOUP
Aprikos och appel soppa

Serve hot in cold weather, or chilled in summertime.

Serves 8–10
500 g/1 lb fresh apricots, stoned, or
375 g/12 oz/4 cups dried apricots, soaked
1 kg/2 lb cooking apples, peeled, cored, cut up
2 sticks of celery, halved
small bunch of parsley
bay leaf
1.5 litres/$2\frac{1}{2}$ pts/$6\frac{1}{4}$ cups light stock
salt
about 200 ml/7 fl oz/$\frac{3}{4}$ cup cream
30 g/1 oz/$\frac{1}{4}$ cup toasted hazelnuts or almonds

Cook the fruit, celery and herbs in the stock for 30 minutes. Remove the celery and herbs and liquidise. Season with salt, stir in the cream and reheat or chill, in either case adding extra stock or water to dilute to the consistency you prefer. Serve scattered with the nuts. Rye biscuits (recipe on page 179) are nice with the soup.

CHILLED BUTTERMILK SOUP
Kaernemaelkskoldskål

Now that we can buy buttermilk at the supermarket, try this Danish soup on a hot summer day. Serve it at the pudding stage, with small oatcakes.

Serves 4–6
2 eggs
60 g/2 oz/$\frac{1}{4}$ cup sugar
juice and finely grated zest of 1 lemon
generous litre/2 pts/5 cups buttermilk, plus extra (see method)
250 ml/8 fl oz/1 cup whipping cream, stiffly whipped
FOR THE OATCAKES
125 g/4 oz/$\frac{1}{2}$ cup butter
125 g/4 oz/$\frac{1}{2}$ cup sugar
500 ml/$\frac{3}{4}$ pt/1 cup measure of porridge oats

Whisk the eggs with the sugar until very thick (use an electric beater). Add the juice of the lemon and the finely grated zest, then the buttermilk. Chill for 1 hour. If you leave the buttermilk soup for a long time, it will grow thicker and thicker, in which case

Apricot soup can be served all the year round, but is best in summer

dilute it with more buttermilk. Just before serving, heap the whipped cream on top.

To make the oatcakes, melt the butter in a pan and stir in the sugar; then when it is dissolved, stir in the oatmeal. Cook until a nice golden brown, stirring all the time. Pack into egg cups, rinsed out with water, and chill until firm. Put the oatcakes into soup bowls, break them up a little and pour over the soup.

YELLOW PEA SOUP
Gulärtsoppa/Arter med fläsk

Yellow pea soup is claimed as a national dish by both Denmark and Sweden. It is their equivalent to the olla podrida of Spain (see page 75) for example, with pulses and meat cooked together, then served separately but in close conjunction. There is no one correct recipe—a Swedish friend said to me briskly, 'The poor add sausage to their yellow peas, the rich smoked bacon and pork'. So take your choice, a smoked pork item of some kind is all that you need.

Danes serve dark rye bread, lager and schnapps with their pea soup (gule aerter). The Swedes drink a glass of hot Punsch, their sweet rum-based liqueur, with their pea soup and follow up with pancakes and waffles. Ginger rather than thyme can be the flavouring, with more or less of the other vegetables than the peas, which may or may not be sieved.

Serves 8
300 g/10 oz/1¼ cups yellow split peas, soaked
2½ litres/4½ pts/11¼ cups water
500 g/1 lb piece of smoked or green streaky bacon, or salt pork
small celeriac, peeled and diced, or 4 stalks of celery, chopped
3 leeks, trimmed and sliced, or 2 bunches of spring onions, trimmed and cut up
250 g/8 oz peeled, diced carrots
500 g/1 lb peeled, diced potatoes
6–8 small onions, peeled
6–8 gammon chops, green or smoked
bouquet of thyme sprigs, or level teaspoon powdered ginger
boiling sausage and/or 4 frankfurters

Cook the peas slowly in 1 litre (2 pts/5 cups) water, without salt, until very tender (about 1½–2 hours). Sieve or process if you like, then season. Meanwhile, simmer the piece of bacon or pork in the remaining water for 2 hours, adding the vegetables after an hour, and the chops, thyme or ginger and boiling sausage, if using, after 1¼ hours.

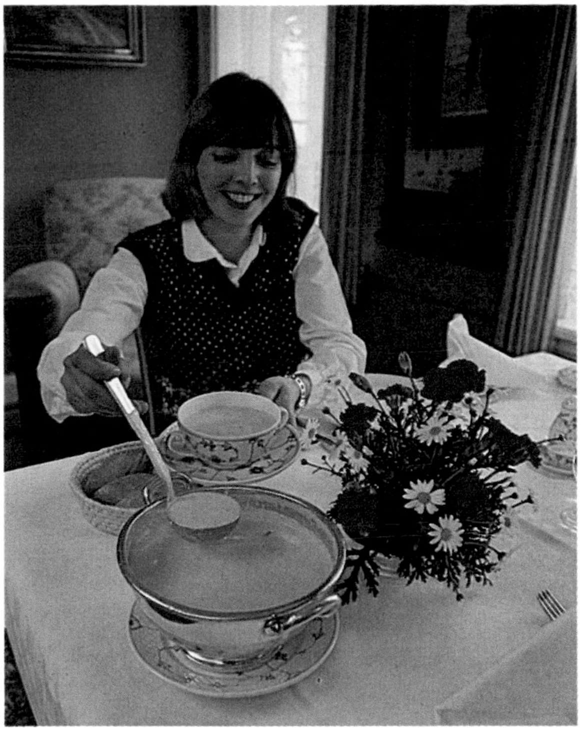

Yellow pea soup is a popular dish for family lunch

Remove the bacon or pork, the chops and boiling sausage, cut them as appropriate and keep warm. Stir the pea purée into the bacon pan, and add extra water if the soup is too thick for your taste. Correct the seasoning. Heat, adding frankfurters 5 minutes before serving the soup.

Ladle out the soup, then, as people finish, bring in the meat to eat on side plates, with a second helping of soup.

BERGEN FISH SOUP

In Bergen fish market, on the quay, cod and coley and other fish are kept in tanks of sea water. You can choose which you want. There is not an enormously wide choice, but the fish shine with freshness and one can buy prawns of a quality we never see. At first I resisted making the local soup because our fish is not so brilliantly fresh, but now, I find its creamy white delicacy, set off by shreds of carrot and leek and tiny fish balls, irresistible. Coley is the main fish required, but ask for trimmings of other white fish as well and a slice of haddock for the fish balls. Other fish of the cod type can be used instead of coley, with good results.

Serves 8
1 kg/2 lb coley fillet, cubed
1 kg/2 lb fish bones, skins, heads etc.
large onion, finely chopped
large leek, trimmed, sliced
2 medium bay leaves
salt, pepper, teaspoon sugar
white wine vinegar
2 medium carrots
white part of 2 leeks
level tablespoon flour
2 level tablespoons butter
3 egg yolks
150 ml/¼ pt/⅔ cup each double and soured cream
chopped chives
FOR THE FISH BALLS
250 g/8 oz skinned, filleted haddock
½ teaspoon salt
2 level teaspoons each flour and cornflour
2 level tablespoons/1 oz/2 tbs cold soft butter
pepper, nutmeg
225 ml/7½ fl oz/good ¾ cup cold boiled milk
4 tablespoons/2 fl oz/⅓ cup cold boiled cream

Put first 5 ingredients into a large pan. Cover generously with water. Simmer for 45 minutes. Strain into a clean pan. Season with salt, pepper and sugar. Add a teaspoon vinegar, taste and add more: the sharpness should be light, but remember the softening effect of cream. Pour off enough stock into a small pan to make a 2 cm (¾ in) depth for poaching the fish balls while the soup is cooking.

To the larger pan of stock, add carrots and leeks cut into thin matchstick shreds (using a mandolin for carrots saves time and fingers). Simmer until almost cooked but still crunchy.

Meanwhile, mash flour and butter together. Add to soup in small quantities, keeping it below boiling point from now on. When it is used up and the soup slightly thickened, beat yolks and creams together and pour in a ladle of soup. Whisk well and return to the pan. Stir for another 5 minutes—do not overheat. Finally add the fish balls (see below), their stock and some chives. Taste for seasoning, adjust and serve.

To make the fish balls, liquidise haddock and salt to a fluffy purée, or mince fish and beat with salt for 5 minutes. Still liquidising or beating, add the remaining ingredients one by one. Form tiny balls with two teaspoons and poach in the barely simmering stock reserved for the purpose. After 2 minutes, taste one—if all trace of flouriness has gone, and it feels light and soft, the fish balls are done. Beginners are advised to try an experimental fish ball first, to see how they go: this also means that extra seasoning can be added if necessary.

CUCUMBER SALAD
Agurkesalat

This cucumber salad accompanies a number of hot dishes in Scandinavia, especially in Denmark, and appears on the cold table or on open sandwiches as well.

Serves 6
large cucumber
level tablespoon salt
rounded tablespoon sugar
150 ml/¼ pt/⅔ cup wine vinegar or cider vinegar
pepper
chopped parsley or dill leaves

Score the cucumber down with a fork or canelle cutter, then slice thinly on the wide grater blade. Put the slices into a colander and sprinkle with the salt. Leave them for an hour or two, then squeeze them dry in a clean cloth. Spread them out in a dish. Mix sugar and vinegar together and pour it over them. Grind on plenty of pepper. Chill for a couple of hours. Taste and adjust the seasoning, then pour off the liquid and serve with the chopped herb.

OPEN TABLE OR COLD TABLE
Smörgåsbord

The smörgåsbord—not to be confused with smørrebrød which is a Danish open sandwich—is a complete meal, including hot main course dishes and a simple dessert. Somewhere I read a folksy explanation that it started with parish picnics, when everyone came with a dish they had made to be put on a common table. I am more inclined to believe that it developed from the brannvinsbord, the aquavit table, which was laid out in a separate room as a curtain-raiser to a special meal of celebration, like the Russian zakuski.

The centre of the whole spread was an immense aquavit container, a huge urn with various compartments and taps for people to draw off the flavoured aquavit they liked best. Aquavit is still the drink of the smörgåsbord, usually anise-flavoured, with beer as a chaser. To outsiders, the most delectable part is the range of pickled fish. Cheese is important too, so that in its smallest form the smörgåsbord will be like the herring course I had at Den Gyldene Freden restaurant (see spiced herring recipe on page 167); in other words, smör, ost och

A stunning smörgåsbord in Stockholm, topped by an aquavit urn: herring dishes are in the foreground

sill—butter, cheese and herring—with bread, of course.

The most delicious smörgåsbord I ever ate was at Roskilde, in Denmark, since the hot dishes were as good as the cold ones, and it was set down in courses the length of a table of 30.

The most spectacular table was laid out in the golden and painted Operakällaren restaurant in Stockholm. The huge table has two rounded ends. One holds ice, into which the pickled fish containers are set, the other has a bain marie system for keeping the hot food hot. At the cold end were four plain pickled herring dishes, together with an escabèche of trout, rollmops, smoked eel, marinated salmon (gravad lax, recipe on page 169), smoked salmon, fish pâté in the modern style, and bowls of soured cream and chives. Down one long side there were stuffed eggs on golden-yellow pollan caviar, black lumpfish caviar and bright pink salmon caviar; four bowls of shellfish salads, a bowl of shrimps, rectangles of thin cheese, Bayonne or Westphalian ham and melon, and a round board with a central spike, like a dark bone, which kept great wheels of rye crispbread in a neat pile. The other side was covered with cold meats—pink-centred beef, tongue, salted veal, ham, pâtés, salami and several sausages, and smoked reindeer, which is softish and between tongue and beef in texture, with a slightly goaty, but delicious, taste. To go with these meats were pickled vegetables and fruit, including lingonberries, apple sauce, red currant jelly, and black, green and stuffed olives.

The dishes at the hot end I did not like so much; they suffered from keeping. There were meat balls of two different kinds, Jansson's temptation (recipe on page 175), mushroom omelette, salt herring baked with lines of potato slices in between and several hot vegetables.

Above this remarkable smörgåsbord running down most of the table, is a raised shelf with a huge aquavit urn in the centre, chased and decorated, and very 19th century in its squat opulence.

The way to tackle a spread like this is to start with the herring end, taking a small selection and returning. It is not wise or polite to heap the plate as if it were the last meal of one's life; if things are messed up, you cannot taste them. Then go for the egg and caviar dishes, with the herring mixed salads, and a few shrimps. Then the cheese or ham and melon.

Apart from the reindeer, I would leave the meat section altogether—beef, tongue and ham are no different from ours. Try a little of one of the hot dishes, but leave room for a light cake or some fruit salad to end up with and, of course, coffee, which seems to be good everywhere in Scandinavia.

A plate of pickled herring with onion and sour cream

To make your own smörgåsbord, all of the cold dishes in this chapter are suitable, and the open sandwich fillings can be adapted or served on small buttered rounds of bread or cocktail-pumpernickel. In the sauces box (see opposite), you will find ways of of changing the basic mayonnaise.

Here, though, are a few more cold table ideas for you to try:

Westcoast salad (Västkustsallad) This consists of roughly equal quantities of lobster, shrimp and mussels, a half quantity of raw sliced mushrooms, some thinly cut tomato wedges and petits pois. Serve with vinaigrette dressing, made with a little French mustard and garlic. Lobster can be left out, or scampi used instead. The salad is served in a bowl, lined with lettuce leaves, or on a dish.

Bird's nest (Fågelbo) In the centre of a square dish, make a mound of chopped parsley and shredded lettuce. At the four corners pile chopped onion, chopped pickled beetroot, capers, and Swedish an-

SAUCES

With the smörgåsbord, Scandinavian cooks have developed their own variations of mayonnaise, and some good sauces for fish.

Curry mayonnaise Flavour 250 ml (8 fl oz/1 cup) mayonnaise with $1\frac{1}{2}$ level teaspoons curry powder and $1\frac{1}{2}$ teaspoons chopped chutney. Serve with dried fish, or prawns of different kinds.

Light mayonnaise Add 60–90 ml (2–3 fl oz/$\frac{1}{4}$–$\frac{1}{3}$ cup) soured cream to mayonnaise, at the end of making it. Chopped green herbs make a good addition, chives in particular. Goes well with all foods.

Paprika mayonnaise Flavour 250 ml (8 fl oz/1 cup) mayonnaise with 1 level tablespoon tomato paste, 1 tablespoon chilli sauce and a finely shredded red pepper. Serve with hot or cold dried fish.

Gastronome mayonnaise Mix 150 ml ($\frac{1}{4}$ pt/$\frac{2}{3}$ cup) mayonnaise with 100 ml (4 fl oz/$\frac{1}{2}$ cup) soured cream, 1 level tablespoon each tomato paste and chopped tarragon, plus 1 teaspoon tarragon vinegar. Serve with cold fish, particularly turbot and sole. (This and the three sauces above are taken from Bengt Petersen's *Delicious Fish Dishes*, published by Wezäta Förlag, 1976).

Apple mayonnaise Mix together an equal quantity of mayonnaise and slightly sweetened apple purée. Flavour with horseradish and rosé wine. Serve with cold pork, duck, ham, beef or veal.

Dill and mustard sauce Mix together 2 level tablespoons (3 tbs) Swedish, German or Dijon mustard, 2 level teaspoons sugar, and a large egg yolk. Slowly whisk in 150 ml ($\frac{1}{4}$ pt/$\frac{2}{3}$ cup) oil as when making mayonnaise. Finally, whisk in about 2 tablespoons (3 tbs) wine vinegar and a generous teaspoon of chopped dillweed. Season to taste. Serve with gravad lax (recipe on page 169).

Fine shrimp sauce Shell 250 g (8 oz) shrimps or prawns. Dry the shells in a cool oven or under a low grill. Process shells to a rough powder, then put them into a pan with the butter and hot water or fish stock to cover. Strain, pushing all the juices through the strainer into a bowl. Leave to cool, then remove the solid cake of shrimp butter. Melt this in a pan, stir in 30 g (1 oz/$\frac{1}{4}$ cup) flour and cook for 2 minutes. Moisten with 150 ml ($\frac{1}{4}$ pt/$\frac{2}{3}$ cup) stock, and milk or single cream. Simmer for 10 minutes. Then add 2 dessertspoons dry white wine and simmer for a few minutes longer. Put in the shrimps or prawns to heat through but do not boil again. Serve with poached or steamed fish, or fish pudding (recipe on page 170).

chovies or pickled spiced herring. On the greenery, arrange egg yolks, in broken half-shells. Depending on the rest of the table, each person has a yolk and what he wants of the other items, or somebody tips out the yolks on to the greenery and mixes all the ingredients into a general salad.

Pink rice salad (Rissallad) A rice salad moistened with a little vinaigrette and drained. It is embellished with pink shrimps, thin shreds of different coloured peppers, stoned olives and lightly blanched cauliflower sprigs. Finally, mix with mayonnaise (recipe on page 112), or cream sharpened with lemon juice, and coloured to a gentle pink as well as flavoured with tomato purée.

Asparagus salad Make with cooked asparagus, dressed with vinaigrette, and chopped hard-boiled egg and parsley.

Hard-boiled egg halves or slices Serve on black lumpfish caviar, with a swirl of cream and chives. Avocado slices can be added, but turn them in vinaigrette first so that they do not discolour.

Cheese mousse (Ostfromage) Thicken 3 egg yolks and 150 ml ($\frac{1}{4}$ pt/$\frac{2}{3}$ cup) of single cream over a low heat (do not boil). Stir in 100 g ($3\frac{1}{2}$ oz) sieved blue cheese. Dissolve 2 level teaspoons powdered gelatine in 8 teaspoons hot water, and mix in. Whip 125 ml (4 fl oz/$\frac{1}{2}$ cup) whipping cream until firm, and fold in. Set in a ring mould—about 900 ml ($1\frac{1}{2}$ pts/$3\frac{3}{4}$ cups) should be adequate. Turn out and surround with radishes, tiny sticks of celery, half-slices of cucumber, etc.

SPICED HERRING
Kryddsill

One evening in Stockholm's old city, I went to Den Gyldene Freden (Golden Peace) restaurant to pay my respects to Carl Bellman, Sweden's great poet of the 18th century. It was his particular haunt, where he sang his songs of the good life, of love and hate and humour, of the watery landscape and the islands of Stockholm, of picnics and drinking parties. The whole place was dark and comfortable,

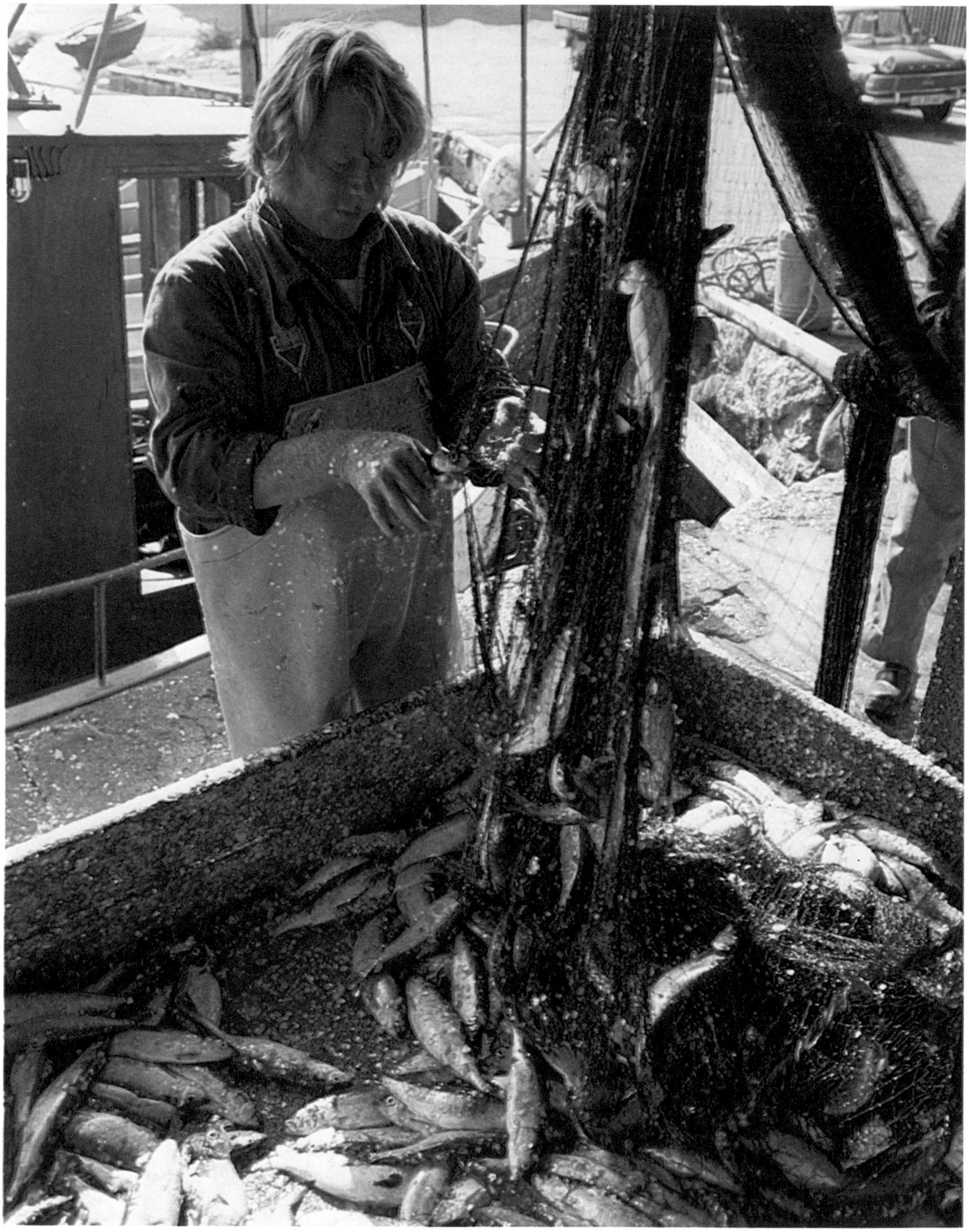

Fish are always fresh in Scandinavia—the catch is landed at Bornholm

low arched, the furniture heavy, with occasional gleams of copper and brass and candles.

Bellman has his plaque on the wall and I ordered things he liked. The herring came in two bowls with fresh sprigs of dill, one at each end of a wooden board. Between them was a plate with two large thin slices of cheese—västerbottenost and herrgårdsost—and a few boiled potatoes with dill. Rye and white bread were put on the table, too. Aquavit was served in a glass pressed down into a bowl of ice, with its flask laid on its side in the ice.

You could serve this and the pickled herring of the next recipe, overleaf, in the same way, substituting Danish and Dutch cheeses: it makes an admirable first course or main lunch dish.

Serves 10
2.5 kg/5 lb fresh herrings, cleaned
10 white peppercorns, crushed
5 bay leaves
5 almonds, slightly crushed
200 g/7 oz/$\frac{7}{8}$ cup sugar
200 g/7 oz salt
10 allspice berries, slightly crushed
tablespoon Greek rigani or dried marjoram

Soak the herrings for 24 hours in one part vinegar to two parts water.

Mix the remaining ingredients. Drain and layer the herring and pickle mixture into a stoneware or glass pot. Cover. Keep cool for 2–3 weeks. Serve as above, or with potatoes boiled in their skin, with soured cream and chives.

PICKLED SALT HERRING
Inlagd sill

A sweet onion pickle makes particularly good herrings. Use large salted fillets (6–8) from the delicatessen, or matjes herring fillets. If you can get neither, quick-salt fresh herrings, after boning them, in a brine made by dissolving 60 g (2 oz) salt in 600 ml (1 pt/2$\frac{1}{2}$ cups) water: in 3 hours, they will be salted enough and will need no soaking.

Drain and dry the fillets and lay them in a refrigerator box, interspersed with 2–3 sliced onions and 2–3 small bay leaves. Make a pickle by simmering together for 3 minutes 250 g (8 oz/1 cup) sugar, 150 ml ($\frac{1}{4}$ pt/$\frac{2}{3}$ cup) wine or cider vinegar, 8 lightly crushed peppercorns, and 1 rounded teaspoon pickling spices, including a small chilli. Cool and pour over the herrings. Cover and refrigerate for 5 days, turning occasionally. Drain and put in a dish, whole or cut into strips. Garnish with the onion, a bay leaf or two and the chilli.

MARINATED SALMON, MACKEREL, TROUT OR HERRING
Gravad lax, makrill, forell, sill

When I first gave this recipe in the *Observer Magazine* some 12 years ago, it seemed daring. Nowadays, such things have become a commonplace of the nouvelle cuisine, and we are used to the idea of fish 'cooked' by lemon, vinegar or salt.

Serves 6–8
1 kg/2 lb fish
heaped tablespoon sea salt
rounded tablespoon sugar
teaspoon coarsely ground black peppercorns
level tablespoon dillweed

Ask the fishmonger to scale and fillet salmon, or to behead and fillet smaller fish. Leave the skin on.

Mix together the rest of the ingredients. Scatter one-quarter of the mixture in the base of a dish, and half on to the cut sides of the fish, which should then be sandwiched together. Put into the dish and sprinkle the last of the mixture on top. Cover with foil and weight down. Leave for 12 hours in the refrigerator or up to 6 days in a cool place. Turn the fish over occasionally.

To serve, drain well, trim off any hard edges, and cut into thin slices on the bias or parallel to the skin. Serve with a dill and mustard sauce (see page 167).

The fish skin should be cut into strips and fried crisp in a non-stick pan with barely any oil, or sealed in a very hot oven. Serve with the fish: for some people it is the best part.

SMORREBROD

In Danish, smørrebrød means simply buttered bread. The idea of putting something on to it, the topping or pålaeg, occurred long before the Earl of Sandwich's gambling parties. By the end of the 19th century, restaurants had printed lists of their open sandwiches, which customers ticked to avoid muddles in the serving.

The genius of the open sandwich was Axel Svensson, who took over the list at Oskar Davidsen's restaurant in Copenhagen early this century. He turned it into a four-foot long fantasy, with new toppings that were to become classics, together with topical allusions such as the Union Jack sandwich, invented to celebrate Denmark's liberation in 1945. Sad to say, Oskar Davidsen's is closed now, but everywhere in Denmark you will find open sandwiches, including some of the ones Axel Svensson invented.

Everything can be used for open sandwiches, but a few rules help to prevent them becoming family dustbins. Of course leftovers are used—open sandwiches are the midday meal of every family—but with restraint. Here are some tips:

1 Danes use rye bread, ranging from light to dark, for its close texture, and wholemeal bread sometimes for shellfish. Crispbread or lightly toasted white bread are also suitable.

2 Use soft bread for firm fillings and firm bread for soft fillings. Butter it right to the edge: on occasion spiced lard, goose or duck fat will be more appropriate than butter, e.g. with pressed rolled pork (rullepølse—recipe on page 173), smoked goose breast, cold roast duck and pork, etc.

3 Genteel lettuce leaves are rarely used between butter and topping.

4 Restrict yourself to three items when you start inventing your own toppings, and make sure always to include some kind of piquancy—smoked fish or meat, capers, anchovies, spiced herring, apple sauce, pickled cucumber and other vegetables, horseradish, or lemon.

5 One of the novelties at Davidsen's was the use of a whole raw egg yolk in open sandwiches. It looks good in the arrangement, and when broken with a fork provides a sauce—just the right amount—for the other ingredients. Go easy with mayonnaise and vinaigrette, as they can cloud the clear textures and flavours.

Open sandwiches are the great Danish speciality for midday meals

Here are a few ideas from Axel Svensson's list:

Union Jack This consists of a layer of scraped, raw fillet steak, as in steak tartare. In the centre place an egg yolk, set inside an onion ring. Radiating to the corners from the yolk, place rows of pink shrimps close together, backs up.

Rush hour Make two complete layers of shrimps, with two individual rows of shrimps on top, so that each sandwich uses between 80–100 shrimps.

Smoked eel Place smoked eel fillets close to each long edge, with scrambled egg in the middle.

Roast beef Make with thin slices of roast beef, crisply fried bacon bits and crisply fried onion rings, or beef with cold béarnaise sauce, or with lines of black lumpfish caviare, or with horseradish. The beef should be underdone.

Smoked Bornholm herring Place herring fillets in strips, with an egg yolk on top, set inside an onion ring. Bornholm herring are the best in Scandinavia. They are caught and smoked the same day, but with their light cure they do not travel well and are rarely to be found outside Denmark. Substitute good kipper fillets, or bloaters.

Smoked salmon Top slices of smoked salmon with an egg yolk, sat inside a tomato ring. Or top with a diagonal stripe of scrambled egg, or with egg yolk, shreds of horseradish and finely chopped onion.

FISH PUDDING
Fiskepudding

The main smoked fish seller in the Saluhall in Stockholm's Ostermalms Square, devotes a corner of his stall to objects that looked like collapsing kugelhupf cakes, interspersed with plastic tubs of shrimps and shrimp sauce.

When I asked what they were, he replied that they were fish puddings. People buy them, wrap them in foil to carry home and reheat them. They are usually served with shrimp sauce. Not one of the most appetising of the gastronomic sights of Scandinavia.

When I returned to England, I looked them up dutifully and realised that they are very similar to French fish quenelles, and just as delicious. The recipe is not difficult if you have a processor, and a good fishmonger.

Serves 6
325 g/12 oz white fish fillet (very fresh cod, hake or haddock)
130 g/generous 4 oz/½ cup butter, softened
2 large egg yolks
2 level tablespoons/3 tbs flour
150 ml/¼ pt/⅔ cup each double cream and milk
1½ level teaspoons salt
level teaspoon sugar
pepper
2 large egg whites, stiffly whisked
extra butter, for greasing
2 level tablespoons/3 tbs fine breadcrumbs
1 level tablespoon chopped parsley
1.25-litre/2 pt/5-cup kugelhupf pottery mould or tin or ring mould

Scrape the fish from the skin, removing any bones, and weigh out 250 g (8 oz) or slightly more. Process the fish with the butter, yolks, flour, cream and milk and the seasoning, in batches, if necessary. When very smooth, fold into the stiffly whisked egg whites. Taste and correct the seasoning.

Grease the mould with a butter paper; put in the breadcrumbs and parsley, rolling them around to coat the sides.

Put in the fish mixture, cover with buttered foil or greaseproof paper and steam or cook in a bain marie in a moderate oven, 180°C (350°F), gas 4, for a generous hour till firm to the touch. Ease with a knife, turn out on to a hot dish and serve immediately with fine shrimp sauce (see page 167).

NORWEGIAN BOILED COD
Helkokt torsk

Norwegians are disgusted by our poor fishmongers; they buy their fish fresh from tanks, which are replenished daily. There the cod is so fine that it is the special Christmas Eve dish—a whole young cod weighing 1.5 kg (3 lb) or so, boiled and served with hollandaise sauce.

The Norwegian way is to scrape the fish, and remove the cod's liver and roe for separate cooking. Then dissolve enough salt in a bowl of water for an egg to float in it, and soak the fish in this brine for 15 minutes. Drain, then place the fish on the tray of a fish kettle, back up, the underpart spread where it has been cut for cleaning. Cover with cold water and add 1 level dessertspoon salt to each 600 ml (1 pt/2½ cups) water, plus a couple of slices of onion. Bring to simmering point, cover and simmer for 15 minutes until the fish is tender but not overcooked; *do not boil.* When the fins can be pulled out easily, the fish is done. Drain for a moment, then serve with hollandaise sauce.

Cook the chopped liver with a little stock from the pan towards the end of cooking time, adding a splash of vinegar and a bay leaf. This sauce is put on the table with the hollandaise. The roe can be used separately, e.g. for an open sandwich; simmer it in salted water until firm, then cool, slice and fry in butter.

To boil cod steaks Tie them with thread. Put under the cold tap, or soak in a bowl of water with ice cubes for an hour or two. This crisps and contracts the flesh. Bring 1 litre (1¾ pts/scant 2½ cups) water to the boil with 2½ level tablespoons salt. Slide in the cod steaks. The water will go off the boil. By the time it returns to the boil, the fish will be done. Serve with cod liver sauce (recipe above), hollandaise sauce (recipe on page 114) or shrimp sauce (recipe on page 167).

TURBOT FROM COPENHAGEN

The best fish I ever ate was at Krogs Fiskerestaurant, right on the quay of the Gammel Strand, in Copenhagen. It was plain poached turbot, with a lightly heaped tablespoon of freshly grated horseradish shreds on top, and a jug of melted butter to go with it. There were also a few boiled new potatoes.

Why was it so good? The fish had been caught

Poached turbot with grated horseradish

Krogs is the best place for fine fish cookery in Copenhagen

that morning, and had just been cooked, not overcooked. If you buy fish of that quality, try the Krogs way of doing it. The turbot can be steamed rather than boiled. Remember to grate down the horseradish root, not across, since the centre can be astoundingly hot.

HIGGLER'S POT
Hökarepanna

I had the recipe for this old dish from a Swedish friend, who lives in England. She makes it for the main course at Sunday lunch very often. First come little round open sandwiches, very fresh tasting, with shrimps and golden caviare and egg.

After the higgler's pot, we have a buttery Swedish cheese, cut in thin slices, and as pudding, vanilla ice-cream with hot Punsch (a Swedish liqueur) to pour over it and more Punsch to drink.

The only problem you may encounter with hökarepanna is finding the veal kidney. Order it in advance from your local veal butcher; it is a great delicacy.

Serves 8
1–1.5 kg/2–3 lb potatoes, fairly thickly sliced
2 pork tenderloins, sliced 1 cm/½ in thick
2 veal kidneys, sliced 1 cm (½ in) thick
500–750 g/1–1½ lb onions, sliced
salt and pepper
300 ml/½ pt/1¼ cups lager
glass of sherry

Cook the potatoes for 3 minutes in boiling salted water. Drain them well. Grease a deep flameproof pot with a butter paper, then put in a layer of potatoes, then some tenderloin, kidney and onions with seasoning. Repeat, and finish with a top layer of potatoes. Pour over the lager. Cover tightly and cook gently until the meat is tender, either on top of the stove or in a low oven, 150°C (300°F), gas 2. Maintain a simmer with the occasional bubble, by lowering the heat after a while. Since neither tenderloin nor kidneys are tough, this dish takes 1½ hours, but test earlier.

Taste the liquid, add extra seasoning if necessary, and pour in the sherry. Cook gently for another 5 minutes.

HAMBURGERRYG

This is now exported from Denmark and sold as smoked pork loin, luxury bacon loin and so on. Cooking instructions are sometimes on the packaging, but I do not follow them myself as the cooking times are generally far too long and result in tough dry meat. In the first instance, hamburgerryg does not need cooking at all and can be eaten like Parma ham (though it does not taste the same). This is not indicated on the packaging neither is it recommended by the exporters. Indeed the cure is slightly different from the hamburgerryg sold in Denmark, but as the loin is heat treated to a sufficiently high temperature to make it bacteriologically safe, one can still serve it in the same way as the Danes do. I often eat in this way.

When it comes to cooking hamburgerryg—and many Danes do cook it as a dinner-party or Sunday dish—I follow the instructions in *Cooking with a Danish Flavour*, by Pauline Viola and Knud Ravnkilde. Miss Viola manages the Consumer Advisory Service of Danish Agricultural Producers in England and knows what she is talking about.

Her way is to put the hamburgerryg into a pan of water, bring it to the boil and then simmer the meat gently for 10–15 minutes. Switch off and leave another 10 minutes. Really it is heated through, which keeps it tender. Her instructions are for a

750 g ($1\frac{1}{2}$ lb) piece; smaller pieces need 10 minutes simmering, then the 10 minutes rest. To serve, cut in slices and serve on a long dish, surrounded with young vegetables and whipped butter sauce (butter whisked to creaminess, perhaps with some chopped herbs added). Or with poached apple halves, the cavities filled with a little tart jelly.

Sugar-browned potatoes are a favourite with hamburgerryg, but are equally good on their own. You need small firm potatoes of a nice even shape, and enough to make a single, not too tight, layer in your sauté or frying pan. Scrub, boil and peel them, being careful not to overcook them. For a 500 g (1 lb) or slightly more potatoes, melt 45 g ($1\frac{1}{2}$ oz/3 tbs) butter in the pan, stir in sugar and cook until they caramelise together. Put in the potatoes, turning them in the glaze to brown and heat them through.

PRESSED ROLLED PORK
Rullepølse

What with pigs and open sandwiches, the Danes should produce excellent charcuterie. This rullepølse is particularly good and undemanding to make at home. You might just as well cure a whole side piece of pork belly and serve it with dry meats, such as chicken, at a party, and the quantities for 10 or more are intended for this. If you must try a smaller piece, reduce the ingredients proportionately.

The curing mixture below comes from *The Oskar Davidsen Book of Open Sandwiches*, and beef, veal or lamb can be used instead of pork. Choose a flat piece, e.g., the breast or brisket, in which lean and fat are inter-larded, weighing about 2 kg (4 lb).

Serves 10–12
whole side piece of pork belly
FOR SPICE MIXTURE
$\frac{1}{2}$ level teaspoon each allspice and ground cloves
2 level teaspoons black pepper
4 level teaspoons salt
2 medium onions, grated
FOR THE CURE
30 g/1 oz/2 tbs brown sugar
90 g/3 oz salt
15 g/$\frac{1}{2}$ oz saltpetre

Skin and bone the pork, or give the butcher time to do this for you. Cut the skin into small pieces, roll and freeze them for later use in stews and stocks; keep the bones for stocks, too. Lay the meat flat and beat out, skin side down. Mix the spice ingredients together, and scatter evenly over the meat. Roll up from one long side, and tie firmly with string.

Mix the cure ingredients together, then rub all over the meat; put everything into a pot. Cover and leave for a week, turning the meat twice a day, and rubbing the liquid which will form in the pot into the meat. If you have a cool larder and it is winter, there is no need to refrigerate the pork, though it is prudent to do so.

Remove the meat, rinse it quickly and put into a deep flameproof pot, adding enough tepid water to cover it generously. Bring to simmering point, cover and cook for $1\frac{1}{2}$ hours, skimming off any foam. Switch off the heat, put a dish on top of the pork and weight it down hard, then leave to cool. Drain, dry and cut in thin slices to serve (dill pickled cucumber goes well with rullepølse).

SWEDISH HASH
Pytt-i-panna

One of Europe's better recipes for Monday leftovers, and a good family dish. The two secrets of its success are the piquancy of the ham or bacon, and the fried eggs.

Scandinavia produces a wide range of cured meats

Serves 4
250 g/8 oz cold cooked beef or veal
about 125 g/4 oz ham, bacon or cooked salted meat
750 g/1½ lb cooked potatoes
2–3 onions, finely chopped
butter
salt and pepper
chopped parsley
4 eggs or 4 egg yolks

Cut the meats and potatoes into tiny dice—avoid mincing. Fry the onions gently in a little butter. Fry the meats in another pan and the potatoes in a third, also in butter, with seasoning. Turn, with a slice, from time to time, always frying gently until all is nicely browned. Mix together and add the parsley. Turn on to a hot dish and keep warm. Either fry the eggs in the remaining fat and put them on top of the hash or put yolks in their half-shells in the centre and serve with pickled beetroot (see opposite) or cucumber salad (see page 164).

TENDERLOIN STUFFED WITH APPLES AND PRUNES
Mørbrad med aebler og svedsker

Tenderloin is the undercut of large bacon pigs, which means it is a speciality of Danish cooking. I particularly like this version of a favourite dish; not only does it taste good, but it can be prepared in advance and quickly cooked.

Serves 6–8
2 pork tenderloins, trimmed of fat
12 large prunes, soaked
level teaspoon each powdered cinnamon and sugar, mixed
2 level teaspoons salt
½ level teaspoon black pepper
250 g/8 oz peeled, sliced apple
butter
150 ml/¼ pt/⅔ cup soured or whipping cream
watercress, optional
red currant jelly, or other sharp jelly

Split the tenderloins down their length, without cutting quite through. Open out and beat them into flat rectangles. Put prunes on to simmer with their soaking liquor, plus extra water to cover them generously. Mix together the cinnamon mixture and the seasonings and sprinkle equally on the meat. Arrange the apple on the meat, then the drained, stoned prunes, cut in half. Keep the prune liquor.

Roll up each tenderloin, starting from one narrow end. Tie the two rolls into shape. Brown all over in a little butter, then put together in a close-fitting saucepan. Pour over the prune liquor and two-thirds of the cream. Cover and simmer for 30 minutes, turning once.

Slice and arrange the meat (having removed the string) on a dish, tucking in sprigs of watercress, if you like. Keep hot. Strain the cooking juices into a wide pan and boil down, if necessary, to concentrate the flavour. Stir in the rest of the cream and add bits of jelly to enhance the flavour. Finally, swirl in a few little knobs of butter. This finishing process should be carried out without the sauce boiling. Pour it over the meat and serve.

GAME OR BEEF WITH NORWEGIAN GOAT'S CHEESE

A taste for gjetost (Norwegian goat cheese) wrote one English food writer of the Thirties, 'a chocolate block of most unusual aspect, is perhaps only to be acquired in the fjords; one tries it and is glad to have extended one's experience, but personally I should not pass that way again.' Certainly the toffee-coloured brick, in its foil wrapping, has a sweet toffee taste which is cloying, if you unwisely cut it any thicker than wood shavings. But, as a cooking cheese with game or well-hung beef, it can be most successful, adding a rich piquancy that is harmonious.

For feathered game (pheasant, partridge, ptarmigan or grouse) Brown the birds in butter. Fit them, breast down, into a close-fitting pot. Pour in single cream to come 1 cm (½ in) up the pot. Cover tightly and cook in a moderately hot oven, 190°C (375°F), gas 5, until tender, turning them at roughly half time and lowering the heat. Carve or cut up, if large, and place in a circle of buttered rice. Put the pot over a low heat, and add slivers of gjetost to the curdled-looking juices, alternating with double cream—up to 125 ml (4 fl oz/½ cup) of both, according to taste. The sauce should smooth out (process and reheat it, if you like). Season and strain over the birds. Serve with rowan or red currant jelly.

For furred game (venison, reindeer) **or beef** Lard a 2 kg (4 lb) boned, roasting joint. Butter it like toast. Place on a rack in a roasting tin and cook in a hot oven, 220°C (425°F), gas 7, for 15 minutes until lightly browned. Pour in 375 ml (¾ pt/scant 2 cups) game or beef stock, then pour 2 tablespoons (3 tbs) soured cream over the meat. Turn the oven down to 180°C (350°F), gas 4, leave for 1 hour. This gives pink-centred meat.

Meanwhile, cook 2 level tablespoons (3 tbs) butter until nut brown. Stir in 2 level tablespoons flour (3 tbs) to make a roux. Pour in 225 ml (8 fl oz/1 cup) game or beef stock. Stir and cook for 2 minutes. When the meat is done, put on to a dish and keep warm in the switched-off oven. Skim the fat from the juices and strain into the sauce. Heat through, adding about 30 g (1 oz) gjetost cheese in slivers, stirring, 200 ml (7 fl oz/good ¾ cup) soured cream and 1 level tablespoon rowan or red currant jelly. Taste and add more seasoning if you like. Serve with the meat. Potatoes and watercress are good companions, as well.

You do not really need the roux. Boil down the stock if you want a more concentrated flavour, whisk in the cream, cheese and jelly, and season, adding plenty of pepper. For most people, this consistency is quite thick enough.

PICKLED BEETROOT

3 large boiled or baked beetroots, peeled and thinly sliced
150 ml/¼ pt/⅔ cup wine or cider vinegar
125 ml/4 fl oz/½ cup water
60 g/2 oz/¼ cup sugar
level teaspoon salt
black pepper
2 rounded teaspoons caraway seeds, or 1 tablespoon shredded horseradish

Put the beetroot into a bowl. Bring the next four ingredients to the boil, and pour hot over the beetroot. Add plenty of black pepper, and scatter either with the caraway seeds (as in Denmark) or with the horseradish (as in Sweden). This makes a pleasant mild pickle.

JANSSON'S TEMPTATION
Jansson's frestelse

My favourite potato gratin, which makes a good Saturday lunch. The name, I think, means no more than 'Smith's Temptation', i.e. everyone's temptation. Which it certainly is. You should make it with Swedish anchovies, which are really spiced cured sprats. I have tried them, but—to Swedish digust—prefer the true anchovies that come in little cans, in oil, or salted. Salted, pickled anchovies of all kinds need to be filleted and soaked in water for 30 minutes before using, but for this dish Swedish anchovies and anchovies in oil can be used directly.

Serves 6
8 Swedish anchovies, filleted or 3 cans anchovies
3 large onions, sliced
1 kg/2 lb potatoes, cut into matchstick lengths
pepper and salt
250 ml/9 fl oz/good cup each single and whipping cream
90 g/3 oz/⅜ cup butter
large gratin dish

Grease the large dish with a butter paper. Fillet the anchovies if necessary, split each fillet in half and keep the liquor or oil. You can soften the onions and potatoes in butter, but it is unnecessary. Set at hot, 220°C (425°F), gas 7.

Put half the potato sticks into the dish, then half the onions. Make a criss-cross of anchovy strips all over, cover with the remaining onions and the remaining potato sticks last of all. Pepper the layers and add a *little* salt (remember anchovies are very salty). Pour over the anchovy liquor or oil, if you have it, then the single cream and dot with butter. Bake in the heated oven for 15 minutes. Then reduce the heat to 190°C (375°F), gas 5. When the dish looks nicely browned and the potatoes are tender, pour over the rest of the cream and keep at a low heat until required.

When you first check the dish, you will notice that the liquid of the gratin looks curdled. This is why you hold back some cream for the very end. I find that gratins improve if they have a chance to mellow in a very low oven, but this is not essential. In any case, Jansson's temptation is good to eat.

CAN'T-LEAVE-IT-ALONE PUDDING
Kan ikke lade vaere

I like the name of this pudding, which is light and refreshing and simple—and irresistible, especially after yellow pea soup or some substantial meat dish. It improves with a little keeping and is best two days after it is made.

Serves 6
5 egg yolks
125 g/4 oz/½ cup sugar
packet/2 level dessertspoons powdered gelatine
4 tablespoons/⅓ cup very hot water
finely grated zest and juice of 2 lemons
5 egg whites, stiffly whisked
900 ml–1.25-litre/1½–2-pt/3¾–5-cup soufflé dish

Using an electric whisk if possible, beat the egg yolks and sugar until very thick and billowy. Sprinkle the gelatine on to the very hot but not boiling water, leave for a minute, then stir gently to dissolve it. Add the zest and lemon juice to the gelatine liquid, then stir into the egg mixture. Finally fold in the whisked egg whites. Pour into the soufflé dish to set. Serve with whipped cream, or double cream beaten until it is very thick but still just pourable.

PEASANT MAID IN A VEIL
Bondepige med slør

Use dark rye bread to make the crumbs for this dish. For me, its success depends ultimately on the amount of cream you eat it with. Cooking apples are used to make the purée, as a rule, but try it with aromatic Cox's or Reinette apples which give an extra richness to the flavour.

Serves 6
175 g/6 oz dark rye breadcrumbs
4 tablespoons/$\frac{1}{3}$ cup melted butter
30 g/1 oz/2 tbs caster sugar
3 large apples, peeled, cored, sliced
250 ml/8 fl oz/1 cup double cream
granulated sugar
125 ml/4 fl oz/$\frac{1}{2}$ cup whipping cream
egg white, stiffly whisked (optional)

Put the breadcrumbs into a pan and pour over the butter, then sprinkle on the sugar. Set over a moderate heat, stirring, until the crumbs are crisp. Leave to cool while you cook the apples. When they are tender, mix in the granulated sugar to taste. Sieve the apples, if you like. I think they are better left in an uneven purée, but Danish cooks prefer them smooth.

Layer crumbs and apple purée into a dish—a glass one shows off the pudding layers nicely. Whisk the creams together, then fold in the egg white, if you like, to lighten the texture. Heap on to the pudding.

JULGRÖT

Before I tried this recipe, I wondered why anyone in Scandinavia should choose a rice pudding for Christmas Eve, to follow the fish (in Sweden, lutfisk which is ling pickled in lye, not to everybody's taste). But now I have tried the recipe I understand. There can be no better rice pudding for combined richness and lightness. It's a winner. A small additional pleasure is the hidden almond: whoever finds it will be the next to get married.

150 g/5 oz/$\frac{3}{4}$ cup Caroline rice
100 g/3$\frac{1}{2}$ oz/scant $\frac{1}{2}$ cup butter
300 ml/$\frac{1}{2}$ pt/1$\frac{1}{4}$ cups double cream, whipped
level teaspoon salt
level tablespoon sugar
an almond

Rinse the rice and simmer it for up to an hour in a litre (1$\frac{3}{4}$ pts/scant 4$\frac{1}{2}$ cups) water, until it is really soft. At this stage it will look odd, even unpleasant. Pour off any abundance of water, if necessary. Stir in the butter and it will begin to improve, then fold in the cream. Heat through without boiling and add salt and sugar. Taste to see if more is needed. Rinse and dry the almond and put it into the rice. Serve with thin cream. The pudding should not be too sweet, more like a porridge.

KRINGLE

A Danish cake made especially at Christmas time. It is easy to recognise as the long strip of yeast dough is bent round into a pretzel shape. The yeast dough is straightforward, not as complex as the yeast puff dough used to make Danish pastries. The lovely flavour comes from cardamom: extract the seeds from the pods, then crush them with a pestle in a mortar.

Serves 6
250 g/8 oz/2 cups strong plain flour
2 level teaspoons Harvest Gold dried yeast
level teaspoon ground cardamom
2 rounded tablespoons/3 tbs granulated sugar
90 g/3 oz/6 tbs Danish butter
1 egg, beaten
75 ml/2$\frac{1}{2}$ fl oz/6 tbs warm milk
FOR THE FILLING
90 g/3 oz/6 tbs Danish butter, softened
2 heaped tablespoons/3 tbs sugar
2 level teaspoons powdered cinnamon
TO FINISH
beaten egg
2 heaped tablespoons/3 tbs chopped almonds
heaped tablespoon sugar
glacé icing

To make the dough, mix the flour, yeast, cardamom and sugar together. Melt the butter and when warm, pour into the middle of the flour mixture and add the egg. Mix to a dough, adding the milk gradually. You may not need it all. The dough should be soft but not tacky. Knead well. Oil the bowl, put the dough back into it and tie into a polythene bag or stretch clear film over the top. Leave to double in size.

Meanwhile, mix the filling ingredients together. Break down the dough and roll it into a strip about 80 × 12 cm (32 × 5 in). Spread the filling down the centre, then flip the two long ends over, one on top of the other, to enclose it. Set oven at 200°C (400°F), gas 6.

Grease a baking sheet, or line it with non-stick baking paper. Fold the dough roll lightly in three and transfer rapidly to the prepared baking sheet. Shape the two ends round and up to the centre to form a giant pretzel, as if you were folding your arms across and up to your shoulders. Tie back into a polythene bag, ballooning it well up so that the dough cannot rise and stick to it. Leave in a warm place to prove for 20–30 minutes.

Brush the dough with egg, sprinkle with almonds and sugar. Bake in the heated oven for 20–25 minutes, or until golden brown. When cold, run trails of glacé icing over the kringle like snow.

NAPOLEON CAKE

The usual Scandinavian Napoleon cake is a type of mille feuilles made with puff pastry. I found this excellent shortbread version in *Good Food from Sweden*, by Inge Norberg (Chatto, 1935), a book worth looking out for in secondhand book shops.

Serves 6–8
250 g/8 oz/1 cup caster sugar
250 g/8 oz/2 cups ground almonds
250 g/8 oz/1 cup butter, softened
250 g/8 oz/2 cups flour
FOR THE FILLING
apple purée or red currant jelly
TO FINISH
whipping cream or glacé icing
slices of candied peel

Mix together the sugar and almonds. Cream the butter until white and soft. Add the almond mixture and the flour. Divide into two equal parts. Set oven at moderately hot, 200°C (400°F), gas 6.

Roll each piece of dough into thin rounds, roughly the size of dinner plates. Bake in the heated oven for about 15 minutes. When cool, sandwich with apple purée or jelly. Cover the top with whipped cream or icing just before serving, and decorate with slices of candied peel.

DANISH PASTRIES
Wienerbröd

These familiar pastries, often so badly made outside Denmark, are made with a yeast puff dough that was originally introduced to the Danes by Viennese pastrycooks. They had been brought to Denmark to break a strike about a hundred years ago. There are a number of shapes which are well described in *Cooking with a Danish Flavour* by Pauline Viola and Knud Ravnkilde. It is their instructions that form the base of the following recipe, though of course all recipes are very close to each other.

To make 12 pastries
250 g/8 oz/2 cups strong plain flour
15 g/½ oz fresh yeast or 2 teaspoons dried yeast
80 ml/3 fl oz/scant ½ cup tepid water
1 egg, beaten
teaspoon sugar
salt
30 g/1 oz/2 tbs lard
150 g/5 oz/⅔ cup lightly salted butter

Fruit snail filling
1 egg, beaten
30 g/1 oz/2 tbs butter, softened
30 g/1 oz/2 tbs caster sugar
teaspoon ground cinnamon
30 g/1 oz/3 tbs sultanas
60 g/2 oz/¼ cup icing sugar
teaspoon water

Cockscomb filling
30 g/1 oz/2 tbs butter, softened
30 g/1 oz/2 tbs caster sugar
30 g/1 oz crushed macaroons or 3 tablespoons lemon curd or apple purée
1 egg, beaten
15 g/½ oz/⅛ cup almonds, blanched, chopped

Put the flour into a large bowl. Mash yeast or sprinkle dried yeast on to the water, let it stand for 10 minutes until foamy. With dried fermipan yeast, stir it straight into the flour. Mix the egg into the yeast, or into the tepid water (fermipan yeast). Stir sugar and salt into the flour, then rub in the lard and mix to a soft dough with yeast liquid or water and egg. Knead into a smooth dough—about 10 minutes, or considerably less if you are using an electric dough hook. Put the dough back into its bowl, tie it into a polythene bag, or stretch plastic wrap over the top. Chill for 20 minutes.

Next soften the butter with a palette knife and shape it into a rectangle. Roll out the dough on a floured board to approximately 25 cm (10 in)

You need to go to Denmark to eat the best and lightest Danish pastries

square. Spread out the butter down the centre to within $2\frac{1}{2}$ cm (1 in) of the edges. Fold the sides over so that they only overlap in the middle by 1 cm ($\frac{1}{2}$ in). Press bottom and top edges to seal them. Roll out into a rectangle about 45 × 15 cm (18 × 6 in) and fold in three. Put dough on a plate and into a plastic bag before returning it to the refrigerator to chill; balloon up the bag so that it does not touch the dough, or else oil it inside. Leave for 10 minutes, then roll it out on the board, turning it as you do with puff pastry. Repeat the chilling and rolling out process twice more, being sure to turn the dough each time. Put back into the fridge for the last time and leave overnight or for at least 4 hours. Now it is ready for shaping.

Fruit snails Take half the dough and roll it out to a 35 × 15 cm (15 × 6 in) rectangle. Brush the two shorter ends with egg to make a $2\frac{1}{2}$ cm (1 in) rim. Cream butter, sugar and cinnamon, then spread over the dough, inside the rim, and scatter on the sultanas. Roll up from one short end, and slice down to make six pin wheels. Put on to a buttered baking tray. Press them down gently and brush with egg. Prove in a warm place for 30 minutes, or until nicely risen, before baking. Again make use of a plastic bag to create the warm steamy atmosphere that encourages yeast doughs to rise.

Cockscombs Roll out the last of the dough into a 30 × 30 cm (12 × 8 in) rectangle. Cut into six squares. Cream butter, sugar and then mix in the macaroons, curd or purée. Place some in the middle of each square. Brush the rest of the dough with beaten egg. Fold each square in half to make oblong shapes, then cut down 6 to 8 times so that when you bend the uncut side you have a lot of teeth making a crest or cockscomb. Put on to a buttered tray and prove as for fruit snails.

Bake in an oven preheated to 200°C (400°F), gas 6 for 10 minutes, then lower the heat to 180°C (350°F), gas 4 and give the pastries another 10 or 15 minutes. They should be golden brown. To ice the fruit snails, mix icing sugar with a teaspoon of water and dribble it over them when they are cold.

RYE BREAD AND HOLE CAKES
Rågbrod och hålkakor

For open sandwiches you must have rye bread, for the sake of its close texture as well as the taste. Rye flour is not easy to manage—you have to add strong bread flour if it is to rise at all. If you want dark loaves, use treacle or molasses, and leave out the aniseed or fennel if this kind of flavour does not appeal to you in bread. The dough is the same for both rye bread and hole cakes but for the cakes, just make it a little softer by adding more liquid.

500 g/1 lb rye flour
about 350 g/11 oz/$2\frac{3}{4}$ cups strong white bread flour
2 level teaspoons salt
packet Harvest Gold dried yeast
500 ml/18 fl oz/$2\frac{1}{4}$ cups milk, blood heat
2 tablespoons each aniseed and fennel seed
30 g/1 oz/2 tbs dripping
2 level tablespoons/3 tbs treacle or golden syrup

Mix the rye flour with two-thirds of the white flour, the salt and the yeast. Make a dough using the milk, kneading it well and adding more flour if necessary. Tie the bowl into a polythene bag and leave to double in size in a warm place. With rye flour, this can take longer than an hour. Warm together the seeds, dripping and treacle or syrup. Add to the risen dough, kneading well and adding more flour as required.

FOR THE BREAD Divide the dough between warm, greased loaf tins, or form into loaves and put on a baking sheet. Prove for 30 minutes, tied in a polythene bag. Meanwhile, set the oven at hot, 200°C (400°F), gas 6. Then bake in the heated oven for about 30 minutes. Brush the tops with hot water, and put back in the oven for a minute or two; remove, turn out of the tins and cool on a wire rack.

FOR THE HOLE CAKES Divide the dough into four or five equal parts. Roll or pat them into rounds the size of dinner plates. Make a central hole with a 5 cm (2 in) scone cutter and prick all over with a fork. Prove for 30 minutes. Meanwhile, set the oven at hot, 200–220°C (400–425°F), gas 6–7. Bake in the heated oven for 15–20 minutes. Brush over with hot water, and put back for a minute or two; remove and cool on a wire rack.

RYE BISCUITS
Rågkex

A plain biscuit that is good with butter, or butter and cheese, and interesting bits and pieces. Make the biscuits as thin as you can, rolling the dough to occupy $1\frac{1}{2}$ baking trays. This recipe comes from the *The Great Scandinavian Cookbook*, which mainly concerns Swedish food, though a good number of dishes are common to all the countries.

125 g/4 oz/1 cup rye flour
60 g/2 oz/$\frac{1}{2}$ cup plain flour
level teaspoon salt
$\frac{1}{2}$ level teaspoon ground cumin
75 g/$2\frac{1}{2}$ oz/5 tbs butter, melted
100 ml/$3\frac{1}{2}$ fl oz/scant $\frac{1}{2}$ cup milk

Mix the ingredients in the order given. Knead the dough smooth and chill it. Set the oven at moderate, 180°C (350°F), gas 4.

Roll the dough out thinly, then put on to the baking sheets and roll again so that it stretches from side to side. Cut into 6 cm ($2\frac{1}{2}$ in) squares with a pastry wheel or knife, then prick with a fork. Bake

Presentation and setting make eating out a pleasant experience

in the heated oven until crisp—15–30 minutes, though the time will depend on how thin you managed to roll the biscuits. Leave the oven on while they cool—this does not take long—then you can judge whether they need to go back to cook a little more.

LACE BISCUITS
Kniplingskaker

France's tuile amande is famous, but this lacy Scandinavian biscuit, bent over in the same way, is better if less well known. Serve it with ices and cold soufflés.

75 g/2½ oz/5 tbs butter
75 g/2½ oz/⅔ cup porridge oats
125 g/4 oz/½ cup caster sugar
egg
level teaspoon each flour and baking powder, mixed

Melt the butter in a wide pan and immediately stir in the oats. When barely tepid, beat in the sugar and egg. Just before you are ready to bake, mix in the flour and baking powder.

Set oven at moderate, 180°C (350°F), gas 4.

Grease two baking sheets with butter and drop 4 teaspoons of the mixture on to each one, wide apart. Bake in the heated oven until a pale brown. The mixture will spread and, if you are not used to making brandy snaps, you would be wise to bake a trial biscuit to see how things work out.

Run a butter paper over a rolling pin or clean bottle. Working quickly, remove the biscuits, one at a time, with a slice, and drape them over the pin or bottle to shape them before they cool and turn brittle and crisp. If the biscuits stick to the trays before you manage to remove them, put them back in the oven for a few seconds so they become pliable again.

GERMANY

The Westphalian breakfast of ham, sausage, pumpernickel, schnapps and beer

What I love about travelling in Germany is that whenever you visit something special, there is an eating place nearby where you can reflect on the experience over good coffee or beer and decent simple food. Go and see the bog corpses at the Schleswig museum—afterwards you can recover in the neat restaurant tucked into a corner of the huge building. After wandering about the great standing rocks and holy grotto of the Externsteine in the Teutoburgerwald, you can get your breath again at a small guesthouse nearby.

The Germans have this great sensitivity to place and what is needed for the best enjoyment of it. Seemliness is an old-fashioned word but it describes the tone well. Montaigne noticed it in 1580, on his journey into Italy. The pretty towns with big clean squares, wide streets, many fountains with running water. He liked the duvet on his bed, the stove that kept his bedroom warm, the cleanliness and service, the polished and painted wooden rooms where all classes ate (at separate tables). He wished he had brought his cook with him from France to learn how to make the dishes he enjoyed so much: the combination of meat and game with fruit, apple added to beef soup, cabbage salads, sauerkraut and the sweetmeats that ended every meal. He was amused by earthenware pots made to imitate pie crust and the way that people solemnly offered each other crayfish.

Montaigne praised the bread—he was the most open-minded of all Frenchmen—especially when it was flavoured with caraway. Today we put French bread at the top, but German bread and baking is of an equally high quality. Our image of German bread goes little beyond black Westphalian pumpernickel and such relations as Leinsamenbrot (linseed mixed with rye) or Vollkornbrot (wheat grains mixed with rye), but there are over 200 kinds of bread, a thousand different buns and rolls. Bakers deliver in time for breakfast, I believe, and bake twice a day as they do in France. Cakes are of a style and creaminess that should not be investigated too conscientiously if you have a waistline to cherish, though you might try a piece of Black Forest cherry cake made by a Black Forest baker with proper kirsch and the right cherries. It can be a surprising experience after the disgusting imitations on sale in England.

If you go anywhere near Hanoverisch, visit the bread museum at Mollenfelde—mill field—where the long past of the baking trades is exhibited. Wafer irons, wooden moulds, picture breads or rather bread sculptures of animals, people and symbols, pretzels, the documents and literature of bread, show a world of skill that we can barely imagine these days.

German food has the reputation of being heavy and bland. Certainly this can be so. Like ourselves they eat too much very often. I remember the shock when an enormous bone was put down in front of me at Dusseldorf, in an old inn—a bone covered with meat, very crisp outside from its roasting on a spit, the famous Schweinsaxe or pig's hock. Even a busy morning spent half in the great food basement of the Kaufhof store, had not given me appetite enough to eat so much. Or perhaps I was overwhelmed by the opulence of the Kaufhof, extraordinary outside a capital city. Sausages and hams stretch, tightly clustered, for yards and yards and yards. In Germany this was partly to be expected. What was less expected was the fruit and vegetables which were piled up in enticing heaps like an open market, with kiwi and passion fruit rolling into neighbouring trays of oranges, and bulging boxes of salad.

One felt the prosperity of Germany, and the trend towards lightness which has strongly influenced the grand restaurants. With the arrival of new ideas from France, flour is cut down or banished, dumplings made small, which only enhances the German skill of marrying sweet and savoury. Another German taste which harmonises well with the nouvelle cuisine is woodland mushrooms, in particular the yellow chanterelle or girolle and the cèpe. As in all countries of northern Europe except Great Britain, mushroom hunting is the autumn passion of family life. And it is big business as well, with a thriving export trade in canned, bottled and dried mushrooms.

Food manufacturers in Germany do go for quality since people there understand and will pay for it. Profits are invested in architecture and embellishment, out of pride. For example, Bahlsen's old biscuit factory, near Hanover, is an art-nouveau building of colour and gaiety. In the modern Herta factory where so much of our Westphalian ham and salami comes from, the vast open-plan office building has filing cabinets set among sculptures, and mobiles hanging beside the typewriters; there are things to touch, things to look at. It is a bright world of zany shapes, but there is nothing zany about the big sheds behind, where the pork is turned into many forms of charcuterie. You see very well why Germany is a country where food is taken seriously and honourably, with much enjoyment and appetite.

HAMBURG EEL SOUP
Hamburger Aalsuppe

Of all fish soups, this is one of the best. Dried pears and eel sound strange, but the taste is delicate and delicious without being in the least bizarre. Alan Davidson, in his *North Atlantic Seafood*, points out that it is really just a German Saure Suppe (sour soup), with eel added. So you can leave the eel out, if you like. But don't. Here is his recipe, with the addition of wine.

Serves 6
large ham bone
1.5 kg/3lb vegetables, prepared and cut up (cauliflower, peas and carrots are essential, plus leek, kohlrabi, Hamburg parsley or white turnip, celery or celeriac, string beans)
200–300 g/7–10 oz dried fruit, predominantly pear, with apple, prune, apricot, soaked in water
150 ml/¼ pt/⅔ cup dry white wine
2 bay leaves
sprig of savory
2 sprigs each of parsley and thyme
vinegar
500 g/1 lb eel, skinned, cleaned, cut in pieces
sugar and salt
FOR THE DUMPLINGS
225 g/8 oz/2 cups flour
pinch of salt
1½ tablespoons/2 tbs beef marrowfat, suet or butter
1 egg
150 ml/¼ pt/⅔ cup water

Put on the ham bone to simmer in plenty of water. Skim as necessary and, after about 20 minutes, put in the vegetables, adding the most tender items last. Simmer slowly until the vegetables are cooked. Meanwhile, simmer the dried fruit with any soaking water and the wine. When softened, add to the vegetable pan, with their liquid.

Put the herbs and a splash of vinegar into the now empty fruit pan with the eel. Just cover with water and simmer gently until the eel is ready to part easily from the bone.

Remove the ham bone, cutting off any little bits of meat and putting them into the soup. Put in the eel pieces, then strain in its cooking liquor. Season to taste with sugar and/or salt.

Mix the dumpling ingredients together, then roll into little balls. Poach them in the soup for 5 minutes, covered, or better still in a separate pan of simmering salted water (dumplings can cloud soup), then serve.

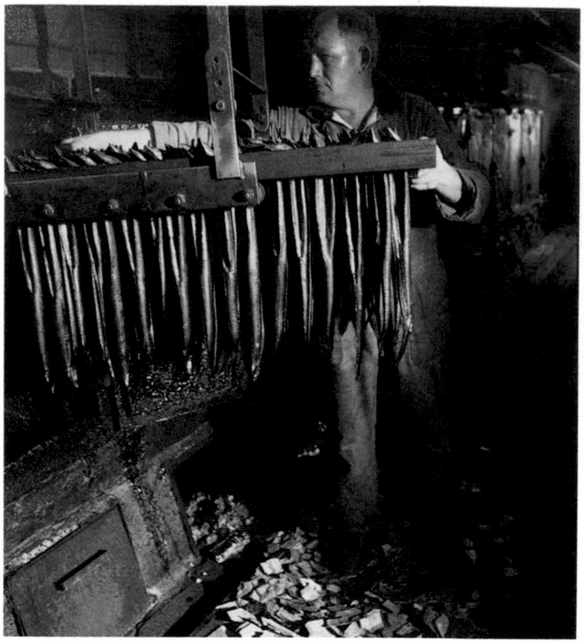

Baltic eel at a Bad Zwischenahn smokery near Bremen

RED WINE SOUP
Rotweinsuppe

A dish from the wine district in the south-west. The best German wine is white, as everyone knows, but red wine is also made in the Ahr valley, south of Bonn. It is not very distinguished wine, so do not imprudently uncork a bottle of your best claret for this soup.

Serves 6
4 level tablespoons tapioca
scant 500 ml/¾ pt/scant 2 cups water
scant 500 ml/¾ pt/scant 2 cups red wine
small stick of cinnamon
2 level tablespoons/3 tbs sugar
thinly cut zest of 1 lemon
1 egg white
30 g/1 oz/¼ cup icing sugar

Cook the tapioca in the water. Add the wine, cinnamon, sugar and lemon peel and bring back to simmering point; leave on a low heat for about 5 minutes. Taste and add extra sugar if you like, but not too much. Beat the egg white with the icing sugar. Divide the soup between six warm bowls, and float icebergs of egg white on top. Serve with sponge finger biscuits.

Note white wine can also be used. In some recipes, the soup is thickened with egg yolks and cream, but I think this 'thinner' treatment is better.

CHEESE CAKE WITH CARAWAY
Gekümmelter Schmelzkäsekuchen

Another good German snack from Hessen, Goethe's country—he was born in Frankfurt. It is made from processed cheese (Schmelzkäse), and if you can find one flavoured with paprika, so much the better. The cake can perfectly well be made with ordinary cheese, coarsely grated, and I use Gouda (if it is flavoured with mustard seeds or dried nettles, it all adds virtue).

Caraway is a flavouring we do not use nearly enough. Try the seeds warmed through in butter and served with egg noodles, topped with little bits of cooked ham. Or put them into bread dough, or pound cakes.

Serves 6
75–100 g/$2\frac{1}{2}$–$3\frac{1}{2}$ oz/$\frac{1}{4}$–$\frac{1}{3}$ cup butter
12 thick slices of white bread, crusts removed
500 ml/generous $\frac{3}{4}$ pt/good 2 cups butter
2 level tablespoons caraway seeds
6 large individually wrapped wedges of processed cheese, or 375 g/12 oz/3 cups grated cheese
salt
paprika

Butter two or more baking dishes or tins and arrange the bread on them, close together. If there are gaps, cut extra bread to fit. Pour on half the milk. Leave for 2–3 minutes, then pour off any surplus into a saucepan. Scatter with caraway. Set oven at moderate, 160°C (325°F), gas 3.

Add the rest of the milk to the pan, bring to the boil and, off the heat, add the cheese, stirring until it melts completely like cream. Season with salt and paprika to taste. Pour over the bread and bake in the heated oven for 20–25 minutes or until the top is nicely browned and the edge crisp. Serve with beer and schnapps, cider or wine.

HAMBURG OPEN SANDWICH
Hamburger Rundstück

Germans are good at snacks, such as sausages and a glass of beer, or this open meat sandwich from Hamburg. There are many versions, but I have chosen one from Arne Krüger's *German Cooking*, and one from Werner Seeberg, chef at the German Embassy in London.

Serves 2
FOR KRUGER'S SANDWICH
2 tablespoons/3 tbs mayonnaise
1 tablespoon yoghurt
2 tablespoons chopped parsley, chives, and savoury, or 2 tablespoons dried mixed herbs
salt and pepper
4 slices of bread
butter
4 lettuce leaves
8 slices of cold roast veal or pork, cut thin

Mix together the mayonnaise and yoghurt, flavour with herbs, salt and pepper. Toast and butter the bread, put on the lettuce, then the meat, and cover with the sauce. Serve with pickled Siberian crab-apples and a sprig or two of parsley.

FOR SEEBERG'S SANDWICH
2 large, soft rolls, e.g. sesame rolls
lettuce
butter
2 slices of roast pork
2 slices of roast beef
little jellied gravy from the roast meat
pickled dill cucumber

Split open the rolls but do not cut through completely. Butter them and put a little lettuce on top.

Two versions of the Hamburg open sandwich

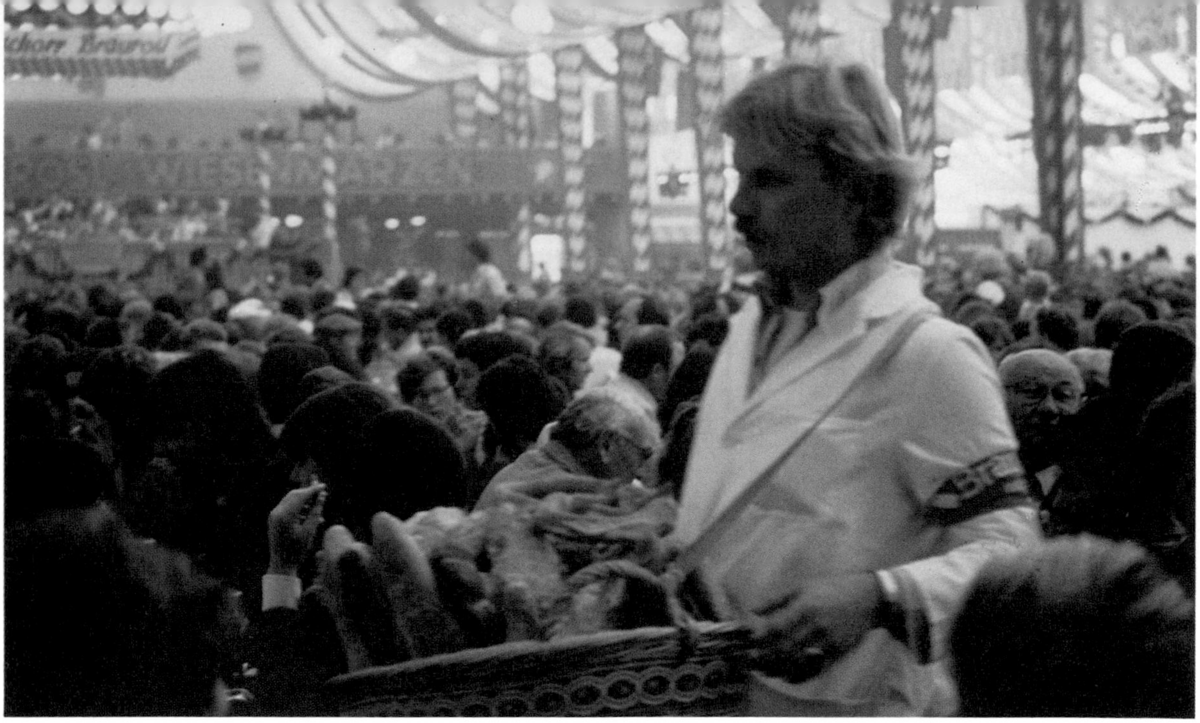

A crowded beer cellar during the October beer festival

Arrange pork on one side of each roll, and beef on the other. Spread over a little jellied meat gravy to moisten it. Serve with pickled dill cucumber.

FRANKFURT GREEN SAUCE
Frankfurter Grüne Sosse

This famous herb sauce is one of the summer triumphs of Frankfurt cookery. There are a number of versions—this one comes from a reader who grew up in Frankfurt—but they all contain seven or eight different herbs.

Serves 6
15 g/½ oz each borage, salad burnet, parsley and sorrel
20 g/⅔ oz each chives and cress or watercress
10 g/⅓ oz each tarragon and chervil
150 ml/¼ pt/⅔ cup mayonnaise
level teaspoon German mustard
2 hard-boiled eggs, chopped
1 small pickled gherkin, with dill, chopped
1 small onion or shallot, chopped
½ clove of garlic, chopped
salt and pepper
grated lemon rind and lemon juice
2 tablespoons/3 tbs soured cream or yoghurt, optional
1 egg yolk

Chop the herbs very finely together. Add the remaining ingredients in the order given, seasoning to taste, and beating in the egg yolk last of all. Serve with fried or poached fish, or cold fish, with hard-boiled eggs, with cold meats, or use as a sandwich filling.

One simpler version is made by mixing the herbs above with a little vinaigrette, and then stirring in 300 ml/½ pt/1⅓ cups soured cream, salt, chopped shallot or onion, 2 mashed hard-boiled eggs.

ASPARAGUS
Spargel

The Germans are crazy about asparagus, which shows their good sense; fat white asparagus with a yellow tip rather than our thinner green kind is what they prefer. In Düsseldorf in the eight weeks leading up to 24 June, one restaurant devotes its menu to asparagus with 209 dishes to choose from.

One popular way of eating asparagus is to serve it boiled, with a thick slice of Westphalian ham, new potatoes and hollandaise sauce. If you can buy thin slices only of the ham, do not let this put you off trying it (hollandaise sauce recipe is on page 114).

SAUERKRAUT WITH PINEAPPLE
Sauerkraut mit Ananas

If you are trying sauerkraut on your family for the first time, I recommend this recipe. You can do it the best, grand way with a whole pineapple, which looks very glamorous, or you can buy canned unsweetened pineapple instead to make a quicker, less fancy version.

Cut the top from a pineapple and set it aside carefully. Cut round inside the fruit, and remove as much flesh as possible to leave a firm shell. Cut the pieces into little chunks, throwing away the hard core, and save any juice. Weigh the pineapple pieces and add 1½ times its weight of rinsed, well-drained sauerkraut (press out the moisture without being too brutal). Mix together with any pineapple juice and olive oil. Put into the pineapple shell and perch the lid on top. A good salad for serving with ham or cold duck, at a party.

The homely version uses drained canned pineapple, mixed with 1½ times its weight of rinsed, drained sauerkraut, plus olive oil, though a tasteless oil can be used instead.

I love the amiable crunchiness of uncooked sauerkraut, but if you are not of the same mind it can be simmered until tender in pineapple juice.

RED CABBAGE WITH APPLES
Rotkohl mit Äpfeln

Like sauerkraut, red cabbage can be served as an accompanying vegetable to a meat dish, or it can provide the basis of a mixed smoked meats and sausage dish, ranging from Bratwurst to Frankfurters or smoked chicken. If you want to make this sort of dish, assemble as good a choice of meats as possible, and add them to the cabbage, according to the time they require for cooking. Smoked bacon belly and hocks should go in from the start, boiling sausages 40 minutes before the end of the cooking time, joints of smoked poultry 20 minutes, and sliced, smoked meats, gammon chops, or sausages 10–15 minutes before the end.

Even if you intend the cabbage as an accompaniment only, it is a good idea to put in a nice piece of smoked pork belly to give flavour, and to provide the nucleus of a meal next day with the leftover cabbage reheated. There are many versions of this simple recipe; most contain vinegar to keep the cabbage red, with apple, sugar and onion added for a sweet-sharp contrast.

Serves 4
red cabbage, trimmed and shredded
4 tablespoons/⅓ cup red wine vinegar
60 g/2 oz/¼ cup dark brown sugar
375 g/12 oz/3 cups sliced onion
60 g/2 oz/¼ cup lard or bacon fat
375 g/12 oz peeled, cored, sliced cooking or sharp eating apples
4 cloves or level teaspoon ground cloves
bay leaf
300 ml/1 pt/2½ cups water or stock
150 ml/¼ pt/⅔ cup red wine, optional
500 g/1 lb piece of smoked bacon belly, rind, and bones included
salt and pepper

Mix the cabbage with the vinegar and sugar. Brown the onion lightly in the fat in a huge pan. Layer in the cabbage and apples, adding the

Piling up the cabbages for making sauerkraut

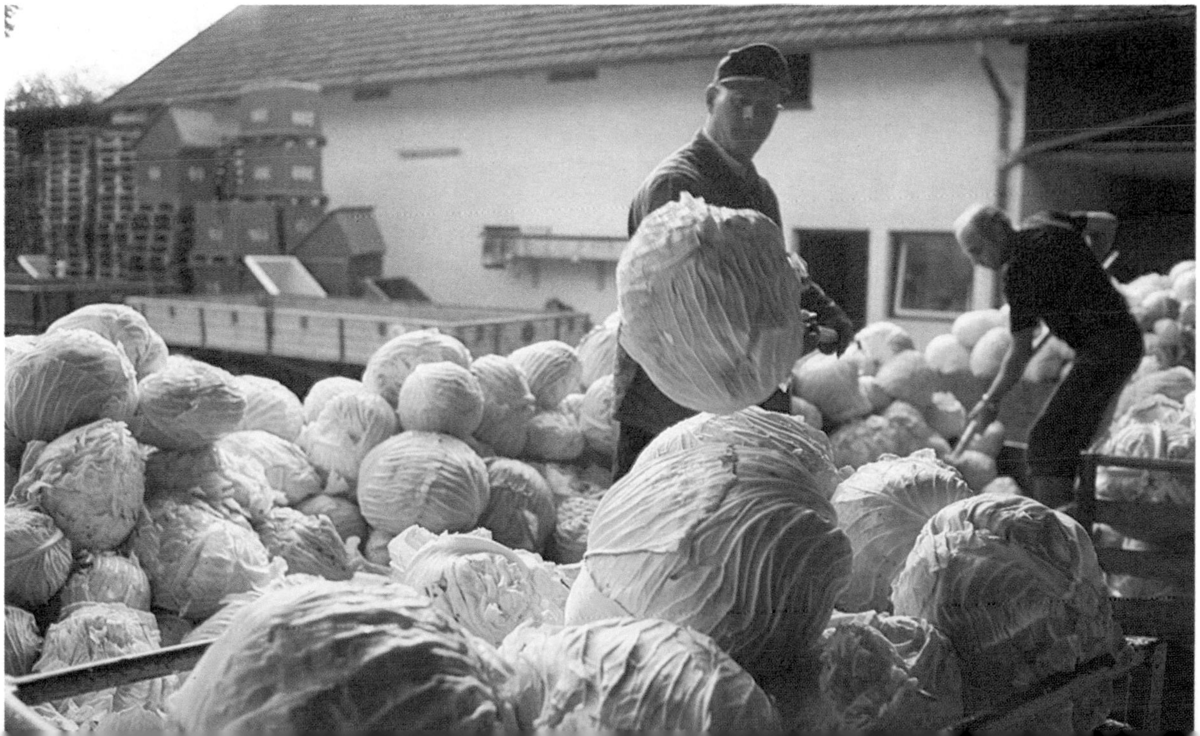

cabbage juices, cloves and bay leaf. Pour in the water or stock and wine, if used, then push the bacon right into the centre. Cover tightly and simmer as slowly as you like, either in the oven, 150°C (300°F), gas 2 or lower, or on top of the stove, for 3–5 hours; stir up occasionally and remove the lid towards the end if there is too much liquid in the pot. Taste and correct seasoning before serving.

WARM POTATO SALAD
Warmer Kartoffelsalat

A good homely dish to serve with sausages or Leberkäse. Make it with waxy new potatoes or Desirée potatoes, in winter.

Serves 8
1.5 kg/3 lb potatoes
few tablespoons hot veal or beef stock
FOR THE DRESSING
175 g/6 oz/1½ cups chopped sweet onion
4 tablespoons/⅓ cup wine vinegar
125 g/4 oz piece of smoked bacon, diced, or rashers, cut into strips
butter
level dessertspoon cornflour
heaped teaspoon brown sugar
4 tablespoons/⅓ cup water
chopped chives and parsley
3 tablespoons/scant ¼ cup soured cream, or whipping cream and lemon juice
salt and pepper

Scrape and steam new potatoes. Or scrub, boil and peel winter potatoes. Slice them into a bowl, add the very hot stock and keep them warm while you make the dressing.

Mix the onion and vinegar. Fry the bacon in a very little butter. Mix the cornflour, sugar and water, then stir into the bacon pan, together with the onion and vinegar. Stir until the mixture clears and thickens slightly, and stops tasting floury—this does not take long.

Off the heat, quickly stir in the herbs and the cream, with lemon juice to taste, if used. Taste and add salt and plenty of pepper. Pour over the potatoes while still very hot. Mix gently and serve immediately.

POTATO DUMPLINGS
Kartoffelklösse

These dumplings are splendid, especially with venison, hare or sauerbraten (recipe on page 193). Try to finish and cook them just before the meal, so that the fried-bread squares stay crisp. This recipe is from Time-Life's *The Cooking of Germany*.

Makes 15–20 dumplings
125 g/4 oz/1 cup fine dried white breadcrumbs
150 g/5 oz/½ cup + 2 tbs butter, or more
3 slices of crustless white bread, cut in 1 cm/½ in squares
60 g/2 oz/½ cup flour
90 g/3 oz/½ cup semolina
level teaspoon salt
¼ teaspoon ground nutmeg
¼ teaspoon ground white pepper
5 medium potatoes (about 1½ lb) boiled, peeled and riced
2 eggs, beaten

Fry the breadcrumbs in 125 g (4 oz/½ cup) butter until golden; remove to a kitchen paper-covered dish and keep warm. Add the rest of the butter to the pan, putting in more if necessary, and fry the bread till brown and crisp; drain on kitchen paper, keep warm.

Mix the next five ingredients and beat them gradually into the potatoes. Beat in the eggs until the potato mixture is light but can hold its shape. If necessary, add extra flour a teaspoon at a time.

With floured hands, form dumplings from a generous tablespoon of the mixture each time. Press a hole into the centre of each dumpling, put in a couple of bread squares and close the dumpling again, reshaping if necessary.

Bring a huge saucepan (or two big saucepans) half-full of water to the boil, and add 2 teaspoons salt, to each one. Put in the dumplings carefully. Simmer them for 15 minutes, stirring lightly once or twice. When they rise to the surface, give them a minute, then remove to a hot dish with a slotted spoon. Sprinkle with crumbs and serve.

POTATO PANCAKES
Kartoffelpuffer

Fun to make as a snack, a Saturday indulgence for the family. The whiskery-brown appearance is a delight, and so is the surprise of eating potatoes with a sweet fruit sauce. Serve soup first, and you have a meal.

Serves 3–4
750 g (1½ lb) peeled potatoes
100 g/3½ oz grated onion
2 eggs, beaten
175 g/6 oz/1½ cups plain flour
good pinch of salt
lard

Shred the potatoes on the coarse side of a grater into a bowl. Mix in the onion, then the eggs, then the flour and salt.

Heat enough lard in a heavy frying pan, to make $\frac{1}{2}$ cm ($\frac{1}{4}$ in) depth. Put in 2–3 heaped tablespoons potato mixture and flatten them together to make a pancake about 12 cm (5 in) across. When the whiskery underside is crisp and nicely browned, turn the pancake and cook the other side.

Taste and decide whether you have got the cooking right: kartoffelpuffer should be crisp at the edge and golden, smoother and paler in the centre and more pancake-like. Cook them in two pans if you can; they are quite easy to manage.

Serve with Preiselbeeren (lingonberries)—available bottled at some delicatessens or in London from the German Food Centre—or apple sauce, or with slices of Cox's orange pippins cooked in butter and scattered with sugar. Preiselbeeren are also good with hare and venison.

POACHED EEL OR FISH FILLETS IN DILL SAUCE

Gedünste Aal oder Fischfilets in Dillsosse

Dill is easy to grow since it does not require good soil. Its special flavour has no equivalent or substitute, which makes it essential to North European cookery where it is much used with fish and vegetables. Freeze-dried dillweed is a successful substitute, but use half the quantity, and always add it gradually to taste. By changing the stock, this dill sauce can also be served with veal, chicken or vegetables.

CABBAGE

The practice of salting down vegetables and leaving them to ferment is ancient, and not particularly German. The Romans did it, and so did every other cabbage-growing people from China to the Atlantic coast of Europe. We are the odd ones out. We never seem to have preserved this vegetable, never had the experience of sauerkraut bubbling gently away in our cellars and sheds. It is easy to make: you need a large wooden barrel, a lot of firm white cabbage and a vast shredder like a giant mandolin. But unless you grow cabbages on a large scale, you should buy it—German sauerkraut if you can, since it is of such high quality.

Rinse and taste the sauerkraut to assess how much soaking it will need to lose its saltiness. Put it into a bowl of tepid water and leave it for 15 minutes, taste and soak again if necessary.

Do not be puzzled by the various cooking times given for sauerkraut. It can be eaten as it is, raw, when it is particularly good mixed with fruit, such as grated apples, bits of pineapple (see page 186), or grapes. Or you can cook it for 15–30 minutes, adding it to onions, browned with a little butter and sugar, and putting in juniper berries and caraway seeds, which are two favourite seasonings for it. Another favourite is cèpes, often in dried form: soak them in a little hot water for 20 minutes, then add the pieces to the pan of sauerkraut and pour in the soaking liquid through a muslin-lined strainer. Serve with pork, sausages, roast duck or goose.

Checking the huge barrels of sauerkraut

Sauerkraut can also make the basis of a slowly-cooked stew, in which smoked meats and game simmer together into a winter dish of hearty delight. Cook it in the same way as the red cabbage in stew recipes. If you have a little sauerkraut to spare, turn it into soup, with ham stock or a ham bone and water and a little smoked pork as a final embellishment.

Serves 6
medium onion, sliced
bouquet garni
2 level teaspoons salt
500 ml/generous ¾ pt/2 cups water
1.5 kg/3 lb eel, skinned, cleaned, cut in 8-cm/3-in pieces, or 1 kg/2 lb white fish fillets (cod, whiting, hake, etc.)
small onion, finely chopped
60 g/2 oz/¼ cup butter
2 level tablespoons flour
2 level tablespoons chopped fresh dill
1 level tablespoon chopped parsley
125 ml/4 fl oz/½ cup soured or whipping cream
lemon juice
sugar
pepper
2 egg yolks

In a wide shallow pan simmer the sliced onion and bouquet garni with the salt in the water for 10 minutes. Slip in the eel or fish and lower the heat so that the water barely bubbles. Remove the eel or fish the moment it is just cooked and keep warm on a serving dish, under a butter paper.

Meanwhile, stew the onion in the butter for 5 minutes over a low heat, stir in the flour and cook for 2 minutes. Strain the fish-poaching liquid into the sauce and boil it hard to reduce the volume, stirring occasionally. When the sauce has cooked down to the consistency of thick cream, add the herbs and cream. Simmer for 5 minutes, then taste and add lemon juice, a pinch of sugar and pepper according to what is required.

Beat a little hot sauce into the egg yolks, then stir back into the pan. Continue stirring for about 2 minutes until the sauce thickens slightly, but do not overheat or the eggs will curdle. Add more chopped dill or parsley, if you like, pour over the fish and serve.

SILESIAN HEAVEN
Schlesisches Himmelreich

Silesia, now divided between Poland and East Germany, has some famous dishes, and this is one of them. I am not sure about the 'Heaven' part—was it inspired by the reaction of bitter poverty glimpsing the elegance of wealthy tables, or was it a name in line with others such as Heaven and Earth (Himmel und Erde) for a dish of apples and potatoes? Perhaps it was a bit of both: fruit in the sky when you die. One thing is certain—nowhere can you eat better pork than in Germany, heavenly pork, properly bred with plenty of fat on it and through the lean meat, making it tender and juicy. Uncooked Kasseler rippenspeer—a smoked cut from the ribs, perfected by a Berlin butcher called Cassel—is an ideal joint for the recipe, after an appropriate soaking. But other kinds of salt pork can be used, or fresh pork.

Of the several versions, I find Arne Krüger's the best (see *German Cooking*). He uses a roast-bag, which works well. I have altered a few details.

Serves 6–8
level tablespoon flour
1 kg/2 lb piece of boned, rolled pork loin or rib, fresh, or lightly pickled or smoked
375 g/12 oz/2 cups dried mixed fruits (apples, pears, apricots, prunes)
30 g/1 oz/2 tbs demerara or soft brown sugar
250 ml/8 fl oz/good ¾ cup dry white wine
salt and pepper
chopped parsley, for sprinkling

Set oven at moderate, 160°C (325°F), gas 3. Shake the flour inside a roast-bag, then put it into a roasting tin.

Cut skin from the pork, and place inside the bag. Pour boiling water over fruit and leave for 30 minutes; drain, put round meat in the bag. Sprinkle with sugar and pour in wine. Close bag and make 4 small holes in it. Bake in oven for 1¼–1½ hours.

To serve, undo the bag, remove the pork and slice. Place the slices on a hot dish, and put the fruit all round. Taste the juice and add whatever seasoning it may require. The flour will have thickened it imperceptibly. Scatter with a little salt, pepper and parsley.

Serve with Semmelknödel (see page 211), or small potato dumplings with a cube of fried bread in the middle of each instead of plums (see page 188).

BRATWURST IN BEER BERLIN STYLE
Bratwurst in Bier nach Berliner Art

Bratwurst is a pale-looking, fresh sausage, made from pork and veal, with plenty of seasoning. Here is one way of cooking it, from Countess Morphy's *Recipes of All Nations.*

Serves 4
500 g/1 lb Bratwurst
large onion, sliced
butter
300 ml/½ pt/1¼ cups beer
2 bay leaves
teaspoon peppercorns
salt
1 tablespoon potato flour (fécule) or arrowroot

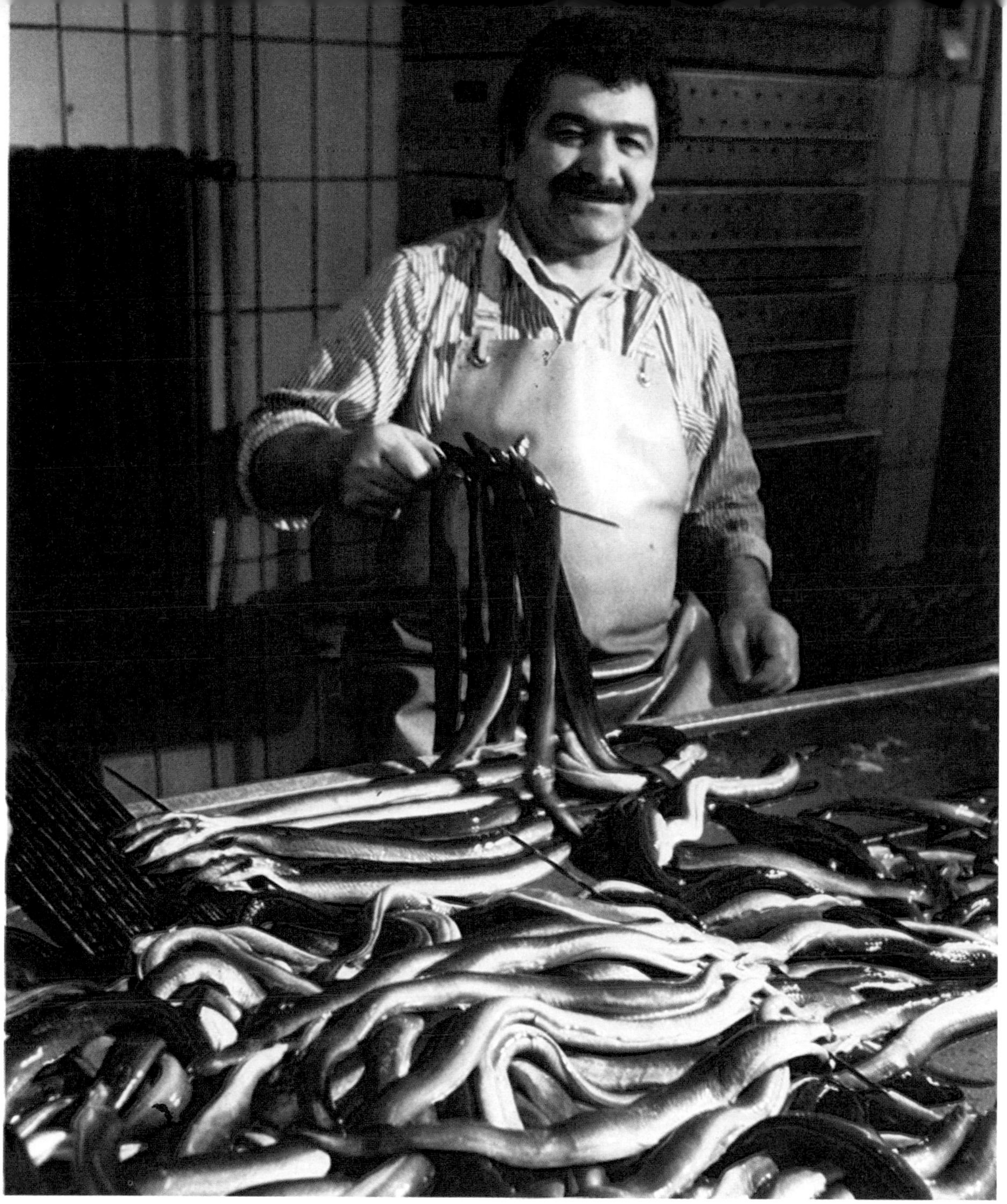

Fresh eels served with a creamy dill sauce are a delicate speciality of German cooking

Pour boiling water over the sausages, leave them for 1 minute, then drain and dry them. Cook the onion in a little butter, and when it softens, without browning, put in the sausages and fry all together. Add half the beer, the bay leaves and peppercorns. Bring quickly to the boil and bubble vigorously for a few minutes. Then add the rest of the beer, and simmer for 15 minutes. Thicken the liquor with potato flour or arrowroot, and serve with boiled potatoes.

Note do not worry if you cannot get potato flour—it is the cheap European substitute for arrowroot, which is easier to find in England.

SAUSAGES

Some of the sausages and cured pork that Germany produces

The superb ham of Westphalia, eaten in transparently thin slices with pumpernickel and pickled vegetables, has been famous in this country for centuries. Less well known, though, is the vast range of German sausages. Antony and Araminta Hippisley Coxe in their *Book of the Sausage,* list over 100, more than twice as many as any other country. Don't write off German sausages because of the abundance of poor hot-dog Frankfurter imitations, but try the coarse-cut liver sausage or extra good salami, for example. Listed below are some of the sausages widely available in England, and in particular from the German Food Centre, near London's Hyde Park Corner:

BRÜHWURST
Smoked and scalded sausages, for immediate consumption. Made from pork, or pork and beef (or veal), and sometimes bacon. This category includes:

Frankfurters No cooking is necessary, eat cold or heat through in hot but not boiling water for 5 minutes. Serve with potato salad, or bread and mustard, or as a garnish for soups and stews.

Bockwurst Like Frankfurters, but not from the Frankfurt area.

Fleischwurst or Extrawurst A larger version of the Frankfurter. Use for open sandwiches, or cold meat platters.

Jagdwurst and Bierwurst Use as Fleischwurst, or cut in strips and make into salad with pickled gherkins, apple, onion, salad vegetables.

Rostbratwurst or Bratwurst Fry or grill.

KOCHWURST
Boiled sausages, sometimes smoked, for immediate consumption. Made from liver or other offal, tongue, blood. It includes:

Leberwurst (liver sausage) No cooking is necessary.

Zungenwurst (tongue sausage) No cooking is necessary.

Sülzwurst (brawn) Made with chunks of meat from pig's head or leg, in aspic.

ROHWURST
Sausages preserved by smoking or air drying; they can be kept for several months in a cool, dry place if the skin is intact. Made from beef and/or pork. Look for:

Salami Use for open sandwiches, cold meat platters or salads.

Cervelat and Plockwurst Use as for salami.

Katenrauchwurst A black-skinned sausage. Cut diagonally in thick, oval slices to serve as for salami.

Teewurst Use as a spread.

RHINELAND MARINATED BEEF POT ROAST
Rheinischer Sauerbraten

A stunning way of cooking beef. The joint of topside is marinated for several days in wine and vinegar with vegetables, then it is braised and served with dried fruit and dumplings or potatoes, or red cabbage. Noodles and lightly-browned breadcrumbs, or larger potato dumplings and breadcrumbs go particularly well with Sauerbraten.

Serves 6–8
2 kg/4 lb piece of topside
lard or bacon fat
small onion and carrot, chopped
inner stalk of celery, sliced
small leek, trimmed and sliced
salt and pepper
150 ml/¼ pt/⅔ cup soured cream and 60 g/2 oz seeded or seedless raisins, or 100 g/3½ oz German honey cake, crumbled, or 100 g/3½ oz/¾ cup gingersnaps, crumbled

FOR THE MARINADE
150 g/¼ pt/⅔ cup each red wine vinegar and red wine, or 300 ml/½ pt/1⅓ cups red wine vinegar
large onion, sliced
2 bay leaves
large stalk of celery, sliced
level teaspoon each lightly-crushed black peppercorns and juniper berries
375 ml/12 fl oz/scant 2 cups water

Place the beef in a deep, close-fitting flameproof pot. Then make the marinade.

Put the vinegar, and wine if used, sliced onion, bay leaves and large stalk of celery into a pan with the peppercorns, juniper berries and water. Bring to the boil, cool and strain over the beef. Cover and leave in the refrigerator or, better still, a cool larder, for five days in winter or three in summer. Turn the beef twice a day. All this is done for German housewives by their butcher: they buy the beef ready-marinated with its juice, tied in a plastic bag.

Drain and dry the meat. Strain off and keep the marinade. Brown the beef in the fat and return to its pot. Brown the remaining vegetables in the fat and put them with the beef. Pour the fat from the pan, deglaze with 500 ml/18 fl oz/2¼ cups of the marinade and pour over the beef. Cover the pot and bring slowly to simmering point (use a heat-diffuser with gas, or cook the beef in an enamelled-iron pan). Simmer gently for 2–3 hours until tender.

Remove the beef to a hot serving dish and keep warm. Strain the liquor into a wide shallow pan, add the remaining marinade and boil down hard. Add seasoning discreetly. Thicken finally by stirring in the cream and raisins, or cake or gingernut crumbs. Pour into a hot jug and serve separately. Surround the meat with cooked mixed dried fruits, or with red cabbage (recipe on page 187); serve with potato dumplings (recipe on page 188) or potatoes.

BEEF OLIVES
Rindsrouladen

Little stuffed rolls of beef, or veal, are made in most European countries, but are a particular favourite in Germany. What makes them delicious is the use of smoked bacon. Some recipes elaborate on the stuffing below, spreading the beef first with mustard and tucking strips of pickled dill cucumber in with the bacon—a good idea if you like a little sharpness of that kind. The only problem here is getting the beef thin enough, ideally it should be cut on a bacon slicer.

Serves 6
12 slices of beef topside
175 g/6 oz/1½ cups finely chopped onion
200 g/7 oz piece of smoked streaky bacon, cut in strips
seasoned flour, paprika
lard
375 ml/12 fl oz/scant 2 cups water
2 medium carrots, cut into sticks
large stalk of celery, sliced
small onion, sliced
white part of 1 small leek, sliced
bouquet garni
salt and pepper
needle and fine thread or wooden cocktail sticks, halved

Beat the topside to make it even thinner. At one end of each slice, put a little chopped onion and bacon, then roll the slices up, starting from that end. Tie with thread or push in toothpicks or halved cocktail sticks to keep the shape. Turn them in seasoned flour, adding about 2 teaspoons paprika, enough to give them a rusty glow.

In a sauté pan, brown the rolls in a little lard. Pour off the surplus, then stir in the water, scraping the base of the pan to dislodge the little brown bits. Add the vegetables and bouquet garni. Bring to simmering point, cover and cook very gently for about 1½ hours or until tender.

At this point you are supposed to strain off the

liquid and make a sauce with a butter and flour roux, in which the beef rolls will be served. But the vegetables look so attractive that I just remove the beef rolls, and boil the pan juices down vigorously to make a concentrated gravy that needs no floury thickening to spoil it. Serve with red cabbage (recipe on page 187) and potatoes or potato dumplings (recipe on page 188).

ROAST GOOSE POMERANIAN STYLE
Pommerscher Gänsebraten

I find the thought of roast goose is often better than the reality. In spite of its reputed fattiness, the meat can be surprisingly tough. But it has a wonderful flavour, especially with this stuffing of apples and prunes with rye bread, from Arne Krüger's *German Cooking*. You can give the same treatment to ducks. Instead of turning the goose over, I drench a muslin cloth in melted goose fat or butter and place it over the breast and legs. The skin browns beneath it beautifully.

Serves 6–8
4–5 kg/8–9 lb goose, with giblets
onion, stuck with 3 cloves
medium carrot
½ bay leaf
sprig of thyme
175 g/6 oz/1 cup pitted prunes, soaked
4 tart apples, cookers or sharp Cox's, peeled, cored and cut in wedges
250 ml/9 fl oz dark rye bread crumbs, or pumpernickel crumbs
2 level tablespoons sugar

Take any lumps of fat out of the goose, chop them and put them in the roasting tin, or melt them over a low heat for drenching the muslin cloth. Put the giblets with the onion, carrot and herbs in a pan with water to cover generously; simmer 1½ hours, while the goose cooks. Set oven at moderately hot, 200°C (400°F), gas 6.

Mix the prunes, apples, crumbs and sugar together and stuff the goose. Put it on a rack in a roasting tin. Place the muslin cloth on top of the breast, or if not using the cloth, place the goose breast down. Put into the heated oven for 45 minutes, then pour off the fat from the roasting tin. Turn the heat down to 160°C (325°F), gas 3 and cook for a further 1½ hours, checking after an hour. The goose is done when the juices are no longer pink; if the goose was breast down, turn it right way up for about 20 minutes before the end of cooking to brown the skin.

Put the goose on a hot serving dish and keep warm. Pour the fat from the tin, and deglaze with the strained giblet stock, boiling it down hard to make a clear, strong-tasting liquid. Pour into a hot jug. Serve the goose with sauerkraut, flavoured with caraway seeds and juniper berries, and cooked with 5 peeled and grated Cox's orange pippins and an onion, browned in lard.

SADDLE OF VENISON OR HARE WITH RED WINE SAUCE
Rehrücken or Hasenrücken mit Rotweinsosse

The two meats can be treated in exactly the same way, but with differences of cooking time and quantity. A saddle of venison is enough for six to eight people, a saddle of hare enough for two or three (keep the legs to make a civet). With the increase in vension farming, we should gradually see more of it in our shops, though much is exported, especially to Germany. It is cheaper than beef and should remain so.

Marinating and larding are good ideas for both venison and hare, though not absolutely essential. Use a strong, large larding needle, the length of a carving knife. These are available here in England, but if you go to Paris you will have an excellent excuse to visit the splendid kitchen shop of Dehillerin by Les Halles and the Forum.

The use of fruit with dark gamey meat is something Germans understand even better than we do. They have a way of cooking game that is very appealing to our taste, which is not really surprising since we owed much to this German practice in the past.

Serves 6–8
2.5 kg/5 lb saddle of venison or 2–3 saddles of hare, well hung and skinned
thick sheet of pork back fat, chilled till firm, then cut into thin strips to fit larding needle
salt and pepper
FOR THE MARINADE
750 ml/1¼ pts/good 3 cups red wine
bouquet garni
teaspoon each juniper berries and peppercorns, lightly crushed
carrot and onion, sliced
tablespoon sherry vinegar, or 2 tablespoons/3 tbs red wine vinegar
750 ml/1¼ pts/good 3 cups water

FOR THE SAUCE
150 g/5 oz carrot, cut into sticks
125 g/4 oz/1 cup onion, sliced
white part of 1 small leek, sliced
2 celery stalks, sliced
60 g/2 oz/¼ cup lard or bacon fat
3 tablespoons/scant ¼ cup port
level tablespoon red currant jelly
100 ml/3½ fl oz/½ cup whipping or double cream
lemon juice
teaspoon horseradish
salt and pepper
TO GARNISH
4 pears, peeled, cored, halved and poached, for venison
lingonberry sauce or red currant jelly, for venison
fried slices of apples or pears, for hare (optional)

Lard the meat with seasoned strips of pork back fat, taking up small 'stitches' if you have a thin larding needle, or pushing the needle right through and drawing back long strips if you have a large needle. Put the meat, fleshy side down, in a close-fitting flameproof pot. Bring marinade ingredients to the boil in a pan, simmer for 5 minutes, then cool and pour over the meat. Cover and leave two days or leave overnight, according to the age of the meat, in a cool place. Then drain and dry the meat. Strain the marinade, reserving bouquet garni and spices.

Set oven at hot, 230° (450°F), gas 8. Brown the sauce vegetables in hot fat, then put in a large cooking pot. There should be enough to make a layer in the base of the pot; if not, add more in roughly the same proportions. Brown the meat and put it on top. Pour in enough of the marinade to come just over halfway up the meat, add the bouquet garni and spices. Cover and put into the heated oven; after 15 minutes, lower the heat to 180°C (350°F), gas 4, and cook 30 minutes for hare, and 50–60 minutes for venison, which should, ideally, be pink.

Put the meat on a hot serving dish, carve and reassemble on the dish, and keep warm. Strain the juices into a wide shallow pan, skimming or blotting away the fat. Add any marinade left over as well. Bring to the boil and boil hard to reduce the liquid to end up with no more than 500 ml (generous ¾ pt/2 cups). Add the port and boil again. Be guided by your taste rather than exact measurement, remembering that cream will be added and that the sauce should taste on the strong side, as it is to be used sparingly with the meat.

To finish the sauce, whisk in the red currant jelly, then the cream; when well amalgamated, sharpen slightly with lemon juice. Finally season with just enough horseradish to give a hint of it in the sauce, plus salt and plenty of pepper.

Surround the venison with halved pears, and drop a spoonful of lingonberry sauce or red currant jelly into the cavities of each one. With hare, omit the pears and add fried slices of apples or pears, if you like, which go better with its smaller size. Pour a little hot sauce over and round the meat, put the rest in a jug. Serve the venison with green beans or red cabbage, the hare with potato dumplings (recipes on page 188) or noodles.

TONGUE WITH PRUNE AND ALMOND SAUCE
Gekochte Ochsenzunge

My own favourite among German sour-sweet dishes. The ideal meat is smoked pickled tongue, but plain pickled tongue does very well, too. If you want to serve the dish in smaller quantities for 3 or 4 people, buy good cooked tongue and reheat the slices in the sauce.

Serves 8–10
ox tongue
onion, stuck with 3 cloves
large carrot, quartered
bouquet garni
light stock
FOR THE SAUCE
level tablespoon butter
1½ level teaspoons flour
125 ml/4 fl oz/½ cup tarragon wine vinegar
6 tablespoons/½ cup red wine
125 g/4 oz/½ cup sugar
powdered cinnamon and cloves
60 g/2 oz/⅓ cup seeded or seedless raisins
20 pitted prunes, soaked
45 g/1½ oz/good ¼ cup blanched almonds, slivered
salt and pepper
lemon juice

Simmer the tongue with the aromatics in water to cover for 2 hours. Cool in the liquor, then remove and skin the tongue. Put it back into the pan with just enough light stock to cover it, and simmer for 2–3 hours until tender.

Meanwhile, prepare the sauce. Melt the butter, stir in the flour to make a roux and cook for 2 minutes. Mix the vinegar and wine and add slowly, stirring all the time, then add the sugar, and stir till smooth. Add a generous pinch of cinnamon and cloves, with the fruit and almonds. Simmer for a few minutes, taste and, if you like, add more spices.

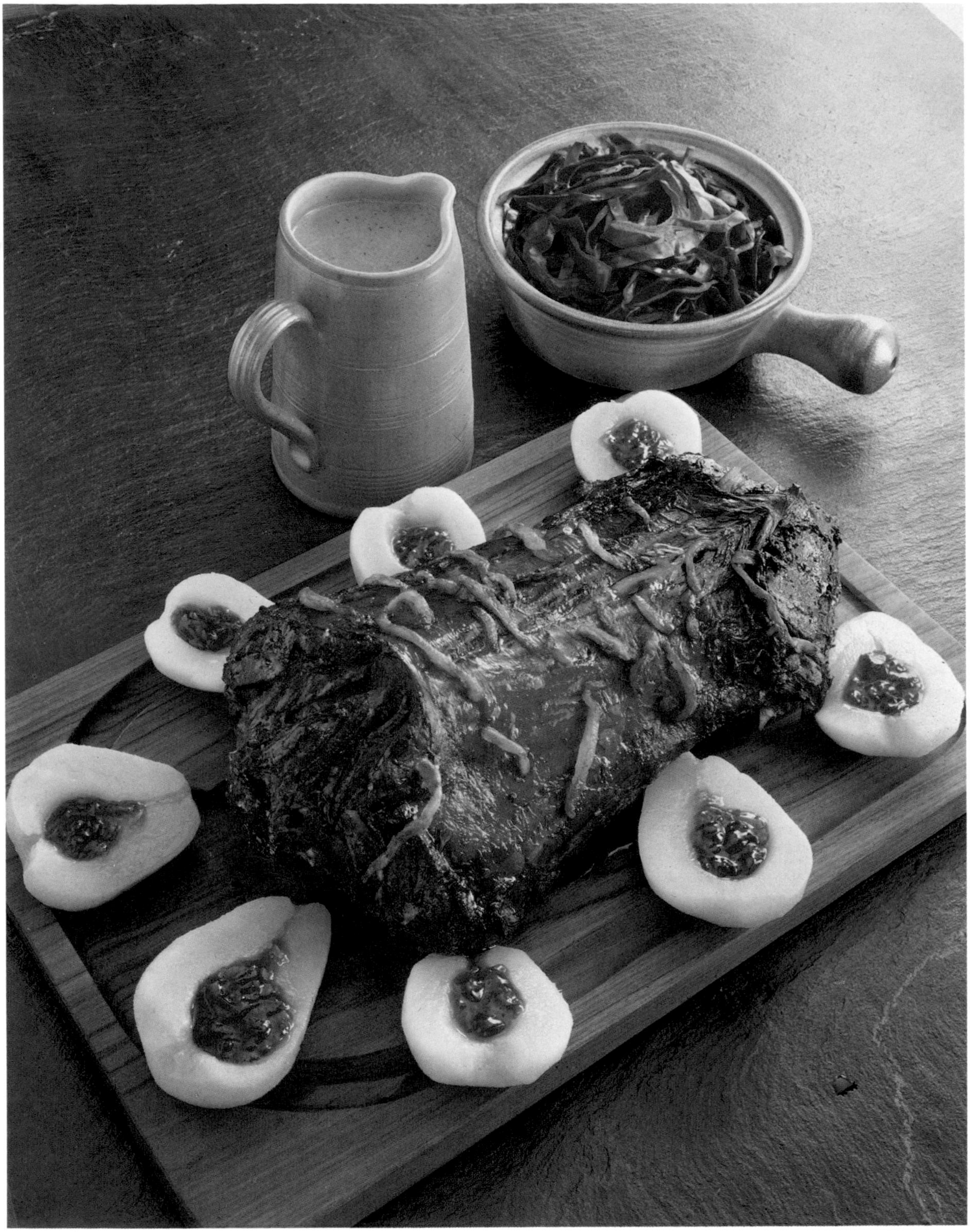

Saddle of venison with red wine sauce, pears stuffed with jelly, and red cabbage

Dilute slightly with some stock from the pan of tongue, and cook very gently for about 20 minutes.

Slice the cooked tongue and arrange it on a hot serving dish. Pour over the sauce, disposing the fruit and almonds around and between the slices. Serve with noodles or potatoes.

LIVER CHEESE
Leberkäse

I am in two minds about Leberkäse. If it comes straight from the oven, warm and juicy, to be eaten in slices in large soft rolls, with warm potato salad (see page 188), or with a tomato or caper sauce I like it very much. Once it is cold, I find it dully unpleasant (and some may find it indigestible). If you are given to meat loaves and the smoothness of Bratwurst and Frankfurters, then you are certain to like Leberkäse.

Hanne Lambley, author of *The Home Book of German Cookery*, on whose recipe this one is based, points out there is not very much liver in it. This is true, but the flavour dominates the other meats. 'Cheese' refers to the consistency, I imagine, as we say damson cheese. Mrs Lambley suggests eating slices of Leberkäse, fried brown in butter and topped with a fried egg, plus roast potatoes and a green or tomato salad.

Serves 8
500 g/1 lb lean beef
500 g/1 lb lean pork
200 g/7 oz calf's or lamb's liver
100 g/3½ oz smoked bacon
medium onion, quartered
1 litre/1¾ pts/4½ cups milk
2 eggs
100 g/3½ oz/scant cup sifted flour
1½ level teaspoons salt
level teaspoon dried marjoram
level teaspoon dried thyme
plenty of black pepper
24-cm/9½-in long loaf tin

Chop roughly and process the meats with the onion in a processor or blender gradually in batches, adding half of the milk to prevent the mixture sticking, together with the eggs. Mix the rest of the milk with the flour till smooth, and add with the seasonings to the meat mixture. Aim to get a very smooth mixture. If you do not have a processor or strong blender, mince the meats twice at least and then mix with the remaining ingredients.

Set oven at moderately hot, 190°C (375°F), gas 5. Line the loaf tin with non-stick baking paper or greaseproof paper, brushed with melted butter. Put in the mixture, brush the top with cold water, and cook in the heated oven for 1¼ hours or until it just tests firm with a skewer. Serve as above.

FRANKFURT BROWN BETTY
Frankfurter Brot Pudding

A German version of our English Brown Betty—the difference coming from the use of little fried bread cubes instead of crumbs, and from the spicing of the apples. In Scandinavia they like the combination of apples and bread so much that they make a Brown Betty like ours, and a cold version called Peasant Maid in a Veil, with rye crumbs (see page 176). The buttery crispness of the hot pudding is its charm; whichever country's version you use, do not be tempted to substitute some other fat. The recipe for this family pudding comes from *The Home Book of German Cookery*, by Hanne Lambley. Use Cox's or other good eating apples: cooking apples would need more sugar.

The wide choice in a German bakery

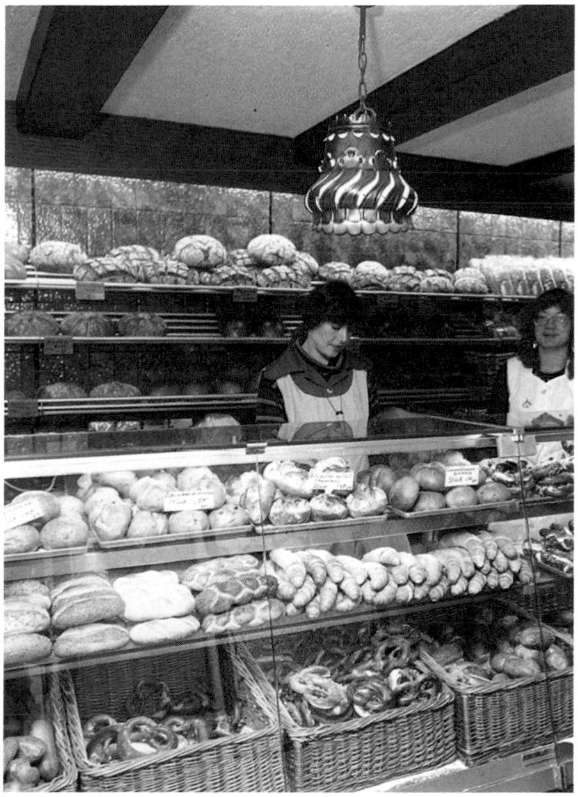

250 g/9 oz cubed white bread
150 g/5 oz/⅔ cup unsalted butter
1 kg/2 lb peeled and sliced apple, Cox's are ideal
50 g/2 oz/¼ cup sugar
¼ teaspoon cinnamon
good pinch ground cloves
150 ml/¼ pt/½ cup white wine or cider
grated rind of ½ lemon
50 g/2 oz/½ cup chopped blanched almonds
50 g/2 oz/⅓ cup sultanas (optional)
30 g/generous oz/2 tbs unsalted butter
icing sugar
whipped cream

Fry the bread in the butter until lightly golden and crisp. Remove to a plate, then fry the almonds (you may need extra butter, unless you use a non-stick pan). Put with the bread. Meanwhile cook the apples in a closed pan with the sugar, spices and wine or cider and lemon rind. When the pieces are tender—Cox's keep their shape, which I like in this kind of pudding, but you can mash them if you prefer—layer them into a buttered ovenproof dish with the bread. Begin and end with bread. My own feeling is to layer them shallow, rather than in a deep dish, so that you get the maximum crispness. Intersperse with the sultanas. Dot with the extra butter and bake for about 30 minutes at 160°C (325°F), gas 3.

To serve, dredge lightly with icing sugar, and put on the table with the cream.

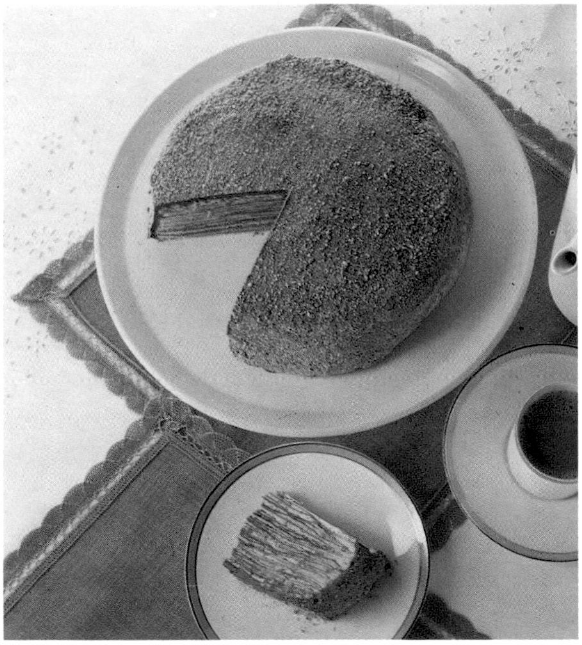

Try counting the layers of this tree cake!

TREE CAKE
Baumtorte

The magnificent layered cake made by professional German pastrycooks on a revolving spit. This is the domestic version, with horizontal layers of cake resembling the inner rings of a tree when each piece is cut.

It sounds laborious, but in fact builds up quickly, and tastes so good that it is well worth the trouble. This particular recipe is based on one by Jolene Worthington in *Cuisine*, the American cookery magazine. What I particularly like about it is the use of apricot jam and finely ground pistachios.

Serves 12–14

FOR THE CAKE

100 g/3½ oz/scant cup pistachios, finely ground
500 g/1 lb apricot jam, sieved and warmed slightly, if necessary, so it spreads thinly
400 g/14 oz almond paste
6 tablespoons/½ cup half cream, coffee cream or single cream
200 g/7 oz/scant cup unsalted butter
135 g/4½ oz/1 cup + 2 tbs plain flour, sifted
100 g/3½ oz/¾ cup cornflour
2 tablespoons/3 tbs rum
teaspoon vanilla essence
level teaspoon grated lemon zest
10 eggs, separated
190 g/6½ oz/good ¾ cup caster sugar
¼ teaspoon salt

FOR CHOCOLATE ICING

90 g/3 oz/⅓ cup unsalted butter
pinch of salt
1½ tablespoons/2 tbs rum
level tablespoon plus level teaspoon golden syrup
90 g/3 oz/½ cup dark or bitter chocolate, broken up small
23–25-cm/9½–10-in springform cake tin; metal base from 20-cm/8-in loose-bottomed flan tin

Put pistachios and jam in convenient bowls near the grill, together with a pastry brush or flexible spatula. Then make the cake.

Start by beating the almond paste and cream to a light, fluffy mixture like mashed potatoes. Cream the butter, fold in the flours, rum, essence and zest, and mix well. Fold in the almond paste mixture. Beat the egg yolks with an electric beater, adding half of the sugar, and continue until the raised

An extravaganza of the biscuit-maker's skill on display at Bahlsen's factory at Hanover

beaters leave a ribbon trail on the surface that slowly disappears; fold into the cake. Beat the egg whites and salt to the soft peak stage, add the remaining sugar, 2 tablespoons at a time, and beat until the whites are stiff but not too dry. Fold the whites, in four batches, into the cake mixture.

Set the grill to top heat. Butter and flour the springform tin, then put a double circle of non-stick baking paper in the bottom.

Put 3 tablespoons cake mixture into the prepared tin and, with the brush or spatula, spread it over the base. Put the tin under the heated grill; leave for 2–3 minutes until the batter has browned and looks rather like a pancake. Remove the tin and repeat layering and grilling. Spread this layer with a thin coat of apricot jam to within 1 cm ($\frac{1}{2}$ in) of the edge and sprinkle with a level teaspoon of pistachios. Make another 2 cake layers, then spread on another layer of jam and pistachios. And so on.

The aim is 30 layers, but I have never quite achieved that. As you grill the layers and the cake rises, you will have to lower the grill shelf so that the mixture does not burn. Cool the cake in the tin, then refrigerate overnight. Next day, unclip and remove the sides of the tin. Centre the tart tin base on the cake. Cut down at an angle to the base of the cake to give it sloping sides. Turn cake upside-down and remove the springform tin base and paper. Turn right way up and place on a cake rack.

Heat remaining apricot jam to 100°C (225°F) and spread with a metal spatula over the top and sides of the cake. Cool for 30–45 minutes.

Make the icing by melting the butter, salt, rum and syrup together. Raise the heat and boil for 1 minute. Take off the heat and stir in the chocolate till melted. Cool until the mixture coats the back of the spoon, then pour over the top and sides of the cake. When it has almost set (about 15 minutes), press remaining pistachios in a circle round the edge and sides of the cake.

This cake keeps well in the refrigerator and freezes beautifully.

CRUMBLE CAKE
Streuselkuchen

A yeast cake with crumble topping that is best eaten with coffee the day you make it. It is perfect when just warm.

Serves 8–10
60 g/2 oz/¼ cup each butter and sugar
2 eggs
375 g/12 oz/3 cups plain flour
packet Harvest Gold dried yeast
75 ml/2½ fl oz/6 tbs warm milk
extra butter, melted
FOR THE CRUMBLE
90 g/3 oz/⅓ cup butter
100 g/3½ oz/scant ½ cup sugar
200 g/7 oz/1¾ cup flour
level teaspoon powdered cinnamon
grated rind of ½ lemon
33 × 23-cm/13 × 9-in shallow baking tin

Cream butter and sugar, add eggs, then the flour mixed with the yeast. Pour in just enough milk to mix to a smooth silky dough, and knead it thoroughly into a ball. Put in a bowl. Tie the bowl into a polythene bag and leave in a warm place until the dough doubles in volume, 1½–2 hours.

Knock the dough down and roll out on a floured board to fit into the baking tin. Brush the tin with melted butter, put in the dough and prick the top with a fork here and there. Brush over with more melted butter. Set the oven at moderate, 180°C (350°F), gas 4.

For the crumble, rub the butter into the remaining ingredients. Sprinkle them over the dough and press it down very lightly. Leave to prove in a warm place for 30 minutes, tied into the polythene bag again. Bake in the heated oven for 30–40 minutes.

Note use rather less crumble mixture and cover the top with sliced apples or halved, stoned plums and sugar before baking, for a fruit tart.

POPPY SEED CAKE
Mohntorte

This favourite German cake originally came from Silesia, which is now part of Poland. Poppy seeds need to be ground; you can buy a special little machine for this, or use an electric grinder. In Germany, shops grind the seeds for you for immediate use as, once ground, the seeds lose their finest flavour quite rapidly.

Serves 6
FOR THE PASTRY
150 g/5 oz/⅔ cup butter, softened
50 g/scant 2 oz/¼ cup caster sugar
pinch of salt
1 large egg
200 g/7 oz/1¾ cups plain flour
FOR THE FILLING
150 g/5 oz poppy seeds, ground
6 tablespoons/½ cup milk
125 g/4 oz/½ cup granulated sugar
60 g/2 oz plain or bitter chocolate, grated
60 g/2 oz seeded or seedless raisins
60 g/2 oz/⅓ cup candied orange peel, chopped
60 g/2 oz/½ cup blanched almonds, grated
large egg, beaten
FOR THE GLAZE
1 teaspoon beaten egg
caster sugar
poppy seeds, unground
20-cm/8-in loose-bottomed flan tin

To make the pastry, cream the butter, sugar and salt. Add the egg, then flour and enough water to make a soft but not sticky dough. Chill for 1 hour. Roll out thinly and cut four circles to fit the flan tin. Put one circle into the tin.

To make the filling, simmer the poppy seeds in the milk for 2 minutes, stirring. Off the heat, add the remaining ingredients except for a teaspoon of the egg which is needed for the glaze. Set oven at moderate, 160°C (325°F), gas 3.

Spread one-third of the filling on the pastry circle in the tin. Cover with a second circle and another third of the filling, then with the third circle and the rest of the filling. Cover with the last circle and press the edge down very lightly. Make a central hole and brush over with the teaspoon of egg. Sprinkle lightly with sugar and poppy seeds. Bake at the top of the heated oven for 45–60 minutes. Serve warm.

MERINGUE LAYER CAKE
Blitztorte

A lovely cake, pretty and varied in texture, not difficult to make. Flavour the filling with tart fruit—pineapple is a favourite, and I've used kumquats cooked in a little syrup with even greater success. Red or white currants, or blueberries, would also do well.

Pretzels come in many sizes and are specially popular in Munich

Serves 8
125 g/4 oz/$\frac{1}{2}$ cup butter
125 g/4 oz/$\frac{1}{2}$ cup caster sugar from vanilla pod-sugar jar
pinch of salt
4 large egg yolks, beaten
3 dessertspoons milk
125 g/4 oz/1 cup plain flour
level teaspoon baking powder
FOR THE MERINGUE
4 large egg whites
175 g/6 oz/$\frac{3}{4}$ cup caster sugar from vanilla jar
60 g/2 oz/$\frac{1}{2}$ cup flaked, blanched almonds
dessertspoon sugar and $\frac{1}{2}$ teaspoon powdered cinnamon, mixed
TO FINISH
250 ml/8 fl oz/scant cup whipping cream, stiffly whipped and sweetened to taste
125–175 g/4–6 oz fruit
two 23-cm/9-in sandwich tins

Cream the butter, sugar and salt together. Add the egg yolks and milk. Sift the flour and baking powder together, and fold into the mixture.

Butter sandwich tins and line with circles of non-stick baking paper. Divide the cake mixture evenly and smoothly between the two tins: there will be a thin layer in each. Set oven at moderate, 180°C (350°F), gas 4.

Whisk the egg whites until stiff, then add the sugar gradually, still whisking. Divide equally in two and spread over both tins of cake mixture. Scatter with almonds, then with the cinnamon sugar.

Bake in the heated oven for 30 minutes. Remove carefully and allow to cool for a minute or two. Ease out on to wire cake racks, covered with greaseproof paper. When quite cold, put one cake, meringue-side facing down, on to a large plate. Fold the fruit into the whipped cream, then spread over the cake. Put the other cake on top, meringue side up.

RUMTOPF

For this rum pot intended as a Christmas preserve, you need a 5-litre (1 gallon or 20-cup) stoneware jar, or a special rumtopf from Germany (or from Austria where they make it as well. In fact, this recipe came from Elisabeth Bond, the Austrian friend who has advised me about Austrian cooking).

There are two things to watch. First, make sure that the rum is the strongest you can buy, and second, avoid using fruit that has been sprayed. Rumtopf sometimes develops mould; I talked over this problem with the Cointreau brothers, who are great specialists in fruit alcohols, at Angers, in France. They had had this mould trouble at home on occasion, and were convinced that sprayed fruit was the cause. You can minimise the risk of mould by preparing rumtopf in a non-porous pot that will fit into your refrigerator. This is contrary to the point of the preserve, which was a way of storing fruit in the days before domestic refrigerators, but it does make success more certain.

Prepare 1 kg (2 lb) strawberries. Make sure they are thoroughly dry before sprinkling them with 500 g (1 lb/2 cups) sugar. Leave overnight. Next day tip the whole thing, juice included, into the pot with 1 litre ($1\frac{3}{4}$ pts/scant $4\frac{1}{4}$ cups) rum. Put a clean plate directly on to the fruit to make sure it stays below the surface: for this reason a straight-sided jar is more practical than the prettier, curvy traditional rumtopf. Cover the top of the jar with plastic film and the lid. Keep in a cool place.

Add more fruit and sugar—half quantities are fine—as the summer fruits come along. You will also need more rum to keep the liquid level up. It should be about 2 cm (1 in) above the fruit. Include sweet and sour cherries (leave stones in); raspberries, loganberries, blackberries; apricots, peaches, greengages and a few plums (leave in the occasional stone); pipped grapes; melon, pineapple, 1 or 2 apples, 1 or 2 pears (peeled and cubed). The currants and gooseberries can go in, too, but the skins tend to toughen up. Add extra rum a month after the pot is full, if you can get it in. Cover for the last time and leave until Christmas.

Serve rumtopf with ice-cream, or a mound of boudoir biscuits dipped lightly in coffee and held together with whipped cream to which a little fine-ground continental roast coffee has been added, or simply in a glass with a whirl of whipped cream on top and a little raspberry juice.

Note Germans will not necessarily approve, but rumtopf can be made with brandy. They do this in some parts of France, where the preserve is known as bachelor's jam.

AUSTRIA & HUNGARY

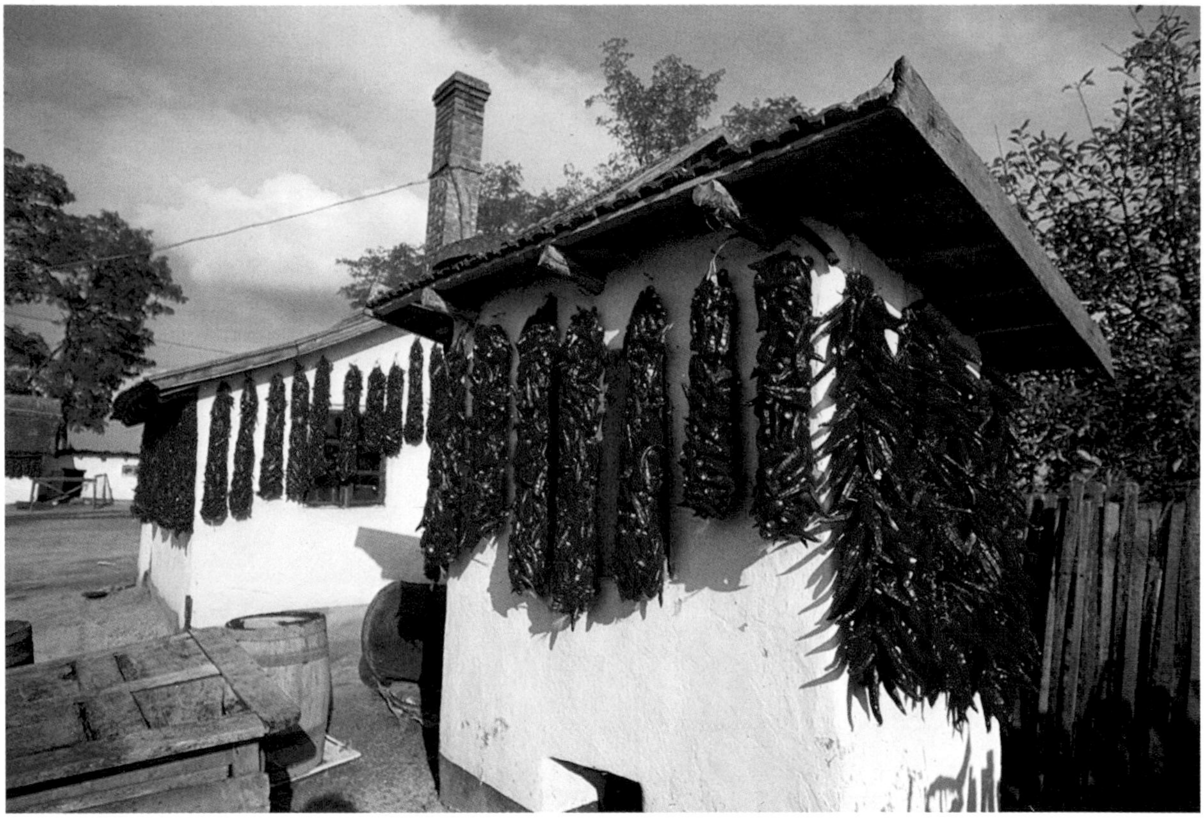

Drying peppers in the old way on the walls of a cottage near Kalocsa

Those supremely grand cities, Vienna and Budapest, were the centres of what was once the Great Austro-Hungarian Empire, set down in Europe's heartlands. Surrounded by Teutons and Turks, Slavs and Italians, the Empire channelled many good things, not least a cuisine, into the Western world through its two capital cities.

Development in Austrian food took place in the 18th century, under French influence. With great families such as the Esterházys, Haydn's patrons, and the benevolent tyranny of Empress Maria Theresa, this style became the rule for the well-off in Hungary, too. Refinement of specifically Hungarian dishes and their acceptance into the Austrian repertoire reached a high point with the setting up of the Dual Monarchy in 1867, when Emperor Franz Joseph I of Austria also became King of Hungary and so ruled over two joined but separate countries. Both capital cities spread with new industry and wealth, Vienna stretched out beyond the new Ringstrasse, and in 1872, Buda and Óbuda joined with the new flat suburbs of Pest on the other side of the Danube to form Budapest. Restaurant and café baroquery of twisted pillars, looking-glasses, gold leaf and round globes of light, belong to this period which ended with the 1914–18 war and the collapse of the Austro-Hungarian Empire.

Although many dishes are common to both countries' menus, they are given a different accent. One must admit and enjoy the fact that Hungarian eating is rumbustious.

For a start everything is red: curtains, tablecloths, napkins, the little embroidered jackets of gypsy musicians, the skirts of the dancing girls, the food itself—red beef, red with paprika and tomatoes, red veal and chickens, pancakes with a rosy sauce. Fogas, the pike-perch special to Lake Balaton, comes golden and rampant on a red-patterned dish. In the Nagycsarnok market in Budapest, one end of the iron building is red from floor to roof with a cascade of peppers, the fall patterned with white garlic.

I drove south one autumn through the paprika harvest—pickers bent double—on the way to the paprika factory at Kalocsa. Fringe after fringe of red peppers hung thick from the eaves of the houses, following the line of gable and porch. Red, everywhere red. I was caught up in this vigour, dreaming of Magyar horsemen and Turks in bright turbans galloping over the distances of the Great Plain. 'You know,' said the girl who was organising the trip, 'that puszta only means field!' But what a field!

Hungarian food also means excellent foie gras which we do not get here, and excellent salami which we do. Nineteenth-century Italian refugees, who were also salami-makers, spotted the old mangalica race of pigs, and saw the similarity to pigs they used back home. Now Hungarian salami has the quality of Italian salami—the best—and is a fraction cheaper.

The delectable cakes of Budapest are for eating on the spot, either at Ruszwurm's, the charming little tea room in Buda, or at grander Vörösmarty's across the Danube in Pest. In Vienna, you can send Sachertorte, Pischingertorte (hazelnut and chocolate wafer) and Mozartkugeln (almond balls) to your friends back home, or boxes of sweets from Demel's. Demel's windows are a fantasy of almond paste sculpture—a pink church, a man in overalls holding a factory tucked under his arm, the Beatles, and coloured desserts that recall an old cookery book.

From such sugar skill, or from the hearty window opposite, a metre deep in roasted calf's knuckles, it is obvious that Austrian cooking has come a long way since the first Austrian hausfrau we know about. She is the Venus of Willdendorf, near Krems, forever in a glass case in Vienna's Natural History Museum. She ate well, obviously, mammoth steak, reindeer, Danube salmon, mountain trout, partridges from the steppes. Her descendants are about still, tidy curls under green hats with little feathers, totting up the price of a crayfish and beer party, in front of a neat round crayfish tank, or tucking into a plump dumpling in the Kärntnerstrasse.

Austria, everywhere, has places to sit down and take a little something. Walks are detours on the way to the pub. Or to the enormous beer cellars that have taken over ancient monastic undercrofts (the most beautiful and famous being Peterskeller, at Salzburg). Every lake has waterside restaurants; great parks like the Prater are dotted with beer gardens. Wine-drinkers will find a 'heuriger' to suit their taste, a pretty decorative sort of place or a few wooden tables and chairs outside a country wine cave. In Tyrol every village has a light, pinewood café, with girls in dirndls to bring you anything from an excellent cup of coffee to smoked pork and sauerkraut. Everywhere an easy willingness to serve refreshments all day (and often in English) makes one realise how sad and grudging and grimy we are here with our public eating-places.

Some people sneer at Austrian 'gemütlichkeit'—genial cosiness—and in the past it must have been stuffy, but in the freer style of today, Austrians manage to get it exactly right. Relaxed comfort is apparent, too, in their home cookery, their hausmannskost, which is simple yet pleasing.

My own complaint in both countries is the difficulty of having a leisurely restaurant meal where you can talk. Music is an obsession. With Mozart, Schubert, Strauss, Haydn, Liszt, Bartók and Kodály, who can blame them?

SAUERKRAUT SOUP
Sauerkrautsuppe/Káposztaleves

In Vienna's Naschmarkt the sauerkraut stall is easy to find, with its big wooden tubs, the graters and piles of cabbage waiting to be salted down. In England you will most likely have to make do with bottled or canned sauerkraut, and I would recommend you go for a German brand. It may be a little more expensive, but the quality is the best. Add your own juniper berries and caraway if they are not included already.

This soup is more of a stew, a meal in itself. Buy properly smoked pork and bacon. If you have to make do with bacon chops instead of a piece of smoked ribs, add it with the sausage and diced bacon, as it does not need much cooking.

Serves 6–8
1 kg/2 lb sauerkraut, washed
1 kg/2 lb piece smoked pork ribs
250 g/8 oz/2 cups chopped onion
2-3 cloves garlic, sliced
level tablespoon chopped dillweed
125 g/4 oz smoked streaky bacon, diced
rounded teaspoon paprika
spiced German boiling sausage
300 ml/$\frac{1}{2}$ pt/$1\frac{1}{4}$ cups soured cream
salt

Put sauerkraut, ribs, onion, garlic and dillweed into a large pan with $1\frac{1}{2}$ litres ($2\frac{3}{4}$ pt/scant 7 cups) water. Simmer for half an hour. Brown diced bacon in its own fat, stir in the paprika off the heat and add to the pan, with the boiling sausage. Bring back to simmering point and cook for another 40 minutes. Remove and cut up pork ribs, discarding any bones, then put meat back into the pan. Stir in cream, add salt if necessary, and bring back to boiling point.

SOUR CHERRY SOUP
Meggyleves

Wonderful cherries—and other fruit—are grown in Hungary. You need dark tart Morellos, or at a pinch Dukes, to make this best-of-all cold summer soups. There are a number of versions, some with red wine, but this one with white wine, seems the best to me: it comes from Victor Sassie, owner of the Gay Hussar restaurant in London's Soho.

Serves 6–8
500 g/1 lb Morello cherries
750 ml/$1\frac{1}{4}$ pts/good 3 cups Riesling
60 g/2 oz/$\frac{1}{4}$ cup sugar
5 cm/2 in cinnamon stick
grated rind of 1 lemon
juice of 2 lemons
100 ml/3–4 fl oz/$1\frac{1}{2}$–$1\frac{2}{3}$ cup brandy, optional
600 ml/1 pt/$2\frac{2}{3}$ cups cream, half soured, half whipping

Put the cherry stalks into a pan. Stone the cherries and add the cracked stones to the stalks. You can crack the stones completely and extract the kernels, which is even better but more laborious. Add the wine, sugar, cinnamon, rind and juice of the lemons. Bring to the boil slowly, simmer for 5 minutes, cover and turn off the heat. Infuse for 15 minutes. Strain into a clean pan, bring to the boil agadnd add the cherries with any juice. Take the pan immediately from the stove and cool.Liquidise or process some of the cherries if you want to give the soup consistency. Stir in the brandy, if using, and adjust flavourings to taste.

Put the cream into a tureen; stir in the soup. Serve well chilled.

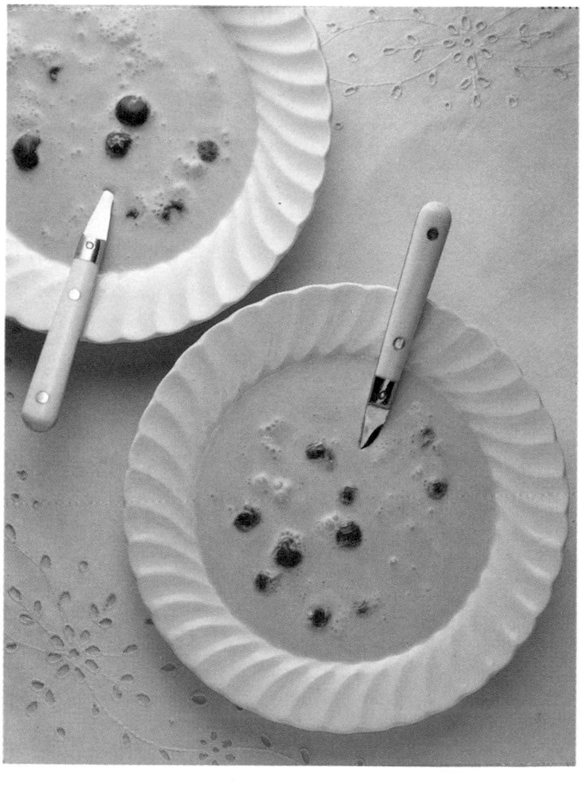

Sour cherry soup is cool on a hot July day

Fogas from Lake Balaton fried in the classic elegant way

KALOCSA FISH SOUP
Halászlé Kalocsai

Before we went round the paprika factory at Kalocsa, we had lunch at the firm's little house beside the Danube. The great river was humping along fast, in sulky shades of brown. The wind blew. The cauldron of fish soup swung gently from a tripod over a gas jet out of doors. We drank wine, watched the deep simmering red bobbing with cherry peppers inside the black pot, listening to the laughter that bursts out from men and women alike in Hungary, with a glorious merriment and noise. 'How do you make the soup?' I asked. 'Well, first you have to catch two carp from the Danube...' obviously my face fell... 'or at the fish farm... or at the market...'. Other river fish can perfectly well be used or white sea fish, though the taste will obviously be different and fishier.

Soups of this kind, or gulyás soups, make the main part of a meal in both countries: in Austria they will be followed perhaps by fruit dumplings (recipe on page 220), in Hungary by a pasta and curd cheese dish (recipe on page 212).

Serves 8

1 kg/2 lb carp, head and tail reserved
15 hot cherry peppers, one broken to expose the seeds, or 2 fresh hot chillies, one broken
100 g/3½ oz/scant cup finely chopped onions
heaped teaspoon tomato paste
rounded tablespoon paprika
1 litre/generous 1¾ pt/4½ cups water
salt

Put the fish head and tail into a pot with the hot peppers or chillies, onions, tomato paste, paprika and water. Bring to the boil, then cover and simmer for 1 hour. Remove the head and tail. Put in the fish, sliced into steaks, and simmer for up to 30 minutes. Do not stir the soup or the fish will break up: just shake the pot occasionally. Season with salt and serve.

FOGAS

Fogas is the most famous Hungarian freshwater fish, and many restaurants around Lake Balaton where it is caught will serve it deep-fried. It looks spectacular having been bent into a triumphant curve before cooking, so that it rears up on the dish. Here is another way of cooking fogas that can be applied to the similar pike-perch or zander, or to salt water fish such as gurnard and mullet of various kinds.

Serves 6
1.5 kg/3 lb fish, cleaned
tablespoon vinegar
salt and pepper
250 ml/9 fl oz/scant $1\frac{1}{3}$ cups each soured and whipping cream
6 egg yolks
90 g/3 oz/scant $\frac{1}{2}$ cup butter, melted
2 tablespoons/3 tbs each chopped tarragon and capers
small onion, finely chopped
level tablespoon anchovy paste
2 tablespoons/3 tbs each chopped parsley and chives
6 egg whites, stiffly whisked

Cover fish with water, add vinegar and 1 teaspoon salt. Bring slowly to boiling point; remove pan from the heat. Cool for 5 minutes, then fillet the fish. Mix remaining ingredients, except the egg whites. Put half in a gratin dish, with the fillets on top. Fold egg whites into remaining sauce and pile on top of the fillets. Bake at 180–190°C (350–375°F) gas 4–5 for about 30 minutes.

KOHLRABI

The long, low Naschmarkt in Vienna, a double alley in the centre of a great boulevard defined by three rows of shop stalls, was originally for dairy produce. Now it is devoted to fruit and vegetables, with an occasional butcher, baker, grocer, pickle merchant and flower seller. In the autumn sun it shone like a never-ending harvest festival. A vegetable in abundance was kohlrabi, which I always associate with the Austrian friend who showed me the best ways to cook it.

Method I Peel, halve and slice into semi-circles 500 g (1 lb) kohlrabi. Melt 2 tablespoons each butter and oil, sprinkle in 1 level tablespoon sugar and caramelise it. Put in the kohlrabi, stirring until the pieces are coated. Cover, lower the heat and leave to cook till tender; there should not be much liquid. Sprinkle on 1 level teaspoon flour and stir in just enough stock or water to make a binding sauce, then cook 3–4 minutes more. Scatter with chopped parsley. Serve with roast or grilled meat.

Shredded marrow is on sale in the markets ready for cooking

Method II Trim 12 kohlrabi of their stalks, keeping the best stalks. Peel and hollow out the kohlrabi. Simmer the shells for 15 minutes in salted water. Add the reserved stalks for the last 2 minutes. Make a meat (beef/pork/veal/chicken/brains) and bread-crumb stuffing and fill kohlrabi. Chop inside parts of kohlrabi and blanched stalks; put in a buttered gratin dish, and place kohlrabi on top. Put a dab of butter on top of each kohlrabi and add enough water to cover stalks etc. Bake at 180°C (350°F), gas 4 until the kohlrabi are tender—about 30 minutes. Pour on cream, fresh or soured, to make a little sauce with the juices in the dish.

YOUNG SWEETCORN IN CREAM
Fiatal tejszines kukorica

A fine dish from George Lang's *Cuisine of Hungary*, creamed sweetcorn to go with fried chicken along with salad. You can serve it on its own, too, in little pots with toast fingers or in pastry cases. I have adjusted quantities to suit large heads of corn.

Serves 6–8 as a starter
5 juicy heads of sweetcorn
125 g/4 fl oz/½ cup double cream
90 g/3 oz/⅓ cup butter
level tablespoon flour
2 large egg yolks, beaten
salt, sugar

Boil the sweetcorn in water to cover until tender, then drain and cool slightly. With a sharp knife, cut the grains of corn off and discard the cobs.

Melt cream and ⅔ of the butter together, stirring, and bring to the boil. Mash remaining butter with the flour and when the cream boils, add the butter-flour mixture in little bits. Whisk and cook for 3 or 4 minutes, without allowing it to boil properly. Off the heat whisk in the egg yolks, and then the corn. Stir and keep over a low heat so that the sauce does not boil again. Add salt and sugar to taste, then serve.

This is very much a last minute dish. If you need to get ahead, complete the cooking and turn the whole thing into a basin or the top of a double boiler. Then you can reheat gently when required.

LECSO

This is the Hungarian ratatouille, eaten as it is, or added to meat and vegetables when making paprikás and other stews. Make it for freezing when peppers and tomatoes are cheap, and you will have the middle stages of a dish always ready.

Serves 4 as a starter
1 large onion, chopped
lard or bacon fat, for frying
60 g/2 oz smoked bacon, chopped
rounded tablespoon paprika
1 kg/2 lb green peppers, deseeded and cut in strips
500 g/1 lb tomatoes, peeled, sliced
salt and pepper
sugar, to taste (optional)
tomato paste, optional

Gently cook the onion in lard or bacon fat, adding the bacon halfway through. When the onion is golden and soft, take the pan off the heat and stir in the paprika with a little water. Put back on the stove and stir in the peppers and tomatoes. Cook fast to make juices run, stirring, then lower the heat and leave to simmer until the lecsó is a pulpy, unwatery stew; this can take an hour. Season to taste, adding sugar and a spoonful of tomato paste, if the tomatoes are on the tasteless side.

SWEET-SOUR CREAMED MARROW
Tökfözelék

I never thought it possible to eat marrow with pleasure, until I had this dish at London's Gay Hussar restaurant one day. In Hungary it is so popular that you can buy the marrow ready shredded. And this I found in the Budapest market I visited. All along the row of pickle stalls, women had placed large mandolin-style graters across tubs. Every time a customer wanted marrow for this dish, they would push the gigantic objects laboriously across the grater blades and it would fall like pale greenish-white spaghetti. Here at home it is difficult to achieve the same thickness or length of shreds, but never mind—the dish is still good even if they are irregular and short.

Serve this marrow as a dish on its own, or with chicken and veal. Or adapt the recipe as I have, over, to cook with meat (tökpaprikás).

Serves 6
2 kg/4 lb marrow, peeled
salt
100 g/3½ oz/scant cup chopped onion
60 g/2 oz/¼ cup butter
heaped tablespoon flour
125 g/4 oz pickled dill cucumber plus
125 ml/4 fl oz of its pickling brine
150 ml/¼ pt/⅔ cup soured cream
pepper
sugar
chopped dillweed

continued on p. 211

PAPRIKA

Paprika is used to cover a whole range of sweet and hot peppers in Hungary, all sub-species, groups and varieties of the New World *Capsicum annuum* (and no relation to *Piper nigrum* which gives us green, black and white pepper*corns*). The pungency of different paprikas depends on how much they contain of the fiery chemical compound, capsicin. Even in sweet-fleshed varieties, the seeds are hot.

How did paprika come to find a second home in the warm south of Hungary, around Szeged and Kalocsa? Nowhere else in Europe, even in Spain, has it reached such a national dominance. Odd plants were grown in grand gardens in the 15th century, but the use of paprika as a universal seasoning among the poor is attributed to the Turks (who are also credited with introducing maize, tomatoes and strudel pastry). Their decisive victory over the Hungarians in 1526 took place at Mohacs, on the present border with Yugoslavia, and not too far north of Serbia whose cookery has contributed lecso—and other dishes—to the Hungarian kitchen. The word paprika came into the Hungarian language, from Serbian, in the 18th century.

Paprika seems to be a rare example of a food making its way up rather than down the social ladder. The poor and wretched of the Great Plain took it first as a medicine against the malaria that came from the undrained swamps. Then it gave a fillip to their scarce and stodgy food. Károly Gundel observes in his *Hungarian Cookery Book* that paprika did not find a place in refined cookery until the middle of the 19th century. What helped was the invention by the Pálffy brothers of Szeged of a machine that stripped paprika fruits of their hot seeds and ribs. These could then be ground separately from the milder, dried fleshy part. By mixing the two, regular grades of paprika seasoning could be put on the market.

Botanists worked on the jumble of varieties—each village seemed to have developed its own—and in 1933 Professor Albert Szent-Györgyi of Szeged University discovered that paprika has 3–5 times as much vitamin C as citrus fruits (and other vitamins, too). For this he got the Nobel Prize.

Today, though, there's also a variety grown that is mild all through without any capsicin at all. So there are six kinds of paprika seasoning in all now available (but not all of them to British cooks).

Exquisite delicate (különleges) So mild it can be used for invalids and in special gastric diets.

Delicatessen A little warmer and very red, used for sauces.

Noble-sweet (édesnemes) The kind most widely used, and the quality exported.

Semi-sweet (félédes) Stronger but not hot.

Rose (rosza) Paler and quite hot.

Cherry peppers are the hottest, used in fish soup

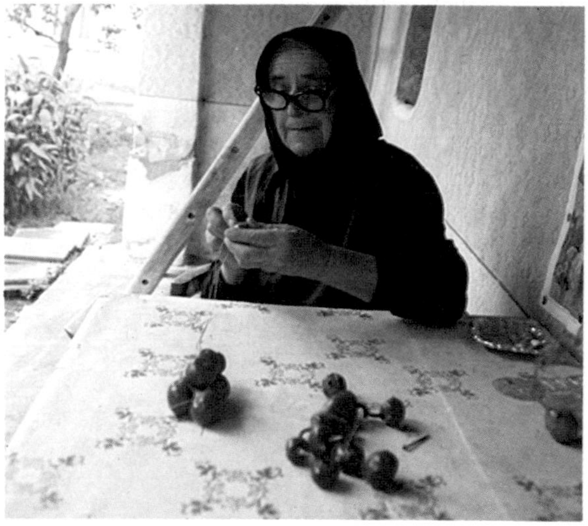

Hot (erös) Brown and very hot, used in small quantities to spice dishes made with noble-sweet or delicatessen qualities. In England its equivalent is cayenne pepper.

Although in most dishes noble-sweet is the paprika intended, cooks do vary the heat to suit their own tastes, and you should do the same. Cayenne or fresh or dried chilli peppers can be used, but unfortunately the delightful fiery little cherry peppers that one sees everywhere on sale in Hungary, are hard to come by here.

As paprika-flavoured dishes grew in popularity, Hungarian chefs classified them into four groups (country versions of these dishes do not always fit exactly into the chefs' neat modern definitions):

Gulyás Made with beef and somewhere between a soup and a stew; often includes potatoes and pinched-off dumplings. No cream is added.

Pörkölt Meaning 'singed' or 'scorched' because little liquid is used for braising the meat. As the small amount of liquid is absorbed, more is added. It has more onions than gulyás. Made with pork, goose duck, red meats and game.

Tokány Like pörkölt, with the meat cut into small oblong pieces, and a reduced quantity of paprika. sometimes ordinary pepper is used instead. Cream and extra vegetables can be put in as well. Made with the same meats as for pörkölt.

Paprikás Pale meats, like chicken, veal and lamb, or fish are cooked with paprika and soured cream. A kind of ratatouille (see lecsó, page 209) is sometimes added.

Shred the marrow into a colander, discarding the seeds. Sprinkle with 1 level tablespoon salt, put a plate on top and leave for at least 1 hour to drain. Squeeze as much liquid as you can from the shreds (the quantity will now be much reduced).

Meanwhile cook the onion in the butter until yellow and soft. Stir in the flour, cook the roux for 2 minutes. Liquidise together the cucumber and its liquid and add to the roux; then add the cream. When smooth and simmering, add the marrow shreds; boil and stir until they are just cooked—not too soft and soggy. Correct the seasoning and turn into a dish. Sprinkle with dillweed. Paprika and caraway can be included with seasonings, and tomatoes used instead of cream.

Variation If you use olive oil instead of butter in the recipe above, and add water, the marrow can be served chilled as a summer soup.

Tökpaprikás Shred 1 kg (2 lb) marrow, and salt it as above. Brown 1 kg (2 lb) cubed tender beef, veal or pork in butter with an onion. Off the heat stir in 1 tablespoon paprika. Add the liquidised cucumber and its liquid and 2 peeled chopped tomatoes. Cover tightly, simmer for 1 hour; add marrow, cover again and cook until the meat is tender. Stir in 300 ml (½ pt/1⅓ cups) soured cream and season to taste with salt and pepper. Serve scattered with chopped dillweed. Enough for 4–6.

DUMPLINGS

One of the pleasures of eating in Austria and Hungary is dumplings. They are not heavy at all, but full of invention and fantasy, and used in many different ways—as snacks, soup or stew garnishes, accompaniments to main courses, and desserts. From the two bread dumpling recipes and from the potato paste given for fruit dumplings (recipe on page 220), you can improvise your own. Often little cubes of fried bread are added to such mixtures, to give a crisp contrast and a surprise.

Bread Dumplings I
Semmelknödel

3 bread rolls
1 egg
100 ml/3½ fl oz/½ cup milk
small onion, chopped
3 tablespoons chopped parsley
30 g/1 oz/2 tbs butter
flour or breadcrumbs

Cube rolls and dry in a cool oven. Beat the egg and milk together. Soften the onion with the parsley in the butter. Mix all together, adding flour or breadcrumbs if the dough is too sloppy to handle. Run your hands under the tap, then form the mixture into little round dumplings. Slip them into a large pan half-full of boiling salted water, cover and cook for about 10 minutes. Taste one, and if cooked, remove the rest.

Left-over dumplings are turned into a homely speciality, *Knödel mit Ei*, which is a great gasthaus favourite. Cut the dumplings in slices and brown them nicely in lard, oil or butter, on both sides. Beat an appropriate number of eggs lightly, with seasoning, and scramble them in the pan with the dumpling pieces. Be sure not to overcook, but serve on the runny side, with a salad.

Bread Dumplings II
Serviettenknödel

4 soft white rolls or baps
50 g/2 oz/¼ cup melted butter
200 ml/7 fl oz/¾ cup milk
salt, grated nutmeg
3 egg yolks
tablespoon chopped parsley
4 rashers of rindless smoked streaky bacon (optional)
3 egg whites, stiffly whisked

Cut the dark crusts thinly from the rolls, if using. Cube and mix the bread with butter, milk, seasonings, egg yolks and parsley. Chop the bacon into bits and fry until crisp in their own fat. Add with their fat, to the bread mixture. Leave 30 minutes. The texture should be moistly spongy—add more crumbs if it is sloppy. Fold in whites.

Butter a cloth in the centre part. Tip the mixture on to it. Fold over the long edges of cloth loosely and secure with safety pins. Tie two ends like a cracker, and then tie the strings round the handle of a wooden spoon. Suspend the dumpling in a pan half-full of boiling salted water, resting the spoon handle across the top. Simmer, covered, for 1 hour. Cool slightly, cut the strings and unwrap; slice the dumpling. (Austrians use a thread; just like a wire for cutting cheese). Fry in butter until golden on both sides.

FLOUR DUMPLINGS
Enough for 6–8

Pinched dumplings (Csipetke) Knead enough white bread flour with a pinch of salt into a beaten egg, to make a firm dough. Form into a flattish roll and place on a board. Flour your fingers and pinch off little bits into simmering soup or salted water. Give them 10 minutes to cook.

Bite-sized dumplings (Galuska) Mix 3 level tablespoons strong bread flour with a large egg and a pinch of salt. Drop small quantities from a teaspoon into simmering soup or salted water; they cook in 4 minutes.

Tarhonya Pasta dough dried in little knobbly pieces that is said to have been carried by Magyar horsemen in the days of the Great Migrations, along with dried beef. All they then needed was water to make a nourishing meal. It is cooked like a risotto, and ends up unmistakeably like pasta but with a rice-like nubbliness. These days it is rarely made at home, but bought in packages.

Cook an onion in butter until golden brown, stir in 250 g (8 oz) tarhonya and when it begins to brown, pour in a ½ litre (¾ pt/scant 2 cups) water. Simmer uncovered, and when the tarhonya absorbs all the liquid, add a little more, and again, and again, until the tarhonya is tender but *al dente*. Serve with gulyás and paprikás dishes, or on its own with butter and grated cheese.

PASTA AND CURD CHEESE GRATIN
Túróscsusza

In Hungary, special broken pasta sheets are sold for making túróscsusza, which is regarded as a dessert or pudding although it is a salty dish. If you have ever wondered how to finish a meal after serving a substantial soup, here is your answer. Buy plain lasagne sheets, the yellow kind not the spinach green ones, and break them roughly into pieces about 3–5 cm (1–2 in).

Serves 6
370 g/12 oz lasagne, broken up
salt
tablespoon oil
butter
250–375 g/8–12 oz piece of rindless smoked streaky bacon, cubed
250 g/8 oz/1 cup curd cheese
150 ml/¼ pt/⅔ cup soured cream

Boil lasagne in plenty of salted water plus the oil to prevent sticking. Drain, mix with a little butter. Set oven at hot, 230°C (450°F), gas 8.

Meanwhile, cook the bacon in its own fat until it's brown and crisp. Add with the fat, to the cooked lasagne immediately after the butter. Spread out in a gratin dish. Mix the curd cheese and cream and spread over the top. Bake in the heated oven until sizzling—about 7 minutes.

PANCAKES
Palacsinta or Palatschinken

These are popular in both countries. But the famous pancake (palacsinta) dishes come from Hungary. The best batter I have found is George Lang's recipe below, from *The Cuisine of Hungary*.

These pancakes, rolled up and cut into strips, are used as a garnish to clear beef soup, like the dumplings.

Makes about 24 pancakes
3 eggs
200 g/7 oz/1¼ cups flour
level teaspoon sugar
pinch of salt
225 ml/8 fl oz/1 cup milk
225 ml/8 fl oz/1 cup carbonated water
clarified butter, for frying
20-cm/8-in omelette pan

Rows of salami drying in a Hungarian factory

Mix the first five ingredients to a smooth, thick batter. This can now rest for an hour or 24 hours. Stir in the carbonated water just before you cook the pancakes.

Heat the omelette pan and brush it with clarified butter. Cook a trial pancake (made with a generous tablespoon of batter), and make any adjustments you think are required. The pancakes should be thin and bubbly in places, but firm enough to hold a filling properly. Brush the pan with butter every three pancakes.

HORTOBÁGY PANCAKES
Hortobágyi palacsinta

The Hortobágy national park, between the Tisza river and Debrecen, is a district of the Great Plain of Hungary now much visited by tourists. There are fairs and horse shows, with the locals acting out the old practice of Magyar herdsmen cooking goulash in their iron pots for people's amusement.

These pancakes filled with stewed veal (pörkölt) are now one of Hungary's national dishes. Since the pörkölt is for pancakes, use a prime veal cut only and cook it briefly. For pancakes, see the recipe above.

Makes 24

FOR THE FILLING

250 g/8 oz/2 cups chopped onion
lard
rounded tablespoon paprika
2 tablespoons/3 tbs water
500 g/1 lb veal, cubed
large green pepper, deseeded and sliced
2 tomatoes, chopped
veal, beef or chicken stock, or water
salt and pepper
150 ml/$\frac{1}{4}$ pt/$\frac{2}{3}$ cup soured or double cream

TO FINISH

beaten egg
breadcrumbs

Stew the onions in a little lard until yellow and soft, take from the stove and mix in the paprika and water. Stir in the veal, cover and stew gently. After 10 minutes, put in the pepper pieces and the tomatoes. Add a little stock or water. Cook uncovered, so that you can keep an eye on things. Stir the meat occasionally, adding extra liquid as the sauce evaporates. Keep to a ragoût moistness. When the veal is just tender, season, take from stove.

Process the meat mixture, or remove and chop meat only. Reheat with the cream. Put a spoonful of filling at the edge of a pancake, spreading it longways. Flip over the sides, then roll up. Repeat until all the pancakes are used.

Dip the pancakes in egg and breadcrumbs, and fry in 1 cm ($\frac{1}{2}$ in) lard until brown and crisp. Serve as a first course with something light to follow, or after a substantial soup.

Variation If you do not wish to fry the pancakes, here is another way of presenting them. Make the veal pörkölt on the liquid side. Drain off the extra gravy before processing or chopping the filling. Mix a little cream into the filling as above, fill the pancakes and place them in a dish. Keep them warm.

Whisk the surplus red gravy into a level tablespoon of flour, and gradually add $\frac{1}{2}$ litre ($\frac{3}{4}$ pt/scant 2 cups) soured cream, or mixed soured and whipping cream. Put into a pan, bring to the boil and simmer for a minute or two. Taste for seasoning. Strain over the pancakes and serve.

WIENER SCHNITZEL

The Viennese are big eaters: the size of their escalopes can be intimidating. The old idea was that the cooked, nicely browned piece of meat should cover a dinner plate completely. I was thankful to find that nowadays moderation prevails: the escalopes we were served only covered most of the plate inside the rim. The veal was a slightly deeper pink and cut a little thicker than for escalopes in France. Slices are taken from the leg, and should be cut on the bias, though few butchers will do this. At home, snip the edges of the meat, to prevent it buckling as it cooks. Then thump it with a rolling pin—not too vigorously, but so that it spreads slightly.

Get everything ready for the meal, and prepare trays of seasoned flour and dried white breadcrumbs, plus a bowl of beaten egg. Melt enough lard in your frying pan(s) to give at least 1 cm ($\frac{1}{2}$ in) depth, and heat it.

Flour the escalopes, shaking off any surplus. Dip them in egg, then press into the breadcrumbs on both sides until they are coated; shake off any excess. Then fry them until they are golden brown in the lard—about 5 minutes, or 4 if the escalopes are particularly thin or small, turning once. Serve immediately with lemon quarters, and a lettuce, cucumber or chicory salad, with strips of pepper and onion, and dressed with vinaigrette, or left plain and dressed with soured cream flavoured with lemon juice, sugar, salt and pepper.

CHICKEN IN A DRESSING GOWN
Huhn im Schlafrock, Backhendl

An old Viennese dish that was the great sign and symbol of prosperous living in Beidermeier Vienna, when it was called chicken in a dressing gown—the dressing gown is the Viennese egg and breadcrumb coating. Today it is called, more prosaically, fried chicken. Like wiener schnitzel, it will be served with a salad and lemon quarters.

Choose the best chickens you can—not frozen ones—weighing 1 kg (2 lb). Cut each one into quarters, or ask the butcher to do it for you. Remove the wing tips. The birds' livers can be used, too: make sure they have no tinge of green gall to spoil the flavour.

Into a wide dish, put plenty of seasoned flour. Into another dish, plenty of fine white breadcrumbs. Into a basin break a small egg per chicken, beat and season.

Prepare the chicken quarters at least an hour before they are to be cooked. Dry them with kitchen paper, dip them in flour rubbing it all over and then gently shake off any surplus. Immerse the quarters in beaten egg, spooning it over the awkward places. Then roll firmly in the breadcrumbs. Do the same thing with the livers. Put on to a baking sheet and chill.

For each chicken, put on a deep pan with enough lard to make a depth of 2 cm ($\frac{3}{4}$ in). Heat them up and put in the quarters, turning them so that they brown nicely. As the colour turns to a warm gold, lower the heat so that the chicken has a chance to cook through. Allow 15–20 minutes cooking time in all. Remove and drain. Fry the livers briefly in very hot lard.

Serve immediately with a lettuce, cucumber or chicory salad as for wiener schnitzel. Creamed sweetcorn is another good accompaniment. As are hot potatoes cut up and served warm with an oil and vinegar dressing, seasoned with a little sugar, much pepper and some chopped onion.

CHICKEN PAPRIKA
Csirkepaprikás

A good recipe for showing how the paprikás method works, the chicken being cooked with small quantities of liquid which are absorbed and concentrated, and continually replenished. This way the sauce is an integral part of the dish. Sometimes lecsó is added to the chicken towards the end. Or you can add bacon, peppers and tomato, the basic lecsó ingredients, to those below: put them in when the onion has softened, adding the bacon first for a few minutes, then the vegetables, chicken and so on.

Serves 4
fresh chicken, jointed
lard
250 g/8 oz/2 cups chopped onion
rounded tablespoon paprika
cayenne (optional)
chicken stock
300 ml/$\frac{1}{2}$ pt/$1\frac{1}{4}$ cups mixed soured and whipping cream
salt and pepper

Lightly brown the chicken pieces in lard in a sauté pan. Remove the pieces, while you put in the onion, lowering the heat so that the onion dissolves to a golden purée.

Take the pan from the stove and stir in the paprika, plus a shake of cayenne, if you like, to add liveliness. Put back and cook for another 2 minutes. Replace the chicken and pour in 125 ml (4 fl oz/$\frac{1}{2}$ cup) stock. Cover and cook until tender. Every so often, turn the chicken and replenish the stock.

Transfer the cooked chicken to a serving dish and keep warm. Bubble the juices in the pan vigorously to concentrate the flavour. Blot away or spoon off surplus fat. Whisk in the cream, bubble slowly for 1 minute and correct the seasoning. This sauce should be a beautiful creamy pink. Strain some over the chicken and put the rest into a serving jug. Serve with egg noodles (fresh ones, if possible) and a cucumber salad.

POOR MAN'S PAPRIKA
Paprikás krumpli

A nourishing dish, the kind mothers make for their children's supper, when time is short.

Cook a chopped onion slowly in lard, put in potatoes, peeled and quartered, and stir in 1 tablespoon paprika, off the stove, with a little water. Put in enough lecsó to make a good stew, or add a green pepper, deseeded and cut in strips and 2 peeled, sliced tomatoes with a piece of smoked bacon. Add a teaspoon of caraway seeds. Cook for 15 minutes, stirring occasionally. Add spicy sausage or good frankfurters, sliced, and some fresh sausage too, if you like. Cook another 10 minutes, allowing the juices to evaporate so that the dish is moist but not wet or soupy.

Cooking gulyás in a rush hut in the Hortobagy national park

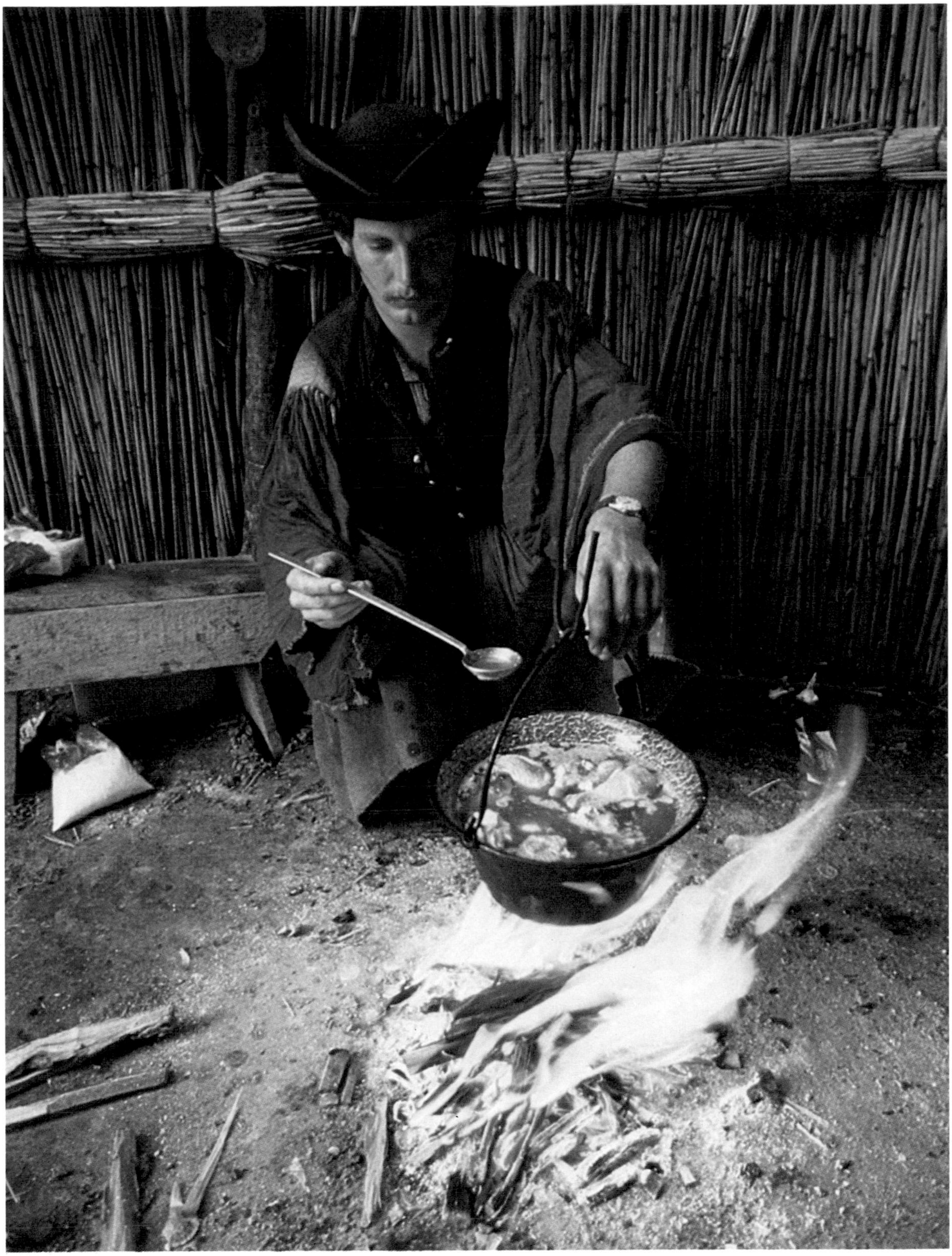

GOULASH
Bográcsgulyás

Bogrács means iron pot, and the same kind of pot that is used for goulash is also used for making fish soup. It hangs over the fire, with its reddish-brown contents bubbling gently. Forget what you may have heard about goulash: it does not contain soured cream and the authentic consistency should be soupy.

If you want to make a proper soup, use shin of beef in half quantity, or slightly less, and add more water still. Gelatinous shin of beef gives a better texture to soup than the more expensive chuck steak.

Serves 6–8
250 g/8 oz/2 cups chopped onion
lard
1–1½ kg/2–3 lb chuck steak
heaped teaspoon paprika
2 large cloves of garlic, smashed
¼ teaspoon caraway seeds
250 g/8 oz green pepper, deseeded and cut into rings
150 g/5 oz peeled, chopped tomato
750 g/1½ lb potatoes, peeled and cubed the same size as the meat
3 or 4 hot cherry peppers or fresh chillies
salt and pepper
flour dumplings dough (recipes on page 221)

Cook the onion slowly in a little lard until soft and yellow. Cut the meat into 2 cm (¾ in) pieces and add to the onion, turning them over and leaving them to fry slowly for a further 7–8 minutes. Take the pan from the heat and stir in the paprika thoroughly. Put back on to the stove and continue to stir for 2 minutes, making sure the paprika does not catch. Add water to cover.

Add the garlic and the caraway seeds to the meat. Simmer for 1 hour. Put in the pepper, tomato and potatoes. Add more water to make a soupy consistency, cover and simmer for 30 minutes more, adding cherry peppers or chillies towards the end. From now on keep tasting, and remove the peppers or chillies once the goulash is fiery enough. Add salt and pepper to taste and more caraway seeds if you like.

Pinch or drop bits of dough into the pot, cover and leave until they are cooked through. Correct the seasoning and serve.

VIENNESE BOILED BEEF
Tafelspitz

The noblest of Austrian dishes, delightful for its combination of solid quality (beef) and frivolous pleasure (sauces). Properly, the name signifies the joint of beef used, a cut including part of the aitchbone and top rump. But brisket, silverside, topside, and rib are also suitable.

The place to eat it is Sacher's, in their splendid comfortable dining-rooms, but we were never there at lunch time and could not face so much meat at dinner. In the end we ate it by accident. We had intended to eat at a heurige in one of the wine villages in the Wienerwald; we drove through slowly but they all looked too knowing and touristical, too hung with pretty quirks and oddities. We ended up at the lonely, busy Fischerhaus in front of the most restoring tafelspitz. As we ate the sun came out, and we set off for Schönbrunn and its long high alleys of trees and statues, and its chinoiserie rooms much fortified by our meal.

Use well-hung beef—Scotch, if possible—and buy dried cèpes to improve the flavour of the stock. It will provide you next day with an excellent clear soup that can be served with little dumplings or pancake strips, in the Austrian manner. You can buy cèpes in packets at delicatessens and good groceries. Don't gib at the idea of apple with beef: when spiked with horseradish, it makes an excellent companion.

Serves 8–10
3 or 4 beef bones
2 litres/4 pts/10 cups water
2–2.5 kg/4–5 lb boned, tied beef
2 large carrots, quartered
Hamburg parsley root or white turnip, quartered
½ smallish celeriac, peeled, or 3 stalks of celery
2 leeks or ½ bunch of spring onions
2 medium onions, each stuck with 2 cloves
2 large cloves, halved
large bouquet garni
large tomato, halved
½ packet of, or a generous pinch of, dried cèpes
level teaspoon peppercorns, lightly crushed

Pour boiling water over the bones, and leave them to cool. Drain and put into a large casserole. Add measured water and bring to the boil. Put in the beef; when the water returns to simmering point, skim well. Add a ladle of cold water and skim again. Put in the remaining ingredients and extra water to cover if necessary. Simmer, with the water barely trembling, for 2½ hours.

While the meat cooks make the two sauces and sauté the potatoes. There are many more sauces, hot ones as well as cold, for serving with boiled beef, but these two are the most common on menus. Serve the accompaniments in separate dishes with thick slices of beef on one large dish.

Apple and horseradish sauce (Apfelkren) Cook 500 g (1 lb) cooking apples, peeled, cored and quartered, with 1 tablespoon sugar and a little lemon juice. Mash to a slightly lumpy purée. When cold add 2–3 tablespoons shredded horseradish from the outside of the root. Or use a proprietary brand of horseradish, but this is a poor second. Taste and adjust seasoning with sugar and lemon juice, perhaps a dash of wine vinegar.

Chive sauce (Schnittlauchsoss) Soak 2 soft rolls or baps in enough milk to turn them into a paste. Sieve with 4 hard-boiled egg yolks. Add 2 raw egg yolks, then whisk in 250 ml (8 fl oz/1 cup) sunflower oil, as if you were making mayonnaise. This can all be done in a processor so far, which saves time sieving. Season with salt, pepper and vinegar. Stir in plenty of chopped chives and put into a bowl.

Sauté potatoes (Geröstete Kartoffeln) Boil 1 kg (2 lb) potatoes in their skins, waxy ones for preference. Or use cold boiled potatoes. Peel and slice. Fry them slowly in lard until brown at the edges, with a little or a lot of onion, which should also brown. The potatoes should not be at all neat and tidy. Drain on kitchen paper and sprinkle with salt. Austrians like this dish so much that it sometimes appears on restaurant menus simply as *Geröstete*—the equivalent, I suppose, to 'fries'.

VENISON ESTERHAZY
Esterházy özfilé

On the bend of the Danube north of Budapest is the old port of Szentendre, now a charming museum town. Above a craft centre is the Aransárkány restaurant.

Cooking is in the charge of one of Hungary's brightest young chefs. In the autumn his menu is devoted to game—venison, moufflon (rather fatty wild sheep), pheasant and wild duck. Here is his recipe for venison Esterházy, which can equally well be made with a piece of beef topside.

Serves 6–8
250 g/8 oz carrot
150 g/5 oz Hamburg parsley root or white turnip
75 g/2½ oz celeriac or celery
large onion, sliced
1½ litres/2¾ pts/scant 7 cups of water
2 large bay leaves
2 slices of lemon
8 juniper berries, slightly crushed
15 whole black peppercorns, slightly crushed
1½ tablespoons wine vinegar with tarragon
1½ kg/3 lb boned haunch of venison, larded
250 ml/8–9 fl oz/generous cup red wine
level tablespoon sugar
400 ml/13 fl oz/1⅔ cups soured cream
level tablespoon German mustard
heaped teaspoon flour; salt

Set aside one-third of the vegetables, having cut them into matchstick strips. Cut up the rest roughly and put into a pan with the onion, water, bay leaves, lemon, spices and vinegar. Boil hard for 5 minutes. Put in the meat, and when the liquid returns to the boil, remove the meat to a close-fitting pot. Cool the marinade, pour over the meat and add the red wine. Keep in the refrigerator for 2 days, turning the meat if it is not submerged.

Remove and dry the meat. Set the oven at moderate, 160–180°C (325–350°F), gas 3–4. Roast the meat for about 1¼ hours—it should be pink in the middle.

Meanwhile strain the marinade into a wide pan and boil hard until reduced to about 125 ml (4 fl oz/½ cup). Add the venison juices from the roasting tin. Mix the sugar, some of the cream, the mustard, flour and salt to taste together. Stir the rest of the cream into the sauce and, when it is bubbling, add the mustard mixture and simmer for a minute or two.

Slice the meat and arrange on a hot serving dish. Pour some of the sauce over and serve the rest in a separate jug. Serve with either one of the bread dumplings (recipes on page 211).

CALF'S LIGHTS IN A PIQUANT SAUCE
Salonbeuschel or Wienerbeuschel

One of the great dishes of Viennese cookery, a favourite of Johann Strauss.

Buy lights (lung) from a butcher who regularly sells veal, and ask for some heart as well. This is not essential but improves the stock and enables you to tell the family—if they are squeamish—that it is a ragoût of calf's heart.

Serves 6
1 kg/2 lb calf's lights and heart
large carrot, sliced
½ Hamburg parsley root or small white turnip, quartered
½ small celeriac, diced
medium onion, stuck with 3 cloves
bouquet garni
½ teaspoon black peppercorns, lightly crushed

FOR THE SAUCE
strip of lemon peel
4 anchovy fillets in oil, or 2 salted anchovies, boned
level tablespoon capers
½ clove of garlic
6 leafy sprigs of parsley
60 g/2 oz/¼ cup butter
45 g/1½ oz/⅓ cup flour
½ medium onion, chopped fine
stock from cooking the lights
lemon juice
150 ml/¼ pt/⅔ cup soured cream
sugar, salt and pepper

Wash the lights and heart. Put into a pan with the vegetables and aromatics. Cover with water. Simmer until the lights are tender, remove them and continue cooking the heart until it is done, too. When the meats are cold, cut them into strips as wide as narrow tape and the length of a matchstick. Strain the stock and reserve. All this can be done in advance.

To make the sauce, chop the first 5 ingredients together. Cook the butter in a heavy pan until it is golden brown and smells nutty. Stir in the flour to make a brown roux of medium colour, not dark. Stir in the onion, then 250 ml (8 fl oz/1 cup) stock. As the sauce becomes thick, add more stock and simmer 30 minutes. Add the chopped ingredients and the meat strips. Simmer for 20 minutes, then finish with lemon juice, soured cream and seasonings to taste. As this is a ragoût, make sure the sauce is neither too liquid nor too copious. It should bind the strips together, but not too firmly. Serve with bread dumplings (recipes on page 211).

STRUDEL PASTRY

The idea of building up thin layers of dough is so basic to Middle Eastern and Balkan cookery that people assume it came to Hungary first with the Turks, then to Austria. Cooks in the two countries claim there is a difference between the Hungarian rétes and Austrian strudel pastries—and no doubt between these two and Greek filo pastry—but I wonder how they would fare at a blind tasting?

Pride in making these pastries so thin that you can read a love letter or a newspaper through their transparency is common to all the countries concerned. I like to think of people at Demel's pastry shop in Vienna, Vörösmarty's in Budapest making their strudel and rétes first thing in the morning, with easy skill, along with every small pastry-maker in Greece.

Although packages of filo pastry sheets are fine for little pasties and the range of Greek pies, you must make your own for a large strudel. In fact it is fun to do, especially if you enlist a helper the first few times. An Austrian friend told me that she saw women at a strudel factory stretching the dough over their shoulders in a confident rhythm, but I recommend a kitchen table, with a patterned cloth, for your first attempt. For the filling, choose any one of the recipes below.

Serves 10
125 g/4 oz/1 cup strong white bread flour or plain flour
½ beaten egg
¼ teaspoon vinegar
30 g/1 oz/2 tbs butter, melted
pinch of salt

Mix all the ingredients to a dough, with an electric mixer if possible, with warm water. It should end up soft and supple, with a silken waxy look. Put on a board and invert a heated bowl over it. Leave 30 minutes while making the filling.

Put the dough on the tablecloth, lightly sprinkled with flour, and roll it out to an oblong. Oil your hands, and if there are two of you, stand at opposite sides of the table. Slip your hands underneath—I find it best with palms downwards, then the dough cannot be damaged by incautious finger movements. Now raise and stretch the dough, partly by its own weight, partly by gentle pulling movements of your hands. When you have a piece about 50 × 60 cm (20 × 24 in) and so transparent you can see the pattern of the cloth through it, it is ready.

Trim off the hard edges with scissors (they can be snipped into soups or stews as pasta), and straighten one long edge. Brush over with melted butter, leaving a wide border at the straightened edge and smaller borders at the other edges. Patch any holes with bits of dough from the edges. Set oven at moderate, 180°C (350°F), gas 4. Spoon over your chosen filling.

Flip three sides of the border, starting with the

long edge with the narrow border, over the filling to enclose it completely. Brush the wide border with water and slip a sheet of non-stick baking paper underneath it. With the aid of the cloth, start rolling up the strudel, starting from the flipped-over long edge. You should end up with a tidy but slightly baggy roll sitting on the sheet of baking paper. Bend the roll slightly if it is longer than your baking sheet. Put on to the baking sheet, brush with melted butter.

Bake in the heated oven for about 35 minutes, until brown and crisp. Baste occasionally with more melted butter. With a sweet strudel, sprinkle with icing sugar and serve with cream. Eat hot or warm, fairly soon after baking to get the strudel at its best.

STRUDEL FILLINGS

Cabbage
1 kg/2 lb smooth hard-headed cabbage
salt
125 g/4 oz/½ cup lard
level tablespoon sugar
175 g/6 oz/1½ cups chopped onion
plenty of pepper

Shred and sprinkle cabbage with plenty of salt—a good tablespoon. Leave for an hour at least, then squeeze out the moisture. Melt the lard in a large pan, sprinkle on sugar and let it caramelize. Stir in onion and cabbage shreds, and fry them slowly at first, then faster, until a rich even brown. Pepper the filling well. No need for breadcrumbs, and the pastry can be brushed with melted lard or bacon fat.

Curd cheese
100 g/3½ oz dried fine white breadcrumbs
butter
375 g/12 oz/1½ cups curd cheese
200 g/7 fl oz/¾ cup soured cream
125 g/4 oz/½ cup caster sugar
grated rind of a lemon
2 egg yolks
2 egg whites

Fry and sprinkle breadcrumbs over the dough. Mix cheese, cream and half the sugar. Add rind and yolks. Whisk whites stiff, add remaining sugar and whisk again until thick and smooth. Fold into cheese. Put over breadcrumbs.

Apple
100 g/3½ oz/scant cup grated walnuts, hazelnuts or fine dried white breadcrumbs
500 g/1 lb sharp cooking apples
100 g/3½ oz/½ cup caster sugar
60 g/2 oz/⅓ cup sultanas, optional
100 g/3½ oz/scant cup chopped walnuts, or chopped toasted almonds/hazelnuts

Fry breadcrumbs—no need to fry the grated nuts—in a little butter. Sprinkle crumbs or nuts over the dough. Peel, core and slice the apples and put over the crumbs. Mix remaining ingredients and scatter over the apples.

Cherry
60 g/2 oz/½ cup fine dried white breadcrumbs
20 g/¾ oz/¼ cup pine kernels
60 g/2 oz/⅓ cup toasted hazelnuts, finely ground
500 g/1 lb sharp cherries, stoned and roughly chopped
125 g/4 oz/½ cup caster sugar
level tablespoon powdered cinnamon
60 g/2 oz/⅔ cup sultanas
sifted icing sugar, for sprinkling

Mix the breadcrumbs and nuts together, then scatter over the dough. Mix rest of ingredients, spread over nut mixture. Roll up and bake. Sprinkle with icing sugar to serve.

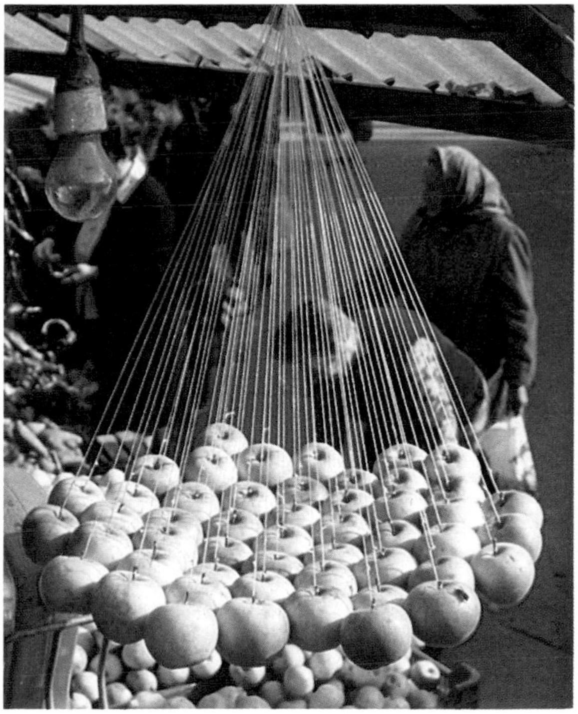

Apples in a Budapest market

Cherry strudel with its ingredients: sugar, flour, breadcrumbs, eggs—and stoned black cherries

FRUIT DUMPLINGS
Powidltascherl

The dumplings we ate in Vienna's Prater Park were semi-circular, but they can quite well be made in a triangular shape. The same dough and cooking method can be used for plums, apricots and small peaches.

The Zwetschke or Quetsch plum, dark blueish-purple, deep-coloured flesh and free stone, is the useful plum of East Europe, Germany, Switzerland and Alsace. I bought some to eat raw from a stall in Vienna's Naschmarkt, and they are delightful for their mildness. They do not make an acid assault on your tongue. They are grown, I believe, in Kent, but I have never seen them on sale in the west of England.

The problem with English plums is, taste apart, the stone: ideally you should push it out with a stoner or wooden spoon handle, leaving the skin unbroken, then you push in a small sugar lump or two. With English fruit you have to cut into them. Apricots work better in this respect, but plum jam, or the Quetsche compote given under the Emperor's pancakes recipe, makes the easiest filling, especially when you are following the recipe for the first time.

NB Plum dumplings of this kind are equally popular in Hungary, where they are known as szilvás gombóc. When you press the dough round the stoned fruit (the cavities are filled with cinnamon and sugar), make sure there are no cracks.

Makes about 20
FOR THE DOUGH
375 g/12 oz old floury potatoes, well scrubbed but not peeled
up to 150 g/5 oz/1¼ cups flour
pinch of salt
30 g/1 oz/2 tbs softened butter
egg yolk, egg white
TO FINISH
300 g/10 oz plum jam
30 g/1 oz/¼ cup fine dry breadcrumbs
30 g/1 oz/2 tbs butter
icing sugar

Boil, then peel the potatoes while still warm. Push through a sieve and mix with about 100 g (3½ oz/

Viennese fruit dumplings scattered with fried crumbs

scant cup) flour, the salt, butter and egg yolk. As you work the dough, add as much of the remaining flour as you need to make a silky soft dough, which is not sticky. Rest for 1 hour.

Divide the dough into 20 or more equal lumps. Roll them out into small circles or ovals. Brush half of the borders with egg white, put a teaspoon of jam in the centre and fold over, pressing the edges gently together. Chill or freeze them at this point, if you like.

Poach them in the same way as for bread dumplings I (recipe on page 211), and serve three or four to each person, on a plate, scattered with the crumbs, fried golden in the butter, and a little icing sugar.

GUNDEL'S WALNUT PANCAKES
Palacsinta Gundel módra

Gundel's restaurant, with its wrought-iron gate, stands solidly on the edge of Budapest's City Park. Károly Gundel took the City Park restaurant over in 1910, and turned a good one into a great one, Hungary's best. Everyone went there: the great, the notorious, the smart, students and middle-class families. The poor who came to his kitchen were fed with an open hand. Gundel wrote several books. Corvina, the state publishing house, keeps a revised edition of one of them in print, the little *Hungarian Cookery Book*. In his introduction, he acknowledges the refining influence of French chefs in the 19th century—'Hungarian cooking became lighter without losing its originality'.

Gundel's has recently been restored, though not I think to its original decor, but the old specialities remain on the menu, like these splendid pancakes.

Serves 4
12–16 pancakes (see page 212)
FOR THE WALNUT FILLING
250 g/8 oz/2 cups walnuts
125 g/4 oz/½ cup sugar
125 g/4 oz/⅔ cup chopped raisins
grated rind of 1 orange
6 tablespoons/½ cup double cream
4 tablespoons/¼ cup rum
FOR THE CHOCOLATE SAUCE
30 g/1 oz/¼ cup cocoa
30 g/1 oz/2 tbs sugar
3 egg yolks
200 ml/7 fl oz/good ¾ cup milk
100 ml/3½ fl oz/⅓ cup whipping cream
125 g/4 oz/⅔ cup dark chocolate, broken up or grated
4 tablespoons/⅓ cup rum
TO FINISH
60 g/2 oz/¼ cup butter
6 tablespoons/½ cup rum

To make the filling, chop about one-third of the walnuts to pinhead size and grate the rest. Mix the two together. Add the other filling ingredients. Put a spoonful in each pancake and fold it in four. Repeat with remaining pancakes.

For the sauce, beat the cocoa, sugar and egg yolks together. Bring the milk and cream to boiling point, then beat into the cocoa mixture. Return to the heat, and cook gently until the custard thickens slightly. Do not overheat, and keep stirring. Then remove from the heat and mix in the chocolate and the rum. Pour into a jug and keep warm.

To serve, melt the butter in a large frying pan and put in the pancakes. Fry them lightly on both sides. Warm the rum in a ladle and set it alight as you pour it over the pancakes. Turn them again, and serve bubbling, with the chocolate sauce.

Note you can omit the flaming if you like, but this is the way they serve them at the restaurant.

SACHERTORTE

Teatime at the Sacher Hotel in Vienna, with Sachertorte in the foreground showing its round seal

Sachertorte is Europe's most famous chocolate cake: I doubt it is Europe's best. In my experience, as far as the actual cake goes, you may find as good and better in many homes or on Women's Institute stalls. What makes it special is the apricot glaze or filling, and the thick flow of chocolate icing that laps over the top and down the side in one smooth movement. The sole decoration of a true Sachertorte is a chocolate seal, a round one if the cake comes from Sacher's, a triangular one if it comes from Demel's, the top Viennese cake shop, in the Kohlmarkt.

Behind these two 'genuine' versions lies a story. Prince Metternich, the great Austrian foreign minister, believed—like his friend Talleyrand—that good food was important to good diplomacy. He demanded high standards in his kitchen and was always expecting something new from his pastry-cook. One day, in 1832, an extra special chocolate cake was produced which met with such approval that it was repeated, and remembered.

Eventually the young man who had made the cake, Franz Sacher, set up on his own near the Opera, in the centre of Vienna. Under his son, even more under his daughter-in-law, Anna, the Hotel Sacher became famous for its restaurant (and private rooms) as well as for its chocolate cake. Indeed the cake became notorious, since Franz Sacher's grandson sold the right to use the genuine seal to Demel's. It was fought out in a long court case. Sacher's won, but both places continued to produce very similar cakes, Demel's with an apricot glaze over the top and sides, Sacher's with an apricot glaze through the middle as a filling. And the seals were a different shape.

However there is—to me, at any rate—a mystery. The contentious recipe was published, other 'genuine' recipes were published. They contain chocolate and a high proportion of eggs. The result is a rich, slightly heavy cake. Yet the cake as bought in Vienna, and as sent all over the world, is dark, but light, even dry, as if cocoa were the flavouring. Perhaps the difference is accounted for by the use of baker's chocolate rather than the high quality plain chocolate which most of us use outside the trade. But whatever the reason, the difference is remarkable. I find it hard to believe that the cake sold in 1983 is exactly the same as the one Franz Sacher first made for Prince Metternich in 1832.

Many bakers today produce decidedly ungenuine chocolate cakes, with the word Sacher written across them in a flowing copperplate style. It has come to mean a plain dark cake with no buttercream filling, the sort of cake that demands the traditional Viennese accompaniment of whipped cream. A cup of black coffee and a glass of water are nearly as essential as the whipped cream, I would say.

EMPEROR'S PANCAKE
Kaiserschmarrn

A fluffy pancake inspired by Emperor Franz Joseph I, and a great Viennese speciality. If you prefer, you can bake the pancake in the oven at 200°C (400°F), gas 6.

Serves 4
200 g/7 oz/$1\frac{1}{2}$ cups flour
pinch of salt
60 g/2 oz/$\frac{1}{4}$ cup caster sugar
4 large egg yolks
3 tablespoons/4 tbs butter, melted
60 g/2 oz/$\frac{1}{3}$ cup sultanas
scant 500 ml/good $\frac{3}{4}$ pt/2 cups milk
4 large egg whites
a little butter
extra caster sugar

Mix the first six ingredients, then beat in the milk. Whisk the whites stiffly and fold them in. Melt butter in two pans. Divide the mixture between them—it should be about 2 cm ($\frac{3}{4}$ in) thick. When golden brown, turn and cook on the other side. Pull apart with two forks in the pan, making rough little pieces, and cook briefly, turning them about. Divide between four hot plates and sprinkle with sugar. Serve immediately with *Zwetschkenröster*:

1 kg/2 lb Zwetschke (Quetsche) plums, or other dark plums
150 g/5 oz/good $\frac{1}{2}$ cup sugar
2 cloves
small cinnamon stick
juice and rind of a lemon

Zwetschke plums can be gently torn apart and the stone picked out, other varieties may need more effort. Simmer remaining ingredients with 125 ml (4 fl oz/$\frac{1}{2}$ cup) water for 5 minutes, then put in the plum halves and stir until thick. The plums should fall into lumpy pieces, the final result being somewhere between a compote and a jam. This mixture can be used for fruit dumplings, too.

Do not give up hope of finding Zwetschke plums in England. I heard of some in Cambridge market two years ago and the friend who bought them wrote to me that 'Austrians do not think of it as just another plum—like Kraut (smooth cabbage) and Kohl (crinkly cabbage), there is the Pflaume (plum) and the Zwetschke.'

SALZBURG DUMPLINGS
Salzburger Nockerln

Not dumplings of the usual kind, but a light soufflé pudding, airy yet filling, which is traditionally baked in three mounds. A chef at the archbishop's palace in Salzburg is said to have invented it, in the 18th century. I find it's best to bake it in two oval gratin dishes, each 25–30-cm/10–12-in long.

Serves 6–8
100 g/$3\frac{1}{2}$ oz/scant $\frac{1}{2}$ cup butter
8 large egg yolks
10 egg whites
150 g/5 oz/$\frac{2}{3}$ cup vanilla sugar
4 level tablespoons/5 tbs sifted flour
grated rind of 1 lemon
150 ml/$\frac{1}{4}$ pt/$\frac{2}{3}$ cup milk
icing sugar

Cream 60 g (2 oz/$\frac{1}{4}$ cup) of the butter, then beat in the egg yolks. Whisk the egg whites until stiff. Add half the sugar and keep whisking. When the meringue is silky, mix a tablespoon in with the yolks, then gently fold the yolks into the whites (if you do not have a very large bowl, do this in two batches). Sprinkle on the flour; fold in, with the lemon rind. Set oven at moderately hot, 200°C (400°F), gas 6.

Bring the milk to the boil with the remaining

Salzburg dumplings are really a souffle

butter and sugar. Divide it between warmed dishes. Heap on the meringue, 3 mounds per dish. Bake in heated oven for 5–7 minutes, until the tops are pale brown and the outside of the mounds just firm. Dredge with icing sugar and serve.

AUSTRIAN NUT PUDDING
Nusspudding

Judging by the lightness and flavour of this steamed pudding, we are not the only ones who know how to make such things. Walnuts come out particularly well, with their bitterness subdued; but the favourite, I think, will always be hazelnuts—toast them in a cool oven first, if you like, until golden all through.

Serves 8
125 g/4 oz/½ cup butter
125 g/4 oz/½ cup vanilla sugar
5 standard egg yolks
2–3 soft baps or white rolls, brown crusts removed, if hard, made into fine breadcrumbs
5 standard egg whites
250 g/8 oz/2 cups nuts
extra butter and sugar
TO FINISH
250 g/8 oz raspberries
icing sugar
300 ml/½ pt/1¼ cups double or whipping cream
1.75-litre/3-pt/7-cup basin or mould

Cream the butter and sugar, then add the egg yolks. Weigh out 60 g (2 oz/1 cup if fresh, ½ cup if dried) crumbs and mix with 2 tablespoons (3 tbs) water to make a crumbly paste. Beat this into the butter mixture.

Whip the egg whites until stiff and fold in. Process or grate the nuts.

Butter and sugar the basin or mould. Turn in mixture; cover, tie and steam or boil for 3 hours.

Meanwhile, make a sauce by sieving, or processing and sieving, the raspberries with icing sugar to taste. Whip the cream very lightly, with enough icing sugar to sweeten it.

When cooked, turn out the pudding. Pour round some of the raspberry sauce to make a moat. Put the rest in a little jug, the cream in a bowl.

RIGO JANCSI

In 1896 the young and far from innocent Princesse de Caraman Chimay ran off with a gypsy musician, Rigó Jancsi (meaning Johnny Blackbird), and set up house in Paris. No case of the raggle-taggle gypsies-O!, for the Princess Clara was the rich daughter of the richest, most illiterate landowner of north–west America (one paper described him as 'the millionaire muskrat catcher'), and there is no record that her distinguished Belgian husband ran after her. With her full lips 'like an open pomegranate', her white plump skin and her restless eyes, she had the look of a saint. Gypsy Johnny was 38. When he drove beside her through the Bois de Boulogne, her hand on his knee, he grinned 'till his strong white teeth showed under his moustache', a twirled moustache. She posed for photographs with a bicycle, like a saucy baker's boy—triangular hat pushed back, cigarette drooping from her mouth and a black velvet knickerbocker suit which showed off her legs in black silk stockings. Paris talked of little else—tut tut, my dear, did you ever?—and Toulouse Lautrec made a lithograph that exactly expressed the fair white Princess 'giving her favour and her purse to a little brown fiddler in the Hungarian band'.

The Hungarians were openly enchanted when their gypsy musician brought his princess home. Enterprising pastrycooks in Budapest made cakes in his honour. This one, with its pale plump filling, became a classic.

Gundel's restaurent on the edge of Budapest's City Park

Makes 24 squares
FOR THE CAKE
6 egg whites
pinch of salt
6 egg yolks
125 g/4 oz/½ cup sugar
2 level tablespoons/3 tbs cocoa
45 g/1½ oz/6 tbs flour
melted butter, for greasing
½ pot apricot jam plus 1–2 tablespoons water
FOR THE GLAZE
60 g/2 oz/⅓ cup dark or bitter chocolate, broken up
2 level tablespoons/3 tbs cocoa
100 g/3½ oz/7 tbs sugar
4 tablespoons/⅓ cup water
½ level teaspoon unsalted butter
FOR THE CHOCOLATE CREAM
2 level teaspoons powdered gelatine
2 tablespoons/3 tbs water
60 g/2 oz/⅓ cup dark or bitter chocolate, broken up
300 ml/½ pt/1¼ cups double cream
300 ml/½ pt/1¼ cups whipping cream
175 g/6 oz/¾ cup vanilla sugar
two baking trays, about 27 × 37 cm/10½ × 14½ in

To make the cake, whisk egg whites with salt and 1 tablespoon water until very thick and firm. Beat in the egg yolks one by one, beating all the time (use an electric beater if possible). Then add the sugar, beating it in thoroughly. Sift together the cocoa and flour. Sprinkle it round the sides of the egg mixture and fold it in carefully. Set the oven at moderately hot, 190°C (375°F), gas 5.

Line the baking trays with non-stick baking paper. Brush it with melted butter. Spread the cake mixture evenly in the trays and bake in the heated oven for about 15 minutes or until cooked.

Invert each tray over a clean cloth. Leave for 5 minutes, then remove the trays and peel away the paper. Warm the apricot jam with the water and, when it boils and begins to disintegrate, sieve it; brush over one cake.

Next make the glaze by melting the chocolate in a basin over simmering water (or the top of a double boiler). Remove the basin (or pan) and cool until tepid. Mix cocoa and sugar to a paste with the water, and add with the butter to the chocolate. Put back over simmering water and stir for 5 minutes. Pour over the chocolate cake without the apricot jam on it. Leave to cool until the glaze is firm. Trim the cake with a heated knife blade, then cut it carefully into 5 cm (2 in) squares, without cutting completely through.

Make the filling. Mix the gelatine with the water. Put the chocolate, creams and sugar in a basin over simmering water (or the top of a double boiler) and heat until thick. Stir in the gelatine and remove the basin (or pan) from the heat. When the cream is almost set but just pourable, whisk it with a rotary beater until it holds a firm shape and becomes pale in colour. Use an electric beater only if you are good at controlling it; but be careful or the chocolate cream will turn to butter. Should it do this, chill the chocolate cream, then soften, and whisk in 115 g (4 oz/½ cup) of unsalted butter, adding the cream gradually.

Spread this chocolate cream filling over the apricot-glazed cake. Chill until just about firm—not hard—and then carefully place the chocolate-glazed squares on top. Leave overnight—chilling again—then cut down between squares to separate the pieces.

RED CURRANT TART
Ribiselkuchen

A strength of Austrian cake-making is the succession of shortcakes, each slightly different, all deliciously crisp and rich. Traunkirchner torte, Linzertorte and this tart are only three out of a magnificent choice. If red currants are not in season, or available frozen, use raspberries or slightly sharp cherries instead.

Serves 8–10
160 g/5½ oz/scant ¾ cup softened butter
160 g/5½ oz/scant ¾ cup caster sugar
4 large egg yolks
100 g/3½ oz/scant cup ground almonds
300 g/10 oz/2½ cups plain flour
FRUIT
about 500 g/1 lb red currants
4 large egg whites
200 g/7 oz/scant cup caster sugar

Cream butter and sugar, add yolks and dry ingredients to make a heavy crumbly dough. Or mix in the processor all together. Spread evenly into a 22-cm/9-in tart or shallow cake tin, preferably one with a removable base. Bake 30 minutes at 190°C (375°F), gas 5. Check after 20 minutes and lower the heat if the edges have begun to brown.

Meanwhile, shred red currants from their stalks and leaves (use a fork). Some Austrian recipes instruct you to cook them lightly, others leave them raw, which I prefer: the advantage of cooking them is that you can control the liquid content by reducing it, in wet summers the uncooked fruit may be so juicy that it overflows the tart. Whisk egg whites stiff, add half the sugar. Whisk again, then add the rest of the sugar.

Take the cake from the oven and turn heat to 190°C (375°F), gas 5. Spread fruit over the cake, leaving a clear rim. Pile on the meringue to the edge of the tin, and put cake into the hot oven for about 15 minutes. Or until the top is nicely caught with brown. Cool and cut into small pieces to serve.

TRAUNKIRCHEN SHORTCAKE
Traunkirchner torte

To the east of Salzburg lies the lakeside town of Traunkirchen where you may eat this delightful shortcake which has become an Austrian classic. The particular egg white filling of this version reminds me of the meringue filling of many Greek cakes.

Serves 8
240 g/8 oz/1 cup butter
90 g/3 oz/6 tbs sugar
280 g/9 oz/2¼ cups plain flour, sifted
3 egg yolks

FOR THE FILLING
3 egg whites
60 g/2 oz/¼ cup caster sugar
90 g/3 oz apricot, strawberry, raspberry jam, sieved

Mix the cake ingredients together in a processor or by hand. Divide into four equal parts. Roll each one into a ball. Chill for 30 minutes. Set the oven at moderate, 160°C (325°F), gas 3.

Roll out and shape them into rounds about 18 cm (7 in) each, on a floured board using flan rings to cut them evenly. Put on to non-stick baking paper-lined baking sheets. Mark one of the rounds into 8 wedges—this will be the top.

Bake in the heated oven for about 20 minutes. The shortbread should end up golden brown and crisp. Check from time to time and turn the heat down if the rounds are catching. Remove and cool; separate wedges along cut marks.

For the filling, whisk the egg whites to a snow with the sugar, then whisk in the jam. Use to sandwich the cakes together, placing the wedges neatly on top. Leave overnight in a very cool place, and eat within 24 hours.

RUSSIA

Compiled by Pamela Davidson

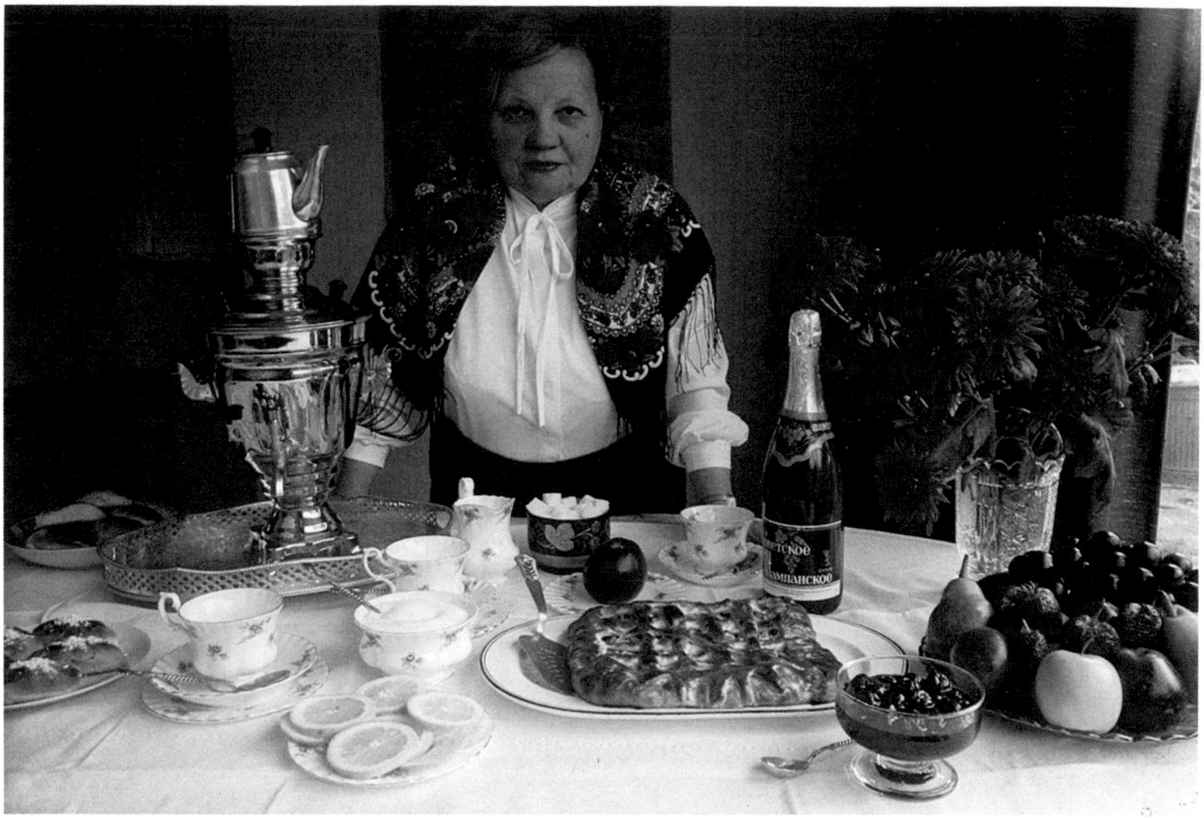

The samovar of boiling water with the teapot on top and a bottle of Russian champagne, preside over a hospitable table

Much of what is written about Russian cookery in the West draws on 19th-century traditions or emigré cookbooks, and bears little relation to the food which is actually prepared and eaten today in Russia. I use the terms Russia and Russian throughout to refer to the European Russian part of the Soviet Union and its Russian inhabitants.

Cookbooks published in the Soviet Union also present a very much more varied and exotic picture of Soviet cuisine than exists in reality. A recent publication, *Everything about Vegetables* (Moscow, 1978), contains recipes for asparagus and artichokes which most Russians today have never even seen, let alone tasted or prepared. Other cookbooks are intent on promoting products which the Soviet populace is failing to buy; *Gifts of the Ocean* (Kaliningrad, 1975), for example, attempts to convert the reader to using a fish paste made from shellfish which has been available for many years now, but has failed to catch the people's imagination.

Between 1976 and 1981, I lived in Moscow and travelled widely in the Soviet Union. During this period, I collected the following recipes which represent the best dishes which I ate at friends and relations. These recipes show clearly how many of the old pre-revolutionary traditions have survived into Soviet times, even though they have often changed quite considerably—usually they are much simpler.

One of the most striking features of contemporary Russian cooking is its remarkable degree of standardisation. The best Russian cooking is done for private or public celebrations of which there are a number, for example: 8 March (International Women's Day), 1 May, 9 May (Victory Day), 7 and 8

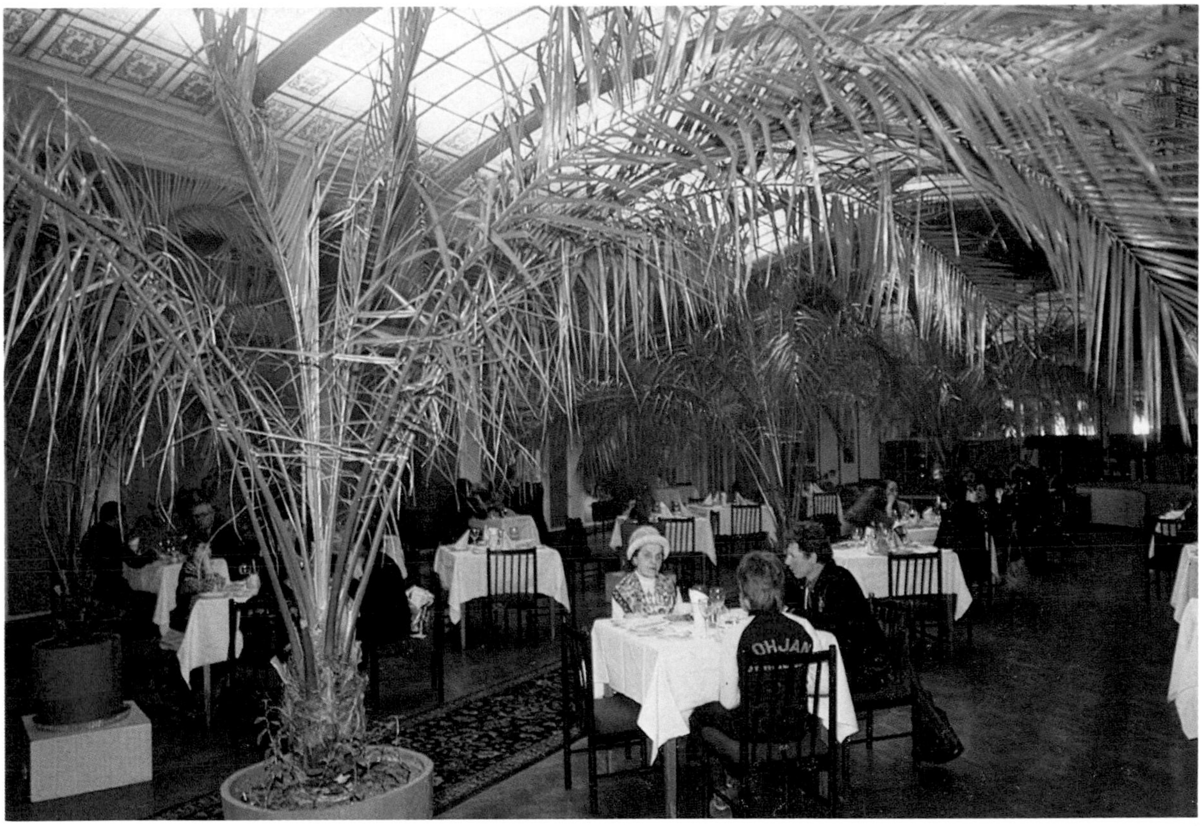

In the restaurant of the Hotel Evropeiskaya, in Leningrad, you will eat dishes that are rare in Russian homes today

November (the Anniversary of the Great October Socialist Revolution) and the New Year. On these occasions, friends and family traditionally gather together and spend a large part of the day sitting around a table loaded with food and drink, pronouncing toast after toast as they eat their way through the food. The remarkable thing about these gatherings from the culinary point of view is that almost exactly the same dishes are served on every occasion in most households.

An important practical reason which contributes to the standardisation of Russian cookery today is the general lack of time available for refined cooking preparations. In most Soviet families, husbands and wives both work full-time; queuing for food takes up a substantial amount of time, and little energy or imagination are left over for the preparation of food.

Furthermore, whereas in the 19th century French chefs worked in Russia and European culinary ideas were readily absorbed into the Russian tradition, Soviet society today is much more isolated in this respect; the only foreign influences which have a marked effect on Russian eating habits are ones which come from within the Soviet Union; thus you find that various Ukrainian, Georgian and Uzbek dishes, for example, have established a permanent place for themselves in the contemporary Russian repertoire. However, there is no equivalent in Russian cooking to the internationalism which has now become common in for example, English cooking.

Part of the reason for the uniformity of Russian cooking lies in a certain streak of conservativism which is strongly rooted in the Russian character.

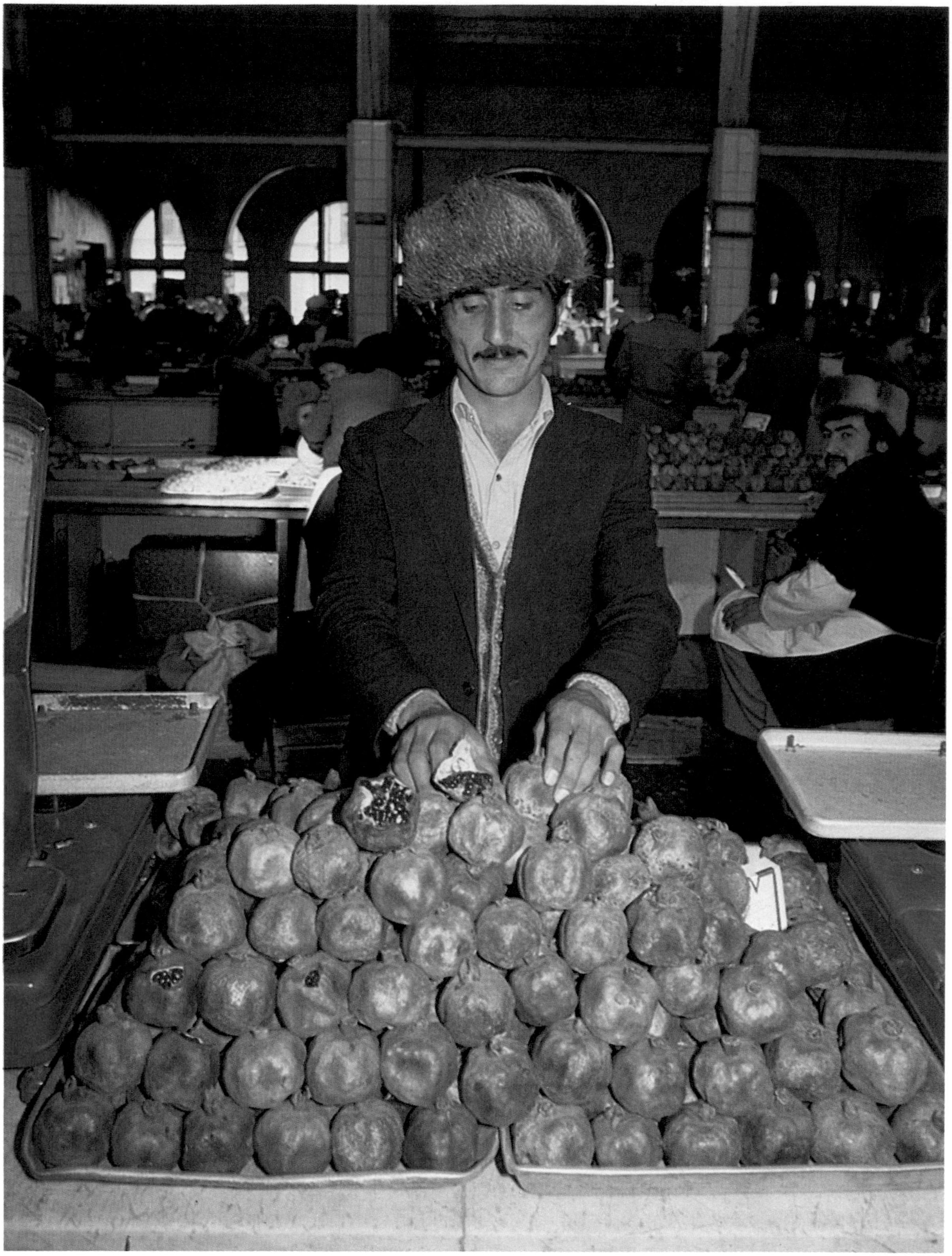

Russians do not seem to regard change or variety in food as an asset; they concentrate on certain well-loved and familiar dishes, and are happy to eat these again and again. Russians cook dishes which they have learnt from their family and friends; they may have one or two standard cookbooks, but they will only use these for reference and to check recipes with which they are already familiar, not as a source of new ideas.

This natural tendency towards conservatism in matters of food is further reinforced by a number of practical difficulties. Food supplies are extremely irregular and cannot be depended on. First you shop, and then you decide what to make. Although food supplies in Moscow are much better than in the surrounding provincial towns and villages, there are nevertheless, frequent shortages of different foods. Staple products such as butter, cheese, sunflower oil or buckwheat kasha may suddenly disappear from the shops; fresh fruit and vegetables are difficult to get during the long winter months. Meat and fish have invariably been frozen for long periods of times before they reach the customer; this has led to the curious practice of smothering them in mayonnaise before cooking them in the oven, apparently in order to give them a bit of taste.

However, most people have ways of getting around these difficulties. Many shops and work places run a system of *zakazy* or orders; this allows you to place an order for a particular combination of foods, either on a regular basis, or before major public holidays. The order will include items which are in high demand and short supply, such as tinned sprats or salmon, salted fish, caviare or good salami. However, it will also include other less desirable items which are not selling well in the shops (even though this practice is illegal according to Soviet law). The second category of items is known as the *nagruzka* or burden, and must be purchased in order to obtain the items which are the true attractions of the order. In recent years, tins of seaweed were regularly included as part of the *nagruzka*; this led to a burgeoning of seaweed salads served in Moscow homes.

You can also shop at the market which represents an officially licensed measure of private enterprise. Many fresh fruits and vegetables, Russian honeys, curd cheeses (tvorog) made from fresh milk, soured cream (smetana), strings of dried mushrooms and exotic foods and spices from the South can be found at the market; these are either unavailable in the shops or are of markedly better quality than official State produce. There are no long queues, but the prices are prohibitively high, and the market remains a luxury which most people can only afford on special occasions.

On the unofficial level, there is the extremely important and extensive network of 'back door' transactions which operates in Moscow. If you have a friend or a contact who works at a cafe, restaurant or shop, you can shop through the 'black entrance' (chernyi khod) as it is called in Russian. Many goods never reach the general public at the front of the shop or in the cafe because they are all sold unofficially to friends and contacts at the back of the shop. To be in some way connected with food or catering in Moscow puts you in a position of considerable importance, and allows you to trade food for other favours. Recent Soviet laws have attempted to tighten up on this practice, but it seems unlikely that it will disappear.

It is for these reasons that the apparent miracle of groaning tables of food in every Soviet household despite the lack of food in the shops is made possible.

The recipes which follow therefore reproduce faithfully the dishes which you would be most likely to be served if you were invited to eat in a Russian home in the Soviet Union today.

The pomegranate seller from the South has opened some of his fruit to show the large juicy grains inside

HOT AND COLD APPETISERS
Zakuski

The Russian verb zakusit' means both to bite into something with one's teeth and to follow a drink down with some food. A zakuska is the name given to this food. It used to be the custom to bring a visitor a glass of vodka and a zakuska on a tray; the guest would first down the vodka in a single gulp to leave the palate cleansed and slightly burning—in an ideal state to receive a zakuska which would immediately follow. The zakuska would be something with a sharp or salty taste such as salted herring or marinated mushrooms.

Nowadays, zakuski are consumed sitting around a table as the first course of a meal. In daily life at home, the meal will start with just one or two zakuski—a salad and some canned fish or salami, for example. However, on special occasions many zakuski are prepared and, although the guests continue to consume further courses, they are usually already more than full after the zakuski.

Typical zakuski served at such occasions would certainly include something salty, such as red or black caviare (red caviare is often served in scooped out halves of hard-boiled eggs), salted herring, salted salmon, salted cucumbers, salted cabbage or salted mushrooms; an enamel pan of hot boiled potatoes is often brought to the table to go with the salted fish; smoked sturgeon, cod's liver pâté, or tinned fish such as sprats or salmon, or salami or ham will also figure on the menu. A hot pie with a meat, fish or vegetable stuffing is likely to be served. In summer, salads made with sliced tomatoes and cucumbers, dressed in sunflower oil or in soured cream, or made with chopped radishes and cucumber in soured cream, covered with fresh dill and parsley, will be served. In winter, one finds salads made of a great number of finely chopped boiled vegetables dressed in mayonnaise, soured cream, or sunflower oil. Here are some typical zakuski served on special occasions.

OLIVIER SALAD
Salat Olivier

Traditional names of dishes from the 19th century have often survived into Soviet times, but their original meaning has frequently been forgotten. I have enjoyed versions of salat Olivier in various Moscow homes, but no one could tell me the origin of its name. I found the answer in an article by Lesley Chamberlain on Russian concepts of food and cooking, published recently in the cookery magazine *Petits Propos Culinaires*: Olivier was a French chef who opened a restaurant in Moscow in the 1880s called the Ermitage, which was popular with the nobility. The modern version is easy to make. The exact proportions of the ingredients can be varied according to what is available. Russians use a type of apple grown in Russia called antonovka for salads; this apple is quite bitter, although it is considered an eating apple rather than a cooking one. The best substitute would probably be a mild cooking apple or a Granny Smith.

Serves 6
2 medium tart apples, peeled and cored
5 medium potatoes, boiled and peeled
5 hard-boiled eggs, shelled
2 pickled cucumbers
½ fresh long cucumber, peeled
200 g/7 oz canned peas, drained
200 g/7 oz canned fish (crab or salmon), or cooked beef, cubed
mayonnaise
salt

Cut the eggs, apples and vegetables, except for the peas, into fine cubes. Mix them with the peas, fish or beef; add enough mayonnaise to bind the ingredients. Season with salt. Keep cool.

BEETROOT SALAD
Salat iz svyokly

Much of what is today most precious to Russians originated in Byzantium: the Russian alphabet and religion, and also the beetroot, which has long been a staple of the Russian diet. The Russian word for beetroot, svyokla, is derived from the Greek word for beetroot, seutlon. Its popularity in recent years has been reinforced because it is one of the few vegetables always available during the long winter months.

Russians use beetroot in the many different salads which appear on the zakuski table. This recipe and the next one are two of the most popular salads based on beetroot.

Serves 4
500 g/1 lb beetroot, cooked and peeled
3 cloves garlic, crushed
120 g/4 oz/1 cup shelled walnuts
mayonnaise or soured cream
salt

Grate the beetroot coarsely into a salad bowl. Add the garlic to the beetroot. Put aside a few walnut halves for decoration; chop the rest of the shelled walnuts very finely, and add them to the salad. Mix all together well and add enough mayonnaise or soured cream to bind everything into a creamy salad. Season with salt. Decorate the top of the salad with a few whole walnut halves.

RUSSIAN SALAD
Vinegret

The Russian word vinegret comes from the French word for vinegar, vinaigre, and was originally used to describe a salad made from cooked chopped vegetables and dressed with oil and vinegar. In today's version of the vinegret, however, the vinegar is missing. The reason is that wine vinegar is not available in Soviet shops; the only kind of vinegar on sale is vinegar essence, which is made from acid spirit, and its taste is rather too sharp for salads. Russians sometimes pour a little over salted herring, or over pel'meni, Siberian ravioli. However, they do not use vinegar as part of a salad dressing, preferring to dress salads simply either with sunflower or olive oil, or with mayonnaise or soured cream.

Today, the term vinegret is most commonly used to refer to a salad made principally with beetroot, althhough one could add a few chopped, boiled potatoes or some salted cabbage.

Serves 6
500 g/1 lb beetroot, cooked and peeled
2 pickled cucumbers, diced
small onion, diced
salt
sunflower or olive oil

Cut the beetroot into fine cubes, and mix with pickled cucumbers and onion. Season with salt, and pour enough oil over the salad to coat the vegetables lightly.

CABBAGE SALAD
Salat iz kapusty

Together with beetroot, cabbage is one of the most important staple Russian vegetables. Fresh and salted cabbage are used in salads, soups or in pies.

The next two recipes were given to me by a friend in Moscow, Anna Solomonovna, who learnt the art of imaginative cooking from her grandmother, who dedicated herself to preparing fine food for the family. This recipe, and the one for cabbage salad with blackcurrants, is thus individual rather than classical. It reflects Anna Solomonovna's Ukrainian upbringing in its combination of vegetables with fruit.

continued on p. 235

Zakuski include (back) salted cabbage, beetroot salad, aubergine caviare, Olivier salad, cabbage salad, and (front) Russian salad, marinated mushrooms, herring in a fur coat, eggs stuffed with caviare, salted cucumbers

DRINKS

Before discussing zakuski, the Russian hors-d'oeuvre course, you need to have a proper grasp of Russian drinking habits, since these are responsible for the form and nature of the zakuski ritual. A zakuska is by definition something which is eaten immediately after a drink; it is natural therefore that drinks should form an essential part of the zakuski course. At any special occasion in Russia, there will always be a variety of bottles on the zakuski table. However, these drinks are consumed in a manner which is totally different from the West. First of all, no drinks are served before the meal or after it; all the drinks are served during the meal, and, in the main, during the zakuski course. Secondly, no distinction is made between different types of drinks with regard to their suitability as accompaniments to various foods; drinks which in the West are regarded as only suitable for cocktails or liqueurs, which are traditionally drunk after the meal, are all drunk throughout the meal with food in Russia. Thus, on a well-stocked zakuski table, when a special occasion such as a birthday or holiday is being celebrated, you would expect to see any combination of the following bottles; almost certainly, a few bottles of vodka; this is the most traditional and popular of Russian spirits. Russkaya vodka is one of the standard and least expensive brands; however, many people consider the more expensive Pshenichnaya vodka made from wheat to be better. You often find a decanter of vodka mixed with the juice of berries, as in the recipe given below. Sweet fortified wines are served, as well as Riesling-type white wines from Bulgaria or Rumania. For some reason, red wine is relatively rare. Georgian and Armenian cognacs are also drunk. On a special occasion, a bottle of fizzy Soviet champagne may be opened. To alleviate thirst, bottles of vodichka (derived from voda, the Russian for water, as is the word vodka), a kind of fizzy lemonade, or bottles of Caucasian spring mineral water such as Borzhomi or Narzan will also be served. Jugs of homemade or shop-bought kvas, and jugs of fruit juice made from berries boiled up with sugar and water are also often served.

At the beginning of the meal, the guests sit down to the zakuski course, and everyone is asked what they will drink. Most people will normally select whichever of the drinks is their favourite, and, providing it does not run out, they will stick to it throughout the meal. This does not apply to champagne which is served as an addition to the regular drinks. The drinking starts off in a rather formal way, following a pattern of ritualized standard toasts to the honour of the occasion which is being celebrated and to the health and happiness of those both present and absent. These toasts are arranged in a well-established order of precedence. Each time a toast is pronounced, the glasses will be refilled. All the guests must participate in each toast, and continue eating the zakuski between toasts. After the initial round of toasts, drinking normally continues in a more informal way, with perhaps only the occasional toast unifying the mixed individual drinking into a single whole. Most of the heavy imbibing is completed by the end of the zakuski course, and many people no longer drink anything alcoholic by the time they get to the main course.

CRANBERRY VODKA
Nastoika na klyukve

Many people like to add variety and taste to vodka by mixing it with the juice of fresh berries; this drink will be stored in a crystal decanter and offered with special pride to guests as something homemade. This is a recipe for one of the most popular of these combinations

300 g/10 oz fresh cranberries
120–200 g/4–7 oz/$\frac{1}{2}$–scant cup sugar
1 litre/1$\frac{3}{4}$ pts/scant 4$\frac{1}{2}$ cups vodka

Check through the berries, discarding any imperfect ones. Remove the stalks and leaves, and wash the berries thoroughly. Put the berries and the sugar (varying the proportions according to how sweet a drink you wish to produce) into a pan, and mash them together with a wooden spoon until the berries are crushed and well mixed in with the sugar. Pour the vodka over this mixture and cover the pan in order to prevent evaporation. Leave to stand overnight.

The next morning, drain the contents of the pan into a jar through a piece of muslin or a very fine sieve. Leave to stand for a while, and then pour into a bottle or decanter (this will allow you to get rid of the sediment which will form at the bottom of the jar).

Put the cranberry vodka into the freezer for an hour or two before serving. The crushed berries left in the muslin can be used to make kisel, (see page 247).

Serves 6
1 kg/2 lb white cabbage, roughly chopped
2 large tart apples, peeled
2 hard-boiled eggs, shelled and chopped
2 spring onions, chopped
fresh parsley and dill, chopped
sunflower or olive oil
lemon juice
salt and pepper
sugar

Put the cabbage in boiling salted water for 3 minutes. Drain it, and then chop it very finely (Russians will put it through their myasorubka or meat grinder to make sure that it is chopped finely enough). Grate the apples coarsely, and add them to the minced cabbage. Mix the eggs, spring onions and herbs with the cabbage and apples. Pour enough oil over the salad to coat it lightly; add a squeeze of lemon juice. Season with salt and pepper, and sugar to taste.

CABBAGE SALAD WITH BLACK CURRANTS
Salat iz kapusty s chyornoi smorodinoi

This recipe was invented 30 years ago by Anna Solomonovna, and illustrates the Russian proverb 'Gol' na vydumki khitra', meaning that poor people are cunning at inventing things. After the war it was difficult to get food in Moscow and the ingredients for this salad happened to be the only ones which Anna Solomonovna could get. However, the salad was such a success that it remained a standard item in her repertoire. It is extremely simple to make (the only effort lies in preparing the cabbage which must be chopped very finely for the salad to be a success) and looks most attractive; the juice from the black currants lends a purplish tinge to the cabbage. You can use fresh or frozen black currants.

1 kg/2 lb cabbage
200 g/7 oz/1⅓ cups raisins
200 g/7 oz black currants
5 tablespoons/6 tbs olive oil
salt

Chop the cabbage up very finely. Wash the raisins, remove the stalks from the black currants, wash them, and add both to the cabbage. Pour on the olive oil and sprinkle on some salt. Mix all the ingredients together well.

CABBAGE PIE
Pirog s kapustoi

Pirogi (pies) or pirozhki (small individual pies) are typically Russian. The word 'pirog' comes from 'pir', meaning a banquet. They were originally baked for special occasions—and still are, although they are most commonly served as part of the zakuski course; they also make a good dish for the evening meal, served with tea.

Pirogi are made with a yeast-based dough, and filled with many different fillings; the most popular are cabbage and hard-boiled egg, meat, fish and rice or mushrooms.

SALADS

The Russian concept of a salad is quite different from the English one. The English salad made with lettuce leaves, tomatoes and cucumbers, dressed in olive oil and vinegar, is not known in Russia. Lettuce is not generally available in Moscow except during the summer months when it appears in the shops in the form of muddy lettuce seedlings packed into paper bags and sold by the half kilo. Some Russians go to the trouble of disentangling these seedlings, washing them several times in water, marinating them in a vinegar and water solution, and mixing them with chopped hard-boiled eggs and spring onions in a soured cream sauce. Large lettuces can be obtained at the market, but they are invariably chopped and shredded, rather than served the English way. The reason for this seems to be that Russians have a deeply rooted sense of the salad as something made from a multiplicity of chopped vegetables, many of which may have been cooked. The nearest that the Russians ever get to the English type of salad is in summer when they serve whole tomatoes, cucumbers, sliced lengthways, washed lettuce leaves, with bunches of dill and parsley on a plate with the zakuski or with the main course as an accompaniment. The basic type of Russian salad is usually dressed in soured cream, mayonnaise, or sunflower oil. Olive oil, although preferred by the cognoscenti, is hardly ever available in the shops, and most Russians therefore content themselves with sunflower oil.

Serves 6

FOR THE DOUGH

30 g/1 oz/1 cake fresh yeast, or 15 g/½ oz dried yeast
4 tablespoons/⅓ cup warm water
level teaspoon sugar
900 g/2 lb/8 cups plain flour
350 ml/12 fl oz/1½ cups warm milk
level teaspoon salt
100 g/3½ oz/scant ½ cup butter, melted
egg, beaten

FOR THE FILLING

1–1.5 kg/2–3 lb cabbage, trimmed and finely chopped
50 g/1½ oz/3 tbs butter
4 hard-boiled eggs, shelled and chopped
salt and pepper
pinch of sugar

TO FINISH

egg, beaten

In a large mixing bowl, blend the fresh or dried yeast with the water, sugar and 1 teaspoon of the flour. Leave in a warm place till frothy—15–25 minutes. Then mix the milk with half of the remaining flour, and combine this with the yeast mixture to make a smooth dough. Cover with a piece of foil and leave to rise in a warm place (about 1–2 hours). When the dough has risen, knead in the rest of the flour, the salt, the butter and the egg until the dough comes away cleanly from the sides of the bowl and your hands.

Meanwhile, prepare the filling. Cook the cabbage in a pan of boiling salted water for 5 minutes, then drain it thoroughly, pressing out any excess moisture. Melt the butter in a pan, put in the cabbage and cook gently for 10–15 minutes, without letting it brown, stirring from time to time. Then add the eggs, salt, pepper and sugar. Set the oven at hot, 220°C (425°F), gas 7.

Divide the dough in half and roll it out fairly thinly into two large oblongs, each 30 × 40 cm (12 × 16 in). Russians usually bake pies on metal sheets which are the size of an average oven shelf. Grease a baking tray or line it with foil; put one piece of dough on it, pile on the cabbage filling quite thickly to cover it, and then top with the other piece of dough. Seal the edges by pinching them together all around. Brush the top with beaten egg, and leave the pie to stand in a warm place for 15–20 minutes. Bake the pie in the preheated oven for 40–45 minutes.

Remove the pie from the oven, brush the top with melted butter, then cover with a clean linen cloth for 15–20 minutes. Remove the cloth and cut the pie into squares; serve warm.

AUBERGINE CAVIARE
Ikra iz baklazhan

This dish, extremely popular among Russians, bears some resemblance to the Provençal ratatouille, but differs in the way in which the aubergines are prepared; rather than being diced, and then stewed, they are first baked, and then their flesh is scraped out. The result is a dish which is closer to a purée than to one of stewed vegetables, as the name ikra, meaning caviare in Russian, indicates.

Serves 6

1 kg/2 lb large aubergines
3–4 cloves of garlic, crushed
2 medium onions, finely chopped
4 tablespoons/⅓ cup sunflower or olive oil
5 medium tomatoes, peeled and finely chopped
small pinch of sugar
salt and pepper
chopped parsley

Bake the aubergines in a moderate oven, 180°C (350°F), gas 4, for about 30 minutes until cooked (the skins will shrivel and the flesh will feel tender if poked). Cut them in half lengthways, and using a spoon, scrape out the flesh from the inside of the skins. Mash the flesh to a pulp with a fork. Set the garlic and onions to cook gently in the olive oil in a deep, heavy pan on top of the stove.

After 2–3 minutes, add the aubergine pulp and the chopped tomatoes to the pan, together with the sugar; season with salt and pepper. Cook this mixture gently for 30–40 minutes.

Turn into a bowl and leave to cool. Serve cold, garnished with parsley, and with plenty of bread and butter, so your guests can make open sandwiches with the aubergine caviare.

GEORGIAN CHEESE PIES
Khachapuri

In Tbilisi, the capital of Georgia, these delicious hot cheese pies are served at special khachapuri cafes straight from the oven. This dish has been widely adopted in Moscow, and it is the simplified Muscovite version that I give here. Russians will use a salty cheese, made from sheep's milk, called brynza for the filling. Feta cheese is a suitable substitute.

Makes 12
FOR THE PASTRY
400 g/14 oz/3½ cups plain flour
½ level teaspoon salt
250 ml/scant ½ pt/1 cup water
200 g/7 oz/scant cup butter
FOR THE FILLING
300 g/10 oz/2½ cups feta cheese, grated or crumbled
60 g/2 oz/¼ cup butter, softened
2 eggs, beaten

Make the pastry by mixing the flour, salt and water together; it should be fairly soft, but dry enough to be able to roll it out. Roll out the pastry into a square, 1 cm (½ in) thick.

Put the piece of butter into the middle of the square of pastry. Fold the edges of the pastry into the middle to form an envelope around the butter. Chill this pastry envelope for 20 minutes. Then roll it out until it is flat; fold it in half, and in half again (reducing it to one-quarter of its original size), and chill again for 20 minutes. Repeat the rolling out, folding and chilling process once more. Then form the pastry into a sausage shape, and cut it into 12 equal rounds. Roll each round out to a width of about 10 cm (4 in)—the size of a medium saucer. Set the oven at hot, 220°C (425°F), gas 7.

Make the filling by mixing the cheese with the butter and eggs. Place a spoonful of filling on each pastry round; pinch the edges together in the middle of each round to seal. Place them on a greased baking sheet.

Bake in the preheated oven for about 40 minutes. The pies will open slightly to reveal their golden brown cheese filling. They should be served hot, straight from the oven.

SLIGHTLY SALTED CUCUMBERS
Malosol'nye ogurtsy

When Russians speak of ogurtsy (cucumbers) they are probably referring to salted cucumbers; if they mean fresh cucumbers, they will specify this by adding the word fresh, svezhie. Salted cucumbers are a standard item found in every Soviet kitchen. They are served whole, to accompany zakuski, chopped up in various salads, or with hot meat dishes; they are also put in to some kinds of soups.

The procedure for making salted cucumbers (solyonye ogurtsy) is quite time-consuming, and most Russians buy them from large wooden barrels in shops or at the market, rather than attempting to make them at home. In summer however, when cucumbers are plentiful, many Russians make their own malosol'nye ogurtsy (slightly salted cucumbers). The procedure for this is quite simple, and the result delicious. Slightly salted cucumbers can be served on their own as an accompaniment to zakuski or meat dishes; they are particularly good when served with hot buttered new potatoes. Sliced up with tomatoes in a little oil, they make an excellent summer salad.

The standard Russian cucumber is short, fat and curly. These are the ideal cucumbers for salting. Choose fresh, firm short ones, discarding any which have yellowed or are bruised. Wash them carefully, and arrange a layer of them in the bottom of a large glass jar. Cover them with sprigs of fresh dill and whole peeled cloves of garlic. Continue building up layers of cucumbers, dill and garlic in this way until your jar is packed full.

Prepare some brine by boiling up water with salt in the proportion of 2 to 3 tablespoons of salt to every litre (1¾ pts/scant 4½ cups) of water. The exact amount you will need will depend on the quantity of cucumbers you wish to salt. Allow the brine to cool, and then pour it over the cucumbers until the jar is full (all the cucumbers must be

Cucumbers, lightly salted with dill and garlic

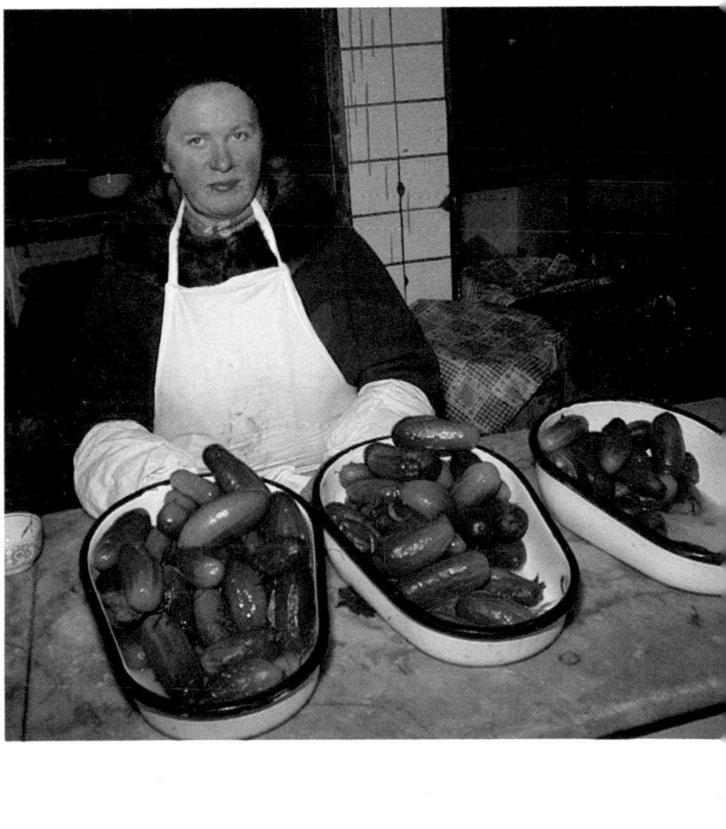

covered by the brine). Cover the jar with a lid, and leave for 2 days. Your salted cucumbers will then be ready. They will keep for some weeks if stored in the fridge.

If two days seems too long to wait, you can produce slightly salted cucumbers in a matter of hours by another method. Slice off the tips of the cucumbers before putting them into the jar, and pour hot brine over them. Then the cucumbers will be ready later the same day.

Elena Molokhovets, the author of the best-known late 19th century Russian cookbook entitled *A Gift to Young Housewifes or A Guide to the Diminution of Household Expenses*, insists that cucumbers should be salted five or six days after the new moon has appeared, and in any case, not later than the full moon; otherwise, she warns, they will be hollow inside, instead of being full and strong.

SALTED CABBAGE
Kvashenaya kapusta

The Russian verb kvasit' means to make something ferment and turn sour. Kvas, the Russian national non-alcoholic drink, is made from rye flour or rye bread which has fermented. In the same way, kvashenaya kapusta is made from salted cabbage which has had a little rye flour added to it to help the fermenting process. Cabbage treated in this way is as much a standard item of Russian kitchens as salted cucumbers; many people buy it in shops, or at the market. Salted cabbage is served on its own as a zakuska, or mixed with other vegetables (frequently beetroot) to form a salad; it is also used for a version of the famous Russian cabbage soup, shchi, which is made with sour cabbage rather than fresh.

The best vessel to use for preparing cabbage in this way is a wooden barrel with straight sides; if you do not have one, or only wish to make a small quantity of cabbage, take a clean large glass jar, and sprinkle a layer of rye flour over the bottom of it. Choose one or several large, firm white cabbages, and use a few of their outer leaves to line the bottom of the vessel (placing the cabbage leaves over the layer of rye flour). Shred the cabbage into long thin strips, and grate a few carrots. You should have roughly seven times more cabbage than carrot. Mix the cabbage and carrot with salt, using 25 g (1 oz) of salt to every kilo (2 lb) of vegetables. Press the salted cabbage and carrot mixture firmly down into the vessel, packing it in as tightly as possible. Cover the top of the cabbage with a few more whole cabbage leaves, place a lid over the vessel and weight it down.

In a few days the cabbage will start to ferment, and foam will appear on its surface. The foam will at first increase, but eventually it will disappear altogether. While the fermenting process is taking place, it is important to poke a wooden spoon down into the cabbage every so often in order to allow the gases which have formed inside the cabbage to escape. The cabbage will be ready when the foam has disappeared; this takes about 5 or 6 days. It will keep for several months.

Elena Molokhovets, the 19th century cookery writer, maintained that the best time for fermenting cabbage was at a full moon. The cabbage would be strong and would squeak between the teeth. For those who prefer their cabbage soft and unsqueaky the last quarter of the moon is the best time to salt it.

MARINATED MUSHROOMS
Marinovannye griby

Mushrooms in Russia are cult objects. Many enthusiasts are prepared to travel out of town after work in order to reach a famous mushroom spot by nightfall, and be ready to begin picking mushrooms there at dawn the next morning. These are then dried, salted or marinated.

Strings of dried mushrooms are sold at markets,

Marinated mushrooms are a great delicacy in Russia

as are fresh mushrooms, and jars of marinated mushrooms are sometimes to be found in the shops. Dried mushrooms are used in soups, and salted and marinated mushrooms are a favourite zakuska served with hot boiled potatoes or as an accompaniment to vodka. Fresh mushrooms are fried with onions in butter and served in a soured cream sauce with hot potatoes, or chopped up to make a filling for pies.

These highly-treasured mushrooms are the kind called cèpes in France and porcini in Italy. Unlike button and field mushrooms, they are not cultivated, but grow wild.

If you cannot find these mushrooms (members of the edible boletus family), use button mushrooms instead. The result will be very successful, but if a subtle flavouring of mushrooms from the boletus family is required, add a dried mushroom of the cèpes or porcini variety to each jar of button mushrooms.

1 kg/2 lb button mushrooms
1–2 dried mushrooms, soaked in water for 2 hours, then drained (optional)
salt
FOR THE MARINADE
125 ml/4 fl oz/½ cup water
125 ml/4 fl oz/½ cup wine vinegar
3 black peppercorns
3 cloves
short stick of cinnamon
bay leaf
1½ level teaspoons salt
level teaspoon sugar
TO FINISH
2–3 tablespoons/3–4 tbs olive or sunflower oil, or soured cream
two 450-ml/¾-pt/2-cup glass jars with lids

Trim the stalks off the mushrooms, wash the mushrooms carefully, and cook them in a pan of boiling salted water for 20 minutes. If you wish, add a pre-soaked dried mushroom. When the mushrooms are ready, pour off the water and leave them to drain in a colander.

Now prepare the marinade. Put the water and the vinegar into a saucepan, and add the spices, bay leaf, salt and sugar. Bring to the boil and simmer for 5–10 minutes. Then add the drained mushrooms to the pan and cook for a further 5–10 minutes, stirring occasionally.

Remove the mushrooms from the heat, and leave them to cool in the marinade. Then spoon them into the clean glass jars. Pour a little oil over the top of the jars, seal with the lids and keep for a week before opening so the flavour has time to mature.

Serve these mushrooms as a zakuska with vodka, covered with a little freshly chopped onion, and with a spoonful of oil or soured cream. Or serve as a supper dish, with potatoes which have been fried with onion, and smothered in soured cream.

HERRING IN A FUR COAT
Selyodka pod shuboi

After knocking back a shot of vodka, Russians must either sniff a piece of black bread, or swallow something sharp and salty, like salted herring.

This recipe is for an elaborate way of serving herring for a special occasion. The triple layer of vegetables, fruit and mayonnaise forms the 'fur coat' of the herring. If you cannot get a salted herring, you can adapt this recipe and use it for marinated rollmop herring.

Serves 2
salted herring, boned
small cooked beetroot, peeled and grated
cooked carrot, grated
cooked potato, cut into small cubes
tart apple, peeled and grated
salt
mayonnaise

Cut the herring into lozenge-shaped pieces, and arrange these like the original fish on a long, oval dish. Cover the fish with a layer of grated beetroot, then with a layer of grated carrot, then with a layer of potato, and finally with a layer of grated apple, using only half of the available vegetables and fruit. Repeat this layering until all the ingredients are used up. Salt if necessary (taking into account the saltiness of the fish which you have used) and finally cover with mayonnaise. This triple layer of vegetables, fruit and mayonnaise forms the 'fur coat' of the herring.

BEETROOT SOUP
Borshch

There are a great number of Russian soups, all of which are very distinctive.

Russians regard soup as an essential part of the main meal taken in the middle of the day; indeed, many are convinced that without soup, it is impossible to digest one's dinner.

Given this strong belief in soups as an essential part of the everyday diet it is strange that they are not usually offered to guests who come on a special occasion for a celebratory meal. Perhaps this is because soup is regarded as a humble, although nourishing and essential part of the daily diet, and is not, therefore, deemed worthy of being offered to guests; or perhaps it is a concession to the finite eating capacities of the guests, who have already filled themselves to bursting-point with zakuski, and could hardly be expected to withstand a triple onslaught of soup, main course and dessert.

Borshch, a soup of Ukrainian origin, has become one of the most popular soups in Russia. Many different types exist; but the Ukrainian, Moscow and Leningrad versions, all made on the basis of a meat stock, are standard types. However, you can make borshch without using a meat stock; this can be a summer borshch, prepared with fresh vegetables, or a mushroom borshch, which uses a stock made from dried mushrooms as its basis. Whatever the type, you will always find beetroot in every borshch. This recipe is for a meat borshch as prepared in Moscow today.

Serves 6

FOR THE STOCK

500 g/1 lb beef on the bone or brisket of beef
3 litres/5 pts/$12\frac{1}{2}$ cups water
2 onions, halved
salt
5 peppercorns
bay leaf

FOR THE SOUP

60 g/2 oz/$\frac{1}{4}$ cup butter
300 g/10 oz beetroot, peeled and diced
1–2 carrots, peeled and diced
1–2 onions, sliced into fine rings
2 tomatoes, peeled and chopped, or 2 level tablespoons/3 tbs tomato paste
tablespoon wine vinegar
tablespoon sugar
$\frac{1}{2}$ medium cabbage, roughly chopped
6 cloves of garlic, crushed with $\frac{1}{2}$ level teaspoon ground black pepper
2 medium potatoes, peeled and diced
6 tablespoons/$\frac{1}{2}$ cup soured cream, to finish

Boil the meat in the water, together with the onions, salt, peppercorns and bay leaf, for 2–3 hours. While the meat is cooking, remove any scum which appears on the surface of the stock. Strain; put aside the meat for later use.

Meanwhile, melt the butter in the bottom of a large saucepan. Put in the beetroot and the carrot, and begin to stew them in the butter. After a few minutes, add the onion, tomatoes or tomato paste, the vinegar and the sugar, and a ladle of the meat stock. Cook this mixture gently for 15–20 minutes.

Then add the cabbage, and cook gently, covered, for another 20 minutes. Pour the strained meat stock over the vegetables, and add more salt or vinegar to taste, if necessary. Add the garlic mixture and potatoes to the soup, and continue cooking the borshch for 5–10 minutes or until the potatoes are ready. (Some people cut off pieces of cooked meat from the bone, chop these up, and add them to the soup.) When the potatoes are ready, turn off the heat, and leave the borshch to stand for 15–20 minutes, covered with a lid.

To serve, put a spoonful of soured cream into each person's soup bowl, then ladle in the hot borshch.

COLD BEETROOT SOUP
Svekol'nik kholodnyi

This is a very popular cold soup, usually served in summer when vegetables and fresh herbs are plentiful

Serves 6

1 kg/2 lb beetroot
2 litres/$3\frac{1}{2}$ pts/$8\frac{3}{4}$ cups water
3 tablespoons/scant $\frac{1}{4}$ cup lemon juice
2 tablespoons sugar
6 hard-boiled eggs, whites only, chopped
4–6 lettuce leaves, shredded
3 spring onions, trimmed and cut into rounds
$\frac{1}{2}$ long English cucumber, finely diced
2 medium potatoes, peeled, boiled and finely diced

TO FINISH

6 tablespoons/$\frac{1}{2}$ cup soured cream
3 tablespoons chopped parsley
3 tablespoons chopped dill

Wash the beetroot thoroughly, and cook them in the water, together with the lemon juice. When the beetroot are tender, remove them from the liquid, peel them, then cut them up into small cubes. Strain the beetroot liquid into a clean saucepan. Chill the chopped beetroot, sugar, chopped egg whites, lettuce, spring onions, cucumber, and the potatoes. Finish with the cream as for borshch and sprinkle with plenty of parsley and dill.

CABBAGE SOUP
Shchi

Shchi is one of the oldest and most traditional of Russian soups. It has two essential elements: a vegetable which is usually fresh or salted cabbage, but can also be sorrel, spinach, beetroot or nettles; the other is a souring agent, which can be soured cream, sour apples or the juice from salted cabbage. This recipe is the standard one made in Moscow today. It uses a meat stock, with fresh cabbage as the main vegetable, and soured cream as the souring agent.

Serves 6
60 g/2 oz/¼ cup butter
2 onions, peeled and cut in fine rings
carrot, peeled and sliced into rounds
Hamburg parsley root or white turnip, or celery root, peeled and diced
strained meat stock, made as for borshch, together with the meat from the stock, cut-up small
500 g/1 lb cabbage, roughly cut into medium-sized pieces
200 g/7 oz potatoes, peeled and diced
100 g/4 oz tomatoes, peeled and chopped
½ level teaspoon ground black pepper
salt, to taste
bay leaf
6 tablespoons/½ cup soured cream, to finish

Melt the butter in a large saucepan. Cook the vegetables gently in the butter for 10–15 minutes until soft. Then add the stock, the meat from the meat stock, and the cabbage. Simmer the soup for 30–40 minutes. Then add the potatoes, the tomatoes, pepper, salt and bay leaf, and cook for a further 10 minutes or until the potatoes are cooked. Finish as for borshch, and serve with rye bread.

DRIED MUSHROOM SOUP
Gribnoi sup iz sushonnykh gribov

The strings of dried mushrooms sold at the market in Moscow seem quite expensive, but a few dried mushrooms go a remarkably long way, particularly when they are used for making a soup. French or Italian dried mushrooms can be substituted for the Russian dried mushrooms.

Serves 6
60 g/2 oz dried mushrooms
generous 2 litres/3½ pts/8¾ cups salted water
100 g/4 oz/good ½ cup pearl barley
4 potatoes, peeled and cut into cubes
4 carrots, peeled and coarsely grated
1 onion, peeled and finely chopped
60 g/2 oz/¼ cup butter
6 tablespoons/½ cup soured cream

Wash the mushrooms in warm water. Then boil them for 30–40 minutes in the measured salted water. Remove the mushrooms from the liquid with a draining spoon, chop them and set aside.

Add the pearl barley to the mushroom liquid, and begin to cook it. Add the potatoes and carrots to the mushroom liquid. Meanwhile, fry the onion and the mushrooms in the butter in a frying pan. When the onions are soft and golden, add them and the mushrooms, together with the buttery juices, to the soup. The soup should have been allowed to cook for about 30 minutes from when the pearl barley was added, to the final stage when the fried mushrooms and onions are added to it. Finish with soured cream as for borshch.

MEAT SOUP WITH SALTED CUCUMBERS AND OLIVES
Solyanka myasnaya

A solyanka is a common Russian soup, which, by Western standards, is extremely unusual. Like shchi, it includes cabbage and soured cream, but its distinctive feature is its sharp, acid taste from the addition of black olives, capers, pickled cucumbers, lemon, marinated mushrooms, or brine from salted cucumbers.

This recipe is for the most usual type of solyanka, using a meat stock but it can also be made with a fish stock or with a stock made from dried mushrooms, or just with vegetables.

Solyanka can also be made in a slightly different way as a solid dish, to be served as a main course. As a soup, it is made to a somewhat thicker consistency than usual.

Serves 6
500 ml/18 fl oz/2¼ cups brine from jar of salted cucumbers
strained meat stock, made as for borshch
400 g/14 oz cabbage
400 g/14 oz boiled beef from the stock, cut up into cubes
200 g/7 oz ham, cut up into cubes
200 g/7 oz frankfurter sausages, sliced into rounds
4 tomatoes, peeled and chopped
4 salted cucumbers, chopped
2 small onions, peeled and finely diced
24 black olives
2–4 tablespoons capers
2 spring onions, trimmed and chopped
2 tablespoons chopped parsley
2 tablespoons chopped dill
10 black peppercorns
salt
6 tablespoons/½ cup soured cream, to finish

Meat soup with pickled cucumber and olives is served with pirozhki (little yeast pasties stuffed with meat)

Boil up the brine from the salted cucumbers, and skim off any foam. Add it to the strained meat stock in a large pan, and simmer on a low heat. Set the oven at moderately hot, 190°C (375°F), gas 5.

Pour boiling water over the cabbage, drain it, and cut it into cubes. Put the cabbage, together with the rest of the ingredients, except the cream, into a large earthenware pot; pour in the stock and put the pot in the heated oven for 10–15 minutes. If you don't have a suitable earthenware pot, use an enamel saucepan, and heat the soup very gently on top of the stove for 10–15 minutes, taking care not to allow it to boil. Finish as for borshch.

Note if salted cucumbers are not available use canned pickled cucumbers instead.

POZHARSKY CHICKEN RISSOLES
Kotlety pozharskie

The word kotleta in Russian can either mean a piece of meat on the bone—a cutlet—or, more commonly today, a rissole made of minced meat, chicken or fish. Some Russian authorities on Russian national cuisine will not tolerate references to kotlety in this second sense; in their view the kotleta which was introduced from abroad into Russian cookery in the 19th century does not deserve a mention alongside truly native Russian dishes. However, the fact remains that kotlety, made of minced beef, pork, chicken or fish, in all shapes and sizes, are one of the most ubiquitous dishes in Russia today.

These rissoles are the invention of a 19th-century cook, Pozharsky, the owner of a restaurant near Moscow. Pushkin ate Pozharsky's rissoles on his way from Moscow to Novgorod and immortalised them in his verse.

Serves 4–6
1 kg/2 lb fresh chicken, undressed weight
100 g/3½ oz white bread
125 ml/¼ pt/⅔ cup milk
75 g/3 oz/⅓ cup butter
salt
2–3 tablespoons toasted breadcrumbs

Remove the giblets and wash the bird thoroughly. Remove the skin and the flesh from the bones (use the bones and the giblets for stock). Mince or process the chicken skin and flesh. Soak the bread in the milk, combine it with the minced chicken, and put this mixture through the mincer or processor once more. Then add 2 tablespoons of the butter, melted, some salt, and mix well.

Form the chicken mixture into oval rissoles; roll them in the toasted breadcrumbs. Melt half of the remaining butter in a frying pan, and fry the rissoles, a few at a time, in the butter lightly on both sides for 4–5 minutes until they begin to turn brown on the outside. Then put them into a preheated moderate oven, 180°C (350°F), gas 4, or cover them with a lid and leave them on the top of the stove over a low heat for another 5–10 minutes until cooked. (Russian frying pans are heavy and round, without a handle; one all-purpose handle is kept handy for gripping frying pans for easy carrying.)

Serve the rissoles with fried potatoes and boiled peas. Pour the rest of the butter, hot from the pan, over them.

SIBERIAN RAVIOLI
Pel'meni

Pel'meni are rather similar to Italian ravioli; they are little envelopes of dough made with flour and eggs and filled with minced meat. They are eaten in large quantities as a main course. They originated in Siberia; indeed, the word pel'meni is apparently derived from pel'nyan' which in the language of the Komi people from near the Urals, on the edge of West Siberia, means 'bread ear'. The crescent shape of pel'meni does recall the shape of an ear.

The popularity of pel'meni has spread to Russia, and one can today get a cheap meal of pel'meni in soured cream or vinegar at a pel'mennaya (a cafe serving pel'meni), or buy readymade frozen pel'meni in supermarkets. Home-made pel'meni are a great treat.

Serves 6–8

FOR THE DOUGH

500 g/1 lb/4 cups flour
2 teaspoons salt
2–3 eggs, beaten
250 ml/9 fl oz/good cup soured cream

FOR THE FILLING

300–400 g/10–14 oz minced beef
300–400 g/10–14 oz minced pork
2 onions, peeled and finely chopped
1–2 teaspoons each salt and pepper

TO FINISH

8 tablespoons butter or 16 tablespoons soured cream, or 6 tablespoons vinegar
freshly ground black pepper
5-cm/2-in pastry cutter

Mix the flour and the salt in a deep bowl; make a well in the middle, and put into it the beaten eggs and cream. Mix to a soft but firm dough, adding, if necessary, a little warm water. Cover it with a cloth and put it to one side for 30–40 minutes.

Meanwhile, make the filling by mixing the ground meats with the onions and seasonings. Add a little cold boiled water to the mixture; it should be less solid in its consistency than ground meat prepared for meat balls.

Take a piece of dough, roll it out very thinly, then cut out small rounds. Repeat until all the dough is used up. Put little spoonfuls of filling on one half of each round of dough, moisten the edges with water, fold over to enclose the filling and crimp the sides together to form a half-moon shaped envelope. The edges must be well pressed together so that they do not come apart during the cooking.

When the pel'meni are all assembled, put them in the fridge for 20–30 minutes to harden.

Bring to the boil a large saucepan of salted water. Cook the pel'meni (in several batches if necessary) in the boiling water until they float back to the surface of the water (about 5–10 minutes).

Serve them in bowls with melted butter, soured cream or a little vinegar; in all cases they should be sprinkled with freshly ground pepper.

Pel'meni are served with soured cream and pepper

The great Russian opera singer, F. I. Shalyapin, invented this dish of mushrooms and vermicelli, flavoured with ham and cheese and garnished with parsley

BEEF STROGANOV
Bef Stroganov

This method of preparing beef takes its name from one of the members of the famous Stroganov family of Imperial Russia. Although this dish has in the West almost come to symbolise the cooking of Russia, it is, in fact, extremely rarely prepared in Russian homes today. Mostly, it appears on the menus of high-class restaurants for foreign tourists.

Serves 4
500 g/1 lb fillet of beef, trimmed of fat and cut into small pieces
2 onions, peeled and finely chopped
3 tablespoons butter
salt and freshly ground black pepper
tablespoon flour
200 ml/7 fl oz/¾ cup soured cream

Flatten the beef pieces by beating them with a meat mallet. Cut each flattened out piece of beef into oblong strips. Fry the onion in the butter in a large sauté pan until soft and golden. Then add the meat, sprinkle with salt and pepper, and fry briskly for 5–6 minutes, stirring and turning the pieces of meat over in the pan. Then sprinkle on the flour, stir well, and fry for another 2–3 minutes. Finally mix in the cream and cook gently for another 2–3 minutes. Taste for seasoning, adding more salt and pepper if necessary. Serve with fried potatoes.

MUSHROOMS SHALYAPIN STYLE
Griby po-Shalyapinski

This recipe describes the way in which the famous Russian opera singer F. I. Shalyapin used to prepare mushrooms. It reached me by a roundabout route. The recipe is unique, and indicates that Shalyapin's artistic genius wasn't confined to singing.

Serves 6
500 g/1 lb button mushrooms, wiped
300 g/10 oz vermicelli
125 g/4 oz/½ cup butter
3 medium onions, peeled and finely chopped
200 ml/7 fl oz/¾ cup soured cream
500 g/1 lb cooked ham, finely chopped
375 g/12 oz/3 cups mild cheese, grated
salt and pepper
5 tablespoons chopped parsley

Chop the mushrooms finely and set aside. Simmer the vermicelli in a pan of salted water for about 10 minutes or until cooked. Drain.

Meanwhile, melt half the butter in a frying pan, put in the onions and mushrooms and cook gently till soft. Then add the cream to the pan.

Mix vermicelli with almost all of the remaining butter and seasoning. Grease a deep round oven-proof glass dish with the rest of the butter and put in the vermicelli. Next add the mushrooms, onion and soured cream mixture; follow this by a layer of chopped ham and then by the grated cheese. Sprinkle with parsley and put in a preheated hot oven, 220°C (425°F), gas 7, for 10–12 minutes or until the cheese has melted and turned golden brown. When serving, use a large spoon and dig right down into the bowl, so that each helping is a cross-section of the dish.

FISH BALLS IN TOMATO SAUCE WITH PRUNES

Tefteli iz rybnogo farsha v tomate s chernoslivom

This is an unusual and imaginative way of preparing fish balls.

Serves 4
700 g/$1\frac{1}{2}$ lb white fish (cod or hake), after boning and skinning
3 medium onions, peeled
60 g/2 oz/$\frac{1}{2}$ cup dried white breadcrumbs
2 eggs beaten
2 teaspoons salt
1 teaspoon ground pepper
300 g/10 oz/good $1\frac{3}{4}$ cups prunes
5–8 tablespoons flour
4 tablespoons/$\frac{1}{3}$ cup olive oil
5 tomatoes, peeled and chopped, or 3 tablespoons tomato paste
1 teaspoon sugar

Mince the fish, and the onions and put into a large bowl. Soak the dried breadcrumbs in a little warm water. When they have swollen up, add them to the minced fish and onion, mix well, add the beaten eggs, and season with salt and pepper.

Pour boiling water over the prunes (if not pre-soaked), and leave them to soak. Form the minced fish mixture into small tomato-sized balls, roll them in flour, and fry them in the olive oil until half-cooked.

Put the tomatoes or the tomato paste into a deep heavy frying pan. Dilute with a little water, add salt and pepper to taste and the sugar, and simmer gently for a few minutes. Put the fish balls in the pan of tomato sauce. Drain the prunes, and add them to the pan. Cook gently over a low heat for 25 minutes. Serve hot, with boiled potatoes, or cold as a zakuska.

YEAST PANCAKES

Bliny

Bliny have traditionally had a strong association with the holiday known as maslenitsa in Russia. Maslenitsa (from maslo, meaning butter in Russian), originally a pagan festival celebrating the passing of winter and the coming of spring, was incorporated by the Russian Orthodox church into its religious calendar, and maslenitsa became a week-long holiday before the beginning of the long Lenten fast. Maslenitsa (like Shrove Tuesday or Mardi Gras) was the last opportunity to indulge in an orgy of eating, and bliny with butter, soured cream, salted fish and many other delicacies were served throughout the week.

Today, few Russians celebrate maslenitsa in its religious sense, but many use it as a good excuse for eating a lot of bliny in the company of family and friends. Needless to say, bliny are eaten all the year round as well.

Bliny can be made from different types of flour—wheat (this makes the lightest bliny), buckwheat, rye, or a combination of these. The batter is made with yeast, and must be allowed to rise twice before the bliny are fried. So allow about 6 hours to prepare bliny before eating them.

Serves 6–8
FOR THE BATTER
900 ml/$1\frac{1}{2}$ pts/$3\frac{3}{4}$ cups milk
30 g/1 oz/1 cake fresh yeast or 15 g/$\frac{1}{2}$ oz dried yeast
500 g/1 lb/4 cups flour
40 g/$1\frac{1}{2}$ oz/good 2 tbs butter, melted
teaspoon salt
tablespoon sugar
egg, beaten
sunflower oil, for frying
15-cm/6-in heavy frying pan

Heat 200 ml (7 fl oz/good $\frac{3}{4}$ cup) milk until it is warm but not boiling. Stir in the yeast till dissolved, add half the flour, and mix well. Cover with a cloth and leave in a warm place to rise for 2–3 hours.

When the batter has risen, add the melted butter, the salt, sugar and beaten egg, and the remaining flour. Mix well to a stiff batter. Then heat the remaining milk till warm and stir it very carefully

Gastronom No 1 in Leningrad has a fine Tsarist interior

into the batter till completely smooth. Cover with a cloth and put aside in a warm place for another 2 hours to rise once more. It should be the consistency of thick cream.

Heat the frying pan and smear it with sunflower oil. Many Russians use half a peeled potato, speared on a fork to do this because it gives an even coating of oil. Pour just enough batter into the pan to cover the surface. When little bubbles begin to appear on the surface of the blin, it is ready for turning. The first blin is often unsuccessful; it takes a little practice to get the pan to the right heat and use just the right amount of oil. There is, in fact, a Russian proverb to this effect—'pervyi blin komom', literally meaning that the first blin is always lumpy—used to encourage people after a first failure. 'Practice makes perfect' or 'better luck next time' are possible English equivalents.

Have a deep round buttered dish by the side of the stove and put each blin into this dish as it is ready; butter the blin, and place the next blin on top. When all the bliny are cooked, cover the dish with a cloth; it is not essential to serve them immediately.

The bliny will be soft, spongy and very light. Serve them piled high on a plate in the middle of the table, surrounded by dishes of accompaniments, e.g. a sauceboat of melted butter, a bowl of soured cream, fine slices of salted herring or smoked salmon, bowls of red or black caviare. Each guest will take a blin, put it on their plate, add an accompaniment, roll the blin into a sausage shape and cut off mouthfuls of blin and filling at a time.

For a light supper in the evening, bliny can be served with a dish of jam, and followed by tea.

SAUSAGE CAKE
Tort-kolbasa

Russians have a great love of kolbasa, a boiled or smoked salami type of sausage in which white rounds of fat are picked out against a pale pink or reddish background. Kolbasa occupies such a firm place in the Russian gastronomic imagination that it has led to the creation of a sweet imitation kolbasa; this dish is made in the shape of a sausage and then cut into rounds; biscuits create the effect of rounds of fat, while a chocolate background serves as the imitation lean meat. I have been served this dish with tea after the main meal in many Moscow homes.

250 g/9 oz/good cup unsalted butter
200 g/7 oz/scant cup sugar
4 tablespoons cocoa powder
200 g/7 oz plain white biscuits
200 g/7 oz/scant 2 cups shelled walnuts
2 eggs, beaten

Melt the butter gently in a pan, and add the sugar and cocoa to it. Stir well, and put this mixture in the fridge to cool. Do not let it harden completely. Crumble or cut the biscuits finely into pieces the size of coffee beans. Chop the walnuts into similar-sized pieces, and mix them with the biscuits.

Stir the eggs into the butter, sugar and cocoa mixture. Then add the walnut and biscuit mixture. Mix well so that the ingredients are evenly distributed.

Cut three lengths of foil, each 15 cm (6 in) wide. Place a third of the mixture evenly down the middle of each piece of foil, leaving about 4 cm ($1\frac{1}{2}$in) of uncovered foil at the end of each sausage. Using the back of a spoon and your fingers, form the mixture into a sausage shape about 3–4 cm ($1\frac{1}{4}$–$1\frac{1}{2}$ in) in diameter. Fold the uncovered ends of foil inwards, and roll the rest of the foil around the sausage, squeezing it until you have a firm evenly-shaped sausage inside. The sausage should be about 42 cm (15 in) long.

Put your three sausages wrapped in foil into the freezer. After an hour they will have hardened sufficiently and can be cut into rounds, arranged on a plate and served immediately. The biscuit mixture will not freeze completely, and, therefore, you do not have to allow for thawing time. The sausages can be stored in the freezer, and cut into rounds immediately before serving.

KISEL'

The regular day-to-day meal at home is usually rounded off with a glass of kompot or kisel'. Kompot is a drink made by boiling up fresh or dried fruit with water and sugar; a few pieces of fruit usually float in the bottom of a glass of liquid. Kisel' refers to a dish made from a fruit-flavoured liquid thickened with potato flour.

The following recipe produces a thickish red or black currant kisel'. It can also be made with soft berry fruits, stoned cherries, cranberries, or soaked dried fruits.

Serves 4
150 g/5 oz red or black currants, fresh or frozen, stalks removed
100 ml/4 fl oz/$\frac{1}{2}$ cup cold boiled water
150 g/5 oz/$\frac{2}{3}$ cup sugar
2 tablespoons/3 tbs potato flour (fécule), dissolved in 250 ml/9 fl oz/1 cup cold boiled water

Crush the currants with a pestle or wooden spoon until the juice runs out. Reserve the juice. Add the water to the currants, and rub them through a sieve, or squeeze out their juice through a piece of muslin into a bowl. Put the fruit pulp in another pan, pour over 500 ml (18 fl oz/good 2 cups) water and boil for 5 minutes. Then strain into another pan. Add the sugar to the strained juice, and bring to the boil.

Meanwhile, sieve the potato flour liquid to make sure it is free of lumps, and add it to the hot syrup. Stir rapidly, bring back to the boil, and then remove from the heat. Add the reserved currant juice to the pan of fruit liquid, stir well, and cool. Serve chilled in glasses.

CHERRY DUMPLINGS
Vareniki s vishnyami

Vareniki are of Ukranian origin, but have become extremely popular and widespread in Russia. They are flour and egg dumplings, most commonly filled with cherries or curd cheese.

Serves 6–8
FOR THE DUMPLINGS
500 g/1 lb/4 cups flour
125–200 ml/$\frac{1}{4}$–$\frac{1}{3}$ pt/$\frac{2}{3}$–good $\frac{3}{4}$ cup ice-cold water
2 eggs
$\frac{1}{2}$ level teaspoon salt
FOR THE FILLING
1 kg/2 lb cherries, stones removed and reserved
200 g/7 oz/scant cup sugar
FOR THE SYRUP
200 ml/$\frac{1}{3}$ pt/good $\frac{3}{4}$ cup water
200 g/7 oz/scant cup sugar

Start by preparing the filling. Put the cherries into an enamelled, glass or china dish, sprinkle them with the sugar, and leave them to stand (if possible in the sun) for 2–3 hours, so the cherries absorb the sugar. Then pour off the juice into a bowl.

Next, make the syrup. Boil the cherry stones in the water for 5–10 minutes; 5–7 of the cherry stones should be crushed. Then strain the liquid,

The Easter kulich is blessed at the midnight Resurrection mass and eaten at home with paskha (centre)

add the sugar to it and heat gently until the sugar is dissolved. Bring to the boil, then reduce the heat and simmer until syrupy. Take off the heat, cool, and mix with the reserved cherry juice. Pour into a jug for serving with the vareniki.

To make the dumplings, mix the flour, water, eggs and salt together to form a stiff but pliable dough. Roll the dough out to a thickness about 3 mm ($\frac{1}{8}$ in), then cut it into 5 cm (2 in) squares.

Put no more than a teaspoon of filling on to each piece of dough (otherwise the vareniki will burst open while they are cooking). Close up each piece of dough around the filling to form triangles. Do not let the seams along the edges become thicker than the rest of the dough; if you do, the joins will not cook properly.

Have ready a large saucepan of boiling salted water (add 1 teaspoon salt for every 750 ml ($1\frac{1}{4}$ pts/ $3\frac{1}{2}$ cups) water). Slip the vareniki into the boiling water, a few at a time, and cook them for 8–10 minutes. When they are ready, the vareniki will float to the surface of the water; lift out with a draining spoon.

Place the vareniki on a shallow dish, and serve immediately, while they are still hot, with the jug of cherry syrup.

Note vareniki are rather substantial, so if prepared in large quantities, they are often served as a main course rather than as a dessert.

EASTER CELEBRATIONS

The most important festival in the Russian Orthodox calendar is Easter, and people flock to church to celebrate the midnight Resurrection service. At this service, the special Easter cakes, kulich and paskha, bearing the letters XB, the Cyrillic initials of the words meaning 'Christ is risen', are blessed.

During the service, members of the congregation, carrying candles, leave the church and parade around it three times, led by the priests and choir. Then, the priests leading the way, return and announce 'Christos voskres!' ('Christ is risen!'), to which everyone replies, 'Voistinu voskres!'—'Truly He is risen!'

After church, Russians return home to a grand

feast to celebrate the breaking of the Lenten fast. It begins with vodka and zakuski and finishes with kulich and paskha.

EASTER CAKE
Kulich

This yeast cake is a little difficult to manage with the egg whites and peel and so on. I find it is best kept in a polythene bag between meals, or until you serve it, with paskha, so that it does not dry out too much.

The recipe below is based on the one in *Russian Cooking*, published by Mir in Moscow, 1974, and translated by F. Siegel.

Kulich is baked in tall, round moulds, so the dough rises and puffs up to give a 'chef's hat' effect. Use two large coffee tins if you do not have tall brioche moulds.

Serves 8–10
600 g/1¼ lb/5 cups flour, sifted
packet Harvest Gold dried yeast
180 ml/6 fl oz/¾ cup warm milk
¼ teaspoon salt
3 egg yolks
150 g/5 oz/⅔ cup sugar
3 cardamom seeds, crushed
150 g/5 oz/⅔ cup butter, softened
3 egg whites, stiffly whisked
75 g/2½ oz/½ cup raisins
25 g/scant oz each candied fruit and blanched almonds, chopped
FOR DECORATION (OPTIONAL)
blanched almonds, candied fruit and peel, chopped, or white glacé icing

Mix 250 g (8 oz/2 cups) of the flour with the yeast in a mixing bowl, then stir in the milk. Put the mixture into a polythene bag, put in a warm place and leave till spongy and doubled in size—about 1 hour.

Then mix in the salt, 2½ egg yolks (set aside about half a yolk for gilding the kulich afterwards), sugar, cardamom and butter. Then add the egg whites and 250 g (8 oz/2 cups) more flour. The dough will be on the wet and sticky side. Add the rest of the flour gradually until you get a dough that leaves the sides of the bowl. If it is a little sticky, do not worry too much. Put in a warm place and leave to rise again—about2–3 hours this time.

Knock down the dough and add the fruits and almonds. Divide between two buttered and floured moulds; the dough should come half or two-thirds of the way up. Leave to prove—about 1 hour.

Set the oven at moderate, 180°C (350°F), gas 4.

Bake the kulich in the preheated oven for about 45 minutes. Check after 35 minutes, by inserting a cocktail stick or thin skewer, which should come out clean.

When ready, turn out and brush with remaining egg yolk and decorate, if you like, with chopped fruit and nuts, or icing, pouring it on so that it dribbles down the sides. Stick a candle in the top of each one if it is Easter.

PASKHA

A rich, creamy cheese mixture, which is traditionally moulded in a tall wooden form, like a cut-off metronome. You can use a tall flowerpot or plastic pot instead.

Serves 8
125 ml/4 fl oz/½ cup double cream
10-cm/4-in piece of vanilla pod, split
2 large egg yolks
90 g/3 oz/good ⅓ cup sugar
125 g/4 oz/½ cup unsalted butter, creamed
750 g/1½ lb/3 cups curd cheese or ricotta cheese
60–90 g/2–3 oz/½ cup candied fruit and peel, chopped
60–90 g/2–3 oz/½ cup blanched almonds, chopped
FOR DECORATION
blanched almonds
cnadied fruit and peel
glacé fruits or raisins

In a small pan, bring the cream, with the vanilla pod, to the boil. Beat the egg yolks with the sugar until creamy, then whisk in the cream. Return the pan to the heat and cook, without boiling, until thick. Remove the vanilla pod and cool the custard. Then mix it with the remaining ingredients.

Pour the mixture into your chosen mould, lined with muslin—this helps you to turn it out, and gives a good surface pattern to the cream cheese. Chill for at least 10 hours or up to three days. Stand the pot in a dish so that the whey can drain (some may ooze out, depending on the type of cheese that is used).

Turn out and decorate. Serve with kulich, or any brioche or kugelhupf mixture you prefer, but flavoured with candied peel and cardamom.

BIBLIOGRAPHY

Information given about books is for British editions. If details differ for US editions these are given in brackets second.

Books covering more than one country:

Arabella Boxer, *Mediterranean Cookbook*, Dent; Elizabeth David, *Mediterranean Food*, Penguin; Alan Davidson, *Mediterranean Seafood*, Penguin (Louisiana State University Press), *North Atlantic Seafood*, Penguin (Viking); *The Cooking of Spain and Portugal*, Time-Life, *o/p*.

GREECE Robin Howe, *Greek Cooking*, Granada; Tess Mallos, *Greek Cookbook*, Hamlyn, *o/p*; Theonie Mark, *Greek Island Cookery*, Batsford (David & Charles); Joyce Stubbs, *Home Book of Greek Cookery*, Faber.

ITALY Alex Barker, *Italian Cooking*, Macdonald; Ada Boni, *Italian Regional Cooking*, Nelson, *o/p*; Elizabeth David, *Italian Food*, Penguin; Marcella Hazan, *The Classic Italian Cookbook*, Papermac (Knopf), *The Second Classic Italian Cookbook*, Jill Norman & Hobhouse (Knopf); Janet Ross & Michael Waterfield, *Leaves from Our Tuscan Kitchen*, Penguin (Atheneum); Jeni Wright, *Encyclopedia of Italian Cooking*, Octopus.

SPAIN Anna MacMiadhachain, *Spanish Regional Cookery*, Penguin; Marina Pereyra de Aznar & Nina Froud, *Home Book of Spanish Cookery*, Faber; Jan Read & Maite Manjón, *Flavours of Spain*, Cassell, *o/p*; Victoria Serra, *Tia Victoria's Spanish Kitchen*, Kaye & Ward, *o/p*.

PORTUGAL Ursula Bourne, *Portuguese Cookery*, Penguin, *o/p*; Maite Manjón, *The Home Book of Portuguese Cookery*, Faber, *o/p*; Carol Wright, *Portuguese Food*, Dent, *o/p*.

FRANCE Pierre Androuet, *Guide du Fromage*, Aidan Ellis (Harper's Magazine Press); Beck, Bertholle & Child, *Mastering the Art of French Cooking, Volumes I* and *II*, Penguin (Knopf); Louisette Bertholle, *French Cooking for All*, Weidenfeld (*French Cuisine for All*, Doubleday); Paul Bocuse, *The New Cuisine*, Granada (*Paul Bocuse's French Cooking*, Pantheon); Michael & Sybil Brown, *Food and Wine of South West France*, Batsford (David & Charles); Robert Courtine, *The Hundred Glories of French Cooking*, Hale; Elizabeth David, *French Provincial Cooking*, Penguin, *French Country Cooking*, Penguin; Jane Grigson, *Charcuterie and French Pork Cookery*, Penguin, (*The Art of Making Sausages, Pâtés and Other Charcuterie*, Knopf); Michel Guerard, *Cuisine Gourmande*, Papermac; Margaret Leeming, *French Family Cooking*, Macdonald; Richard Olney, *Simple French Food*, Jill Norman & Hobhouse (Athencum); Jennie Reekie, *Traditional French Cooking*, Pan; Helge Rubinstein, *French Cookery*, Eyre Metheun; Jean & Pierre Troisgros, *The Nouvelle Cuisine*, Papermac (Morrow); Roger Verge, *Cuisine of the Sun*, Papermac (*Cuisine of the South of France*, Morrow); Anne Willan, *French Regional Cooking*, Hutchinson (Morrow); Anne Willan & Jane Grigson, *The Observer French Cookery School*, Macdonald (*The La Varenne Cooking Course*, Morrow); *The Complete Encyclopedia of French Cheese*, Harper & Row.

BRITAIN Elisabeth Ayrton, *The Cookery of England*, Penguin, *English Provincial Cooking*, Mitchell Beazley (Harper & Row); Lizzie Boyd, *British Cookery*, Croom Helm

(Overlook Press); Catherine Brown, *Scottish Regional Recipes*, Molendinar; Susan Campbell, *English Cookery New and Old*, Hodder & Stoughton; Elizabeth David, *English Bread and Yeast Cookery*, Penguin (Viking), *Spices, Salt and Aromatics in the English Kitchen*, Penguin; Jane Grigson, *English Food*, Penguin; Dorothy Hartley, *Food in England*, Macdonald; Aileen King & Fiona Dunnett, *Home Book of Scottish Cookery*, Faber; F. Marian McNeill, *The Scots Kitchen*, Granada; Mary Norwak, *English Puddings*, Batsford (David & Charles), *Farmhouse Kitchen*, Penguin; Patrick Rance, *The Great British Cheese Book*, Macmillan; Michael Smith, *Fine English Cookery*, Faber; E. Minwel Tibbett, *Welsh Fare*, Welsh Folk Museum; Kathie Webber, *Traditional English Cooking*, Batsford (David & Charles); *Irish Recipes Traditional and Modern*, Mount Salus Press.

SCANDINAVIA J. Audrey Ellison, *The Great Scandinavian Cook Book*, Allen & Unwin, *o/p*; Oskar Jakobsson, *Good Food In Sweden*, Generalstabens Litografiska Anstalt; Inga Norberg, *Good Food from Sweden*, Chatto & Windus, *o/p*; Bengt Petersen, *Delicious Fish Dishes*, Esselte Wezata Forlag AB; Pauline Viola and Knud Ravnkilde, *Cooking with a Danish Flavour*, Elm Tree Books, *o/p*; James R. White, *The Oskar Davidsen Book of Open Sandwiches*, Høst & Søns Forlag, Copenhagen; James & Elizabeth White, *Good Food from Denmark and Norway*, Frederick Muller, *o/p*.

GERMANY Antony & Araminta Hippisley Coxe, *The Book of the Sausage*, Pan, *o/p*; Robin Howe, *German Cooking*, Granada; Arne Kruger, *German Cooking*, David & Charles, *o/p*; Hanne Lambley, *The Home Book of German Cookery*, Faber; Betty Wason, *The Art of German Cooking*, Allen & Unwin, *o/p* (Doubleday).

AUSTRIA & HUNGARY Gretel Beer, *Austrian Cooking*, Deutsch (*Austrian Cookery and Baking*, Dover); Christopher Floris, *The Floris Book of Cakes*, Deutsch; Karoly Gundel, *Hungarian Cookery Book*, Corvina (International Publications Service); George Lang, *The Cuisine of Hungary*, Atheneum; Fred Macnicol, *Hungarian Cookery*, Penguin, *o/p*.

RUSSIA Lesley Chamberlain, *Food and Cooking of Russia*, Allen Lane (Penguin); Nina Nicolaieff & Nancy Phelan, *The Russian Cookbook*, Papermac; Nina Petrova, *The Best of Russian Cookery*, Batsford (Crown); Savella Stechiskin, *Traditional Ukrainian Cookery*, Trident Press, Winnipeg.

INDEX